Case Management and Rehabilitation Counseling

Case Management and Rehabilitation Counseling

Procedures and Techniques

THIRD EDITION

Richard T. Roessler
and
Stanford E. Rubin

Contributors:

Richard J. Baker

Richard Beck

Walter Chung

Roy C. Farley

Reed Greenwood

Weihe Huang

Richard P. Millard

pro·ed
An International Publisher

8700 Shoal Creek Boulevard
Austin, TX 78757-6897

An International Publisher

© 1998, 1992, 1982 by PRO-ED, Inc.
8700 Shoal Creek Boulevard
Austin, Texas 78757-6897

Library of Congress Cataloging-in-Publication Data

Roessler, Richard, 1994–
    Case management and rehabilitation counseling : procedures and
techniques / Richard T. Roessler, Stanford E. Rubin : with
contributions by Richard J. Baker . . . [et al.]. —3rd ed.
        p.   cm.
    Includes bibliographical references and index.
    ISBN 0-89079-741-2
    1. Rehabilitation counseling.   2. Vocational rehabilitation.
    I. Rubin, Stanford E.   I. Title.
HF7255.5.R63   1998
362'.0425—dc21   9735024
                                                              CIP

This book is designed in Goudy and Utopia.

Printed in the United States of America

    4   5   6   7   8   9   10   03   02

To our wives, Janet and Nancy;
our children, Jennifer, Kristin, Penelope, Jenny, and Allison;
and our parents, Kathryn and Ralph and Ruth and Frank

Contents

Preface

The growing responsibilities of the rehabilitation counselor in public and private health care delivery systems create a need for an updated presentation of critical counseling and case management skills. In the third edition of *Case Management and Rehabilitation Counseling: Procedures and Techniques*, we focus on the generic skills of diagnosis, information processing, planning, service arrangement, program monitoring, placement, ethical decision making, and caseload management. Although frequently demonstrated in relation to the demands of public rehabilitation programs, the counseling and case management strategies presented apply equally well to a wide variety of other counseling and case management roles.

In the third edition of *Case Management and Rehabilitation Counseling*, we have added information on multicultural considerations in counseling, family involvement in the rehabilitation process, and rehabilitation services in a managed care environment. Thus, the reader gains an understanding of counseling and case management skills, as well as a familiarity with the context in which these services are provided. Without coverage of these important topics, the text would leave today's students of rehabilitation with only a partial understanding of their roles. Students must appreciate the impact of cultural factors on counseling process and outcomes, the role of the family in improving the results of rehabilitation services, and the effects of managed care policies on the service delivery system.

With its origins in the authors' work on the Facilitative Case Management (FCM) model, the third edition continues to view the rehabilitation counselor as a vocational expert in the community of helping professionals. Thus, counselors complete the evaluation, planning, service, and placement phases of rehabilitation with a commitment to maximum (a) involvement of the person with a disability and (b) use of that person's vocational potential. The essence of the counselor's mission is to enable individuals with disabilities to select, attain, and maintain appropriate vocational goals—that is, jobs that they both can and want to do. Success in the vocational arena is a necessary step in the improvement of the overall quality of life of people with disabilities.

As always, we thank the Arkansas Research and Training Center in Vocational Rehabilitation (H133B30059) and the National Institute on Disability and Rehabilitation Research (NIDRR) for their support. We acknowledge the many contributions of rehabilitation counselors, supervisors, and inservice trainers to the development of the concepts and techniques advanced in the third edition. Assistance in the preparation of the manuscript from the Research and Training Center and the Rehabilitation Institute of Southern Illinois University is much appreciated.

Case Management and Rehabilitation Counseling is an excellent textbook for two courses in rehabilitation education programs: rehabilitation counseling/case management and supervised practicum. As the primary textbook for a course in rehabilitation counseling and case management, the third edition can be used with supplementary materials such as computer simulations of case and caseload management. Instructors may wish to increase application of the principles and practices in the text by directing students in development of a case file consistent with forms and procedures in public or private rehabilitation settings.

For the supervised practicum course, the book structures a series of experiences that students should complete during their field placements. As they study chapters on intake interviewing; medical, psychological, and vocational evaluations; information processing and rehabilitation planning; placement; caseload management; and ethical decision making, they should participate in related field experiences. Hence, students would have an opportunity for first-hand practice of the principles stressed in *Case Management and Rehabilitation Counseling*.

The third edition of *Case Management and Rehabilitation Counseling* is compatible with the fourth edition of our introductory textbook, *Foundations of the Vocational Rehabilitation Process* (Rubin & Roessler, 1995). For example, *Case Management and Rehabilitation Counseling* presents the cases of Shirley Steed, Ted Johnson, and Jed Pierce as they progress through the stages of the intake interview; medical, psychological, and vocational evaluations; information processing; and rehabilitation planning. In the treatment of Shirley, Ted, and Jed, many of the principles in Chapters 7 through 12 of *Foundations* are implemented. Therefore, instructors and students will find the contents of *Case Management and Rehabilitation Counseling* consistent with the practices espoused in an introductory course in which *Foundations of the Vocational Rehabilitation Process* is used. By combining the fourth edition of *Foundations* with the third edition of *Case Management and Rehabilitation Counseling*, rehabilitation educators can effectively coordinate a 2-semester study of the foundations, components, and operations of the rehabilitation process and the role and function of the counselor in managing that process in a wide variety of public and private service settings.

In closing, we wish to thank the individuals who have contributed to this book. Chapter 6 continues to honor the memory and talents of Richard Baker who died in a plane crash in 1983. We thank Richard Beck, Walter Chung, Roy Farley, Reed Greenwood, Weihe Huang, and Richard Millard for their substantial contributions to the third edition. The assistance of the individuals who typed the manuscript, developed the subject and author indexes, and proofed the materials is gratefully acknowledged. In particular, we wish to recognize Anita Owen at the University at Arkansas, Mary Falaster, and Linda Patrick and her staff in the College of Education at Southern Illinois University. Finally, we thank our families for their continued support and encouragement.

Mission, Role, and Competencies of the Rehabilitation Counselor

Rehabilitation counseling can trace its origins as an occupation to the Smith-Fess Act of 1920, which initiated the civilian federal–state rehabilitation program. Although the number of rehabilitation counselors was quite small in the 1920s through 1940s, the growth of their numbers and subsequent professionalization were greatly stimulated by the passage of the Vocational Rehabilitation Act Amendments of 1954. The 1954 legislation authorized a substantial increase in government financial support for vocational rehabilitation activities. It also authorized grants to colleges and universities for training the professional rehabilitation workers needed to fill the many new positions created by the expanded funding.

The rehabilitation service system in the United States can be divided into three sectors: (a) the public sector, (b) the private non-profit sector, and (c) the private for-profit sector. The inception of the public rehabilitation system is typically associated with the passage of the Smith-Fess Act in 1920. While, as indicated above, their numbers were quite small prior to 1954, the great majority of the rehabilitation counselors during the period of 1920 to 1954 were employed in the public sector. However, since 1954, the number of rehabilitation counselors employed in both the public and private non-profit sectors has grown tremendously. The growth in the latter sector has been stimulated by the expansion in the number of rehabilitation facilities over the last 35 years (Danek, Wright, Leahy, & Shapson, 1987). During the 1970s and 1980s, the largest amount of growth in the number of rehabilitation counselors occurred in the private sector (Danek et al., 1987), which includes many for-profit rehabilitation companies.

Since its inception in 1974, the Commission on Rehabilitation Counselor Certification (CRCC) has certified more than 14,000 rehabilitation professionals as Certified Rehabilitation Counselors (CRC) (Commission on Rehabilitation Counselor Certification, personal communication, August 30, 1996). One can gain an idea of the job settings in which certified rehabilitation counselors work by examining information from recent CRCC recertification records. In the 1991–1992 records, data were available for approximately 1,500 counselors seeking recertification. The percentages of counselors employed in a variety of settings were as follows: private for-profit, 43%; state–federal, 18%; private non-profit, 14%; mental health, 7%; medical/hospitals, 5%; college/university, 4%; public schools, 2%; and other, 8%.

Forty-two percent of the sample had graduated from a Council on Rehabilitation Education (CORE) accredited master's degree program in rehabilitation counseling (Leahy, Szymanski, & Linkowski, 1993).

Arguments regarding the role and function of the rehabilitation counselor have filled a great many journal articles and book pages over the past 35 years. Speculative cases have been made for counseling functions as opposed to coordinator functions (Patterson, 1970; Remley, 1993); others have opted for problem-solving (Angell, Desau, & Havrilla, 1969) and case management (Roessler & Rubin, 1992) models. Still others have described the rehabilitation counselor as a rehabilitation clinician (Whitehouse, 1975), a vocational specialist (Hershenson, 1988), or a "demand-side" job developer (Gilbride & Stensrud, 1992).

Empirical evidence bears on the question of the role and function of the rehabilitation counselor. Using the Personal Styles Inventory, Kunce and Angelone (1990) reported that practicing rehabilitation counselors in one sample ($N=56$) resembled either a "case manager" (50%) or a "therapist" (27%) personality type. Regardless of personality profiles, rehabilitation counselors possess core characteristics that influence their work with people with disabilities—for example, an interest in helping others and a desire to use their abilities to help people with disabilities achieve significant life outcomes (Matkin, Bauer, & Nickles, 1993).

This chapter's description of the rehabilitation counselor's mission includes an array of counseling and case management services that result in enhanced quality of life (QOL) for people with disabilities (Roessler, 1995). Strong arguments exist in the rehabilitation literature for adoption of QOL as a primary rehabilitation outcome criterion (Livneh, 1986; PSI International, undated; Schalock, Keith, Hoffman, & Karan, 1989; Wright, 1980). To influence a person's QOL positively, rehabilitation counselors must provide high-quality case management, vocational assessment, vocational counseling, affective counseling, and job placement services. The validity and utility of the counselor's many duties, therefore, are functions of the extent to which they promote the QOL of people with disabilities.

When people judge their QOL, they compare what they have with what they believe they deserve. The resulting discrepancies create either negative or positive affect with negative affect related to feelings of strain and pressure (Campbell, 1981). Through their many job functions, rehabilitation counselors help people remedy the negative discrepancies that they encounter in life as the result of severe disabilities.

Research on the factors associated with the way that persons with disabilities rate their QOL clarifies which domains of a person's life require attention by the rehabilitation counselor. QOL ratings by people with disabilities correlate positively with satisfaction with (a) type of employment, (b) use of spare time (leisure), (c) standard of living, (d) health status, (e) social relationships, (f) level of financial security, and (g) family relationships (Arnold & Partridge, 1988; Kirchman, 1986; Lehman, 1983; Lehman, Ward, & Linn, 1982).

Indicating the need for attention to QOL, several investigators have found that individuals with disabilities rate their QOL lower than do nondisabled groups (Chubon,

1985; Lehman et al., 1982). Hence, conclusions about QOL ratings by people with disabilities contrast sharply with those reported for individuals in Flanagan's (1978) national surveys, " . . . most of the adults in this country report that their needs and wants are well met in the areas most important to their lives" (pp. 140–141). The goal of rehabilitation counselors, then, is to emphasize a QOL orientation in their services to people with disabilities in order to help them satisfy their needs and wants.

The significance of the job role of the rehabilitation counselor should, therefore, be judged in terms of the extent to which it contributes to enhancing the QOL of persons with disabilities. Drawing upon role and function research, we depict the multiple duties of the rehabilitation counselor in a list of job tasks for each of four areas (Emener & Rubin, 1980; Rubin et al., 1984; Wright, Leahy, & Shapson, 1987), combined with the knowledge that counselors need to perform those job tasks (Leahy et al., 1993). By adequately performing these job tasks, the rehabilitation counselor becomes a valuable ally in the client's efforts to improve the quality of his or her life.

This chapter also discusses several stress-producing factors inherent in the rehabilitation counselor's job. Failure to attend to those stress factors could result in a burnout problem in the profession.

RESEARCH ON NEEDED REHABILITATION COUNSELOR JOB TASKS AND COMPETENCIES

Several self-report survey studies provide insights into the role and function of the rehabilitation counselor. These studies report how rehabilitation counselors estimate spending their time and what activities they view as significant parts of their jobs. Table 1.1 shows the results of two survey studies (Zadny & James, 1977; Rubin & Emener, 1979) on how rehabilitation counselors reported spending their work time. At least two significant conclusions are evident in the results reported in Table 1.1. First, rehabilitation counselors have a diverse work role. Second, rehabilitation counselors may spend less time in counseling and guidance than in completing paperwork (recording, report writing, and clerical work). In a national study, Wright et al. (1987) found that rehabilitation counselors rated case recording as a very significant part of their job. More specifically, the rehabilitation counselors in their national sample listed the following activities as highly important parts of their job: (a) "Write case notes, summaries, and reports so that others can understand the case," and (b) "Compile and interpret client information to maintain a current case record" (p. 112). Still, the data in Table 1.1 support the assertion that counseling is a substantial part of the rehabilitation counselor's role. The national sample of rehabilitation counselors in the Wright et al. (1987) study reported spending a similar percentage of their time counseling (i.e., 26.6%), thereby further validating the significant part counseling plays in the rehabilitation counselor's job role.

TABLE 1.1

Results of Two Survey Studies of Rehabilitation
Counselor Estimates of Time Spent in Seven Work Activities

Counselor Work Activity	Percentage of Time Spent	
	Zadny & James (1977)[1]	Rubin & Emener (1979)[2]
Counseling and guidance	27.4	20.65
Recording, report writing, and clerical work	29.4	38.26
Overall planning of work	4.8	9.03
Placement of specific clients	7.2	7.52
Public relations	5.4	5.84
Professional growth	7.4	6.61
Other (e.g., resource development, travel, job development, arranging and coordinating services)	18.3	11.87
Total	99.9	99.78

[1]Surveyed a random sample of 208 rehabilitation counselors from seven Western states.

[2]Surveyed a nationally distributed but small ($N=30$) sample of rehabilitation counselors who attended the 1978 National Rehabilitation Association Convention in Salt Lake City.

Four nationwide mail survey studies of rehabilitation counselors' roles, functions, and competencies occurred in the 1980s. Emener and Rubin (1980) surveyed a national sample of state rehabilitation agency, private rehabilitation facility, and private-practice human-service program rehabilitation counselors regarding the extent that each of the 40 job tasks on the Muthard and Salomone (1969) Abbreviated Rehabilitation Counselor Task Inventory is a part of their job. The results showed that rehabilitation counselors report that affective counseling, vocational counseling and assessment, case management, and job placement tasks are substantial parts of their job.

Rubin et al. (1984) conducted a mail survey using a longer and more comprehensive job task inventory with a national sample of certified rehabilitation counselors employed in state–federal rehabilitation agencies, private non-profit rehabilitation facilities, mental health and mental retardation centers, hospitals, private rehabilitation companies, and private rehabilitation counseling practices. The rehabilitation counselors in their sample also reported affective counseling, vocational counseling and assessment, case management, and job placement tasks as being substantial parts of their job.

Wright et al. (1987) asked a national sample of rehabilitation counselors to indicate on the Rehabilitation Skills Inventory how important it was for them to have the competency to carry out each of 114 different job tasks. They operationally defined importance to encompass "the extent to which a professional skill is important to the respondent's primary work role . . . in the current job setting and how critical the respondent's use of this skill on the job is to the client's rehabilitation" (p. 110). Consistent with the findings of Emener and Rubin (1980) and Rubin et al. (1984), Wright et al. (1987) found that rehabilitation counselors considered it highly important to the client's rehabilitation for counselors to be able to competently perform affective counseling, vocational counseling and assessment, case management, and job placement job tasks.

Beardsley and Rubin (1988) surveyed a heterogeneous group of rehabilitation professionals, including rehabilitation counselors, vocational evaluators, work adjustment specialists, job development and placement specialists, rehabilitation nurses, and independent living service providers. The purpose of the study was to identify job tasks and knowledge generic to the six groups. To provide data for the survey, over 2,000 professionals completed either a job task inventory (Rehabilitation Profession Job Task Inventory, RPJTI) or a knowledge inventory (Rehabilitation Profession Knowledge Competency Inventory, RPKCI). Job functions found to be common for the six groups included service planning and evaluation activities, therapeutic service activities, client staffing activities, and professional study activities. In addition, four areas of knowledge were found to be commonly used by the six groups on their jobs: medical and psychosocial aspects of disability, legal and sociological influences in rehabilitation, rehabilitation and human services, and principles of human behavior.

The research results provided in Table 1.1, as well as the results of Emener and Rubin (1980), Rubin et al. (1984), Wright et al. (1987), and Beardsley and Rubin (1988), support two conclusions. Rehabilitation counselors have a diverse job role, and they need many skills if they are to help people with disabilities improve the quality of their lives. The results of those four studies provide a basis for further clarifying the role of the rehabilitation counselor through the discussion of the following four job task areas: (a) case management, (b) vocational counseling and assessment, (c) affective counseling, and (d) job placement.

The four job task areas are presented in Tables 1.2 through 1.5. These four job task area tables were developed through a two-step process. In Step 1, a list was made of all the rehabilitation counselor job tasks that (a) were reported by Emener and Rubin (1980) or Rubin et al. (1984) as receiving a mean rating by rehabilitation counselors of 3.5 or greater on Scale 1 of those studies (extent task is a part of their job), (b) were reported by Wright et al. (1987) as receiving a mean rating of 2.5 or higher on their competency importance scale, and (c) received a 3.0 mean rating (perform once a month) by all respondents in the Beardsley and Rubin (1988) survey. To be included in the Step 1 list, the item also had to fit conceptually under one of the four job role areas found on Tables 1.2 through 1.5.

With parsimonious communication and description as the goal, the purpose of Step 2 was to reduce the size of the list in each job task area by eliminating redundant items without distorting the role of the counselor as collectively delineated by the four studies. In cases in which an item is associated with more than one source, the wording could have been exactly the same or similar across the sources. To increase conceptual clarity, the authors shifted some job tasks from the category in which they were found in one of the original studies to a category in which they fit better thematically. Since "professional study activities" was a job task area noted only in the Beardsley and Rubin survey, it was not placed in a table. As an important professional development activity, this category included two activities: read professional literature (relevant to business, labor market trends, medicine, and rehabilitation), and read relevant research to enhance personal effectiveness on the job.

Case Management Job Tasks

Table 1.2 presents the counselor's case management tasks in terms of three areas: intake interviewing, service coordination, and case recording and reporting tasks. As is reflected in Table 1.2, good intake interviewing results in the counselors obtaining a clear picture of (a) what the client is seeking, (b) whether the agency might be able to help the client, and (c) what type of evaluations would be necessary to determine client eligibility and feasibility. At the end of an effective intake interview, clients should understand the counselor's role and responsibilities as well as their own responsibilities in the rehabilitation process. They should also understand the extent to which client–counselor communication is confidential. Finally, clients should understand the types of rehabilitation benefits and services that might be available to them.

TABLE 1.2
Case Management

Job Tasks	Sources*
Intake Interviewing	
Conducts intake interviews to determine how the counselor and the agency can help the client.	2, 3, & 4
Determines client's expectations of rehabilitation services.	2
Reviews client background material from the referral source or sources.	4
Determines which special medical examinations the client requires.	1 & 2
Discusses with the client the rehabilitation counselor's role and responsibilities in the rehabilitation process.	2
Explains the extent to which communications between the client and rehabilitation specialist are confidential.	2 & 4

(continues)

TABLE 1.2 (*Continued*)

Job Tasks	Sources*
Ensures that clients understand their rights and responsibilities in the rehabilitation process.	2 & 4
Explains available rehabilitation entitlement benefits to clients.	2
Explains the services and limitations of various community resources to clients.	3
Clarifies for clients mutual expectations and the nature of the counseling relationship.	3 & 4
Provides the client information about community services, recreation, transportation, and so forth.	2

Services Coordination

Job Tasks	Sources*
Identifies rehabilitation facilities, centers, agencies, or programs that provide services to persons with disabilities.	4
Reviews the client's progress in a training program with the client and his or her instructor.	2
Briefs cooperating services or agencies when referring clients.	2
Refers clients to training facilities for development of vocational skills.	2
Establishes working relationships with community organizations and leaders to secure referrals.	1 & 2
Refers clients for work evaluation.	2
Refers clients to rehabilitation facilities to assess clients' physical limitations, work tolerance, motivation, and level of vocational functioning.	2
Refers clients for work adjustment training.	2
Refers clients for medical evaluation.	2
Refers clients for psychological evaluation and testing.	1 & 2
Refers individuals who are ineligible for or unsuited to the agency's services to other agencies.	2
Coordinates activities of all agencies involved in a rehabilitation plan.	1, 2, & 3
Refers clients for psychiatric treatment.	1
Refers individuals who are ineligible for or unsuited to the agency's services to other social agencies.	1

(*continues*)

TABLE 1.2 (*Continued*)

Job Tasks	Sources*
Provides information regarding organization's programs to current and potential referral services.	3
Collaborates with other providers so that services are coordinated, appropriate, and timely.	3 & 4
Consults with medical professionals regarding functional capacities, prognosis, and treatment plans for clients.	3
Participates in diagnostic staffings on clients.	2
Establishes timetables for performing assorted rehabilitation services.	2 & 4
Collaborates with cooperating rehabilitation workers in planning and executing the client's rehabilitation plan.	2 & 4
States clearly the nature of clients' problems for referral to service providers.	3
Refers clients to appropriate specialists or special services.	3
Facilitates clients' cooperation in diagnostic procedures.	2
Monitors clients' progress toward attaining the vocational goal specified in the written rehabilitation plan.	2
Makes sound and timely financial decisions.	3
Negotiates financial responsibilities with the referral source or sponsor for a client's rehabilitation.	2
Evaluates effect of services on individual clients.	4

Case Recording and Reporting

Writes case notes and summaries (including analysis, reasoning, and comments) so that others can understand the client's progress.	1, 3, & 4
Reports verbally on the client's progress to a rehabilitation team or other collaborators.	1 & 2
Prepares a summary report or letter to describe the client to cooperating individuals or agencies.	1
Reports to referral sources regarding progress of cases.	3
Abides by ethical and legal considerations of case communication and recording (e.g., confidentiality).	3
Compiles and interprets client information to maintain a current case record.	3 & 4
Participates in case conferences.	4

*1. Emener & Rubin (1980)

2. Rubin et al. (1984)

3. Wright, Leahy, & Shapson (1987)

4. Beardsley & Rubin (1988)

Analysis of Table 1.2 also indicates that service coordination is a major case management responsibility of the rehabilitation counselor. For example, the rehabilitation counselor must establish contacts with community leaders and organizations to secure referrals. Throughout the evaluation process, the counselor must arrange for client evaluations with physicians, psychologists, and vocational evaluators. The counselor must identify competent professionals in each of these areas. The counselor is also actively involved in arranging for and monitoring the restoration and training services provided for the client. Finally, the rehabilitation counselor has fiscal management responsibilities related to case service coordination.

The job function area of recording and reporting can be readily understood from examination of the contents of Table 1.2. It includes activities pertaining to (a) maintaining client case records, (b) reporting on client progress to appropriate persons both within and outside the rehabilitation agency, and (c) preparing summary reports to describe the client to other individuals and agencies involved in the client's rehabilitation program. Recording and reporting are important activities, particularly with the common use of supervisory case review as a means of evaluating counselor effectiveness. Hence, counselors must attend to these duties carefully. At the same time, researchers have noted that paperwork demands are related to low morale among rehabilitation counselors (Gomez & Michaels, 1995).

Vocational Assessment and Counseling Job Tasks

Table 1.3 presents the rehabilitation counselor's vocational assessment and vocational counseling tasks. As is evident in Table 1.3, the rehabilitation counselor's diagnostic responsibilities call for the soliciting and processing of relevant information. Good diagnostic decisions that require the gathering of comprehensive information on the client shape the final contents of the rehabilitation plan. For example, before the rehabilitation program can be finalized, the counselor must determine the vocational significance of the disability, the compatibility of vocational goals with the individual's personality, and the rehabilitation services required.

TABLE 1.3
Vocational Assessment and Counseling

Job Tasks	Sources*
Vocational Assessment	
Makes logical job, work area, or adjustment training recommendations based on comprehensive client information.	3
Matches client needs with job reinforcers and client aptitudes with job requirements.	3
Uses behavioral observations to make inferences about work personality characteristics and adjustment.	3

(continues)

TABLE 1.3 *(Continued)*

Job Tasks	Sources*
Selects evaluation instruments and techniques according to their appropriateness and usefulness for a particular client.	3
Identifies client work personality characteristics to be observed and rated on an actual job or simulated work situation.	3
Determines the level of intervention necessary for job placement (e.g., job club, supported work, on-the-job training).	3
Uses test results as a diagnostic aid in the process of gaining a thorough understanding of the whole client.	1 & 2
Identifies transferable work skills by analyzing client's work history and functional assets and limitations.	3
Assesses client's readiness for gainful employment.	3
Identifies social, economic, and environmental forces that may adversely affect a client's motivation for rehabilitation.	3
Assesses the consistency of the client's vocational choice with his or her personality.	1 & 2
Elicits information about the existence, onset, severity, and expected duration of a client's disability.	2
Assesses the vocational significance of the client's disability.	1 & 2
Judges the level and type of training of which the client is capable in order to assist him or her in making a realistic vocational choice.	1 & 2
Assesses a client's past training, work experience, past earning level, hobbies, educational level, and socioeconomic factors in relation to vocational choice.	2
Determines appropriate community services for client's stated needs.	3
Reviews medical information about the client to help determine feasible vocational goals.	2
Consults with experts in a particular field, prior to recommending a training or educational program, to determine the potential for client placement in that field.	2
Uses test results as a diagnostic aid in the process of gaining a thorough understanding of the whole client.	2
Appraises the client's psychological readiness for a rehabilitation program.	1 & 2

(continues)

TABLE 1.3 *(Continued)*

Job Tasks	Sources*
Reviews psychological evaluation reports about clients.	2
Decides if medical or psychological services will reduce the vocational handicap.	1 & 2
Selects appropriate adjustment alternatives such as rehabilitation centers or educational programs.	3

Vocational Counseling

Integrates information from vocational, medical, and psychological diagnostic reports.	2
Integrates assessment data to describe client's residual capacities for purposes of rehabilitation planning.	3
Prepares a comprehensive diagnosis incorporating relevant information regarding the client, as a basis for a rehabilitation plan.	2
Interprets diagnostic information to clients (e.g., tests, vocational and education records, and medical reports).	3
Relates clients' stated interests and values to vocational choices.	3
Reviews medical information implications for their functional limitations.	3
Counsels with clients regarding educational and vocational implications of test and interview information.	3
Interprets results of work evaluations to clients.	2 & 3
Suggests to the client occupational areas that are compatible with the vocational, psychological, and social information gathered to improve the appropriateness of his or her choice.	1 & 2
Examines with the client the consequences of his or her disability and its vocational significance.	1 & 2
Explores with the client his or her vocational assets and liabilities in order to assure a realistic understanding and acceptance of them.	1 & 2
Discusses with the client specific vocational alternatives that are compatible with his or her training and experience.	2
Develops mutually agreeable vocational counseling goals.	3 & 4
Counsels with clients regarding desirable work behaviors to help them improve their employability.	3

(continues)

TABLE 1.3 (*Continued*)

Job Tasks	Sources*
Discusses with clients labor market conditions that may influence the feasibility of entering certain occupations.	3
Discusses client's vocational plans when they appear unrealistic.	3
Counsels clients to select jobs consistent with their abilities, interests, and rehabilitation goals.	3
Identifies educational and training requirements for specific jobs.	3
Recommends occupational and educational materials for clients to explore vocational alternatives.	3
Discusses factors related to good work adjustment with clients to help them improve their employability.	1 & 2
Incorporates information covering broad occupational areas and specific jobs into the counseling interview.	1 & 2
Uses the *Occupational Outlook Handbook*, and other sources of occupational information (such as briefs and abstracts) to explain job titles, duties, and requirements that are relevant to the client's general vocational goals.	2
Recommends and makes available occupational information (such as briefs and abstracts) to explain job titles, duties, and requirements that are relevant to the client's general vocational goals.	2
Interprets results (may use test forms and protocols) and answers any questions the client has about group intelligence and special aptitude tests (e.g., General Aptitude Test Battery, Bennett Mechanical, Minnesota Clerical, or Purdue Pegboard).	2
Develops a rehabilitation plan with the client.	2 & 4

*1. Emener & Rubin (1980)

2. Rubin et al. (1984)

3. Wright, Leahy, & Shapson (1987)

4. Beardsley & Rubin (1988)

Vocational counseling tasks are directed at facilitating the individual's vocational choice. During vocational counseling, occupational information and client assessment results are frequently introduced. In addition, the relationship of client strengths and limitations, in relation to the demands of work in general or specific jobs, is discussed. During this process, the rehabilitation plan is also developed with the client.

Affective Counseling Job Tasks

Table 1.4 presents the rehabilitation counselor's affective counseling tasks. Affective counseling is directed at helping people with disabilities deal with their feelings regarding their disabilities, as well as their concerns about participating in a rehabilitation program. Therefore, counselors help individuals explore, understand, and deal with the handicapping implications of their disabilities. Emphasis is placed on facilitating personal awareness of what cannot be changed, as well as what can be changed and how.

In counseling with the client's family, the rehabilitation counselor must often explain the nature of the client's disability, related problems, and rehabilitation services needed. Often, counselors must counsel with family members to resolve family-based barriers to client rehabilitation progress, to encourage family support of the client during the rehabilitation process, and to inform family members of the client's progress in the rehabilitation program.

TABLE 1.4
Affective Counseling

Job Tasks	Sources*
Recognizes psychological problems (e.g., depression or suicidal ideation) that require consultation or referrals.	3
Discusses the client's interpersonal relationships in order to help him or her better understand their nature and quality.	1, 2, & 4
Counsels clients to help them understand or change their feelings about themselves and others.	1, 2, & 4
Counsels with client to clarify economic and social impact of disability.	4
Counsels with the client to help him or her achieve an emotional and intellectual acceptance of the limitations imposed by his or her disability.	1, 2, & 4
Reduces the client's anxiety by helping him or her face and realistically assess problems that seem insurmountable.	2 & 4
Interprets the factors affecting clients' behaviors in order to aid in modifying these behaviors.	2 & 4
Counsels with clients to identify emotional reactions to disability.	3
Employs counseling techniques (e.g., reflection, interpretation, and summarization) to facilitate client self-exploration.	3

(continues)

TABLE 1.4 (*Continued*)

Job Tasks	Sources*
Assists clients in terminating counseling in a positive manner, thus enhancing their ability to function independently.	3
Assists clients in verbalizing specific behavioral goals for personal adjustment.	3
Assists clients in modifying their lifestyles to accommodate functional limitations.	3
Assists clients in understanding stress and in using mechanisms for coping.	3
Uses assessment information to provide clients with insights into personal dynamics (e.g., denial or distortion).	3
Provides information to help clients answer other individuals' questions about their disabilities.	3
Evaluates the client's social support system (family, friends, and community relationships).	3
Explores clients' needs for individual, group, or family counseling.	3
Determines a client's ability to perform independent living activities.	3

*1. Emener & Rubin (1980)

2. Rubin et al. (1984)

3. Wright, Leahy, & Shapson (1987)

4. Beardsley & Rubin (1988)

Job-Placement Job Tasks

Table 1.5 presents the rehabilitation counselor's job-placement tasks. As is evident in Table 1.5, these responsibilities include placement counseling and job-development tasks. Placement counseling functions occur during job search and adjustment to employment periods. Placement counseling can focus on any of the following: (a) job-seeking skills training, (b) supportive counseling while seeking a job, (c) information on available job openings, (d) an orientation to employment agencies in the community, and (e) post-employment counseling to help the client deal with job adjustment problems that occur after employment. Job-development tasks involve breaking down attitudinal barriers to the employment of persons with disabilities by providing employers with relevant client–job match information, and by arranging on-the-job training opportunities.

TABLE 1.5
Job Placement

Job Tasks	Sources*
Placement Counseling	
Gives the client placement-related information (e.g., functions of state and private employment agencies, union policies and procedures, and Worker's Compensation law).	1
Uses supportive counseling techniques to prepare clients emotionally for the stresses of job hunting.	1, 2, & 3
Instructs clients in ways to locate jobs.	2
Discusses with the client alternative ways to respond to employer questions about his or her disability.	2
Provides direct information to clients on available job openings that best suit client's needs and abilities.	2
Interviews an unmotivated client, perhaps over several meetings, to develop his or her motivation for remunerative employment.	2
Interviews the client after he or she is employed to provide support and reassurance.	2
Assists clients in preparing written job applications and resumes.	2
Assesses transferability of client skills across specific jobs or job families.	2
Instructs clients in preparing for the job interview (e.g., job application, attire, and interviewing skills).	3
Applies labor market information pertinent to success in locating, obtaining, and advancing in employment.	3
Informs clients of job openings suitable to their needs and abilities.	3
Uses local resources to assist with placement (e.g., employer contacts, colleagues, and state job services).	3
Instructs clients in methods of systematic job search skills.	3
Job Development	
Discusses the client's work skills with an employer and enumerates specific tasks the client can do.	2
Secures information about the client's performance on and adjustment to his or her new job from the employer and the client.	2
Offers a personal reference for the client who is seeking a job.	2

(continues)

TABLE 1.5 (*Continued*)

Job Tasks	Sources*
Arranges on-the-job training programs for the client.	2
Provides prospective employers with appropriate information on clients' work skills and abilities.	3
Responds to employers' biases and concerns regarding hiring persons with disabilities.	3
Monitors clients' post-employment adjustment to determine need for additional services.	3

*1. Emener & Rubin (1980)

2. Rubin, et al. (1984)

3. Wright, Leahy, & Shapson (1987)

Knowledge Required To Perform Rehabilitation Counseling Tasks

To perform the myriad rehabilitation job tasks described in Tables 1.2 through 1.5, rehabilitation counselors must draw on a broad knowledge base gained through advanced training and on-the-job experience. In a recent study, Leahy, Szymanski, and Linkowski (1993) clarified the dimensions of this knowledge base and the importance attached to these knowledge dimensions by rehabilitation professionals. The authors asked a sample of 1,535 counselors applying for recertification (which occurs 5 years after original certification or previous recertification) to rate 58 knowledge areas relevant to the practice of rehabilitation counseling on a 5-point Likert-type scale (0 = *not important*, 1 = *of little importance*, 2 = *of moderate importance*, 3 = *highly important*, and 4 = *very highly important* to the respondent's role as a rehabilitation counselor in the setting in which he or she works) (Leahy et al., 1993, p. 134). Having at least 5 years of experience in the field, respondents represented a wide variety of job settings, job titles, and educational levels.

To understand the types of knowledge that practicing counselors consider important, one can examine both the overall ratings given to the 10 knowledge domains and the individual ratings of items within each domain. Significantly, all 10 knowledge domains were regarded as moderately to highly important for the practice of rehabilitation counseling. From the perspective of the 1,535 respondents, the 10 domains ranked as follows in terms of importance: medical and psychosocial aspects of disability (3.29); environment and attitudinal barriers (3.25); assessment (3.12); vocational counseling and consultation services (2.96); foundations of rehabilitation (2.89); case management and service coordination (2.80); individual and group counseling (2.77);

family, gender, and multicultural issues (2.72); Workers' Compensation (2.58); and program evaluation and research (2.12).

One can quickly notice the associations between results of the role and function studies and the knowledge study results. The Leahy et al. (1993) data suggest that rehabilitation counselors need knowledge necessary for carrying out the job functions of case management, vocational assessment and counseling, affective counseling, and job placement. The Leahy et al. (1993) results also suggest that it is important for rehabilitation counselors to have knowledge of family, gender, and multicultural issues and of ethical standards for rehabilitation counseling (areas discussed in three chapters in this text).

The authors examined differences in knowledge importance ratings related to variations in the sample of counselors seeking recertification. Although no differences were reported as a result of years of experience or educational levels, factors such as gender, job title, and job setting were associated with different knowledge priorities. For example, respondents who worked in mental health settings rated vocational counseling as less important than did respondents from private for-profit, non-profit, state–federal, and college settings. Respondents from private for-profit settings provided higher ratings for knowledge of workers' compensation than did respondents from all other job settings.

FACTORS AFFECTING THE COUNSELOR'S JOB PERFORMANCE: THE PROBLEM OF BURNOUT

Defining the role of the rehabilitation counselor may be easier than performing that challenging role throughout one's career without experiencing professional disengagement or what is more commonly referred to as counselor burnout. The rehabilitation literature identifies several factors that contribute to rehabilitation counselor burnout.

Payne (1989) discussed stress-producing factors that are inherent in the rehabilitation counselor's job—such as extensive client contact, caseload responsibilities, and negative case outcomes. Many of these factors cited by Payne are reminiscent of Miller and Roberts's (1979) analysis of counselor burnout. For example, they discussed how counselors must, through their services to clients, make service delivery decisions and take actions without certainty of their effect. Counselors must continuously deal with the stress produced by this ambiguity. Dealing with client emotional reactions in the interview, determining the feasibility of the vocational goal in the rehabilitation plan, and deciding whether all necessary evaluation data have been gathered are but a few examples of the tension-producing judgments required of the counselor. Miller and Roberts (1979) also observed that counselors experience tension from constantly having to decide which of their many competing job demands to attend to next. Because of excessively large caseloads containing many individuals who require attention over a long period of time, counselors are never able to complete all the necessary tasks for all their clients. Hence, counselors are constantly confronted by a group of uncompleted case service tasks, many of which simultaneously demand the counselor's attention. Unfortunately, research indicates that the larger the caseload, the more exhausted counselors feel (Maslach & Florian, 1988), a condition that may have a very detrimental effect on performance (Wheaton & Berven, 1994).

Another source of tension has been labeled the "Futility Syndrome," which results from serving people with terminal illnesses (Allen & Miller, 1988). No matter how much the counselor may want a client to succeed, some individuals have only minimal prospects for long-term success in their vocational rehabilitation programs. Rehabilitation counselors who have difficulty dealing with their resulting disappointment may become overwhelmed and depressed by the high odds against being effective with some of their clients who have very severe disabilities.

An element of role strain existing in the rehabilitation counselor's job identified by DeLoach and Greer (1979) and Smits and Ledbetter (1979) is the "quantity versus quality" dilemma. While recognizing that people with severe disabilities require comprehensive services, the system also pressures counselors to move rapidly to accumulate their "quota" of successful case closures. Such pressure can easily preclude the delivery of an optimal package of services. As a result, "any employment" rather than "optimal employment" may become the rehabilitation counselor's case service outcome goal with many clients. This discrepancy between what rehabilitation counselors are reinforced for doing and what they believe they should do creates considerable conflict and stress for these professionals.

Role strain also arises from the tendency of supervisors to treat rehabilitation counselors as though they are not professionals. For example, counselors who reported dissatisfaction with aspects of their job such as promotion opportunities and working relationships with their supervisors also experienced higher levels of emotional exhaustion (Maslach & Florian, 1988).

Research (Bloom, Buhrke, & Scott, 1988) also documents a relationship between the level of expectations for one's performance as a rehabilitation counselor and professional disengagement (burnout). Some counselors who entered the field with high expectations, a condition to be encouraged, eventually reported higher levels of emotional exhaustion and depersonalization after several years of work. To cope with their feelings, they often lowered their expectations for their job performance. Decreased practitioner expectations, however, must be countered in positive ways if the field is to retain its high degree of professionalism.

Because several stress-producing factors are currently embedded within the rehabilitation counselor's job role, the question becomes one of how to deal with them. Research on coping with stress (Allen & Miller, 1988; Cooper & Marshall, 1978; Tache & Selye, 1978) and burnout (Bloom et al., 1988) suggests three broad approaches.

1. *Change the work environment.* Modify conditions so that they are more conducive to human capabilities and needs. Targets might include the social, psychological, and organizational environment of the workplace. For example, attention might be devoted to developing administrative approaches in rehabilitation agencies that enhance the participation and autonomy of the rehabilitation counselor, as well as encourage communication, openness, and trust in the work environment. Agencies can improve their environments by emphasizing and reinforcing professional development for counselors, clarifying work roles and realistic goals for rehabilitation counselors, improve co-worker relationships, and increase clerical resources for counselor use (Gomez & Michaelis, 1995).

2. *Teach counselors how to handle job stressors more effectively.* Change counselors' interpretations or appraisals of problematic situations and/or provide them with the skills and competencies needed to respond more effectively; prepare counselors for coping with terminal illness and death (Allen & Miller, 1988).

3. *Show individuals how to create diversions from stressful aspects of the job that cannot be changed.* One example of a stressful situation that is difficult to change is the continuous tragedy of clients with progressive, severe disabilities whose health fails even with the best rehabilitation services. In order to deal with such unchangeable situations, counselors may need diversions such as meditation, relaxation, exercise, and other types of self-renewal activities.

This book's approach to coping with stress is to teach counselors the skills required for their complex job role. As Landy (1985) noted, one significant way to help individuals deal with job-related stress is to teach them how to be more efficient and productive. In the chapters that follow, many pragmatic guidelines are provided for carrying out the various aspects of the rehabilitation counselor's role. Those guidelines are developed in detail with emphasis also on demonstration of their application through sample rehabilitation client cases.

CONCLUDING STATEMENT

The rehabilitation counseling occupation began when the Smith-Fess Act of 1920 established the state–federal program. The professionalization of the rehabilitation counselor, however, has a more recent origin, dating back to 1954 when the Vocational Rehabilitation Act Amendments authorized grants to universities and colleges for establishing rehabilitation counseling training programs. Since 1954, rehabilitation experts have espoused many divergent opinions about the role of the counselor. With the accumulation of empirical research, it appears necessary to recognize that rehabilitation counseling is a multi-function specialty with a broad knowledge base that has the end goal of improving the QOL of people with disabilities.

To have a positive influence on QOL of people with disabilities, rehabilitation counselors must have core skills in case management, vocational assessment and counseling, affective counseling, and job placement. The rehabilitation counselor's responsibility is to gather and organize relevant evaluation information on the person and to involve the person in the rehabilitation planning process. With the client's involvement, the rehabilitation counselor must develop a plan that integrates both rehabilitation agency services and the services from other agencies and community-based private professionals. Although this is a difficult task in and of itself, it is not enough for rehabilitation counselors simply to develop such plans. They must also see to it that the plans are implemented, that clients achieve their vocational goals, that clients are satisfied with the services received, and that the services result in improved QOL for the person. To continue to perform these multiple tasks, counselors need comprehensive advanced training that provides them with knowledge of vocational counseling and consultation; medical and psychosocial aspects of disability; individual and group counseling; program evaluation and research; case management and service coordination; family, gender, and multicultural issues; foundations of rehabilitation; workers' compensation; environment and attitudinal barriers; and assessment.

To retain their effectiveness, counselors must continue their own professional development through self-study of the trends in rehabilitation and business. Furthermore, they must cope with many job-related stressors that, if ignored, could result in lowered expectations or professional disengagement in some other way. Changes can be made to help counselors avoid burnout and do their jobs more effectively. For example, the process of recording and reporting in vocational rehabilitation has been streamlined via computer software and hardware. Counselors can be given more autonomy in handling their own cases and, thus, be held accountable for meeting concrete outcome criteria, not for adhering strictly to prescribed procedural duties. Counselors can learn how to monitor their reactions to stress and integrate self-renewal diversions into their lives. Finally, counselors can become even more efficient and effective in their work roles. It is the intent of this book to help counselors develop that efficiency and effectiveness in order to help people with disabilities enhance the quality of their lives.

Importance of Vocational Counseling Skills for the Rehabilitation Counselor

Employment and its many benefits are just as important to people with disabilities as they are to the general population. In one study, individuals with disabilities were so committed to returning to work that they preferred that their rehabilitation counselors concentrate on vocational counseling and placement services rather than psychological counseling (Murphy, 1988). While recognizing the need to achieve psychosocial outcomes, they reported seeking many of those services from other professionals. Moreover, they attributed much of their psychological distress to their current unemployment or underemployment.

By stressing that employment is the *sine qua non* for their involvement with rehabilitation, people with disabilities are in no way refuting the earlier argument that the rehabilitation counselor's chief mission is to promote the quality of life (QOL) of persons with disabilities. The myriad services provided by rehabilitation counselors prepare people with disabilities to make important gains in personal independence, health, adjustment, and educational statuses that are necessary prerequisites to acquiring employment, the keystone in their definitions of a quality life. When that preparation is successful and individuals secure employment, they believe that rehabilitation has been a success (Murphy, 1988).

Research on job satisfaction stresses two basic reasons for the significance of the work role. First, extrinsic reinforcers are available through working, such as money, power, and recognition from others. The second reason is intrinsic in nature and manifested in a sense of security, satisfaction, self-realization, and positive time structuring (Kuhnert, 1989). When individuals become unemployed, they are denied access to many extrinsic and intrinsic reinforcers, consequently experiencing considerable stress. Hence, vocational rehabilitation counseling represents a significant stress-reduction strategy in the lives of people with disabilities.

Data in several studies support the strong relationship between employment and QOL for people with disabilities (Crisp, 1990). In an 11-year follow-up study of individuals with spinal cord injury, Krause and Crewe (1987) identified several important variables related to long-term survival. After accounting for the effects of age and age at onset of injury, the researchers found that people who survived spinal cord injury over an 11-year period were initially (i.e., at the beginning of the 11-year period) rated higher on vocational and personal adjustment by a team of psychologists. They also spent more of their time involved in socially active roles—that is, working or enrolled in school during the follow-up period. Other studies document positive correlations between global ratings of well-being by people with disabilities and employment status. Number of hours worked per week, pay per week, and satisfaction with one's current job were positively related to QOL in several investigations (Kirchman, 1986; Lehman, 1983). In one study, people with severe mobility limitations, when contrasted with a nondisabled comparison group, placed greater emphasis on the contribution that social functioning, specifically obtaining a job, makes to one's QOL (Ramund & Stensman, 1988). As Murphy (1988) noted, not 1 of the 14 rehabilitation clients in his study considered rehabilitation successful if he or she was still unemployed.

Empirical findings in several studies, as well as the stated preferences of people with disabilities, therefore, strongly support the contention that rehabilitation counselors must be highly skilled vocational counselors. They must have the training and skills needed to help people with disabilities choose jobs for which they are well matched (i.e., jobs in which they will be both satisfied and satisfactory workers). Evidence supports the positive relationship between job satisfaction and the extent of congruence that exists between personality dimensions of rehabilitation clients and the characteristics of the work environments they enter. In a study of successfully rehabilitated individuals, Jagger, Neukrug, and McAuliffe (1992) found that individuals with disabilities who worked in compatible jobs in terms of Holland's six dimensions of person and environment (realistic, investigative, artistic, social, enterprising, and conventional) reported greater job satisfaction on the Minnesota Job Satisfaction Questionnaire.

To help people with disabilities choose jobs in which they will be both satisfied and satisfactory employees, the counselor often must facilitate greater client "understanding of self within the context of the world of work" (Solly, 1987, p. 297). By structuring a counseling experience that enables the individual to explore and integrate vocationally relevant information about self, educational opportunities, and employment options, the rehabilitation counselor can facilitate that understanding. But first, the counselor should help the person address certain prerequisite issues. According to Amundson (1989), the first step in career planning involves determining the person's readiness for the vocational exploration and choice process. Factors affecting readiness are revealed in questions such as (a) has the individual met basic survival needs, (b) does the person have a sufficient level of self-esteem, and (c) does the person have positive expectations about personal control of his or her life? Affirmative answers to these questions suggest readiness for vocational planning.

Having determined that the person is ready to begin the vocational counseling process, the rehabilitation counselor guides the individual through a systematic vocational choice or decision-making strategy. Such a strategy calls for the identification of possible occupational options for the client, the examination of relevant client and occupational–educational information, assessment of environmental obstacles to entering each identified occupation, possible approaches for overcoming such obstacles, the examination of each occupational option in light of that information, and the selection of a vocational goal. In the vocational counseling process, the counselor must serve as (a) an expert on "sources of occupational–educational information resources and of first-hand information on potential careers" (Solly, 1987, p. 298), (b) a facilitator of client self-exploration, and (c) a guide who enables the individual to consider all information pertinent to selecting an occupational role.

Through the vocational self-exploration process, the rehabilitation counselor helps the person acquire data necessary for vocational decision-making purposes and process that information so that any vocational choice reflects an accurate appraisal of reality factors. Information that must be procured and processed during the vocational counseling process includes both the characteristics of the person and the characteristics of the environment. The appropriateness of a vocational choice cannot be determined solely on the basis of consideration of the capabilities or interests of the individual. The nature of the environment can significantly influence an individual's ability to acquire a particular job, as well as tenure on the acquired job. Dobren (1994) clarified the complexity of this person–environment transaction by describing not only how physical, economic, personal, and social variables influence individual action, but how the event of disability changes some variables and creates new ones. This change results in an increase of adaptational challenges that the individual with a disability faces. Examples of changed variables following disability onset include social attitudes (social) and self-concept (personal). Examples of new variables include financial disincentives (economic) and architectural barriers (physical).

A good fit between the person and the environment should result in high worker performance and satisfaction, as well as low stress (Kulik, Oldham, & Hackman, 1987). Two aspects of fit between the person and the environment are typically considered. These are the fit

1. between the person's needs and values and the opportunities provided by the environment in which he or she operates and

2. between the demands of the environment and the abilities of the person to meet those demands. (Kulik et al., 1987, p. 279)

While matching the person and the job represents the core concern in vocational counseling, determining effective matches is a complex measurement challenge. For example, which personal characteristics and which environmental aspects should be taken into consideration? "Clearly the answer to the . . . question is 'it depends.' If one wishes to be a sumo wrestler or a National Football League player, then weight is important. For most other fields, probably not" (Osipow, 1987, p. 333). At the same time, counselors and clients must remember that this pairing of person and job is not based on rigid thinking about people or settings. Neither is static. Through training and education, people can develop new skills and knowledge. Through modifications and accommodations, employers can alter work environments and their task demands so that they are more compatible with the person's capabilities. In fact, a wide range of environmental (i.e., job modification) strategies exist to bring a person and an environment into harmony—for example, installation and modification of equipment, alteration of schedules and job duties, and provision of readers and interpreters.

Chartrand (1991) captured this more dynamic understanding of vocational counseling in her presentation of Person × Environment assumptions. By following her tenets of trait/factor (T/F) counseling, the rehabilitation counselor can implement a more flexible and comprehensive approach to vocational counseling:

1. Although they are definitely capable of rational decisions, people make decisions that are also influenced by affective factors.

2. People and work environments differ on measurable and meaningful dimensions.

3. The greater the similarity between a person's traits and the work environment's factors, the greater the probability of vocational success.

4. Congruence is not a static concept; people and environments have the capacity to change and to shape each other.

5. People *seek* and *create* environments that allow them to express preferred characteristics.

Thus, individuals with disabilities can become more effective in career decision making if counselors help them (a) develop their understanding of self (traits) and work environments (factors) and (b) master the problem-solving and accommodation skills needed to reduce incongruities between the two.

ENVIRONMENTAL FACTORS IN THE VOCATIONAL CHOICE PROCESS

As clearly stressed in the preceding discussion, the rehabilitation counselor and client should not neglect environmental factors that make one work setting more desirable than another for the individual. These factors include variations among work settings in terms of location, structure, and amount of interpersonal support. For example, work usually takes place in special locations in the community, many of which are at a considerable distance from the client's home. Location, therefore, is a significant consideration for many clients with disabilities because of either the absence of family transportation or deficiencies in public transportation systems, particularly in rural areas.

For many individuals with physical disabilities, structural aspects of the work setting are significant considerations. Modifications at the work site such as the replacement of steps with ramps, the addition of computers with voice output and screen enhancers, or the modification of machinery represent reasonable accommodations for employees with disabilities. The structure of the workday and company policies may include other important considerations, such as frequency of breaks, length of workday, and sick and nonpaid leave regulations.

Limited access to vocational opportunities due to physical barriers is one way the environment influences the vocational choice process. Elaborating on barriers in the physical environment, Mace (1980, pp. 131–132) described how the meaning of accessibility differs depending on the nature of one's disability. For example, accessibility for individuals in wheelchairs includes "hard surfaces, gradual slopes, lower fountains, and wider doors." Individuals limited in the capacity to walk may need "hand rails, a place to sit and rest, or extra time to move about." Individuals with visual impairments require "contrasting tactile or audible information displays and warnings, someone to give directions, or permission to bring a guide dog along." Finally, individuals with hearing impairments need visual information displays or access to an interpreter. Therefore, when structural factors at the job site are a significant factor, vocational choice must take into consideration the feasibility of job modifications. As Marachnik (1970) cautioned, some kinds of work "might not lend themselves to improvisation or specification change because of speed, automated procedure or machine operation" (p. 228). For example, a rancher who has multiple sclerosis may no longer be able to perform duties such as tending cattle, climbing silos, and mixing feed because workable accommodations do not exist. This individual needs to explore vocational options that are much less physically demanding, such as a business manager for a farm or local agricultural cooperative.

The relationship between the amount of interpersonal support to be expected on a particular job and the person's need level in that regard is also an important vocational choice consideration. Individuals requiring significant interpersonal support on the job are good candidates for prevocational preparation or supported employment situations, which provide job coaching and co-worker support. Neff (1985) stated that individuals are ready to explore and act on potential vocational choices when they are able to maintain a balance between independence and dependence and to learn how to do a job successfully without alienating others.

When working with individuals with disabilities, it is very important for the rehabilitation counselor to know the local labor market, not only in terms of available job opportunities, but also in terms of the location, structure, and interpersonal support aspects of the work settings. Counselors must then integrate this reality-based understanding of the world of work into their plans for client evaluation and rehabilitation plan development.

DISABILITY CHARACTERISTICS AS A CONSIDERATION IN VOCATIONAL COUNSELING

The individual's perception of the significance of his or her disability is a relevant consideration in the vocational choice process. For example, Kunce (1969) reported data supporting the following hypothesis: "difficulties involved in rehabilitation vary directly with the interference that the given disability has upon the individual's life style" (p. 205). Specifically, he found that individuals experiencing physical disabilities who valued physical activity highly encountered more difficulties reorienting their lives than did individuals with physical disabilities who placed less value on physical activities.

Rohe and Athelstan (1982) found a significant incongruency between the pre-injury vocational interests and the post-injury vocational capabilities of men suffering paraplegia or quadriplegia as a result of traumatic spinal cord injuries. As a group, these individuals tended to prefer occupations in which physical abilities are used to deal with things such as heavy machinery. Consistent with their lack of interest in academic pursuits, they showed little inclination to enter occupations requiring social interaction or dealing with complex data. Consequently, males with spinal cord injuries may have little interest in abstract vocational planning processes or in rehabilitation plans that call for long-term education without a specific job connected to the completion of that process. According to Rohe and Athelstan (1982), people with spinal cord injuries "who do pursue further schooling probably see it as a means to an end, rather than as intrinsically interesting. It seems desirable, therefore, to make any further education directly relevant to employment and to reduce the length of schooling as much as possible" (p. 290).

Research has also examined the effect that one's medical condition has on vocational outlook. Goldberg, Bigwood, MacCarthy, Donaldson, and Conrad (1972) found several interesting differences between two groups of individuals with end stage renal disease—one group on hemodialysis awaiting renal transplantation and another group who had completed a kidney transplant operation. Although those awaiting transplantation had broader vocational interests, they were more unrealistic in their vocational planning. Goldberg et al. (1972) hypothesized that individuals awaiting renal transplantation may be more unrealistic in their vocational planning due to the uncertainty of the effect of the anticipated transplant operation. In a more unstable psychological state characterized by anxiety and uncertainty, people on hemodialysis who had not had a kidney transplant may be more likely to grasp at false hopes. Goldberg et al. pointed out that those who had undergone the operation tended "to scale down their aspirations to a level . . . congruent with employment opportunities" (p. 33). The findings of Goldberg et al. suggest that for clients with medical conditions that can be further stabilized, it is wise to delay vocational choice until that stabilization has occurred.

Age at onset of disability can be a significant consideration in the vocational counseling process. For example, in the case of congenital or early childhood disabilities, parental or community overprotection may greatly limit the person's capability to understand during adolescence or early adulthood how personal capabilities relate to vocational demands. In such situations, the vocational counseling experience should involve clients in self-analysis with counselors helping them translate personal strengths into useful work skills. This self-analysis should also focus on the client's values and beliefs about work. These can be examined (a) at a general level in terms of a person's orientation toward work itself, (b) at an intermediate level in terms of a person's orientation toward an occupation, and (c) at a specific level in terms of attitudes toward particular job duties and responsibilities (Wise, Charner, & Randour, 1976). Therefore, on one hand, a counselor and client might be discussing the importance of the work ethic itself in the individual's life (to work or not) and, on the other hand, they may be discussing the relative desirability of aspects of one job in the community versus another.

Early onset of disability is significant for yet another reason. Over time, many disabilities develop serious complications. In the case of juvenile diabetes, Stone and Gregg (1981) stressed the importance of anticipating in rehabilitation planning the effects of complications at a later stage of the disability. For example, juvenile diabetes is often related to conditions such as coronary heart disease, hypertension, visual impairment, renal involvement, and diabetic neuropathy. Because of the effects of these conditions, the individual should avoid "jobs or occupations requiring keen sense of sight, irregular work hours or work routines, and heavy physical exertion" (Stone & Gregg, 1981, p. 288). Jobs requiring the operation of heavy machinery are dangerous if the person experiences dizziness or related diabetic symptoms. In the vocational counseling process with persons with juvenile diabetes, it is imperative for the counselor and client to determine whether job-related stress could cause complications or blood sugar imbalances to reemerge (Franz & Crystal, 1985).

When economic disadvantage is paired with early onset of disability, the challenge to the rehabilitation counselor may be increased. For example, Smith and Chemers (1981) found that economically disadvantaged "hard to employ" job trainees tended to view employers, supervisors, and managers as hostile, uncaring, and unfriendly. In addition, these individuals tended to be deficient in the assertive, independent behaviors usually associated with job advancement and upward mobility. Hence, self-defeating misperceptions and certain behavioral deficits can become important areas for exploration during vocational counseling.

Finally, when the early onset disability is mental retardation, the individual may lack the decision-making skills needed to make an independent vocational choice. When this is the case, the rehabilitation counselor may have to teach decision-making skills to the client before the vocational choice process is initiated (Solly, 1987). With many such clients, parent involvement may be crucial in the vocational counseling process. Solly (1987) has stressed that "parent involvement can be critical in facilitating the decision-making process, developing rapport, and in aiding the flow of communication between the counselor and the mentally handicapped client" (p. 297).

Later onset of disability creates a set of negative circumstances for the individual as well. For example, mid-life disability disrupts the correspondence that the person has established in a certain job or career (McMahon, 1979). The counselor and client must, therefore, collaborate in a process of career redevelopment. Numerous significant areas must be examined in light of the effects of the disability, such as the impact of disability on functioning, accuracy of the individual's current self-assessment, realities of work, and changes resulting in the person and job fit.

Hershenson (1996) elaborated on the impact of midcareer disability on the person's coping outcomes by explaining that disability first negatively affects the person's work competencies, which subsequently influences his or her work goals and work personalities. The counselor can help the client reestablish correspondence through Hershenson's (1996) "4 R" approach of (a) "reintegrating the work personality, (b) restoring or replacing competencies that were lost or failed to develop, (c) reformulating work goals, and (d) restructuring the work environment to maximize supports and to minimize barriers" (p. 7). Fundamental to use of the "4 R" approach is an understanding that the entire process of vocational counseling occurs in the context of other system influences as well. Historical and contemporary experiences in one's family, educational, and social environments shape the person's values and priorities and enhance or limit the person's capacities to respond to the demands of independent living and work environments (Hershenson, 1996).

Later disabilities in life can have negative effects on personal outlook and work stability. Some clients may lower their levels of aspiration educationally and vocationally as evidence of pessimism regarding their current condition (Goldberg & Freed, 1973; Thurer, 1980). In a survey of individuals who had bypass surgery, Thurer speculated that excessive concern with "taking it easy" may have contributed to a low rate of returning to work after recuperation. Engblom et al. (1994) reported that individuals who experienced coronary artery bypass surgery were more likely to return to work if they had a shorter absence from work and if they held positive expectations regarding work and their capabilities to return to work.

In reviewing research in the area of disability and vocational development, Goldberg (1992) provided a useful synopsis of the career development impact of both early and late onset conditions. Counselors may use the following observations from Goldberg's research to guide them in their vocational counseling with people with disabilities:

1. Vocational plans, interests, and work values held prior to disability influence vocational choice more than severity of disability.

2. Because they are related to the probability of returning to and maintaining employment, motivation to work, realistic self-assessment of capacities and limitations, and optimism about future recovery (collectively referred to as vocational development) are critical variables in vocational evaluation.

3. Periods of hospitalization, medical treatment, therapies, and other time taken for adjustment to disability interrupt the career pattern.

4. People with invisible disabilities make more specific, realistic plans than do people with visible disabilities, since invisible disabilities evoke less social stigma and less employment discrimination.

5. Cultural expectations and parental and teacher expectations have a marked effect on the vocational plans of people with disabilities.

6. People with disabilities from higher socioeconomic situations have more mature

vocational plans than do people with disabilities from lower socioeconomic situations.

7. People with physical disabilities tend to score higher in educational plans, realism, initiative, work values, and average vocational development than do people with developmental disabilities.

8. Because they have prior work experience, people with acquired disabilities tend to choose occupations consistent with previous goals, interests, and values.

9. Due to their limited work histories, people with congenital disabilities choose occupations consistent with parental aspirations and social class.

MINNESOTA THEORY OF WORK ADJUSTMENT

An important theoretical and empirical elaboration of the person–environment match concept in vocational counseling can be found in the research-based propositions of the Minnesota Theory of Work Adjustment (Dawis & Lofquist, 1984; Hesketh & Dawis, 1991; Osipow & Fitzgerald, 1996; Rounds, Dawis, & Lofquist, 1987). The theory's basic assumption is that individuals seek to establish and maintain correspondence with their environment. This correspondence implies not only that the individual is capable of meeting the demands of the environment, but also that the environment is capable of meeting the needs of the individual. To be more specific, the individual enters the work situation with skills that must be compatible with the skill demands of the job if the individual is to be a satisfactory worker. At the same time, the job must provide the worker with sufficient levels of preferred reinforcement if the worker is to be satisfied. As Dawis and Lofquist pointed out, when requirements of the individual and environment are met, the situation is in balance or is "correspondent."

Two key terms in the Minnesota Theory for the rehabilitation counselor are "satisfactory" and "satisfied." If individuals are to persist on the job (referred to as tenure), they must be satisfied and satisfactory. In other words, in the process of fulfilling the demands of the work role (satisfactory), the individual receives sufficient personal rewards for doing the work (satisfied). Therefore, the Minnesota Theory of Work Adjustment stresses the importance of matching person and job in order to increase the likelihood of worker satisfaction and satisfactoriness. By assessing the client's aptitudes, skills, and interests and the reinforcers and ability requirements of the job, vocational rehabilitation counselors can help individuals make appropriate plans for job training and placement.

In estimating the individual's potential satisfaction with work, the counselor must help the person consider a number of sources of reinforcement from work such as extrinsic rewards, intrinsic rewards, and social rewards. Extrinsic rewards are clearly important. Monetary compensation enables individuals to meet basic needs and to pursue enjoyable activities during non-working hours. However, work is done for more than simply extrinsic rewards, such as the paycheck. Intrinsic rewards that refer to personal satisfactions derived from work are important too. Finally, social rewards (e.g., contact with others in the workplace) are also significant. Developers of the Minnesota Theory summarized these "pay offs" from employment in terms of six value dimensions: achievement (feedback from and accomplishment of the work task), comfort (a comfortable, nonstressful work environment), status (recognition from others and prestige), altruism (harmony with and service to others), safety (a stable and predictable work environment), and autonomy (exercise of self-control and initiative in work) (Hesketh & Dawis, 1991, p. 10).

In vocational counseling, therefore, rehabilitation counselors should recognize the following:

1. Jobs differ in the amount of intrinsic, social, and extrinsic rewards they offer.

2. People differ in their preferences for these different rewards.

Hence, the counselor and client should carefully assess the individual's reward preferences and the availability of preferred reinforcers in different jobs. Compatibility between the two is an important feature of job satisfaction.

As one of the propositions in the Minnesota Theory of Work Adjustment (Dawis & Lofquist, 1984) states, "Satisfactoriness is a function of the correspondence between an individual's abilities and the ability requirement of the work environment" (p. 60). Therefore, the counselor and client must carefully consider the relationship of current and potential capabilities to work demands. The skills needed to meet work demands can be construed in several ways. For example, Herr (1987) stressed that basic literacy, responsible attitudes toward work, the ability to communicate, and the ability to learn often were more important to job success than training in specific occupational skills.

Since the relationship between worker characteristics and job characteristics is rarely static, tenure on a job reflects not only an initial "match" between person and job, but also a continual series of efforts on the part of person and situation to adjust to each other (e.g., provision of reasonable accommodations). Therefore, client tolerance for discorrespondence, as well as his or her style of dealing with discorrespondence, become relevant considerations in the vocational planning process. For example, some individuals may be more tolerant of discorrespondence (e.g., flexible) than others. The more flexible individuals are, the greater the amount of discorrespondence they might tolerate before attempting to decrease it (Hesketh & Dawis, 1991).

Individuals may also differ in their strategies for decreasing discorrespondence. Some may take an "active" orientation and attempt to change the environment to meet their needs. Others may take a "reactive" stance and modify their own needs in order to adjust to the environment (Osipow & Fitzgerald, 1996). Through effective vocational diagnosis, the counselor can determine the client's style of responding to discorrespondence in the work situation. In this regard, Dawis (1976) stated, "It is recognized that most if not all people use both modes . . . (*activeness* and *reactiveness*) . . . at one time or other in their work careers, and that utilization of one or the other depends in part on situational factors. However, it is reasonable to assume that, in the course of one's response and reinforcement history, a person develops a more or less stable preference for one mode of adjustment" (p. 243). Therefore, when working with clients with a tendency to take the "active" orientation, the counselor would be wise to steer away from job openings in which both discorrespondence and a "rigid" employer are present.

In summary, the Minnesota Theory of Work Adjustment stresses that the counselor's role is one of helping the individual identify correspondent employment situations. Correspondence between person and job indicates that the individual is satisfied with the job and that the employer is satisfied with the individual. Many factors affect the extent of correspondence between the individual with a disability and the job, and it is the rehabilitation counselor's responsibility to determine the interventions needed to create better job–person fits. On one hand, interventions may need to focus on enhancement of individual knowledge and skills. On the other hand, interventions may need to focus on clarifying the employer's obligations under the Americans with Disabilities Act of 1990 (ADA) to provide reasonable accommodations in job application and employment processes (Mullins, Rumrill, & Roessler, 1995).

THE CRUX MODEL

The Crux Model (see Figure 2.1) depicts the dynamics of the vocational counseling process in rehabilitation. Divided into two major phases, evaluation and planning, the model directs the counselor's efforts in collecting significant social–vocational history information and relating it to work demands. The relationship between the evaluation and planning phases is also delineated in the Crux Model.

Through the intake interview and the medical, psychological, and vocational evaluations, the counselor gathers information regarding the client's past, current, and potential capacities in physical functioning, psychosocial functioning, and educational and vocational skill development. The rehabilitation counselor should also gain a clear picture of the client's current economic situation. When rehabilitation counselors can answer most of the questions in Table 2.1, they are in a good position to fill in the boxes above the dotted line on the Crux Model.

Rather than questions that the client can answer directly, the concerns in Table 2.1 can be resolved only through careful consideration of information yielded by the intake interview, medical evaluation, psychological evaluation, and vocational evaluation. By studying the questions in Table 2.1, counselors can identify remaining

(*text continues on p. 35*)

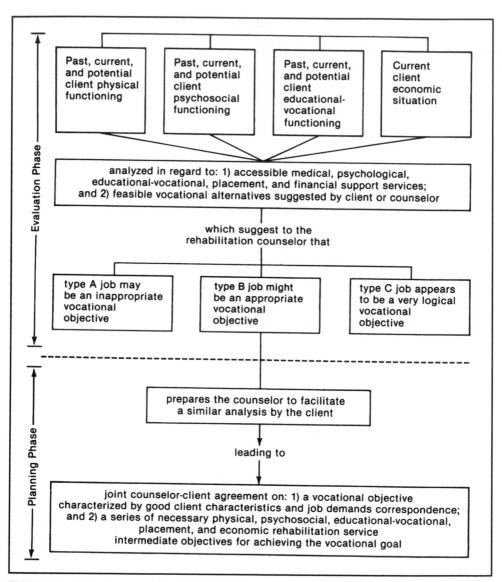

FIGURE 2.1. The Crux Model. *Note*. From *Goal-Setting: Guidelines for Diagnosis and Program Development* by R. Roessler and S. Rubin, 1980, Fayetteville: University of Arkansas, Arkansas Research and Training Center in Vocational Rehabilitation. Reprinted with permission.

TABLE 2.1
Program Development Information Needs

Physical Factors

Extent of Disability

1. How does the disability handicap employment potential?

2. Is the disability progressive or stable?

3. Can the person's functioning in activities of daily living be improved?

4. How much assistance in activities of daily living will the individual always need?

5. Is the disability stable enough to initiate rehabilitation programming?

Services

1. Which physical restoration services are needed to reduce the handicapping effects of the disability (e.g., surgery, orthotic and prosthetic devices, physical therapy, and occupational therapy)?

2. Can job modifications reduce the extent of the client's physical handicap for employment?

Psychosocial Factors

Psychological Reaction to Disability

1. To what degree has the client adjusted to the handicapping aspects of the disability?

   a. Does the person use "disability" as an excuse for failure?

   b. Are any physical symptoms psychologically based?

   c. Is the client excessively concerned with personal health?

   d. What secondary gains is the individual receiving from remaining unemployed?

   e. Does the client have the emotional stability to engage in a vocational rehabilitation program at the present time? In the near future?

Family and Friends

1. What positive or negative role will the individual's family and friends play in the rehabilitation process (e.g., be supportive, overprotective, or unrealistic regarding client potential)?

Services

1. Which personal counseling and/or family counseling services will be necessary (e.g., psychotherapy, personal adjustment training, relaxation training)?

(continues)

TABLE 2.1 (*Continued*)

Educational–Vocational Factors

Educational Considerations

1. What types of vocational training or jobs does the client's educational history suggest?

2. Are the person's vocational aspirations and educational history compatible?

Vocational Skills and Interest Considerations

1. What vocational skills does the client currently possess?

2. What vocational skills can the person develop that could limit the functional impact of the disability?

3. Has the individual developed new vocational skills that have vocational relevance?

4. Are client vocational goals consistent with current vocational interests?

Vocational Self-Concept

1. Does the client have a realistic perception of current

    a. strengths and weaknesses as a worker,

    b. potential for vocational skill development, and

    c. reasons for being unemployed?

Job Acquisition

1. Can the person independently locate job openings?

2. Can the person satisfactorily fill out job application blanks?

3. Can the person make a good impression on an employer?

Job Retention Considerations

1. Can the client satisfactorily meet the demands of competitive work (e.g., accepting supervision, working independently, getting along with co-workers, and maintaining an adequate production rate)?

2. Would the client's present use of leisure time adversely affect job retention?

(continues)

TABLE 2.1 (*Continued*)

Services

1. Which educational and vocational services are needed (e.g., remedial education, vocational training, work adjustment training, job-seeking skills training)?

Economic Factors

Financial Considerations

1. Do disability-related financial benefits (SSI, SSDI, Medicaid, Worker's Compensation) create disincentives to the individual's rehabilitation?

2. Could current debts affect the completion of the person's rehabilitation program?

3. Can the person manage personal finances?

4. Does the person have sufficient financial support at present?

Services

1. What economic support will the client need during and after the rehabilitation program (e.g., SSI, food stamps, or low-rent housing)?

---

information gaps in their client evaluation. If possible, these remaining issues should be resolved before moving to plan development with the client.

Next, the counselor must study the implications of the evaluation data for different vocational options. In order to do this task well, the counselor must understand the strengths and limitations of the client, the influence of sociocultural factors on the person's development (i.e., social class, race or ethnicity, gender, and sexual orientation), and the characteristics and demands of local jobs.

Vocational possibilities generated during the counselor's analysis of evaluation information should not be viewed as "vocational imperatives," but rather as suggestions for consideration during vocational planning. Vocational planning involves the counselor and client in discussing potential vocational choice possibilities with the objective of selecting a vocational goal in which client characteristics and job demands are compatible. Moreover, this discussion should focus on the rehabilitation services necessary (i.e., physical, psychosocial, educational–vocational, placement, job modification, and economic support for achieving the goal). Each service should be directed at meeting an intermediate objective, which is considered to be an essential stepping stone toward the final goal—that is, becoming a satisfactory and satisfied employee in a particular work role.

CONCLUDING STATEMENT

In the minds of many people with disabilities, vocational counseling and placement services are top priority reasons for seeking assistance from a rehabilitation counselor. The outcome of the rehabilitation process should be a job that is commensurate with the individual's training and experience (i.e., suitable employment). The suitability of employment is, however, affected by many factors—characteristics of the person and characteristics of the environment. Although an initial level of compatibility is required, both person and environment can adjust to more adequately meet each other's needs. Facilitating this process of accommodation is an important part of the rehabilitation counselor's role.

Chapter 2 has stressed the importance of the match between person characteristics and job characteristics and the role of the counselor in facilitating examination of these factors during the counseling process. Described in terms of satisfactory and satisfied, a good job–person match implies that the person with a disability can meet the skill demands of the job (satisfactory) and that the job activities meet the needs of the person (satisfied).

To meet the needs of the person, the job must provide certain preferred reinforcers. Reinforcement needs of the individual fall into three broad categories—intrinsic, social, and extrinsic satisfaction. Intrinsic satisfaction results from the way in which the work activity itself gives individuals feelings of self-fulfillment and competence. Involvement in work also provides individuals with rewards of a social or interpersonal nature. Extrinsic values of work include wages and fringe benefits. Counselors must help clients clarify their needs for these intrinsic, social, and extrinsic satisfiers as well as the opportunities to acquire them in the world of work.

The individual's capability to satisfy the demands of the job is another important factor. Indeed, for some rehabilitation clients, the first task is to develop basic employability skills, and, hence, prevocational training and work adjustment activities are valuable. Some individuals learn these on-the-job skills readily and are good candidates for supported employment programs. Others may not have achieved medical stability and should delay vocational choice for a period of time. These individuals must realize that their impatience to attain a vocational objective is a type of defense or protection against confronting the full implications of the disability. And, finally, some clients may have readily transferable skills for skilled to professional positions and be able to return to their previous or related occupations with only minor modifications. By understanding the wide range of vocational readiness possible, rehabilitation counselors can better direct the counseling process to meet the individual needs of their clients. A considerable amount of information must be reviewed during vocational counseling. Both the client and the counselor must consider the individual's disability, aptitudes, psychosocial development, interests, and values and the influence of natural, social, and work setting environmental factors.

Although this chapter focuses on determining the fit between client and job as an outcome of vocational counseling, the information it discusses should not be used by the counselor in such a way as to develop an "occupational imperative" for the client. Rather, these factors should be thought of as relevant areas of consideration in occupational exploration (see the Crux Model in Figure 2.1). By helping the client understand the role of these factors in affecting vocational success, the rehabilitation counselor plays a truly facilitative role in helping people with disabilities make sound vocational choices. That facilitative role means not only that the counselor must use evaluation techniques such as the medical examination, work evaluation, and standardized educational and vocational tests, but also that the counselor must help the client process that information for vocational choice purposes.

Helping people make their own vocational decisions wisely is clearly the main goal of the vocational counseling process. To build up to that goal, the counselor must carefully structure and manage a comprehensive medical, psychological, and vocational evaluation of the client. Counselors then must help clients process the resulting evaluation information in order to select a feasible vocational goal. But, even after the vocational choice is made, the rehabilitation process is not complete. Restoration, vocational training, placement, and job analysis and modification services are usually still needed. Therefore, while they must also be skilled vocational counselors, rehabilitation counselors must also be competent case managers.

As the remaining chapters of this book unfold, the necessary interaction between the case management and vocational counseling roles will become clearer. Further, the unique competencies and role of the rehabilitation counselor in the community of helping professionals should also become quite apparent.

The Intake Interview

Roy C. Farley and Stanford E. Rubin

Regardless of the specific setting, the rehabilitation client will complete an intake interview. The intake interview can be defined as a conversation between a counselor and a client with a definite mutually acceptable purpose. Because it must establish a foundation and climate for an effective working relationship, the intake interview is of critical importance. It has been viewed as the "most challenging of all interviews," requiring intense concentration on the part of the rehabilitation counselor (Nugent, 1990, p. 70).

The content of the intake interview should be chosen to accomplish prescribed goals. Because achieving intake interview goals is the rehabilitation counselor's responsibility, he or she must be prepared to direct the interaction. Being prepared to direct the interaction and having a clear goal plan for the intake interview are somewhat synonymous.

Certain general goals should be addressed in the intake interview of every client. These include (a) providing the client with necessary information about the role of the agency, available services, and client responsibilities; (b) initiating the diagnostic process (information collection); and (c) developing adequate rapport. Adequate rapport exists if the client feels he or she has freedom of expression; feels understood by the counselor; and has trust in the counselor and confidence in the counselor's ability to help. The following general questions can help guide rehabilitation counselor planning for the intake interview:

1. What are my goals for the interview (see previous three goals)?

2. What information should be provided to the client during the intake interview?

3. What information do I need to collect from the client during the intake interview?

4. What is the most efficacious manner to exchange that information?

Rehabilitation counselor pre-intake interview planning should facilitate the information exchange process. The absence of effective planning for the intake interview may very well result in wasted time, inadequate information, and possible damage to rapport. Effective intake interview planning requires more than determining the information that should be collected from or disseminated to a client. It also requires a clear realization of the purpose that such collected or disseminated information will serve for facilitating the client's ultimate rehabilitation. The remainder of this chapter discusses the three general goals for the intake interview. They are (a) orienting the client to the agency and its services, (b) initiating the diagnostic process, and (c) developing adequate rapport.

THE INTAKE INTERVIEW AS A SERVICE ORIENTATION SESSION

During the intake interview, the client should be oriented to (a) the agency's purpose and services, (b) service eligibility criteria and client rights, (c) the rehabilitation counselor's function, and (d) his or her (the client's) responsibilities. The content of the orientation in these four areas is likely to depend on the problems experienced by the client and the client's expectations of the agency and rehabilitation counselor. That knowledge allows the rehabilitation counselor to personalize the orientation, with the counselor sounding more like a helping professional than a recording.

> The client does not want a discussion of agency policy and services in general. She wants to know only of those services appropriate to her situation and those policies relevant to her problems, communicated in a way which translates services and policies in terms of these particular concerns. (Kadushin, 1972, p. 31)

Therefore, rehabilitation counselor statements on agency purpose, services offered, and eligibility criteria should be specifically worded for each client applying for services. Making the content of the service orientation highly relevant, specific, and meaningful to the client's needs will improve the client's long-term memory of such information. Health care research suggests that patients have less than optimal recall of information they are provided in health care interviews (Stewart & Cash, 1994).

During the intake interview, the rehabilitation counselor should explain his or her role as a direct provider of services, as an arranger or coordinator of services for the client, and as a client advocate. Clients who are aware of the rehabilitation counselor's capability to arrange for necessary services (e.g., medical services, vocational training, and maintenance payments), as well as to provide counseling (e.g., personal and vocational) services, are in a better position to actively participate in their rehabilitation planning. Put most simply—they become cognizant of what might be possible.

Early in the intake interview, the client should be made aware of the extent to which the counselor–client discussion is confidential (Okun, 1987). Failure to inform the client of confidentiality can result in much information of a personal nature being denied (Nugent, 1990). To the extent that the client can be guaranteed that any revelations of unflattering material will not be "available to a wider public," his or her level of ego threat should be reduced, with the result being freer client communication (Kadushin, 1972, p. 54). Any limits to confidentiality should also be made clear to the client. In this regard, Benjamin (1981) stated,

> We cannot, morally, encourage disclosure about values, attitudes, and behaviors unless we are certain that we can guarantee confidentiality. If we cannot, it is essential to state this clearly, for the client has every right to know what will be kept confidential, what may be kept so, and what will not. Given this information, he will decide how to proceed. (p. 56)

During the intake interview, clients should also be informed of the reason for any necessary post-intake interview participation in diagnostic activities, as well as be provided a brief description of those activities, including what will occur, when it will occur, and where it will occur. Such information can reduce client apprehensiveness about upcoming evaluation activities. Explanations by the counselor that describe how specific diagnostic services can help achieve rehabilitation objectives can be helpful. For example, because vocational evaluation services might facilitate appropriate client vocational choice, the rehabilitation counselor might say, "Your participation in vocational evaluation can help us to better understand your interests and abilities so that together we can arrive at a suitable vocational objective."

It is also important to explain the contents of any form that the client will be asked to sign during the intake interview. Explaining the purpose of each form and why the client's signature is necessary should be the typical modus operandi of the rehabilitation counselor.

There is no reason for the rehabilitation counselor to not inform the client of the objectives of the intake interview. In fact, structuring the intake interview experience for the client could result in the client also approaching the intake interview in a systematic goal-oriented manner. Although there is a paucity of research on the relationship of rehabilitation counselor structuring and client outcome, several studies in the psychotherapy literature have shown early structuring of the psychotherapy relationship for clients to have a significant positive effect on treatment outcome (Goldstein, 1973; Hoehn-Saric et al., 1964; Jacobs, Charles, Jacobs, Weinstein, & Mann, 1972; Sloane, Cristol, Pepernik, & Staples, 1970; Strupp & Bloxom, 1973; Truax & Wargo, 1969; Warren & Rice, 1972). Research in the social work literature (McIsaac & Wilkinson, 1965; Schmidt, 1969) shows a relationship between the interviewer's lack of structuring the purpose of the interview for the client and the client's uncertainty and confusion regarding the purpose of the interview. This finding supports the value of rehabilitation counselors structuring the intake interview with their clients. When clients better understand their interviewee role responsibilities, they are also likely to be less anxious during the interview. Overall, effective structuring of the intake interview results in the client having greater confidence in the rehabilitation counselor's competence (Kadushin, 1972).

As can readily be seen at this point, much information must be communicated to the client during the intake interview. Therefore, it is not beyond the realm of possibility that the client could become overwhelmed by it and end up more confused than truly informed. Two ready "rules of thumb" that can help the rehabilitation counselor avoid that negative outcome are as follows:

1. Use language that corresponds with the client's background. Avoid the use of confusing terminology and jargon.

2. Guard against providing the client too much information at "one shot" during the interview. Clients provided too much information at once can be overwhelmed.

Because providing information does not guarantee that it has been comprehended before the intake interview ends, the rehabilitation counselor should determine whether the client has understood the information provided. One check is to ask the client to give his or her interpretation of the information provided to determine level of comprehension (Stewart & Cash, 1994).

It is wise to summarize the significant content of the intake interview discussion as the interview approaches its end. Via the summary, the rehabilitation counselor should make clear to the client those steps they agreed the counselor would take and those steps the client would take prior to the next interview. The purpose of subsequent interviews can also be touched upon via this summary.

INITIATING THE DIAGNOSTIC PROCESS

In order to obtain a diagnostic understanding of the client, the rehabilitation counselor must collect much information from the client. The intake interview is a significant vehicle for information collection, because it affords clients an opportunity to provide the counselor with the social and vocational history necessary for diagnostic and prognostic purposes. When the picture of the client's social and vocational history has been "insufficiently developed" during the intake interview, the rehabilitation counselor may be inadequately equipped to determine the unanswered questions that must be addressed via subsequent outside evaluations. The following undesirable conditions may occur when information gaps about the client exist at the end of the intake interview: (a) failure to realize the need to arrange for a medical, psychological, or educational–vocational evaluation, and (b) development of a less than optimally designed rehabilitation plan. A comprehensive social and vocational history has been obtained once the rehabilitation counselor can answer the following questions, plus most of the questions in Table 3.1.

a. Does the client have a specific vocational objective?

b. Does the client have more than one potential vocational goal?

c. How optimistic or pessimistic is the client about his or her ability to achieve each vocational goal?

d. Is the client interested in vocational training?

e. Is the client interested in any specific type of vocational training?

TABLE 3.1
A Topical Information Collection Guide for the Intake Interview

Physical Factors

1. What specific physical impairments are present?

2. What caused the disability?

3. How long has the client had a disability?

4. Has the client received any disability-related treatment in the past (e.g., physical therapy, occupational therapy, prosthetics, or orthotics)?

5. Has the client's disabling condition become worse over the past year?

6. Is the client currently receiving any disability-related treatment?

7. Is the client taking any medication with potential side effects?

8. Do any recent medical test results clarify extent of physical impairment?

9. How does the client's physical disability handicap daily functioning?

Psychosocial Factors

1. Personal Adjustment

   a. Do recent psychological test results pertain to the question of client psychological adjustment?

   b. Is there any agency or professional from whom the client is presently receiving psychological services?

   c. Has the client ever received professional treatment for a personal adjustment problem?

   d. Is the client taking any tranquilizers or sleeping pills?

   e. Does the client report unnecessary avoidance of work or social situations since acquiring a disability?

2. Relationships with Family and Friends

   a. What is the client's marital status?

   b. Is the client living with his or her family?

   c. Does the client have any dependent-age children?

   d. Will the most significant family members (e.g., spouse) be supportive of the rehabilitation plan?

(continues)

TABLE 3.1 *(Continued)*

e. How does the client feel about his or her home environment?

f. How does the client get along with other members of the family?

g. Does the client have any close friends?

h. Is the client satisfied with his or her social life?

i. How does the client fill the hours of the day?

j. Would the client's family be willing to relocate geographically for him or her to acquire work?

Educational–Vocational Skills Development Factors

1. Educational History

   a. How far did the client go in school?

   b. What did the client like or dislike about school?

   c. Why did the client leave school (graduate, other)?

   d. If the client did not complete high school, has he or she passed a high school equivalency exam?

   e. Has the client received vocational training that has prepared him or her to enter a particular occupation?

2. Work History

   a. What were the last three jobs held by the client?

   b. For each of those jobs, determine the following items.

      i. Weekly earnings.

      ii. Length of employment (Was it long enough to acquire specific skills?).

      iii. Time since job held (Has sufficient time passed for significant skill loss to take place?).

      iv. Aspects of the job performed well and poorly by the client.

      v. Aspects of the job liked most and least. Why?

      vi. Reasons for termination of employment.

   c. Prior to onset of disability, were there any significant interruptions in work history? Why?

   d. Is the client presently unemployed? If yes, for how long?

   e. Has the client been employed since acquiring a disability?

(continues)

TABLE 3.1 *(Continued)*

Economic Factors

1. What is the client's primary source of support?

2. Does the client have other sources of support?

3. Does the client have any unpaid debts of significant size?

4. What fixed living expenses such as medication costs cannot be reduced?

5. Does the client have a Worker's Compensation case pending?

6. Is the client receiving or has the client applied for welfare or SSI benefits?

7. Does the client have any medical insurance?

8. Is the client concerned about his or her economic situation?

9. What minimal level of earnings from work must the client receive?

Note. From *Intake Interview Skills for Rehabilitation Counselors* (pp. 64–66), by S. E. Rubin and R. C. Farley, 1980, Fayetteville: Arkansas Rehabilitation Research and Training Center. Copyright 1980 by the Arkansas Rehabilitation Research and Training Center. Reprinted with permission.

For an example of the result of a comprehensive intake interview, read the Intake Interview summary for Shirley Steed below.

 # CASE STUDY: SHIRLEY STEED

Summary of Intake Interview

Shirley Steed is a 38-year-old white divorced female. She has four children; two sons, ages 15 and 17, and two married daughters, ages 19 and 20. Married at age 16, Shirley did not work during the first 10 years of her marriage. At age 26, she went to work in a fabric shop. She worked in the fabric shop for 6 months, at which time she took a job in a print shop where she worked for 8 years. She then took a job in a second print shop, where she had been employed until 2 weeks ago. She had to quit her last job because of illness. She is currently under considerable financial strain and is applying for public assistance.

Mrs. Steed seeks rehabilitation services to gain the vocational skills needed to become a secretary. Due to her present health condition, she is no longer able to do the heavy work required in a print shop. She describes her major symptoms as bad varicose veins, chronic bronchitis, emphysema, nervousness, and depression.

Although Mrs. Steed has no formal work experience as a secretary, she did have secretarial training in high school. Her employment history is largely confined to work in print shops and clerking in a fabric shop. She worked in one print shop for over 8 years.

Although she quit school in the 12th grade, Mrs. Steed earned her high school diploma by passing a GED examination 3 years ago. During high school, she completed a typing and shorthand course and reported her skill levels at 55 wpm on the typewriter and 60 wpm with shorthand. However, she has not typed or taken shorthand for the past 22 years.

Mrs. Steed's medical complications developed when she began work 12 years ago in a fabric shop. At that point, her health began to deteriorate due to an asthmatic condition that was aggravated by an allergy to wool. As was noted above, Mrs. Steed worked in the fabric shop for only 6 months. She then left the fabric shop and began working for Top Notch Printing. At that job, she operated an AB Dick offset press, did some darkroom work, and some collating. She was able to handle the job physically and liked working there. However, during her 8 years of employment at Top Notch Printing, Mrs. Steed was frequently absent from work due to acute health problems. After she had been employed there for 4 years, she contracted double pneumonia that triggered a chronic bronchitis condition. During the remainder of her employment at Top Notch Printing, she was frequently absent from work due to recurring lung infections from the chronic bronchitis. Approximately 3 years ago, Mrs. Steed was hospitalized for physical and nervous exhaustion that was the end product of marital conflicts, her husband leaving her, and deteriorating health. At that point, she was fired from her job at Top Notch Printing because of her frequent absences from work.

She divorced her husband at that time. She related that her husband started drinking from the time that she developed chronic bronchitis and that he often physically abused her. In fact, about a month before she lost her job in the print shop, she had her husband jailed for assault and battery. She has not seen or heard from him since he was released from jail.

The crushing combination of these factors brought on a depression in Mrs. Steed, for which she was treated by a counselor at a mental health center throughout the following 12 months. She felt that the counseling helped her adjust to her divorce, overcome her depression, and return to work.

Mrs. Steed was employed for 3 months following the loss of her job at Top Notch Printing. She then acquired a job at T and J Printing as a press assistant and also did the collating necessary for producing a weekly newspaper. She operated a Heidelburg and Davidson offset printing press. She handled all the paper cutting and the entire printing process. The job was extremely difficult for her. She often had to lift a case that the type was locked in, which ranged in weight from a minimum of 10 pounds to a high of 40 pounds with the full form locked into it. The work wore her down, and she experienced several successive illnesses. Her bronchial condition deteriorated, and she developed emphysema. Mrs. Steed has also developed very bad varicose veins in both legs, and it bothers her to be on her feet all day. Two weeks ago, she finally had to quit her T and J Printing job for health reasons.

Mrs. Steed's emphysema rules out strenuous work, and her varicose veins make it extremely difficult for her to work on her feet for long periods. In fact, she commented that she needs a flexible work routine in which she can alternate sitting and standing in order to be as comfortable as possible. She also indicated that until her health improves, she will probably lack the stamina necessary for a 40-hour work week.

Overall, Mrs. Steed's ability to work seems to be good, with the exception of the health-related limitations. She worked successfully in the print shop and the fabric shop, mastering the tasks involved in printing and clerking.

Mrs. Steed also related that she enjoys interpersonal relationships at work, and she particularly appreciated those that she experienced at the print shop. However, she does not enjoy working in high-pressure, competitive situations such as the sales position at the fabric shop. She disliked the competition for customers that her immediate supervisor encouraged among the clerks at the fabric shop. Mrs. Steed said that there would have to be no other job available before she would consider returning to work as a sales clerk.

She reports no conflicts with peers or supervisors other than her negative reactions to workers with excessively competitive attitudes whom she encountered in the fabric shop. Mrs. Steed has good work habits and—health permitting—wants nothing more than to work regularly.

Although Mrs. Steed's two daughters have married and left home, she feels close to them both. In fact, she is currently living with one of her daughters. However, she must find a new residence before her daughter's husband returns from the service next month.

Mrs. Steed still has a 15-year-old son directly in her care. She is concerned about her son's interest in quitting school and entering Seaman's School. Although he is having difficulties in high school and would probably get along better at Seaman's School, he cannot leave high school for another year. Her older son, who is 17 years old, is currently in jail for grand larceny. Although he originally received a 1-year sentence for stealing a car, he did escape and has had additional time added to his sentence. These complications with her two sons made Mrs. Steed very tense and worried.

As previously indicated, Mrs. Steed will soon need a residence of her own. She has no insurance of any type and is currently paying medical bills that run about $50 a month. Because Mrs. Steed is currently unemployed, she has no money coming into the family and needs to receive some financial support.

Mrs. Steed's current options for dealing with her problems appear to be limited to applying for public assistance and completing a vocational rehabilitation program. She says she does not want to be dependent on welfare and hopes that she can return to work very soon as a secretary. She feels that she could earn adequate wages as a secretary to meet her needs and the needs of her younger son until he can enter Seaman's School.

The intake interview affords clients the opportunity to describe their situations and their perceived rehabilitation needs to the rehabilitation counselor. The rehabilitation counselor's role is to listen effectively and to ask questions when necessary. Stewart and Cash (1994) characterize effective listening as active listening. They define active listening as listening "carefully and critically to words, arguments, and evidence, and observ[ing] . . . all nonverbal clues from voice, face, gestures, eye contact, and movements" (p. 31). However, listening effectively does not necessarily mean being totally silent. Cormier and Cormier (1979) discuss the following four counselor responses as listening responses: (a) clarification—"a question beginning with 'do you mean that' or 'are you saying that' plus a rephrasing of the client's message," (b) paraphrase—"a rephrasing of the content of the client's message," (c) reflection—"a rephrasing of the affective part of the client's message," and (d) summarization—"two or more paraphrases or reflections that condense the client's messages or the session" (p. 64). All four responses have at least three common purposes. First, they communicate that the counselor is "hearing" what the client is saying. Second, they serve as a check on the accuracy of the counselor's understanding of what the client is saying. Third, they serve to facilitate client clarification of that which he or she wishes to communicate. The rehabilitation counselor's effective use of these four responses, plus the use of properly timed questions phrased in an open-ended exploratory manner (e.g., "Can you tell me about the things you liked or disliked about your last job?"), should facilitate sufficient client self-exploration during the intake interview. These responses should provide the counselor with answers to most of the previously noted intake interview questions without the counselor having to ask the majority of them. The optimal outcome of an intake interview is both greater rehabilitation counselor understanding of the client's situation and increased client understanding of his or her situation.

Saying that insufficient information collection could yield a social–vocational history that is incapable of providing the counselor with the insights necessary to sufficiently understand his or her client for future planning purposes is not analogous to saying that the rehabilitation counselor should collect every conceivable piece of social and vocational history information from the client. Some bits of information will simply be superfluous to counselor achievement of diagnostic accuracy. Not only is the collection of irrelevant information from the client a waste of valuable intake interview time, it could also negatively affect the level of client–counselor rapport if the client begins to perceive the rehabilitation counselor as an "information voyeur" or a "grand inquisitor." Therefore, the rehabilitation counselor must be capable of discriminating between significant and superfluous information. Significant information enables the rehabilitation counselor or the rehabilitation team to make differential predictions across potential alternative rehabilitation plans with respect to (a) likelihood of successful completion and client satisfaction, (b) potential difficulties that might arise, (c) interventions necessary for overcoming such difficulties, and (d) probability of the success of such interventions overcoming difficulties (Rubin & Farley, 1980).

Donald Jones's case below illustrates the effect of counselor failure to collect a piece of information relevant to making differential predictions.

 ## CASE STUDY: DONALD JONES

Donald Jones would like to enter a 2-year computer programming training program. His interests and aptitudes are compatible with that occupational choice. However, the counselor does not inquire about Donald's wife's attitude toward that rehabilitation goal. The client drops out of the training program 6 weeks later. The counselor wonders why. The counselor checks with the client and finds out that the client's wife resented the poverty lifestyle for a year. She threatened to leave him if he remained in the program. Had the counselor been aware of the wife's attitude, he might have arranged for family counseling or suggested that Donald prepare a vocational objective achievable via on-the-job training.

The Donald Jones example also indicates the danger of a superficial rehabilitation counselor information collection style. By helping the counselor identify significant unanswered questions prior to and during the intake interview process, the content of Table 3.1 enables the rehabilitation counselor to avoid a superficial information collection style. For example, the list in Table 3.1 can help the counselor generate covert questions about the client that can tend to guide his or her intake interview focus. A general example would be:

a. "What do I know about the client?"
b. "What do I still need to know about the client?"

Such questions tend to provide direction for guiding the interview interaction. They can aid the rehabilitation counselor in knowing where he or she is (what is already known) in the intake information collection process and where to proceed next (what still needs to be known).

Many covert questions are stimulated by hypotheses that the counselor has generated about the client or the client's situation based on previous information collected. These covert questions stimulate overt information collection behavior directed at confirming or disconfirming the hypotheses. Therefore, covert questions can act as a "scientific" guide to the rehabilitation counselor's overt information collection behavior. These questions act in such a way that the probability of achieving a better understanding of the client is greatly increased (Miller, 1985). Two examples of the generation of relevant covert questions can be observed below (Rubin & Farley, 1980).

1. The following covert question could be triggered by an awareness that the client has recently been fitted for a functional hand prosthesis to replace his

nonfunctional cosmetic hand: How does the client feel about wearing the functional prosthesis in public? (For example, does the client feel too self-conscious to wear it in many social situations?)

2. Knowing that a client has been receiving psychotherapy for adjustment problems for the last year is an important fact that could stimulate the following covert question: Does the client think that he has been helped by the psychotherapist? In what ways?

As can also be readily realized from the above examples, the rehabilitation counselor's failure to either generate significant covert questions or be guided by them during the intake interview can result in eventual diagnostic inaccuracy.

Superficiality of focus is more likely to occur when the rehabilitation counselor becomes more interested in filling out agency forms than in truly *getting to know his or her clients*. This can be observed in the sample conversation below, in which the completion of a form appears to have been the dominant consideration controlling the intake interview interaction.

COUNSELOR: How old are you now?

CLIENT: 28

COUNSELOR: Have you been trained for any jobs?

CLIENT: Yeah, I had secretarial training in high school.

COUNSELOR: I see. Have you had contact with vocational rehabilitation before, uh?

CLIENT: No.

COUNSELOR: Who is your family doctor?

CLIENT: Dr. Russell.

COUNSELOR: What type of medical problem do you have?

CLIENT: I'm a nervous wreck.

COUNSELOR: Are you taking anything?

CLIENT: Yes, I'm on librium.

COUNSELOR: Are you in therapy?

CLIENT: Yes.

COUNSELOR: With whom?

CLIENT: Dr. Mildred Sorvino at the mental health clinic.

COUNSELOR: How long have you lived in this area?

CLIENT: I was born here.

COUNSELOR: I see.

CLIENT:	But I haven't lived here in years though.
COUNSELOR:	Are you renting now?
CLIENT:	Uh-huh.
COUNSELOR:	Okay. Have you worked since you moved back here?
CLIENT:	Yeah, I worked for the Kelly Services for about a month.
COUNSELOR:	Uh-huh. Did you work for anybody before that?
CLIENT:	Not since we moved here.
COUNSELOR:	I see. And before you moved here?
CLIENT:	Sales-clerked at a Speedi-Mart food store.
COUNSELOR:	Uh-huh. When was that?
CLIENT:	I imagine that was around '83.
COUNSELOR:	Did you do this for a long period of time?
CLIENT:	No, just a short time.
COUNSELOR:	All right. Are you receiving any welfare aid now?
CLIENT:	Just, uh, $155 a month for my daughter.
COUNSELOR:	This is through welfare?
CLIENT:	Yeah.
COUNSELOR:	Did you graduate from high school?
CLIENT:	I took the GED test in 1989.
COUNSELOR:	How far did you go in formal education?
CLIENT:	I quit school in the 9th grade.
COUNSELOR:	All right, did you work at that point?
CLIENT:	No, just dropped out of school.
COUNSELOR:	By any chance are you a veteran?
CLIENT:	No.
COUNSELOR:	I would like you to sign this application form right here.
CLIENT:	Okay.

DEVELOPING ADEQUATE RAPPORT

Counselor–client rapport does not develop in a vacuum. Rather, its development is greatly dependent on the effectiveness of counselor preparation for the interview and his or her interview response style after the client arrives. It is likely that the rehabilitation counselor has prepared well for the interview and has responded effectively in the interview when the client likes the counselor, perceives the counselor as competent, and feels that the counselor cares about him or her.

Preparation for the Interview

The physical arrangement of the interview setting can facilitate or retard the achievement of intake interview diagnostic goals and the development of counselor–client rapport. When the first contact with the client is in a place other than the office, rehabilitation counselors may be limited in the things they might do to structure the setting. However, when that first contact is in the office, there are several things that rehabilitation counselors can do to enhance rapport and communicate interest and concern. These include (a) effective furniture arrangement, (b) preventing unnecessary interruptions, and (c) proper time planning.

Effective Furniture Arrangement

While some studies (White, 1953; Widgery & Stackpole, 1972) show a relationship between furniture arrangement and level of rapport in an interview setting, much more research is needed before definitive conclusions can be drawn. Therefore, one must presently turn to commonsense conclusions of writer–practitioners for guidance on furniture arrangement. Such writers (Benjamin, 1981; Kadushin, 1972) seem to suggest that as a general rule (as opposed to an absolute rule) of thumb, counselors should avoid placing physical barriers such as a desk between themselves and their clients. Barriers between the counselor and the client can become barriers to open communication. This would be especially the case in regard to nonverbal communication. In this regard, Kadushin (1972) states,

> A desk between the interviewer and the interviewee means that half of the interviewee's body is nonobservable. Any gestures of the lower part of the body—tapping feet, knees clamped together, tensely clasped hands in the lap—are masked from view. However, some people need the limited protection from interviewer observation which the table or desk permits. They are made anxious if too much of themselves is accessible to observation. (p. 117)

While the exception to the rule pointed out by Kadushin (1972) above is likely valid, the findings in the Widgery and Stackpole (1972) study on desk position and interviewee perception of interviewer credibility are not supportive of it. These researchers found that high-anxiety interviewees perceived greater interviewer credibility when no desk separated them than when one did. However, it should be pointed out that Widgery and Stackpole (1972) used a highly artificial experimental situation with college students as subjects. Until more research has been done, rehabilitation counselors will have to draw upon their "common sense" in determining how to arrange their office furniture in a manner most facilitative of counselor–client rapport. One easily drawn "commonsense" conclusion for those rehabilitation counselors who work with persons with physical disabilities is to arrange the office to avoid barriers to accessibility (e.g., rearrange furniture such as a desk and file cabinets so that the client will not be bothered with running an obstacle course just to get into the office). An interview setting with accessibility problems for a client with a physical disability can make the person feel like a "second class citizen."

Other Pre-Interview Considerations

Another commonsense rule of thumb is to put away things that could distract the client or that the counselor does not wish the client to see, such as case files, papers, forms, and medical or psychological reports. Rehabilitation counselors should also meet with clients in a place where confidentiality can be assured. Clients are less likely to provide much meaningful and relevant personal information in a meeting place devoid of sufficient privacy (Stewart & Cash, 1994).

Rehabilitation counselors should allow sufficient time to achieve their interview objectives. Therefore, scheduling too many people for too short of a period should be avoided.

Once clients arrive, it is important that they see themselves as recipients of the rehabilitation counselor's attention. Therefore, removal of potential distractors such as phone calls and knocks at the door should be taken care of prior to the scheduled interview (Nugent, 1990). Even when such arrangements have been made with the secretary beforehand, reminding the secretary about it in the presence of the client clearly communicates to the client that he or she is entitled to, and will have, the counselor's total attention during the interview (Bernstein, Bernstein, & Dana, 1974).

Rehabilitation Counselor Interview Response Style

If rehabilitation counselors are to be successful in meeting the goals of the intake interview (e.g., providing information, initiating the diagnostic process, and developing rapport), they must have an effective interview response style. That style should be pervaded by both nonverbal and verbal counselor responses that facilitate the development and maintenance of counselor–client rapport. Optimal counselor responses are those that communicate understanding, warmth, respect, and genuineness, and that encourage client freedom of expression and self-exploration.

Nonverbal Behavior

Once he or she has entered the counselor's office, the client should receive the counselor's full attention. The counselor should also do what is necessary to make the client comfortable. For example, proper distance should be established between the counselor and client. Proper distance is a comfortable distance for both the counselor and client. Carkhuff and Anthony (1979) suggested that the optimum distance between the helper and the helpee "is three to four feet in a one to one seating situation" (p. 39). Research on the relationship between physical proximity and individual comfort level show that Americans tend to get uncomfortable when they get within 2 feet of another person (Argyle & Dean, 1965).

Facing the client squarely, inclining his or her upper body slightly toward the client, and maintaining proper eye contact can communicate counselor involvement with the client. Research has shown that leaning toward the helpee is positively related to the helpee perceiving the counselor as being attentive to him or her (Genther & Moughan, 1977). Eye contact is a more complex issue.

> In Western culture, eye contact is an indication that the counselor is paying attention . . . . People tend to use more eye contact when they have positive feelings for someone. However, persistent eye contact, such as a steady gaze of more than 10 seconds (staring) is likely to make a client anxious and could be interpreted as a sign of hostility . . . . As a counselor, you want to maintain eye contact with a client without staring. (Cormier & Cormier, 1979, p. 43)

As the counselor assumes a comfortable distance, faces the client squarely, leans his or her body toward the client, and establishes proper eye contact, he or she should maintain an open, relaxed posture. The importance of an open posture (avoid folding arms, crossing legs, and so forth) and support for the slogan "open body—open mind" are indicated in a study by McGinley, LeFevre, and McGinley (1975). They found that not only do people seem to *like* an individual with an open body position, they also are more likely to allow that person to have more influence in changing their opinions than someone with a closed body position.

The counselor should also refrain from distracting movements. Distracting gestures may include shaking a pointed finger, yawning, closing eyes, frowning, sneering, fidgeting, swinging arms wildly, tapping fingers, and swinging legs (Okun, 1976). Many of these gestures can communicate lack of interest, disapproval, or impatience. On the other hand, proper movements may communicate those things important to the establishment of rapport. Okun (1976) listed occasional head nodding and hand movements as positive communication behaviors. Bayes (1972) found body, head, and hand movements, as well as smiling, to be indications of high warmth rating. LaCrosse (1975) found counselor positive head nods, gesticulations, and smiling to be positively related to ratings of counselor attractiveness and persuasiveness.

The foregoing discussion clearly indicates the importance of nonverbal behavior to the counselor's goal of developing adequate rapport with the client during the intake interview. Proper counselor distancing, body positioning, body movements, smiling, and eye contact help communicate respect, involvement, interest, warmth, and understanding, all of which are important to the development and maintenance of rapport.

Verbal Behavior

Like nonverbal behavior, the rehabilitation counselor's verbal interview behavior can affect the level of counselor–client rapport. Nugent (1990) pointed out that attempting to put the client at ease via social chit-chat at the beginning of the intake interview is not recommended. For many clients, any delay by the rehabilitation counselor in getting to the reason they have sought services can produce the opposite effect of raising the client's anxiety. Nugent (1990) suggested opening with a simple statement such as, "Tell me what brings you here for rehabilitation counseling services." However, the recommendation against informal chit-chat may not be equally valid for clients in all cultures. For example, Zuniga (1992) recommended the opposite approach with some Hispanic clients who are likely to prefer that the counselor communicate in a more personable and less task-oriented style, at least initially.

A number of writers (Benjamin, 1981; Capuzzi & Gross, 1995; Evans, Hearn, Uhlemann, & Ivey, 1989; Landefeld, 1975; Miller, 1972) have classified counselor verbal interview responses into various categories. Since the classification systems tend to use different category labels while covering many of the same verbal responses, to report them all here would tend to both bore and confuse the reader. Because of its clarity, the authors have chosen Miller's (1972) classification system as the basis for the following discussion. Miller identified five classes or types of verbal responses. Three of the responses can be used by the counselor to collect information from the client. These are identified as continue responses, focus responses, and check responses.

Continue responses (e.g., "um-hmm," "yes," "I see," and "yeah") are remarks that encourage further speech by the client with no particular topic or form indicated. They indicate to the client that he or she has the counselor's full attention; continue responses are "green lights" for the client to continue talking (Rubin & Farley, 1980). Continue responses not only indicate that the counselor is listening but also can communicate interest, involvement, acceptance, warmth, and positive regard. By encouraging client self-expression, continue responses also serve to maintain the interview discussion without interruptions.

Focus responses prompt the client to provide more speech on a topic already presented. Miller (1972) classified these responses as either binary focus or nonbinary focus. A binary-focus response is a closed-ended question that calls for a yes-or-no answer. It indicates to the client that the counselor is seeking specific information and tends to guide the client's verbal behavior in a restricted manner. The nonbinary-focus response is an open-ended question and requires a narrative answer. It allows for more flexibility than the binary-focus response in the client's verbal behavior by allowing him or her more freedom of expression. Research on the effect of counselor open-ended questions on the frequency of client affective self-reference statements in initial quasi-counseling interviews (Highlen & Baccus, 1977; Hill & Gormally, 1977) suggests that counselor nonbinary-focus responses should promote client discussion of feelings in rehabilitation counseling intake interviews.

The third type of counselor information-collection response, the *check response*, functions to indicate that a "check" on communication is being conducted. Often referred to as reflections, the check response communicates to the client that the counselor understands what is being said and that the client should continue giving information. Research on the effect of check responses on the frequency of client affective self-reference statements in initial quasi-counseling interviews (Highlen & Baccus, 1977) suggests that counselor reflection of feeling responses should also promote client discussion of feelings in rehabilitation counseling intake interviews.

Rehabilitation counselor verbal responses that keep the focus on the client's concerns and allow the client the greatest freedom of expression facilitate rapport development. Open-ended questions and statements such as "Tell me more about . . . ," questions such as "How did you feel about . . . ," and reflections such as "You appear to be saying that you did not like that job because . . . ," encourage the client to talk and explore his or her thoughts and feelings. These questions require a narrative statement from the client (as opposed to short answers) and allow more freedom of expression. Therefore, they facilitate client self-exploration.

Open-ended statements and questions are also helpful in opening the intake interview. A statement such as "Let's begin by you telling me what brings you here," immediately focuses the interview on the client's concerns. Statements that reflect the counselor's understanding of the client are also useful verbal responses to keep the interview client centered. Frequently communicating understanding should build, strengthen, and maintain rapport.

The counselor should avoid *excessive* use of closed-ended questions (i.e., responses that call for short, quick client replies). These responses have their place in the intake interview—in instances in which specific bits of information are needed for filling out forms. Closed-ended questions are the most direct means of gathering factual information such as name, age, address, social security number, and so on. However, closed-ended questions should not be the predominant or most frequent response used to gather information from the client. The extensive use of this type of responding may result in clients perceiving the counselor as someone who is only after the facts and not very interested in how they think, feel, and act. Therefore, clients would learn very quickly not to go into any depth with information, and much pertinent and relevant information would not be shared.

Miller (1972) refers to counselor responses that function to present outside information to the client as declarative responses. When it becomes necessary for the counselor to disseminate information to the client, this type of response is used.

The fifth category offered by Miller (1972) is called a *switch response*, a response that directs conversation from one topic to another. The topic switched to may be one newly introduced or a reintroduction of an old one. This type of response is highly appropriate for moving a client off an exhausted subject and is sometimes necessary if the counselor is to achieve interview goals.

Merely using all of the above responses to guide the intake interview discussions will not necessarily promote rapport. However, the appropriate use of the various responses should positively influence the development of adequate rapport. Appropriate use is likely synonymous with "proper balance," which probably always will be determined by the situation and the client, and therefore is determined through good rehabilitation counselor judgment.

As the foregoing discussion indicates, the counselor's use of verbal responses is important to the development of adequate rapport. Keeping the interview focused on the client's concerns; using responses that allow the greatest freedom of self-expression; avoiding the excessive use of closed-ended questions; using reflective responses and short, quick verbal responses that indicate listening help communicate the concern, involvement, interest, respect, warmth, genuineness, and understanding that facilitate the development, enhancement, and maintenance of rapport.

CONCLUDING STATEMENT

Exchanging information and developing rapport with a person with a disability are the primary focuses of the rehabilitation intake interview. The counselor is responsible for directing that exchange of information and, therefore, must be prepared to interact with the client in a manner that will facilitate orienting the client to the agency, initiating the diagnostic process, and developing adequate rapport.

During the intake process, the client needs much information. To decide if the rehabilitation agency can meet his or her needs, the client needs information about the rehabilitation agency, its role and function, services that are offered, the objectives of those services, and eligibility requirements. The counselor's role and the client's rights and responsibilities are other areas to be discussed with the client during the intake interview. The counselor is more likely to effectively orient the client to the agency by knowing the information the client needs, as well as the most effective and efficient way to communicate that information.

The client has much information that the counselor must collect during the intake interview. The collection of that information can be facilitated when the counselor is aware of all the information collection areas that should be explored and when he or she is effective in promoting client self-expression and self-exploration.

Information exchange and rapport development can be greatly facilitated through effective rehabilitation counselor nonverbal and verbal intake-interview behavior. They are also facilitated through proper rehabilitation counselor preparation for the intake interview.

Medical Evaluation

The purpose of the medical evaluation in the rehabilitation process is to determine client medical limitations and remaining capacities. In particular, the rehabilitation counselor is interested in information regarding the client's capabilities to fulfill various types of vocational demands. The vocational implications of medical findings comprise a significant part of the diagnostic data base essential for the development of the rehabilitation plan (Brodwin & Brodwin, 1993). Focusing on medical evaluation, Chapter 4 addresses several important concerns: (a) choosing a physician for the medical evaluation, (b) making an effective medical referral, (c) knowing what to expect from evaluating physicians, and (d) using the medical consultant.

CHOOSING A PHYSICIAN

Since selection of an inappropriate physician will likely result in an inadequate medical report, the first guideline for effective medical referral would be to choose the evaluating physician wisely. One criterion to consider always is the physician's ability to develop rapport with his or her patients. The effectiveness of the communication between the referred client and the physician depends somewhat on the level of rapport between them. Therefore, the level of rapport can have an effect on the quality and sufficiency of the information on which the validity of the written medical evaluation report rests (Felton, 1993b).

An appropriate physician can be one who has treated the client in the past. The degree to which this physician is an appropriate choice depends on three factors: (a) knowledge of the client's medical history, (b) medical expertise with the specific disability(ies) present, and (c) level of established rapport with the client. Of course, even without previous contact with the client, a specialist in the treatment of the client's particular disability who is also capable of developing rapport with the client, usually is considered an appropriate physician. Hence, rehabilitation counselors must be familiar with the many existing medical specialties. In the process of acquiring medical evaluations of their clients, rehabilitation counselors may interact with a variety of medical specialists. Table 4.1 (based on information obtained from the American

Medical Association [1989], Felton, Perkins, & Lewin [1969], and Good Housekeeping [1989]) presents a description of many of these specialties.

TABLE 4.1
Medical Specialists

Specialist	Function
Allergist	Diagnoses and treats any type of allergy or allergic reaction.
Cardiologist	Diagnoses and treats diseases of the heart and associated blood vessels (cardiovascular system). Disorders treated include "coronary heart disease, hypertensive heart disease, rheumatic heart disease, infectious heart disease, and heart defects present at birth" (Good Housekeeping, 1989, p. 352).
Dermatologist	Treats diseases of the skin, hair, and nails.
Endocrinologist	Diagnoses and treats diseases caused by a hormone imbalance such as diabetes mellitus or thyroid disorders.
Gastroenterologist	Diagnoses and treats diseases and disorders of the digestive system such as stomach ulcers, stomach cancer, pancreatic cancer, ulcerative colitis, and disorders of the liver and gallbladder.
Gynecologist	Diagnoses and treats disorders of the female reproductive system.
Hematologist	"Specializes in disorders of the blood, and, to some extent, those affecting the closely associated lymphatic system" (Good Housekeeping, 1989, p. 359).
Neurologist	Treats diseases of the nervous system.
Neurosurgeon	Performs surgery on the brain, spinal cord, and the peripheral and autonomic nervous system.
Oncologist	Diagnoses and treats tumors or new growths, both benign and malignant.
Ophthalmologist	Diagnoses and treats disorders of the eye.
Orthopedist	"Perform(s) many tasks, including setting broken bones and putting on casts; treating joint conditions, such as dislocations, slipped disks, arthritis, and back problems; treating bone tumors and birth defects of the skeleton; and surgically repairing or replacing hip, knee, or finger joints" (American Medical Association, 1989, p. 752).
Otolaryngologist	Medically and surgically treats diseases of ear, nose, and throat.
Pediatrician	Specializes in the medical care of children.

(continues)

TABLE 4.1 (*Continued*)

Specialists	Function
Plastic Surgeon	Performs reparative surgery to restore "function and, when possible, appearance following tissue loss and damage by injury or disease, especially burns, cancer and automobile accidents" (Good Housekeeping, 1989, p. 374).
Physiatrist	Tests and establishes a rehabilitation program for "patients recovering from or overcoming disabilities or impairments caused by injury (especially of the joints and muscles), illness, or neurological conditions such as paralytic strokes" (American Medical Association, 1989, p. 793).
Psychiatrist	Diagnoses and treats emotional and behavioral problems.
Rheumatologist	"Diagnoses and treats arthritis, rheumatism, and other afflictions of the joints, muscles, or connective tissues" (American Medical Association, 1989, p. 871).
Thoracic Surgeon	Performs surgery on lungs, esophagus, and trachea.
Urologist	Treats diseases of the genito-urinary system.

Note. Table 4.1 is based on information obtained from American Medical Association (1989), Felton et al. (1969), and Good Housekeeping (1989).

MAKING AN EFFECTIVE REFERRAL

In an effective medical referral, rehabilitation counselors should specify the information they need from the physician. These information needs can be communicated through a list of referral questions. Although referral questions should be tailored to the individual case, some general issues are relevant for all clients. For example, referral questions should touch on the following issues: (a) the client's general health; (b) the progressive nature, stability, or controllability of the disability(ies); (c) recommended medical treatment and appropriate source and location of treatment; (d) type of life situations or stressors that may exacerbate the condition(s); (e) disability-imposed limitations on daily activity; (f) potential effects of prescribed medication on work performance; (g) potential future complications stemming from the disability(ies); and (h) additional medical evaluation needed.

The basic issue to consider during the medical evaluation is the extent to which disability-related limitations affect the person's capability to satisfy certain job demands. For example, both upper and lower extremity based functional limitations have a bearing on person and job fit. Functional limitations of the upper extremities affect fine hand movements, grasping, pinching, working over the shoulders, tactile discriminations, pushing, reaching above or below shoulder level, and writing. Functional limitations of the lower extremities affect kneeling, stooping, standing, balancing, climbing, and walking (Andrew, 1994). Other functional limitations frequently pertinent to the medical evaluation are those that affect tolerance for sitting, carrying, or lifting, and tolerance for environmental conditions such as dampness, fumes, cold, heat, dust, mold, or dryness (Andrew, 1994).

Using the case of Shirley Steed as an example (see Chapter 3 for Shirley's Intake Interview Summary), the rehabilitation counselor should provide referral questions similar to those in Table 4.2. That list demonstrates a request for relevant, comprehensive, and specific feedback from the physician. Therefore, the contents of Table 4.2 can serve as a model for rehabilitation counselors to follow when soliciting medical evaluation information about a client.

In addition to appropriate referral questions, the counselor should provide the physician with relevant medical and social–vocational history on the client (Velten & Bondi, 1973). This history should include not only a synopsis of personal, social, psychological, and vocational data collected during the intake interview, but also relevant medical records from medical treatment that occurred within the past year (or earlier in the case of chronic conditions). Physicians can perform their evaluations more effectively if also provided information regarding the client's tentative vocational objectives. That information allows the physician to speak more specifically to client–job fit considerations from a medical viewpoint.

TABLE 4.2
Some Questions for the Physician: The Case of Shirley Steed

Pertaining to Respiratory Condition

1. What is the current severity of Mrs. Steed's pulmonary emphysema?

2. Are any conditions in Mrs. Steed's life exacerbating her respiratory conditions?

3. To what extent will Mrs. Steed's respiratory conditions become more severe over the next 5 years? 10 years?

4. Are there specific work conditions (e.g., lifting, standing, allergens, or work schedule, that Mrs. Steed should avoid?

5. Are there any immediate, intermediate, or long-term medical treatments that will improve Mrs. Steed's respiratory conditions?

6. What level of stability in her respiratory condition should be reached before she seeks employment?

Pertaining to Circulatory Condition

1. What are the medical recommendations for the treatment of Mrs. Steed's varicose veins?

2. Are there specific work conditions (e.g., long periods of standing, sitting, or walking) that Mrs. Steed should avoid due to her varicose veins?

KNOWING WHAT TO EXPECT FROM EVALUATION PHYSICIANS

As a result of the medical evaluation, the rehabilitation counselor should have detailed responses to all medical referral questions that help the counselor determine (a) the presence of a physical or mental disability, (b) the degree to which the condition limits the activities that the individual can perform, and (c) the extent and means by which the disabling condition may be corrected or ameliorated through physical restoration services (Hylbert & Hylbert, 1979). Via a survey of the medical evaluation process, Nagi (1969, p. 210) identified information that can be expected from the medical evaluation. For example, the course of pathology should be identified as "single incident, recurrent acute incident, long-term dysfunction, or long-term dysfunction with recurrent acute incidents" (Nagi, 1969, p. 210). Course of pathology might also vary along another scale that follows this pattern: "acute stage, convalescent, acute stage controlled, acute stage controlled but requires continuous supervision to remain stable, acute stage controlled but liable to reactivate, metastasize or involve other functions, uncontrollable—slowly progressive, uncontrollable—rapidly progressive" (Nagi, 1969, p. 210).

The medical evaluation report should also discuss the extent of residual effects from the condition that might range from "none, partial residuals, residuals of undetermined nature, determined stable residuals" to "progressive residuals" (Nagi, 1969, p. 210). When discussing prognosis in the medical evaluation report, the physician should indicate whether the disorder is "fully controlled with no future recurrence, controllable by continuous supervision, currently controllable but liable to later complications, compensable through provision of prosthesis and training in use . . . , partially compensable, improvable only, undetermined (outcome based on present knowledge of physical therapy)," or whether "no improvement is possible with best known methods" (Nagi, 1969, p. 210).

Rehabilitation counselors must have a level of understanding of medical terminology that is adequate for understanding both oral and written reports of physicians on their clients. Felton (1993a) has pointed out that,

> Many physicians have difficulty expressing themselves in lay terms and rely on technical words, phrases, and sentences. When speaking with an individual who understands the nomenclature, the physician will speak more readily and more completely, to the advantage of the counselor who needs an understanding of the client's medical conditions. (p. 21)

Accumulated medical information becomes valuable to the degree that it helps the rehabilitation counselor and client make practical decisions regarding the individual's work potential and tolerance. For example, depending on the type of limitations associated with a physical disability, the individual might be capable of work at the different levels that follow.

1. Heavy manual work—digging, lifting, or climbing regularly as main occupation

2. Manual work including incidental or occasional heavy work

3. All work except heavy labor, subject to regulated regimen

4. Sedentary work with regular hours and meals

5. Work under specified conditions

6. Work at home only

7. Not fit for work

Work capability also differs by extent of endurance, and an individual might be capable of part-time work only or of full-time work.

In the evaluation of some people with severe physical disabilities, the physician must provide the counselor with information pertinent to the individual's independent living capabilities. For example, any disability-related limitations on the individual's capacity for carrying out activities of daily living (personal grooming, eating, dressing, toileting, and mobility) and medical self-care, as well as medical services (prosthetics and orthotics) that can increase independent functioning, should be addressed in the medical evaluation report. Homebound clients present additional diagnostic questions that should be addressed in the medical evaluation. For homebound clients, the physician can help the counselor determine those out-of-home activities that the client might undertake with the assistance of proper support services.

Unfortunately, medical evaluation reports do not always provide clear prognoses. It is not unusual to find an absence of clear statements by the evaluating physician on the client's capacities, limitations, or environmental tolerances. When this is the case, it is the counselor's responsibility, with the help of the medical consultant, to interpret the vocational implications of medical information as a basis for planning and service provision (Swisher & Hylbert, 1973).

USING THE MEDICAL CONSULTANT

To use the medical consultant effectively, rehabilitation counselors should have a basic understanding of the effects of disability, disease, and injury. Furthermore, they must have knowledge of the process of medical diagnosis and treatment, and of the role of medical specialists in that process, as well as a sufficient understanding of medical terminology as previously indicated. But, a grounding in medical facts alone is insufficient; counselors must also understand how clients perceive their disabilities in terms of short- and long-range limitations in independent living and vocational functioning.

A counselor must also take some very practical steps to prepare for the session with the medical consultant. First, counselors should review all of their cases to determine those to present to the medical consultant. In addition, they should specifically identify the questions to be answered by the medical consultant. Normally, cases presented to the medical consultant are those of people who have multiple disabilities or need specialized medical treatment, surgery, or prosthetic devices. In some instances, counselors may need the medical consultant's assistance to deal with conflicting information in the case file. Differing opinions about the client's limitations and prognosis may emerge when the counselor compares data from the physician, the client, and the intake interview (McGowan, 1969).

During the session with the medical consultant, counselors can expect help in a number of ways (Hylbert & Hylbert, 1979). The medical consultant can clarify aspects of the medical report that contain technical data regarding the client's functional limitations, prognosis, and vocational handicaps. By reviewing existing case data, the medical consultant can also recommend further diagnostic or treatment services from medical specialists. Other benefits from sessions with the medical consultant include (a) teaching counselors about the nature of disease, diagnosis, and treatment; (b) helping counselors coordinate their medical services and, therefore, minimize the amount of time the client must stay in the medical phases of rehabilitation; and (c) assisting counselors in selecting rehabilitation facilities that have competent medical programs.

CONCLUDING STATEMENT

The physician's role is to help the counselor better understand the relationship between the client's current and potential disability-related limitations and the demands of various jobs. In order to plan the medical evaluation process and use the resulting findings, the counselor must have an understanding of medical terminology and services, as well as implications of different disabling conditions.

The medical referral process itself is more likely to result in desirable outcomes if the rehabilitation counselor follows certain guidelines. The rehabilitation counselor should refer clients to physicians who have treated the client in the past or who are specialists in the client's medical condition. To interpret the vocational significance of the client's limitations, the physician should know what job or jobs the client is considering. In addition, information regarding the client's vocational, social, and medical history can assist the physician in making some determinations.

Most importantly, the rehabilitation counselor should provide concrete requests for information. The data that the rehabilitation counselor should request from the physician include the client's general health; the extent and stability of the existing disability; functional limitations related to the disability; additional medical tests required; recommended medical treatment as well as its source, location, and expected effects; work conditions to avoid; and prognosis for return to work. Some or all of these questions may be appropriate depending on the individual client. Providing specific questions improves the likelihood that the medical evaluation will result in clear-cut statements regarding the way the disability limits or impairs the functioning of the individual. Therefore, the counselor will be better able to identify the services required to overcome the vocationally relevant aspects of the disability.

Again, using the case of Shirley Steed for purposes of illustration, Table 4.3 presents a model medical evaluation report from a physician. If medical reports fail to reach the thorough standards demonstrated in Table 4.3, the rehabilitation counselor is either providing insufficient guidelines to the physician or referring clients to the wrong physician.

TABLE 4.3
Medical Report for Shirley Steed

Mrs. Shirley Steed was examined in my office for problems related to pulmonary and vascular functioning. The examination revealed that she is currently in the early stages of chronic obstructive pulmonary emphysema and is suffering from varicose veins in the lower extremities.

From visual inspection of her legs, it is obvious that Mrs. Steed has developed large, distorted veins. Varices are particularly noticeable on the right leg. Mrs. Steed complained of frequent leg muscle fatigue with occasional symptoms of swelling in the ankles and nocturnal leg cramps. If Mrs. Steed will wear elastic stockings, avoid undue standing, and elevate her legs periodically, it is highly possible that surgery can be avoided. However, the varices of the right leg are more pronounced, and the veins may eventually require ligation, stripping, or both. Careful attention should be paid to signs of further enlargement of the veins or to changes in the condition of the skin. Obviously, Mrs. Steed cannot return to heavy work that requires her to be on her feet for extended periods of time.

Early signs of impairment of the lung's ventilation functions are present. Based on spirogram readings, Mrs. Steed's expiration rates are below normal. It appears, therefore, that she is in an early stage of obstructive pulmonary emphysema. Many causes have contributed to this condition; most significant, of course, are chronic asthma and bronchitis with attendant lung infections. While exhibiting some coughing followed by shortness of breath, Mrs. Steed is able to return to unlabored breathing within a short period.

Purulent discoloration plus an abnormal white blood count indicate the presence of a lung infection. I have prescribed achromycin for 3 weeks for her. The bacterial infection should be cleared up within 2 weeks.

Mrs. Steed also reported being in both a mildly anxious and depressed state lately and has been having trouble sleeping. I have prescribed a Valium dosage of 5 mg four times daily to help relax her. However, Valium should be viewed as a short-term measure. Therefore, psychological evaluation followed by any recommended psychological treatment should be arranged as soon as possible.

Based on the interaction of her depressed psychological state and her general rundown physical condition resulting from chronic obstructive pulmonary disease, I would place her at Level III of the American Lung Association's (AML) classification for emphysema patients. Though not confined to her home and still capable of self-care, Mrs. Steed is incapable of a normal activity pattern and is, therefore, unable to work. However, it appears that her physical condition can be improved considerably through the careful regulation of her diet and physical activity plus the taking (via inhalation) of a bronchodilator drug, isoetharine metaproterenol. A weight loss of 15 pounds should ease her return to a more normal activity

(continues)

TABLE 4.3 (*Continued*)

level. Assuming Mrs. Steed's strict compliance to these medical recommendations, her prognosis for moving to a Level II AML classification within 30 days is good. While she will still have some restrictions on her physical activity at that point, Mrs. Steed should be able to return to work in a sedentary job requiring little physical exertion (light work). This prognosis is also dependent on a distinct improvement in her psychological state.

Mrs. Steed reports allergic reactions to lint on fabrics and clothes and to clothing dyes. Therefore, she should avoid work environments containing those allergens. Mrs. Steed's respiratory condition will also require careful selection of work sites as free as possible from industrial fumes or other foreign substances. She should also avoid work settings characterized by dampness, cold, or excessively dry heat.

While obstructive pulmonary emphysema is a progressive disease, with proper medical supervision, healthy living habits, and a relatively low-stress and light-work job, Mrs. Steed's prognosis for soon achieving and sustaining vocational rehabilitation for at least 5 to 10 years is good.

Claude R. Rasmussen, M.D.
Rehabilitation Consulting Physician

Psychological Evaluation

This chapter discusses the following issues: (a) knowing what to expect from psychological evaluation, (b) choosing a consulting psychologist, (c) making an effective psychological referral, and (d) using the psychological report. The purposes for securing psychological information range from substantiating the existence of disabling conditions such as mental retardation, learning disability, and emotional disturbance to developing a better understanding of the relationship of the person's intellectual, neuropsychological, and personality and behavioral functioning to the demands of vocational roles. Results of the psychological assessment help counselors identify client needs, select services to meet those needs, and, finally, suggest vocational roles that hold the potential for "good or sufficient" person–job match.

KNOWING WHAT TO EXPECT FROM PSYCHOLOGICAL EVALUATION

The ultimate objective of psychological evaluation is to determine a person's ability to cope with life demands. Hence, psychological assessment should result in predictive statements about the individual's behavior in a wide range of situations. The rehabilitation counselor's responsibility is to determine the appropriateness of those predictions and secure the services the person needs to develop behavioral competencies in vocational and social roles.

In making a referral for psychological evaluation, the rehabilitation counselor is interested in specific information regarding the person's interpersonal skills, ability to learn new jobs, emotional stability, and commitment to vocational goals. Therefore, descriptions of psychological functioning stated in jargon or theoretical terminology (e.g., "libidinal forces" or "intrapsychic conflicts") have little meaning for the rehabilitation counselor (Gill, 1972, p. 475). The counselor needs concrete statements from the psychologist predicting the person's reactions in specific situations, where and how the person will likely function effectively and ineffectively, and the type of situations or rehabilitation services that could augment effective functioning (Bush, 1992; Plummer, 1976).

Psychological evaluation should provide leads as to the "fit" between the individual's personality and situational demands—in particular, the relationship among what a person wants from a job (desired reinforcers), the reinforcers available from particular jobs, and the person's abilities and job demands (Dawis & Lofquist, 1984). Therefore, rather than focus broadly on the way in which client strengths, weaknesses, conflicts, and defenses affect personal functioning, psychological reports should specify the extent to which the person can meet the interpersonal and skill demands of various vocational roles. The psychologist's report should describe potential client problems in adapting to work in general and, when requested by the counselor, to particular work roles. Diagnosed psychological problems should be followed by recommended rehabilitation services.

CHOOSING A CONSULTING PSYCHOLOGIST

The rehabilitation counselor should use psychologists who understand the effects of disability on psychological adjustment and personal functioning. They should recognize that the behavioral effects of disabilities can be psychogenic or organic in nature. They should also be cognizant of behavioral effects attributed to the disability itself. Problems such as brain damage, end stage renal disease, or damage to the central nervous system (as in cerebral palsy) may produce certain characteristic behavioral reactions. In addition, a disability such as traumatic head injury calls for examination by a psychologist who specializes in neuropsychological examinations. Inclusion of an intelligence test or a memory test in a psychological battery does not constitute a neuropsychological evaluation. Neuropsychological evaluations focus on the abilities that higher brain functioning affects by measuring cognitive functions as well as intelligence, verbal comprehension, verbal reasoning, memory and learning, visual and spatial abilities, and problem solving. Physical functioning (tactile, auditory, and visual perception), motor coordination, and emotional functioning are other important components of the examination. Common test batteries used in neuropsychological evaluations include the *Halstead-Reitan Neuropsychological Test Battery* and the *Luria-Nebraska Neuropsychological Battery* (Hallover, Prosser, & Swift, 1989, p. 3).

The psychologist should also be capable of helping the rehabilitation counselor differentiate between temporary adjustment reactions that are disability specific and those that are a function of social learning. For example, an individual's attitude toward his or her disability depends largely on experiences prior to acquiring the disability, the anxiety and fear experienced during the onset and duration of the illness or accident that led up to the disability, the information the individual has regarding the disability, how the person is treated by family and friends, and the individual's hope for recovery (Rubin & Roessler, 1995).

The rehabilitation counselor should select consulting psychologists who do not harbor rigid defeatist attitudes toward disability. By placing an excessive emphasis on being realistic, some psychologists may unnecessarily limit the potential of people with disabilities. In addition, psychologists should be encouraged to avoid excessive emphasis on the client's problems. In overlooking many of the individual's assets, psychologists run the danger of lapsing into what Wright (1980) referred to as the "succumbing" perspective. Instead, psychologists should continually remind themselves of certain principles, such as, "People with disabilities are not passive—they do and must actively take charge of their lives; they are highly differentiated as individuals. Severity of a disability is as much a function of physical and social environmental barriers, if not more so, than of personal impairments" (Wright, 1980, p. 279).

In regard to the latter principle, considerable research has demonstrated that psychological response to disability is partially a function of the attitudes and behaviors of others toward the person with the disability (Bolton, 1981; Safilios-Rothschild, 1970; Wright, 1968). Negative reactions toward individuals with disabilities stem from a cultural emphasis on perfection, physical appearance, and similarity (Kolata, 1993). As Vandergoot and Engelkes (1980) found in the case of employment, the more visible the disability, the more the individual with the disability experiences discrimination. When interacting with individuals with visible disabilities, nondisabled people may feel anxious and attempt to avoid further social contact (Bolton, 1981) or react with overconcern or oversolicitousness (Safilios-Rothschild, 1970). These negative reactions from others result in a sense of devaluation and, hence, lowered self-esteem on the part of the individual with a disability.

The psychologist should also have specific knowledge of the way the disability affects test-taking ability, and, therefore, the results on a variety of psychometric assessments. For example, the use of paper and pencil tests that require a certain amount of eye–hand coordination to mark responses may not provide an accurate estimate of the aptitudes and potential of individuals with disabilities (stroke and cerebral palsy) that affect coordination. Other problems, such as visual impairment and language or communication limitations (as in the case of individuals with hearing impairments), also result in biased assessments. In fact, the National Association of the Deaf contended that all standardized psychological–educational tests for individuals with hearing impairments are invalid unless administered in the language of the person— for example, American Sign Language (ASL) (Bolton, 1981).

The psychologist should also possess an understanding of the goals and objectives of the rehabilitation process. Because rehabilitation's goal is vocational placement, the consulting psychologist should be prepared to answer referral questions regarding the vocational significance of the person's strengths and limitations in the psychological, social, and intellectual areas. Overall, the psychologist should help the counselor and the person identify feasible vocational roles for consideration during the planning process.

Finally, psychologists who do not provide competent evaluations should not be used. One indication of incompetence is similar psychological evaluation reports provided on all clients referred. Bush (1992) provides the following as an example of an instance in which a state rehabilitation agency stopped using a psychologist:

> . . . 98% of all . . . [his] . . . psychological evaluations included the diagnosis: "mixed personality disorder". Not only was the psychologist making a diagnosis on very limited observations (and sometimes very limited data), he was essentially affixing a "garbage can" diagnosis with little meaning and questionable usefulness. (p. 101)

MAKING AN EFFECTIVE REFERRAL

Several considerations are relevant in making a referral to a psychologist. First, the counselor must identify the individuals for whom a psychological evaluation is needed. Second, the counselor must properly prepare the person for referral to a psychologist. Finally, the counselor must provide the psychologist with significant social history information about the person and important referral questions that should be addressed.

Determining the Need for Psychological Evaluation

Information regarding abilities, aptitudes, interests, and personality–behavioral patterns is necessary for several different types of people. For eligibility purposes in state vocational rehabilitation agencies, psychological evaluation is required to document either mental retardation or emotional disturbances and, since 1985, the diagnosis of specific learning disability (Biller & White, 1989). Psychological evaluation is also suggested with clients when (a) long-term or expensive training is involved for areas in which the individual has no work history; (b) no feasible vocational alternatives are clearly apparent for the individual; (c) the individual has several vocational objectives that seem appropriate; (d) the counselor believes that the client's vocational objective is not feasible and needs information to confirm or disconfirm its appropriateness; (e) either conflicting information or significant information gaps exist in the educational or vocational history in the case file; (f) the counselor suspects the client may have certain unidentified limitations or talents; or (g) the client has disabilities necessitating "specialized evaluation of capacities, abilities, skills, interests and personality such as brain or head injuries, blindness, deafness . . . and damage to the central nervous system" (McGowan & Porter, 1967, p. 66; Patterson, 1960).

For other individuals, psychological evaluation would be of very limited value. For example, clients with a positive work history who intend to return to their previous jobs upon completion of medical rehabilitation services would not usually need a psychological evaluation. Other people may be so uncooperative and negative regarding psychological testing that it would be counterproductive to send them to a psychologist as long as that attitude persists.

Preparing the Person for Psychological Evaluation

In preparing a person for psychological evaluation, the counselor should describe the purposes of psychological testing, including what questions it can help answer in the process of developing a rehabilitation plan. The counselor should also explain who will pay for the evaluation, when and where it will take place, and the name of the psychologist. In down-to-earth terms, rehabilitation counselors should explain that the results of psychological assessment can help individuals (a) increase their level of self-awareness, (b) identify behavioral strengths and limitations, (c) develop vocational goals and plans, and (d) determine future testing and treatment programs (Groth-Marnat, 1984).

The preceding explanation may be adequate for some people. Others may feel that being sent for a psychological evaluation indicates that they are seriously disturbed. To avoid prompting such feelings, the counselor should emphasize that the psychological evaluation will help the person and his or her counselor identify and resolve problems that might interfere with successful vocational training and placement.

Information To Provide the Consulting Psychologist

To increase the probability of a thorough psychological evaluation, the rehabilitation counselor should provide the psychologist with specific information about the social–vocational history, medical history, and vocational objectives of the person being referred. Rather than have the psychologist waste time by acquiring information from the individual that has already been collected by the counselor, the counselor should provide brief synopses in the following areas: (a) physical—history of person's disability, previous treatment, current medication, and recent medical test results; (b) educational–vocational—number of years of education, courses liked and disliked, previous vocational training, past jobs, and type of work liked and disliked; (c) psychosocial—history of previous psychological treatment, current medication, and quality of relationships with family and friends; (d) economic—current financial situation, sources of financial support, current and anticipated debts as a result of disability and other reasons, and other sources of support such as Social Security or worker's compensation; and (e) vocational choice—expressed vocational interests and vocational objectives, desires for certain types of vocational training, perception of ability to achieve vocational objectives, and level of earnings desired (Maki, Pape, & Prout, 1979; Rubin & Roessler, 1995). It is also important that the counselor inform the psychologist about tentative service and vocational objectives.

To increase the utility of the psychological report, the rehabilitation counselor should also provide specific referral questions. These questions should focus on areas of ambiguity regarding the person's physical functioning (neurological), psychosocial functioning (characteristic personality–behavior patterns, responses to different situational demands), intellectual functioning, and vocational interests and goals. Pertinent questions for the psychologist in each of these areas include (note that the vocational evaluator can provide valuable insights regarding many of these questions) the following.

Physical Functioning

1. Do psychological test results indicate damage to the brain or central nervous system? How would this damage affect the person's functioning?

Psychosocial Functioning

1. How does the individual's current psychological adjustment present barriers to rehabilitation?

2. How is the person's level of judgment, reasoning, or comprehension affected? How are these effects manifested in behavior?

3. Is there evidence of emotional disturbance? How severe; what type?

4. In what ways might personal adjustment problems affect performance in and completion of vocational training as well as subsequent vocational functioning?

5. What aspects of the person's perception of his or her environment might affect adjustment to a work situation (e.g., how does the individual perceive authority figures)?

6. Is there evidence of interpersonal skill deficiencies, past and present, that could interfere with work adjustment?

7. What aspects of the person's nonwork life situations are important to work adjustment (e.g., are there unusual family stresses)?

8. How do personality characteristics affect the job selection process (e.g., is the individual too anxious for certain work settings)?

9. Are there certain behaviors that might affect work performance (e.g., is the person's attention span appropriate for certain types of work)?

10. Is the individual better suited for certain work environments (e.g., would a large group situation be appropriate)?

11. Can the person adjust to a competitive work situation (e.g., can the person work under pressure to meet expectations for production rates, commissions, and so forth)?

Intellectual Functioning

1. Does evidence of mental retardation exist?

2. Is there any evidence of a learning disability?

3. What aspects of the client's intellectual functioning should be considered in rehabilitation planning?

4. How does the person's intellectual capacity affect his or her ability to learn new work skills? What limits should be set on the level of vocational training?

Vocational Interests and Goals

1. What are the person's vocational interests?

2. Are the individual's vocational interests consistent with expressed vocational goals?

3. Are the person's interests and goals reasonably compatible with his or her level of functioning in other areas (educational–vocational, psychosocial, and physical)?

The counselor may develop a format for regularly providing the psychologist with the information recommended in the previous paragraphs. One possible approach is a standardized form sent to the psychologist containing appropriate background information, as well as specific referral questions for the psychologist to address. Such a form is presented for Shirley Steed in Table 5.1.

TABLE 5.1
Sample Psychological Referral Form

Client Name: Shirley Steed

Synopsis of Intake Information

Physical

History of chronic bronchitis, emphysema, and varicose veins. Respiratory condition aggravated by allergy to fabrics. Poor health resulted in frequent absences from work. Currently unable to tolerate heavy work. Taking Valium, Librax, or both at present time.

Psychosocial

Frequent episodes of depression and nervousness tied in with hospitalization for exhaustion. Treated by a counselor approximately 2 years ago for depression related to marital and family difficulties. Currently seems too anxious to work.

Educational and Vocational

Interested in working as a secretary. Completed her GED 3 years ago. Had typing and shorthand instruction in high school approximately 20 years ago. Has worked successfully in a fabric shop (short term) and two print shops (long term). Forced to leave work because of her health.

Economic

Presently has no financial support. Will apply for public assistance but also needs work to pay living and medical expenses. Younger son still dependent on her financially for 1 more year.

Vocational

Seeking clerical or secretarial work. Appears feasible given light physical demands of the job.

Tentative Objectives

Rehabilitation Services

Needs to control respiratory problems through medication, diet, and proper working environment. Depression and anxiety may require additional therapy. Varicose veins appear controllable.

(continues)

TABLE 5.1 (*Continued*)

Vocational

Secretarial or clerical training with placement in a local business.

Referral Questions

Physical (Neurological) Functioning

1. N/A

Psychosocial Functioning (characteristic personality-behavior patterns; responses to different situational demands)

1. Does Shirley have an identifiable emotional disorder? If so, what?

2. How will Shirley cope with the stresses of office work?

3. What conditions precipitate Shirley's tension and depression?

4. Is Shirley too disturbed at the moment to work? If so, how long will it take before she is ready for work?

5. Does Shirley see herself as able to upgrade her clerical skills and work successfully in an office?

6. What type of treatment is suggested for Shirley's anxiety and depression?

7. What type of treatment is suggested for the family problems Shirley is experiencing?

Intellectual Functioning

1. Does Shirley have the intellectual capacity for clerical work?

2. Are Shirley's aptitudes compatible with those required for clerical work?

Vocational Interests and Goals

1. Are Shirley's vocational interests consistent with clerical work?

USING THE PSYCHOLOGICAL REPORT

Isett and Roszkowski (1979) identified 12 common areas of the psychological report. These areas were:

1. Background information (developmental history, educational history, and social history)

2. Behavior during the psychological assessment

3. Behavior during other contacts the psychologist has had with the person

4. IQ test results

5. Perceptual–motor functioning information

6. Social skills and social maturity

7. Academic achievement data

8. Objective personality test results (behavior rating scales, behavior charting)

9. Projective personality test results

10. Summary and conclusions

11. Recommendations for remediation of educational deficits

12. Recommendations for behavior management

Groth-Marnat (1984, p. 366) provided a briefer outline for the psychological report. Recommended areas included (a) discussion of the referral questions, (b) listing of tests given and other evaluation procedures, (c) behavioral observations, (d) relevant history, (e) test results, (f) impressions and interpretations, and (g) recommendations. Of course, the psychologist could incorporate much of the information identified by Isett and Roszkowski (1979) in the format suggested by Groth-Marnat.

Past survey data have indicated that rehabilitation counselors and administrators are generally satisfied with the psychological evaluations they receive (Amble & Peterson, 1979; Cull & Levinson, 1977). However, those same studies identified several specific areas of dissatisfaction. Rehabilitation administrators criticized some reports for their ambiguity regarding the relationship of psychological data to the day-to-day social and vocational functioning of the individual. The length of time that the psychologist required to report to the counselor was also cited as a major problem (Cull & Levinson, 1977, p. 204).

Reviews of the content of psychological reports reveal a number of specific problems. For example, some reports are too long, too technical, and too theoretical. They are pervaded with jargon and are poorly written (Rennick, 1975). They may summarize the results of different assessment tasks without providing any integration of the findings into a comprehensive vocational prognosis (Amble & Peterson, 1979). A small percentage of the Amble and Peterson sample (12% to 17%) also noted problems with the interpretations and recommendations of the reports. For example, some goals suggested by psychologists were either unrealistic or impossible, such as recommending that a person living in a rural area become involved in group therapy. Counselors also noted that some recommendations were too general to be of help. In addition, a few counselors (12%) commented on a "recognizable sameness from one report to another" (Amble & Peterson, p. 129).

Counselors in the survey conducted by Amble and Peterson (1979) listed characteristics of effective psychological evaluations. First, they recommended concise reports, preferably three to five pages, completed within 2 weeks. The reports should provide concrete responses to the counselor's referral questions. Several counselors in the survey (15% to 30%) also indicated that effective reports should include information concerning (a) vocational recommendations for the person, (b) specific interpersonal and vocational skills, (c) compatible job opportunities in the local community, and (d) the anticipated limitations in functioning identified in the evaluation. Other counselors requested recommendations for specific psychological treatment such as family therapy, work adjustment, and psychotherapy. Gill (1972) suggested that the psychologist identify the appropriate sources and locations of treatment.

Past research with people with mental retardation (Isett & Roszkowski, 1979) documented the importance of psychological evaluation, particularly the phase of the report that provided recommendations for behavior management. In a study of common problems presented by individuals with mental retardation, Wittman, Strohmer, and Prout (1989, p. 12) broadened the list of desirable information from the psychologist. They emphasized the need for information relating to the following areas:

1. General interpersonal coping and social skills
2. Psychological functioning issues such as self-esteem and image problems
3. Work-related adjustment problems
4. Family adjustment and social support systems.

A sample psychological report for Shirley Steed is presented in Table 5.2. The report has certain positive and negative points. On its behalf, one can say that it is brief and to the point. With a minimum of jargon, the report establishes the existence of a psychiatric diagnosis (acute depressive reaction). Some attention is devoted to discussing appropriate work settings for Shirley given the accomplishment of certain psychological treatment goals. Although her capabilities appear sufficient for clerical work, Shirley will experience tension in several job-related situations. Services to help her deal with these tensions, as well as with existing family problems, are also presented.

After reviewing the report, a group of rehabilitation counselors noted some deficiencies. They expressed the need for more information on Shirley's reactions and feelings. From the report, the counselor learned little about Shirley's goals. The counselors also expressed a desire for a profile of the scores on the various tests.

The Responsibility of the Rehabilitation Counselor

Given that the psychologist has submitted a specific report in a prompt manner, the rehabilitation counselor has an obligation to be an intelligent consumer of the report. In other words, the rehabilitation counselor must have a sufficient understanding of the techniques used, their reliability and validity, and the types of norms used for judging client performance (Maki, Pape, & Prout, 1979). Such an understanding will enable the counselor to make appropriate judgments regarding psychological information as the counselor and client move into the planning phases of the rehabilitation process.

TABLE 5.2
Mrs. Shirley Steed: Psychological Report

Tests Administered

Wechsler Adult Intelligence Scale (WAIS-III) (Wechsler, 1997), *Minnesota Multiphasic Personality Inventory* (MMPI) (Hathaway & McKinely, 1970), *Thematic Apperception Test* (TAT) (Murray, 1993)

Observations During the Interview

Mrs. Steed was pleasant, well groomed, and cooperative. She expressed a desire to deal with her problems, return to work, and be self-supporting. She reported improvement in her physical health as a result of recently prescribed medication. Mrs. Steed did become particularly tense and anxious, however, when we discussed her two sons. She expressed a great deal of concern about being viewed as a failure "as a parent" if her two sons did not "turn out well." Obviously, the current situation with one son in prison and the other threatening to drop out of school only increased Mrs. Steed's concerns.

Test Results

Mrs. Steed's scores on the WAIS–III were as follows: Verbal, 113; Performance, 106; Full-Scale IQ, 111. A WAIS–III Full-Scale score of 111 places Mrs. Steed in the high average range of intelligence. Her verbal functioning was somewhat better than her performance, but the difference is not significant.

Mrs. Steed's scores on the MMPI revealed moderate levels of anxiety and neurotic personality features. This profile on the MMPI (2, 7), characterized by anxiousness regarding the future, is frequently associated with somatic symptomology (chest pains, nervous stomach, diarrhea, and dizziness). Nervousness, tension, weakness, depression, and obsessions are also frequent complaints.

Individuals with the 2–7 profile tend to set high standards for themselves and, as a result, perform well. Because of their high standards and chronic anxiety, however, they find it very difficult to deal with multiple sources of stress in life. Mrs. Steed's uncertain financial, vocational, and health conditions, as well as her relationship with her sons, create considerable stress in her life.

Based on her MMPI profile, the TAT was administered. An analysis of the material in Mrs. Steed's stories reveals a level of insecurity coupled with feelings of tension and anxiety. She expressed numerous times a need to do well and meet the expectations of others. She often focused on how other people are evaluating the central character in the story and how that affects the individual. Her stories also included a "self-fulfilling prophecy," or comments about wanting to succeed but knowing "deep down" that the person will fail. It obviously would be important for Mrs. Steed to explore further her unrealistic and self-defeating expectations. As with the MMPI, anxiety and depression were underlying themes in the TAT.

Results of the MMPI, TAT, and our discussion in the interview suggest that Mrs. Steed is experiencing personal adjustment problems such as depressive reactions that fit the diagnostic category of dysthymic disorder (DSM–IV, 300). Mrs. Steed could benefit from personal counseling to help her deal with her reactions to tension and anxiety and training in relaxation and other stress management techniques.

(continues)

TABLE 5.2 *(Continued)*

Conclusions and Recommendations

Mrs. Steed had few complaints about her past employment experiences. Given her high to average level of intelligence and history of adapting well to the demands of work, Mrs. Steed definitely has employment potential. Several problems currently stand in the way, however.

Mrs. Steed has a depressed–anxious profile on the MMPI and TAT, which is corroborated by her energy level and affect, as demonstrated in the interview. Coupled with her recurrent respiratory problems, this psychological state is not conducive to resuming and maintaining work. Mrs. Steed must, therefore, improve her medical and psychological status. In addition to the medical regimen, I also recommend that Mrs. Steed begin personal counseling.

Attention should also be given to the work situations Mrs. Steed should avoid. Jobs with high-pressure performance or sales and commission demands would not be suitable. Work with a steady pace requiring clerical or office work skills would be appropriate for Mrs. Steed.

Of course, tension will develop in any job situation and may lead to adjustment problems. Hence, she will need assistance in learning how to manage stress. For example, she will experience job stress in (a) handling interruptions such as answering the telephone while typing or filing, (b) meeting deadlines, and (c) shifting from task to task as requested by her supervisor. Until she gains confidence in her clerical skills, Mrs. Steed will work best with a supportive supervisor.

Mrs. Steed and her younger son need to participate jointly in family counseling. Her younger son should continue consultation with a rehabilitation counselor regarding his educational and vocational plans. Psychological services for Mrs. Steed could be secured at minimal cost from the Larkspur Mental Health Center.

Summary

Currently, Mrs. Steed manifests symptoms of a psychoneurotic depressive reaction. If she receives counseling services and is able to resolve family problems, she should be a good prospect for vocational training and placement in office and clerical work.

CONCLUDING STATEMENT

Psychological evaluation can provide valuable information regarding the existence of a disability, the vocational significance of that disability, recommendations for psychological services, and the person's potential level of intellectual and psychosocial functioning. The basic objective on the counselor's part is to interpret the implications of this information for the individual's capability to meet the demands of various vocational roles. Of course, not everyone seeking rehabilitation services should be referred for psychological evaluation. Some people may have a successful work history and, upon receiving rehabilitation services such as medical restoration and case management, be capable of returning to the same job. For others, the counselor may have certain questions that can be answered only through psychological evaluation.

Desirable characteristics of a consulting psychologist include an understanding of the vocational rehabilitation process, as well as of the effects of the disability on vocational functioning. Hence, the psychologist's report should provide not only a profile of the individual's intellectual functioning, personality, and behavior, but also an indication of the extent to which that profile is related to functioning in specific vocational roles. The psychologist must also understand the psychological effects of the disability itself, the psychological effects of the individual's perception of his or her disability, and the psychological impact of negative reactions from others.

In making referrals to psychologists, rehabilitation counselors should provide synopses of the person's functioning in physical, psychosocial, and educational–vocational areas. By providing such information, the counselor not only saves the consulting psychologist time, but also enables the psychologist to concentrate on describing the psychological functioning of the individual as it is related to vocational potential. By providing specific referral questions, rehabilitation counselors also increase the likelihood of a more appropriate and specific evaluation from the psychologist.

The counselor also must prepare the person for psychological evaluation by explaining the purpose and nature of psychological testing and assessment. The counselor should also discuss specific reasons for referring the person to a psychologist, such as (a) to help the individual define problems, (b) to enable the person to gain a better understanding of personal strengths and limitations, and (c) to aid the individual in making reasonable plans and decisions.

Finally, the counselor should have some definite expectations for the psychological report. The report should be written in concrete, specific terms and should culminate in a series of recommendations regarding psychological services and appropriate vocational roles for the individual. Suggestions regarding psychological services should also include the source and location of the services in the community. In making vocational recommendations, the consulting psychologist should keep in mind the realities of the local world of work, including the fact that these recommended vocational roles must actually exist in the community. To avoid unnecessary case processing delays, psychologists should submit their reports promptly (in approximately 2 weeks). In addition, it is helpful if the report is kept as brief as possible, preferably 3 to 5 pages in length.

Vocational Evaluation

Richard T. Roessler and Richard J. Baker

Chapter 6 discusses the purpose of vocational evaluation and those characteristics of an evaluation program considered to be desirable. It also provides suggestions for effectively using vocational evaluation resources for making an effective referral. To help demonstrate points made throughout the chapter, an evaluation plan and an evaluation report are included for the case of Shirley Steed.

THE PURPOSE OF VOCATIONAL EVALUATION

The purpose of vocational evaluation is to assess the client's vocational aptitudes, interests, and behavior in order to determine potential employment goals and the services needed to achieve them. The final objective of the evaluation service is to specify the most feasible vocational goals based on a synthesis of relevant client and service information.

The rehabilitation counselor should expect vocational evaluation to (a) generate information on the client's current vocationally relevant levels of social, educational, psychological, and physiological functioning; (b) estimate the individual's potential for behavior change and skill acquisition; (c) determine the client's most effective learning style; (d) identify jobs the client can do without additional vocational services; (e) identify educational or special training programs that might increase vocational potential; (f) identify potentially feasible jobs for the client with further vocational services; and (g) identify community support services that might augment job retention following successful client placement. Of course, a vocational evaluation does not supply all of the answers, and an evaluator does not have rehabilitation programming responsibility for people referred by the rehabilitation counselor. Rather, similar to medical evaluation and psychological evaluation, vocational evaluation is yet another information resource that contributes to effective development of the rehabilitation program.

Whereas the diagnostic purpose of vocational evaluation is to gather data needed to identify employment goals and related services, its purpose from a client-centered perspective is to facilitate the person's understanding of his or her current functional capacities in various situations, as well as the potential benefits of involvement in further services. When individuals contribute to planning the evaluation and they understand how the ensuing information about vocational abilities and limitations, work-related behaviors, and skill potential can relate to their success, they are more likely to take a proactive role in future rehabilitation programming (Cutler & Ramm, 1992; Vash, 1984). Unfortunately, the client-centered purpose of vocational evaluation is sometimes overlooked. In their zeal to involve the individual in services, the rehabilitation counselor and the vocational evaluator can easily forget to help the person understand the rationale for the evaluation program. When this happens, true client involvement in rehabilitation planning is significantly curtailed.

DESIRABLE CHARACTERISTICS OF A VOCATIONAL EVALUATION PROGRAM

The quality of an evaluation is determined by the interacting effects of (a) the professional skills of evaluation staff, (b) the availability of evaluation tools and techniques, (c) the ability of evaluation staff to involve the client in the evaluation process, and (d) the ability of an evaluator to report evaluation results effectively.

The Vocational Evaluator

Because the effectiveness of a vocational evaluation program greatly depends on the professional skills of its staff, the importance of staff trained in vocational evaluation cannot be overstressed. Although graduate training for vocational evaluators and rehabilitation counselors is similar in many ways (e.g., both receive training in basic rehabilitation philosophy, medical and psychological aspects of rehabilitation, and various aspects of psychometric testing and interpersonal skill training), the vocational evaluator should have received specialized training in the use and interpretation of work samples, behavioral observation and analysis in work-related settings, specialized individual and group psychometric tests, interpretation and synthesis of evaluation data, and development of comprehensive written evaluation reports. Vocational evaluators are certified by the Commission on Certification of Work Adjustment and Vocational Evaluation Specialists (Certified in Vocational Evaluation, CVE). Although the presence of certified personnel at a facility should indicate the quality of available vocational evaluation services, it does not assure the appropriateness of a program for a given referral. The counselor must consider a number of other factors as well, such as client needs and availability of specific types of evaluations.

General Programmatic Considerations

Although most evaluation programs serve people with a wide range of disabilities, they are not all equally equipped to assess the vocational potential of a diversified clientele. Before that is possible, the evaluation facility must have a large variety of verbal and performance tests capable of providing meaningful information on low-functioning as well as higher functioning individuals. The evaluation program also needs access to in-house and community work sites that allow for situational assessments appropriate for male and female, as well as ambulatory and nonambulatory individuals. The most limited programs are those that only use standardized paper and pencil tests because they are incapable of evaluating client work aptitudes via the observation of the individual's performance in a variety of work-like environments or situations. Such programs are, therefore, especially limited for assessing young clients who have not done well in school testing situations and who tend to react negatively to paper and pencil tests when their relevancy is not obvious (Weldon & McDaniel, 1982). Because many standardized paper and pencil tests elicit reactions of test anxiety and fail to consider either differences in learning style or the effects that specific handicapping conditions have on their predictive validity (Power, 1991; Rosenberg, 1973; Schlenoff, 1974), the negative performance of some individuals on those tests may be somewhat misleading from a diagnostic point of view.

Evaluation programs that incorporate work samples, simulated work settings, and on-the-job evaluation are more likely to validly pinpoint functional work problems. Such programs are more capable of fully exploring the functional implications of a person's disability and of identifying specific work adjustment problems (i.e., deficits in specific vocational skills and generic skills of the good worker) that must be ameliorated before placement can be recommended. Even these more diversified work evaluation programs are not without limitations, however, because their range of recommended vocational options is restricted by the kinds of work samples or work settings available to the facility. Too often, the work evaluator's recommendations can be heavily determined by work programs available in the same facility. If the work tasks available to the program are limited to low-level vocational activities, the evaluation program may be inappropriate for assessing higher functioning individuals.

To broaden a facility's capability to assess vocational functioning, Ditty and Reynolds (1980) advocated an individualized and community relevant approach to vocational evaluation. To yield better estimates of an individual's learning potential and limitations, they recommended simplifying and recombining segments of standardized ability tests and work samples. The researchers also stressed the need to develop community referenced work samples that simulate local job options for which the person might qualify. The client is pretested on the tasks (which parallel critical job functions in real jobs) and evaluated regarding strengths and limitations. Enrollment in individualized and accommodated vocational training should follow such a prescriptive evaluation.

The time involved in completing a comprehensive evaluation is another consideration in choosing an evaluation program. Programs that rely on more traditional testing procedures usually take less time to complete evaluations than programs using work sample and situational assessment techniques. In the final analysis, however, the rehabilitation counselor must become knowledgeable about the strengths and limitations of evaluation programs available in the community and make a selection based on program suitability given the special evaluation needs of the client in question.

When time is an issue, counselors should know that a variety of efficient computerized evaluation systems are available such as Opticon, Insight, and MESA. In a very short period of time, individuals can respond via the computer to a battery of aptitude and interest measures. Moreover, the computerized system can provide profiles of the person's vocational aptitudes and relate them to a series of feasible job titles in a very brief amount of time. These job titles are useful additions to the vocational evaluation report. Of course, computerized systems are expensive and require frequent updating. Evaluators should keep in mind that a client's lack of familiarity with the computer or anxiety about using one may affect the validity of the results (Cutler & Ramm, 1992).

Development of the Evaluation Plan

Vocational evaluation begins with the referral questions submitted by the rehabilitation counselor. The counselor's referral questions help the vocational evaluator develop the overall evaluation plan, which in turn should direct evaluation activities toward addressing those referral questions.

Programs that use questions and written goals in their plans to determine the evaluation tools and techniques are more likely to provide efficient and effective services (Cutler & Ramm, 1992). In the case of Shirley Steed (see Case Study, Chapter 3), the basic referral questions (Table 6.1) are about her potential for (a) working in clerical and other types of employment, (b) benefiting from further vocational training, and (c) seeking a job independently. Although guided by the counselor's request, the evaluation plan (Table 6.2) details the information needed to answer the referral questions and the tools and techniques to be used to gather the information. The plan deals with assessing vocational aptitudes, physical tolerance, present skill levels where applicable, interests, interpersonal skills, reactions to various stress situations, possible effects of medication, and job-seeking skills. Table 6.3 provides a brief description of the tests administered to Shirley Steed during the vocational evaluation process.

TABLE 6.1
Referral Questions for Shirley Steed's Vocational Evaluation

1. What is Shirley Steed's potential for clerical employment?

2. What potential benefits can she gain from further vocational training?

3. What is her potential for occupations other than clerical employment?

4. Name the effects that Shirley Steed's medication could have on her potential to engage in training and work.

5. Does she have enough physical stamina to work in a competitive work environment?

6. How well does Shirley Steed react to stress created by various work environments?

7. To what extent is Shirley Steed capable of independent job seeking?

TABLE 6.2
Evaluation Plan: Initial Questions and Evaluation Methods
See Table 6.3 for a brief description of each test administered.

Initial Questions Evaluators Might Ask	Evaluation Method—Techniques Used To Gather the Information
1. What are Shirley Steed's present aptitude levels?	*General Aptitude Test Battery*
2. What potential benefits can she gain from further education or training?	*Differential Aptitude Test* (Verbal, Numerical, Spelling)
3. What is her tolerance for sitting and standing?	*Valpar* Simulated Assembly, Behavior Observation on Sedentary Tasks
4. What is her present typing speed?	*Typing Test for Business*
5. What is her present level of dictation?	Dictation Test for Business (not administered)
6. Can she operate office machines and use software (e.g., photocopier/collator; microcomputer, word processing, and spreadsheet software)?	On-the-job evaluation in facility
7. What are her work environment expectations and interests?	*Minnesota Importance Questionnaire; Career Assessment Inventory*
8. What is her specific aptitude for clerical tasks?	*General Clerical Test*
9. Are her interpersonal skills and general appearance appropriate for competitive employment?	General observation of her behavior with staff, clients, taking phone messages, and so forth
10. What are her reactions to stress and work pressure?	Behavior observation on work samples, tests, and so on
11. Does her medication have any apparent effect on work performance?	Behavior observation, personal interview, and medical report
12. How might her nervousness or depression (should it continue) affect vocational planning?	Personal interview and psychological report
13. Is she capable of completing a job application quickly and accurately?	*Job Seeking Skills Assessment*
14. Are her job interview skills adequate for independent job seeking?	*Job Seeking Skills Assessment*

TABLE 6.3
Brief Description of Tests Administered to Shirley Steed
During Vocational Evaluation

Career Assessment Inventory (CAI)

The CAI is a 305-item inventory patterned after the *Strong Campbell Interest Inventory* (SCII) and designed to assist in career counseling of high school students and adults seeking immediate career entry, as well as individuals interested in careers requiring some post-secondary education such as technical or business school or some college training.

Differential Aptitude Test (DAT)

The DAT assesses aptitude levels in the following areas: verbal reasoning, numerical ability, abstract reasoning, clerical speed and accuracy, mechanical reasoning, space relations, and spelling and language usage. Results are generally used for helping students choose appropriate coursework and for helping individuals select realistic occupational goals.

General Aptitude Test Battery (GATB)

Developed by the United States Employment Service, the GATB, consisting of 12 subtests, yields scores on nine significant aptitudes pertinent to performance in a wide range of occupational groups. Further occupational information relevant to GATB results is provided in the *Dictionary of Occupational Titles* (DOT).

General Clerical Test

This instrument was designed to measure aptitudes that are of importance in clerical work of all kinds. The test consists of nine parts that are grouped to produce subscores related to clerical, numerical, and verbal aptitudes.

Job Seeking Skills Assessment (JSSA)

The JSSA is a behavioral assessment of skills required to complete the job application and interview.

Minnesota Importance Questionnaire (MIQ)

The MIQ is a 210-item paired comparison instrument designed to measure 20 vocationally relevant need dimensions that refer to specific reinforcing conditions that have been found to be important to job satisfaction.

Typing Test for Business (TTB)

The TTB was designed as a multi-unit test to assess competence within various areas of typing. Each of the five test units is based on a common typing task and is designed as an independent measure of a particular typing skill.

Valpar Component Work Sample Eight (VCWS 8)

The VCWS 8 was designed to measure a person's ability to work at an assembly task requiring repetitive physical manipulation and evaluate a person's bilateral use of upper extremities.

As is evident in Tables 6.2 and 6.3, a comprehensive evaluation program uses a variety of evaluation tools and techniques. By explaining the rationale for each question and corresponding tools and techniques, the evaluator increases the person's motivation for participation throughout the evaluation experience. An additional benefit of this client-centered approach is greater client understanding of evaluation results and recommendations for services.

Even with a client-centered approach, evaluators may not be sensitive to the important effects that cultural and gender variations have on the evaluation process. In a review of this issue, Parker and Schaller (1996) identified several factors that can negatively influence the validity of vocational aptitude and interest testing for women with disabilities and people with disabilities from minority backgrounds. Influential variables include "performance motivation, acculturation, inappropriate norms, and gender restrictiveness" (Parker & Schaller, p. 135).

Performance motivation is the willingness to expend effort in responding to an evaluation such as a paper and pencil test. Mistrust of the evaluator or evaluation instrument arises when respondents question the eventual use of the results (i.e., "Will the results be used to discriminate against me in some way?"). This mistrust leads to decreased performance motivation and, thus, to inaccurate test outcomes.

Testing outcomes are also affected by fluency in English, one criterion of acculturation. Certainly, results from aptitude and interest measures in English are questionable when administered to persons with minimal proficiency in English. Hence, evaluators should first determine the person's level of English usage by interviewing the person, person's family, or counselor. A test of language proficiency is also suggested to determine the person's skills in "word recognition, word meanings, comprehension, and spelling" (Martin & Swartz, 1996). Data from such a variety of sources enable evaluators to determine the appropriateness of their typical test battery. Unfortunately, responding to language barriers is not solved as easily as simply translating the assessment instrument into the person's native language. Information on reliability, validity, and appropriate norms is also needed on the translated version of the assessment (Parker & Schaller, 1996).

Acculturation is, however, a broader concept than simply language proficiency. Acculturation has to do with values and belief systems that differ from culture to culture and have a bearing on important issues in vocational assessment such as the importance of work, the decision-making patterns in the family, and the meaning of disability and gender-related variables in one's life. Hence, evaluators must learn about the priorities and customs of people from the various racial–ethnic groups they serve (Martin & Swartz, 1996).

Using appropriate norms to interpret scores of people with disabilities, particularly women with disabilities, is often impossible because the norms are based on the combined male and female scores of people in a majority sample who have no disabilities. People with disabilities who have limited experience in a given vocational area may fare poorly when compared to individuals without handicaps who have some experience in a field. Moreover, norms based on combined male and female samples may not yield accurate conclusions regarding a woman's preferences for nontraditional occupational roles and probable success in those roles. Same-sex norms, norms based on groups of people with disabilities, and norms from measures with "sex-balanced" items (i.e., items reflecting gender-role socialization differences between men and women) are feasible solutions to norming problems (Parker & Schaller, 1996, p. 137), and thus to the problem of invalid evaluation reports.

The Evaluation Report

The evaluation report is the final product of vocational evaluation services. It reflects the true utility of the evaluation referral. The evaluation report is the counselor's record of the client's evaluation and should specifically address the rehabilitation counselor's purpose(s) for referring the client to the program.

A comprehensive evaluation report should contain (a) a short summary of the reason(s) for the referral; (b) disability and other pertinent background information, (c) significant behavioral observations and their vocational significance; (d) the results of tests and work samples administered during the evaluation and the functional vocational significance of these results; (e) information pertinent to daily living or social functioning skills; (f) a summary statement synthesizing the observations and results into a general statement of assets, transferable skills, limitations, and needed accommodations to be considered in future programming; and (g) a recommendations section that identifies potential options, vocational or otherwise, that seem most feasible in light of available information along with suggested steps for achieving such options (Cutler & Ramm, 1992; Thomas, 1986).

Recommendations should be specifically related to the initial referral questions and should identify options that are most feasible if no further services are provided, as well as options that would only be feasible given the successful completion of additional services. Recommendations stated in this way not only give the rehabilitation counselor a clearer understanding of the potential vocational benefits of further services, but also serve to help the client understand the relationship between possible service outcomes and long-range vocational objectives. The evaluation report for Shirley Steed (see Table 6.4) shows how such an evaluation was carried out in relation to the initial referral questions (Table 6.1) with recommendations related to employment opportunities available with and without further training.

Power (1991) and Thomas (1986) provided the essential elements for a checklist for evaluating the quality of an evaluation report. Effective vocational evaluation reports receive high marks in regard to such questions as:

1. Does the report respond to the referral questions?

2. Are the rehabilitation planning implications of the report clear?

3. Are the recommendations well documented?

4. Are there inconsistencies between data and recommendations?

(text continues on page 94)

TABLE 6.4
Vocational Evaluation Report for Shirley Steed

___

To: Rehabilitation Counselor

From: Vocational Evaluator

Re: Evaluation Report for Shirley Steed

Disability: Varicose veins, chronic bronchitis, emphysema, psychoneurotic depressive reaction

Evaluation Period

3 weeks (because of Mrs. Steed's physical condition, she only spent 4 hours a day in evaluation)

Reason for Referral

Shirley Steed, a 38-year-old Caucasian female, was referred for vocational evaluation to determine her feasibility for clerical or other employment, as well as her potential to benefit from further vocational training. Mrs. Steed's past work history includes 11 years of employment as an offset press operator preceded by 6 months as a sales clerk in a fabric shop. Increasing recurrence of lung infections from chronic bronchitis and the subsequent development of emphysema, however, have caused her to quit her job for health reasons. In addition, she was briefly hospitalized about 3 years ago for physical and nervous exhaustion resulting from a combination of stresses caused by marital problems and increasing physical problems.

At present she is divorced and has four children: two married daughters (one with whom she is living), a 17-year-old son in prison, and a 15-year-old son living with her. Mrs. Steed's medical report indicates that she is taking 5 mg of Valium (Diazepam) four times a day to help her relax and that she is not capable of working at the present time because of her emphysema. If her present treatment regime is successful, however, she is expected to be able to do sedentary work in settings that do not expose her to lint, industrial fumes, dyes, or other substances that might induce an allergic reaction. She should also avoid work settings characterized by excessive dampness, cold, or dry heat.

Behavioral Observations

Mrs. Steed was not absent during the evaluation period, and she was punctual at all times. At the onset of evaluation, she appeared to be very nervous and upset, but she seemed to relax as the evaluation progressed. Mrs. Steed was troubled with drowsiness from time to time, a factor she attributed to the Valium. One day when she did not take the medication, however, she was considerably more anxious and nervous.

When Mrs. Steed was asked to work faster on tasks, she became noticeably more anxious and her performance deteriorated somewhat. At the point when she felt she was not doing well, she began to cry and asked to go home early. She seemed to be under a great deal of stress and, in a personal interview, spoke of her concerns about her two sons and her need to be able to support them and herself. She is very concerned about an upcoming move from her daughter's home and having to go on welfare.

Throughout the evaluation period, Mrs. Steed was appropriately dressed in clean, plain, well-worn clothing. After her initial nervousness passed, she related well to staff and other

(continues)

TABLE 6.4 (*Continued*)

evaluates. She was able to ask for help on evaluation tasks when necessary and was quick to inform the evaluators when she completed various tasks. It seems that much of her anxiety is related to her concerns about family and her living situation, rather than concern about her image as a worker.

Evaluation Results

The tests administered were: *General Aptitude Test Battery* (GATB), *Differential Aptitude Test* (DAT), *General Clerical Test, Typing Test for Business, Valpar Simulated Assembly, Career Assessment Inventory, Minnesota Importance Questionnaire* (MIQ), and *Job Seeking Skills Assessment.*

Mrs. Steed's scores on the GATB indicate she has above average intellectual (116), numerical (108), and clerical perception (115) abilities, and her other scores are close to average (100), with the exception of finger dexterity (82) and manual dexterity (85), which were somewhat below average. It is possible, however, that these last scores are somewhat depressed by the effects of the medication coupled with anxiety.

She was also given the DAT to check for academic potential and achieved a verbal and numerical score at the 70th percentile and a spelling score at the 80th percentile using 12th grade female norms. This is consistent with her GATB performance and indicates she has the ability to pursue further academic or vocational training requiring good verbal and numerical ability.

On the *General Clerical Test,* when compared to clerical workers, Mrs. Steed scored at the 70th percentile on clerical subtests, at the 65th percentile numerically, and at the 90th percentile verbally. When compared to secretaries and stenographers, her clerical score was at the 60th percentile, numerical at the 55th percentile, and verbal at the 50th percentile. This performance suggests that she is highly competitive for employment in clerical occupations and has average clerical ability as compared to general secretaries and stenographers.

Mrs. Steed was able to type 30 wpm with four errors, which was considered to be quite good considering that she has not typed to any extent for 20 years. She would, however, have to increase her speed to at least 40 wpm for employment as a clerk typist, and to 60 wpm for general employment as a secretary.

She declined to take the shorthand test as she could not remember enough to make testing feasible. As part of the evaluation, Mrs. Steed was given the opportunity to operate a variety of office machines in the facility and learned without difficulty to operate a photocopier with a collator, a word processing program for desk computers, and a six-line PBX switchboard. During her short on-the-job evaluation on the switchboard, she was able to handle incoming and outgoing calls appropriately, take messages, and make general announcements over the PA system. She did seem to tire rather easily, however, and expressed some concern as to whether she could learn to manage all the activities going on in the office.

Her performance on the job application and job interview simulations was basically acceptable; however, a few problem areas were noted. While she completed all sections of the job application correctly, she required more than the recommended 15 minutes to finish the form. With practice in completing applications and the use of application aids (an index card with background and employment data on it), she should complete most forms in a satisfactory amount of time.

(continues)

TABLE 6.4 (*Continued*)

Mrs. Steed's behavior in the simulated job interview revealed several strengths and weaknesses. She adequately described her educational training, employment history, and specific work skills. She does need to improve her presentation of her disability-related conditions and the way they affect and do not affect her work potential. She also appeared nervous (gestures, voice tone) during the interview and must remember to speak up throughout the interview (voice volume).

Mrs. Steed's biggest deterrent to employment and training at the present time is her physical and nervous condition. As soon as her physical condition improves and her medication can be reduced to levels that do not cause her to become drowsy, she could be capable of engaging in or receiving training for sedentary clerically related occupations.

Regarding levels of employability, Mrs. Steed has demonstrated the interest and ability to pursue secretarial jobs and learn fairly complex business machine and software operations. As employment in an entry level clerical position would pay little more than minimum wage, and Mrs. Steed is very concerned about being able to care for herself and her son financially, training and eventual placement in higher level positions seems most appropriate. Consistent with the recommendations in her psychological report, it is also felt that counseling to help her deal with her personal and family problems would most likely speed her ability to become ready for competitive employment. She will also need assistance in learning to manage stress. Until she gains more stability in her home life and her medication can be reduced, she will most likely work best in a relatively low-stress work environment with a supportive supervisor.

Recommendations

1. That Mrs. Steed pursue admission to the local business school to increase typing speed, learn common word processing software, shorthand, and receive training in office machine operation and office management.

2. That upon completion of training, Mrs. Steed consider employment in one of the following areas:

Administrative secretary	169.167-014
Accounting clerk	216.482-010
Cost Clerk	216.382-034
Billing machine operator	214.482-010
Word processing machine operator	203.382-030

3. If it is decided that Mrs. Steed needs to seek employment as soon as possible, then it is recommended that she take a short course in keyboarding and use of word processing software and that she seek employment in one of the following areas:

Credit clerk	205.367-022
Insurance clerk	219.367-014
Administrative clerk	219.362-010
Contact clerk	209.387-010
Civil service clerk	205.362-010
Hotel and motel desk clerk	238.367-038
File clerk	206.367-014
Medical records clerk	245.362-010

(continues)

TABLE 6.4 (*Continued*)

Thank you for referring this individual to our program. Please feel free to contact me should you have additional questions regarding your client.

Cynthia I. Seall
Vocational Evaluator

5. Are these inconsistencies among results of different assessments?

6. Are the recommendations specific and realistic; do they provide an understandable profile of the individual's vocational potential and readiness to work?

7. Are the training and employment recommendations consistent with local opportunities?

8. Is the report brief but concise?

MAKING AN APPROPRIATE REFERRAL

The appropriateness of a referral for vocational evaluation rests primarily on the counselor's knowledge of two factors—the characteristics of the person referred and the characteristics of available vocational evaluation programs. For example, inappropriate referrals may result because some vocational evaluation programs are designed to evaluate the vocational potential of individuals with physical disabilities with average or above intellectual abilities. With their primary emphasis on evaluating people for entry into skill training, ongoing educational programs, or direct entry into the labor market, these programs may be poorly equipped to evaluate individuals with severe intellectual or psychiatric disabilities. People with such characteristics are more appropriately referred to vocational evaluation units capable of evaluating general employability factors such as ability to accept supervision, get along with co-workers, maintain an adequate production rate, and tolerate frustration. Ensuing recommendations should focus on entry into the employment market via supported employment or work adjustment programs designed to teach clients basic work skills.

Although it is frequently difficult for a counselor to know who (or which type of client) a program is capable of serving most effectively, a check with other counselors or referral sources can often yield this information. In the case of Shirley Steed, an appropriate evaluation program had the tools and personnel necessary for assessing clerical or related occupational skills and vocationally related behavior. A vocational evaluation program limited to assessing general employability behaviors was inappropriate.

Clearly, the rehabilitation counselor's knowledge of a person is absolutely essential for determining an appropriate evaluation program. An understanding of the individual's expectations of the rehabilitation process and any special considerations related to the individual's disability, interests, past vocational experience, and present vocational capability plays an important role in the determination of questions to be addressed during the vocational evaluation. In the final analysis, selection of an appropriate vocational evaluation program is determined by the content of the client's social–vocational–medical history and the potential rehabilitation plan objectives previously discussed by the client and rehabilitation counselor.

At referral, the vocational evaluation unit should be provided with a clear statement of the type of information needed by the rehabilitation counselor. The vocational evaluation unit should also be sent all client information that could help the evaluator develop an effective evaluation plan (Power, 1991). For example, when the vocational evaluator is aware of the person's medical condition, evaluation activities that are compatible with this client's physical and emotional condition are more likely to be selected. Moreover, the vocational evaluation report is more likely to discuss appropriate medical implications. In the case of Shirley Steed, the information specifying her medication dosage allowed for a more accurate interpretation of her drowsiness and her lower scores on tasks requiring motor coordination and work speed. Information about her respiratory condition and varicose veins helped ensure that Shirley would not be asked to perform potentially harmful tasks during vocational evaluation. It also affected the kinds of jobs recommended by the vocational evaluator. Similarly, an understanding of Shirley's family situation and emotional condition was also important to the vocational evaluator. Analysis of this information, along with other evaluation data, suggested the need for placement in an emotionally supportive work environment. It also suggested the value of training Shirley for a level of employment that could subsequently result in her greater ability to provide more adequate financial support for her family. Other information related to her education and employment history contained clues about the typing level and shorthand speed that she might be expected to regain through vocational training, presuming continued motivation for retraining.

Failure of the rehabilitation counselor to provide the vocational evaluator with relevant social, vocational, educational, and medical history information can be serious. It can set the stage for the person being put through a number of unnecessary evaluation procedures before the already available information is used, or possibly even worse, the formulation of recommendations by the vocational evaluator that do not take all relevant issues into consideration.

Because evaluation information used to make recommendations for continuing services is based on a client's current functioning, it is also important that the individual be relatively stable physically and emotionally at referral for vocational evaluation. If this is not entirely possible, a statement of the client's probable physical and emotional functioning in the near future following available restoration services should be developed. This will make the evaluation information much more valid as a basis for recommending the design of work adjustment or vocational training plans as well as for predicting future client potential. For example, if the individual acquired prescription glasses after completing vocational evaluation, there is no way to judge how having the glasses during evaluation would have affected his or her performance. Similarly, if significant changes in the person's living situation, physical condition, medication, and other factors are imminent, referral to evaluation is more appropriate after the change has occurred and the person has had a chance to adjust. If this delay is not possible, the timing and possible effects of the change should be communicated, along with other referral information, to the vocational evaluator.

In summary, an appropriate referral involves not only determining the appropriateness of the evaluation program for meeting the needs of the client, but also communicating relevant medical, emotional, educational, economic, and vocational information to the evaluation program—along with a clear statement of evaluation goals that reflect the expectations of the counselor and the client. Referrals made as a routine matter, or simply as activities to occupy the client, are of little value (Power, 1991).

PREPARING THE CLIENT FOR VOCATIONAL EVALUATION

Because expectations of vocational evaluation stem from the rehabilitation counselor's description of the operations and purpose of the evaluation service, the counselor's orientation must accurately reflect the client's subsequent evaluation experience. Inconsistencies between the two can confuse individuals and seriously affect their motivation to participate fully in the vocational evaluation or subsequent aspects of the rehabilitation program. For example, unnecessary demoralization can occur if the client expects placement in employment to directly result from the evaluation when both the predictable and actual outcome is a recommendation for a specific type of work adjustment training. Another problem can result from the pass–fail syndrome. If an individual expects to fail or pass the evaluation—that is, if the counselor leads the person to believe that further services depend on how well he or she does—then the individual may approach the vocational evaluation process with a great deal of anxiety. Anxiety can affect a person's ability to perform up to potential.

The effective preparation of the client for vocational evaluation by the rehabilitation counselor is extremely important. In the orientation, the rehabilitation counselor should cover the following:

1. *An explanation of the purpose of vocational evaluation.* The counselor should stress the assessment of vocational assets in order to help identify realistic vocational goals. Care should be taken to point out that one cannot pass or fail the evaluation and that efforts are designed to determine the most suitable jobs and training programs for the person.

2. *The specific goals of the evaluation.* The counselor should discuss with the client the specific information needed and how the vocational evaluation program will help provide this information. For Shirley Steed, such a discussion might have

centered on the need to determine her potential for employment in clerical or secretarial occupations and the most appropriate types of training or retraining. Finding out more about her sitting and standing tolerance and exploring job settings that would be most appropriate given her respiratory condition may have been other points covered during the counselor–client discussion. Shirley should also understand that the overall goal of the evaluation is to provide her and the counselor with useful information for planning future vocational programming.

3. *The kinds of techniques the client may experience.* Paper and pencil tests, computerized evaluations, work samples, and situational assessments should generally be discussed to allay fears and correct any misconceptions. It is important that this information be consistent with the actual techniques used by the evaluation program in question.

4. *Procedural issues.* Prior to the referral, counselors should clarify issues such as probable starting and ending dates of the evaluation; maintenance, transportation, and living arrangements; expectations related to attendance; and whom to call if problems should arise. Careful discussion and resolution of these procedural issues can do much to ensure that the person's participation in the evaluation will proceed smoothly.

Preparation of the client, therefore, primarily consists of helping the individual develop realistic expectations of the evaluation process, and assuring to the greatest extent possible, that potential problems external to the evaluation process are kept to a minimum.

HOW TO GET MORE FOR YOUR MONEY

Generating good lines of communication between the counselor and evaluator, as well as fostering mutual professional respect, can greatly increase the likelihood of the rehabilitation counselor and the client receiving the "most for their money." The following list of Do's and Don'ts will help the rehabilitation counselor establish a beneficial relationship with the vocational evaluator.

Do's

1. Discuss the client's goals and needs with the vocational evaluator prior to the referral. Point out special concerns and reiterate the points in a cover letter accompanying the referral. Clarify expectations before—not after—the evaluation is completed.

2. Send pertinent background information to the evaluator before the client begins evaluation. This will be of considerable help for developing the evaluation plan with the individual.

3. Attend the initial evaluation staffing, if invited. If not, see that an invitation is forthcoming.

4. Give the evaluator(s) constructive feedback regarding the utility or appropriateness of evaluation reports and recommendations. This will help communicate how well their service is meeting referral expectations.

5. Give evaluators feedback on the long-term rehabilitation outcomes of people they have evaluated. This kind of information can help evaluators examine the validity of vocational recommendations.

6. Ask for clarification of recommendations that are incompatible with the evaluation data presented in the report.

Don'ts

1. Do not tell evaluators how to do their job. Evaluators take as much pride in knowing their job as do rehabilitation counselors. Suggestions for improved evaluation services should be couched in terms of how the client might be better served.

2. Do not communicate dissatisfaction about services to persons other than the evaluator in question unless problems cannot be resolved any other way.

3. Do not believe negative feedback from clients without first checking out the situation with other persons involved.

4. Do not criticize the evaluation process unless positive suggestions can be offered.

5. Do not be afraid to ask for answers to questions perceived as not having been dealt with during the evaluation.

While this is by no means an all-inclusive list, adherence to the intent of these Do's and Don'ts can do much to build a strong sense of rapport between the rehabilitation counselor and the vocational evaluator. This is extremely important as disagreements or lack of communication between these two professional groups generally result in less effective rehabilitation services.

CONCLUDING STATEMENT

In conclusion, the use of vocational evaluation resources is necessary to assess the vocational potential of many people with severe disabilities. The purpose of the evaluation is to assist in the establishment of realistic vocational goals and the identification of the most effective services for helping persons reach stated goals.

This evaluation must be compatible with the client's rehabilitation goals. Whenever possible, the counselor should help the client relate evaluation results to these potential goals. For this to occur, the rehabilitation counselor must be able to match client needs to appropriate evaluation resources and develop the necessary level of professional rapport with both clients and vocational evaluators for the most effective use of this valuable rehabilitation service.

Vocational Alternatives
for Clients Not Referred
for Vocational Evaluation

Shirley Steed's case illustrates the use of multiple evaluation sources. For example, Chapters 4 and 5 present her medical and psychological evaluations. Chapter 6 demonstrates the way in which vocational evaluation, when coupled with social–vocational, medical, and psychological information, can result in identification of vocational alternatives for the client. Vocational evaluation programs, however, are not available in every community. Hence, even when needed, comprehensive vocational evaluation may not be a possibility. In other cases, the characteristics of the individual may allow the counselor to identify feasible vocational alternatives without referring the person to a vocational evaluation unit. For these reasons, rehabilitation counselors must have vocational analysis skills that include the use of both interest measures and occupational information resources. By combining information from these sources, they can prepare clients for making vocational choices and participating in rehabilitation planning.

In the past, rehabilitation counselors reported that they devoted approximately 13% of their time to the area of assessment, a function that they considered to be a moderately important aspect of their job (Leahy, Shapson, & Wright, 1987). If anything, the counselor's assessment role will become even more important with the dawning of the 21st century. As cultural, economic, and technological changes occur, people must cope with a rapidly evolving workplace. To help people with disabilities enter this expanding and demanding world of work, rehabilitation counselors need accurate knowledge of "job demands, work opportunities, reasonable accommodation, and the social context of work" (Vander Kolk, 1995, p. 45) as well as of critical vocationally relevant characteristics of the person, such as aptitudes and interests.

To demonstrate one counselor's approach to vocational analysis—the use of occupational information resources and interest measures—the case of Ted Johnson is introduced. A summary of the information known by the counselor at the completion of the intake interview (see case study) and the medical evaluation (see Table 7.1) follows. To begin the vocational analysis for Ted, the counselor reconsidered the vocational significance of data from the intake interview and medical examination.

CASE STUDY: TED JOHNSON

Summary of Intake Interview

Ted Johnson, a 31-year-old African American male, graduated from high school in 1983. Married shortly thereafter, he and his wife live in a community of 200,000 people. Ted, his wife, and three children live in an apartment. On the average, Ted makes about $500 a week from a small barber shop he operates; however, his earnings lately have dropped to about $375 a week. He is a licensed driver and owns his own car. Mrs. Johnson works full time as a medical records clerk.

Ted first heard of vocational rehabilitation from his uncle who received rehabilitation services approximately 5 years ago for a respiratory condition. Ted has come to rehabilitation because he feels he can no longer work as a barber due to diabetes-related circulatory problems. After standing for long periods, he needs several doses of an over-the-counter anti-inflammatory medication (two or three tablets) during the day and evening to ease the pain in his legs.

After completing vocational training, Ted went directly into barbering. He has worked as a barber for 12 years and now owns two barber chairs, a back bar, mirrors, and several waiting chairs. He also leases a small shop in a suburban location.

Ted characterized himself as a "goof-off" in high school. Although he is a high school graduate, his high school classes were generally not college preparatory—such as shop, business education, and printing. He received Bs and Cs in these courses but realizes now that he could have done much better. He also wishes he had taken college preparatory courses and at least tried to get an associate degree from the local community college.

Ted had medical problems with his legs as early as 8 years of age, when he was diagnosed as having inflammatory rheumatism. He experienced inflammation of the knee joints in junior high school and in high school to the extent that he was frequently excused from physical education. Eight years ago, his knees swelled to the point at which he could not turn over in bed or walk without assistance.

Ted first learned that he had diabetes a little over 5 years ago when the family doctor found that his father had a diabetic condition. The doctor then checked the rest of the family and found that Ted was a borderline diabetic. To date, he has been able to control his blood sugar level through managing his diet and oral medication. Insulin injections have not been necessary, but his doctor has told him to expect to start soon because of the progressive nature of his disease.

Ted reported to vocational rehabilitation on his own initiative and was neatly dressed in slacks and sport shirt. He manifested good verbal and social skills. His personality obviously contributed to his success as a barber over the past 12 years.

Ted expressed an interest in motorcycle repair, an occupation he had frequently observed at a motorcycle repair shop next door to his barber shop. He noted that motorcycle repair involved bench work, which would allow him to sit or stand as needed during the day. As an occupation, small engine repair would allow him eventually to open his own shop and be his own boss, a possibility that is very important to him.

He also suggested bookkeeping as a possible vocation. He had, in fact, enrolled in an accounting course at the local junior college last year. Ted pointed out, however, that bookkeeping would not be his first choice because he would have to stay in an office all day and would not be able to be his own boss. Ted wants a job in which he would spend only part of the week in his office. This was one of his complaints about barbering—he could never leave the shop.

Ted thought a position as a recreation specialist or camp counselor working with children might be one way to work in various settings. Although he likes that kind of work and coaches a little league baseball team, he recognized drawbacks such as starting at a low-level position with little possibility of advancement.

Ted also expressed an interest in furniture reupholstery. He has relatives in the furniture reupholstery business who would be willing to train him and eventually sell him their equipment. He also indicated that his wife could help in this type of work.

Ted has also thought about exploring social work positions. He believes that he would enjoy this work and that it would allow him to spend some of his time in the office and some in the field.

Fully realizing the seriousness of circulatory problems associated with diabetes, Ted understands that he can no longer work in any job where he must stand all day. He discounts the utility of any of the adaptations to barber chairs that would allow him to sit while he cuts hair. Ted feels that the medical signs clearly indicate that he must change to a more physically compatible occupation before circulatory deterioration reaches the point that amputation becomes the only feasible treatment.

Fortunately, Ted has a positive work history with demonstrated ability to manage his own small business. Drawing on his basic skills as a worker and on his aptitude for skilled work, Ted should have the capabilities to meet the demands of a wide range of jobs.

Currently, Ted's family situation poses no problems to his rehabilitation. His wife helps him cope with his medical problems and also works to help support the family. His children seem to be well adjusted and are having no problems in school.

Ted shows no evidence of anxiety or depression regarding his present situation. In fact, he appears to have made up his mind that he must begin a vocational training or educational program as soon as possible in order to start a new type of work. He has apparently developed ways over the years to adjust to the problems presented by rheumatism and diabetes. The proof of his ability to cope with these stresses is apparent in his long and stable work history.

*Ted would like to start a rehabilitation program in which he receives voca-
tional or educational training and some financial support while in training. He
commented that he would rather not be on welfare but that he has paid enough in
over the years to deserve some support now that he needs it. He cannot maintain
his barber shop while in training because rent and utilities make it an unfeasible
part-time operation.*

With an understanding of Ted's strengths and limitations, the counselor screened
additional vocational possibilities identified through perusal of information resources
such as the *Dictionary of Occupational Titles* (U.S. Department of Labor, 1991), the
Enhanced Guide for Occupational Exploration (Maze & Mayall, 1991), and the
Occupational Outlook Handbook (U.S. Department of Labor, Annual). The counselor
also administered Holland's *Self-Directed Search (Form R)* (Holland, 1994). Each of
these resources can provide valuable information for expanding the counselor's and
the client's thinking regarding feasible vocational objectives. Of course, as pointed out
in Chapter 9, the counselor must temper conclusions drawn from such resources with
personal knowledge about the nature of work in the local community.

TABLE 7.1
Ted Johnson's Medical Report

Mr. Johnson has had diabetes mellitus for 6 years at a controllable level, with the exception
of recently developed circulatory problems in both legs. Circulation difficulties are manifested
in pain and limited mobility at times.

Swelling of the knees was also apparent as a result of rheumatoid arthritis. The patient
complained of stiffness and pain, particularly during the morning hours. I have prescribed a
medical regimen of ibuprofen and corticosteroids, as needed, to combat the pain and swelling.

Given these two conditions affecting his lower extremities, Mr. Johnson must avoid any
work with excessive standing or walking. For this reason, his current occupation as a barber
is extremely inappropriate. Physical stress factors of any job—standing, walking, lifting, or
stooping—should be carefully evaluated. In addition, Mr. Johnson should not be exposed to
extremes of coldness or dampness or wide temperature variations.

Although Mr. Johnson's blood sugar level is controllable through diet, existence of the
circulation problem suggests that he may soon require insulin on a regular basis. At this
point, Mr. Johnson must maintain a regular work pace, rather than one that fluctuates in
terms of demands and hours. Mr. Johnson also requires a work style that allows him a regular
eating schedule.

At present, Mr. Johnson's general health, with the exception of the problems mentioned
above, is good. No evidence exists of further complications from the diabetes, such as vision
or upper extremity complications. The rheumatoid arthritis is currently confined to the legs.
Mr. Johnson reports no problems with his hands, elbows, or shoulders.

Given proper working conditions and health habits, Mr. Johnson should be capable of
full-time work. I am also recommending regular medical examinations to monitor his diabetic
and arthritic conditions.

THE *DICTIONARY OF OCCUPATIONAL TITLES* (DOT)

The 1991 Revision of the Fourth Edition of the *Dictionary of Occupational Titles* (DOT) provides a general description of approximately 20,000 jobs found in the American economy. Each of these jobs is assigned a nine-digit occupational code that precedes a comprehensive definition of the job. Job definitions are presented in terms of nine occupational categories:

0/1. Professional, technical, and managerial occupations

2. Clerical and sales occupations

3. Service occupations

4. Agricultural, fishery, forestry, and related occupations

5. Processing occupations

6. Machine trades occupations

7. Benchwork occupations

8. Structural work occupations

9. Miscellaneous occupations

These nine categories are further subdivided into 82 specific occupational divisions and 559 homogeneous groups. The resulting three-digit code (the first three digits of the occupational code) enables the counselor to enter the DOT and find jobs the client has held as well as related jobs in those industries. To locate job definitions, the counselor can also use an alphabetical index of occupational titles at the back of Volume II. If the counselor knows the industry in which the job exists, he or she can use the occupational titles arranged by industry designation as well.

Functional demands of each of the jobs described in the DOT are provided in part of the nine-digit code identifying the occupation, as well as in the definition of the job itself. For example, the second set of three digits refers to demands of the job in regard to worker relationship categories—Data, People, and Things. For each of the jobs described in the DOT, these worker function ratings indicate the characteristic demands of the position. The lower the number, the more complex the function. A brief overview of the skill levels in the Data, People, and Things areas is provided in the list to follow:

Data: Information, knowledge, and conceptions related to data, people, or things, obtained by observation, investigation, interpretation, visualization, and mental creation. Data are intangible and include numbers, words, symbols, ideas, concepts, and oral verbalizations.

People: Human beings (and animals, when dealt with on an individual basis as if they were human).

Things: Inanimate objects as distinguished from human beings, substances or materials, machines, tools, equipment, and products. A thing is tangible and has shape, form, and other physical characteristics.

Data (4th digit)	People (5th digit)	Things (6th digit)
0 Synthesizing	0 Mentoring	0 Setting-up
1 Coordinating	1 Negotiating	1 Precision working
2 Analyzing	2 Instructing	2 Operating–controlling
3 Compiling	3 Supervising	3 Driving–operating
4 Computing	4 Diverting	4 Manipulating
5 Copying	5 Persuading	5 Tending
6 Comparing	6 Speaking–signaling	6 Feeding–offbearing
	7 Serving	7 Handling
	8 Taking instructions–helping	

(U.S. Dept. of Labor, 1991, p. xix)

Using the DOT, the counselor can learn more about the nature of the work involved in the jobs mentioned by Ted during the intake interview. For example, because of some questions about the physical demands of the job, the counselor might seek additional information on small engine or motorcycle repair work. To enter the DOT, the counselor must first determine the occupational classification and DOT number for motorcycle and small engine repair. The easiest way to generate this information is to use the alphabetic index at the back of Volume II of the DOT. On page 1325 of the alphabetical index of occupational titles, the counselor learns that motorcycle mechanic has a DOT number of 620.281-054. This number indicates that the motorcycle mechanic is a machine trades occupation (6), further specified as mechanics and machinery repairers (62) with a special focus on motorized vehicles (620). The counselor also learns that being a motorcycle mechanic requires fairly high levels of data-related (2=analyzing) and things skills (1=precision working), but low levels of people skills (8=taking instructions–helping).

The DOT presents the following description of motorcycle mechanic:

620.281-054 **MOTORCYCLE REPAIRER** (automotive ser.) alternative titles: motorcycle mechanic

Repairs and overhauls motorcycles, motor scooters, and similar motor vehicles. Listens to engine, examines vehicle's frame and confers with customer to determine nature and extent of malfunction or damage. Connects test panel to engine and measures generator output, ignition timing, and other engine performance indicators. Dismantles engine and repairs or replaces defective parts such as magneto, carburetor, and generator. Removes cylinder heads, grinds valves, and scrapes off carbon, and replaces defective valves, pistons, cylinders, and rings, using handtools and power tools. Hammers out dents and bends in frame, welds tears and breaks, and reassembles and reinstalls engine. Repairs and adjusts clutch, brakes, and drive chain. Repairs or replaces other motorcycle and motor scooter parts, such as spring fork, headlight, horn, handlebar controls, valve release, gear lever, gasoline and oil tanks, starter, brake lever, and muffler. May specialize in repair of motor scooters and be designated Motor-Scooter Repairer. (U.S. Dept. of Labor, 1991, p. 563)

Given Ted's medical report, several aspects of the job of a motorcycle mechanic concerned the counselor, including dismantling engines, hammering out dents, welding tears and breaks, and possibly working on his feet in a damp, cold garage during winter months. Hence, the counselor reviewed other jobs in the DOT that Ted mentioned to identify options that are less likely to exacerbate Ted's physical condition, for example, recreation supervisor (187.167-238).

187.167-238 **RECREATION SUPERVISOR** (profess. + kin.) alternative titles: area supervisor; district director; recreation specialist

Coordinates activities of paid and volunteer recreation service personnel in public department, voluntary agency, or similar type facility, such as community centers or swimming pools: Develops and promotes recreation program including music, dance, arts and crafts, cultural arts, nature study, swimming, social recreation and games, or camping. Adapts recreation programs to meet needs of individual agency or institution, such as hospital, armed services, institution for children or aged, settlement house, or penal institution. Introduces new program activities, equipment, and materials to staff. Trains personnel and evaluates performance. Interprets recreation service to public and participates in community meetings and organizational planning. May work in team with administrative or other professional personnel, such as those engaged in medicine, social work, nursing, psychology, and therapy, to ensure that recreation is well balanced, coordinated, and integrated with special services. (U.S. Dept. of Labor, 1991, p. 146)

The counselor can use the DOT in several other useful ways. First, the counselor might review jobs related to work that Ted has expressed an interest in such as upholstery, social work, or bookkeeping. Second, the counselor could use the DOT to scan job listings in areas where Ted has worked successfully. For example, the counselor might wish to review the broad category of service occupations that includes barbering. A detailed list of service occupations can be found in the DOT. Finally, the counselor may examine job titles closely related to an area of interest for Ted. For example, neither Ted nor the counselor may be familiar with the wide range of jobs related to a recreation specialist. Since recreation specialist is in the *187* occupational category (service industry managers), both Ted and the counselor could read about jobs adjacent to recreation supervisor such as manager of recreation facility, bowling alley, storage garage, and theater. Some of these positions may have excellent employment potential in Ted's community.

By using Ted's expressed interests and past work history, the counselor can introduce Ted to a wide variety of potential vocational objectives using the DOT. Equal partners in the vocational counseling process, Ted and his counselor can consider these vocational objectives during the initial stages of the planning process. For each potential job, the counselor must help Ted clarify the relationship of intake and medical evaluation data (physical, psychosocial, and educational–vocational functioning) to job demands. The end result of this process is a vocational goal that Ted selects as the basis for his individualized written rehabilitation program (IWRP). However, Ted does not need to stop his vocational exploring with the DOT. Other useful tools exist such as the *Enhanced Guide for Occupational Exploration* (Maze & Mayall, 1991) and Holland's (1994) *Self-Directed Search–Form R* (SDS).

TED'S VOCATIONAL INTERESTS: USING THE *ENHANCED GUIDE* AND THE SDS

Research reveals that work provides access to sources of satisfaction that encompass intrinsic reinforcers such as the opportunity to (a) use abilities, (b) achieve, (c) be busy all the time, and extrinsic reinforcers such as the opportunity to (a) advance, (b) be paid well, and (c) receive recognition for accomplishments (Dawis & Lofquist, 1984). An individual's preference regarding these intrinsic and extrinsic reinforcers is implicit in the vocational choices they have made and the jobs they have enjoyed. Therefore, the counselor can help Ted expand his vocational horizons by identifying jobs that he would be interested in either because of their relationship to past work he has liked or to an interest profile generated by a reliable and valid interest assessment. Both of these vocational exploration strategies are described using the *Enhanced Guide* and Holland's SDS.

Using the *Enhanced Guide for Occupational Exploration*

The *Enhanced Guide* (Maze & Mayall, 1991) contains a description of 2,500 of the most important jobs in the American economy. These occupations are organized within the occupational clusters consistent with the Department of Labor's 12 major interest factors—artistic, scientific, plants and animals, protective, mechanical, industrial, business detail, selling, accommodating, humanitarian, leading–persuading, and physical performing. The *Enhanced Guide* is useful because it allows the counselor and the client to locate jobs that the person has enjoyed and to consider other related jobs that may represent better options given the person's current status.

In Ted's case, the counselor knows that he enjoyed his work as a barber. Hence, the counselor could locate the interest category including barbering and review other similar types of work with Ted. Two strategies are available for finding the proper interest category for barbering. First, the counselor can use the alphabetic index at the back of the *Enhanced Guide* (p. 477) and find that barber is in the personal service area of the economy, which is consistent with the accommodating (09) interest area. The counselor could also review the 12 interest categories at the beginning of the *Enhanced Guide* and locate barbering within the accommodating area (09.02-02). With this information, Ted and his counselor can explore accommodating (09) job titles for possible vocational goals.

Initially, Ted was pleased to learn that the accommodating vocational interests that he satisfied through barbering could also be met in other accommodating jobs that he had mentioned in his intake interview, such as camp counselor, social worker, and recreation leader and aide. He also learned that *accommodating* included the sales professions as well, an idea he had not given much consideration to in the past. He did not, however, wish to pursue sales because he did not like the idea of persuading other people that they needed a product or service that he was selling.

Using the SDS

If Ted and the counselor were still not satisfied with the range of occupations available through use of the DOT or the *Enhanced Guide*, they might decide to incorporate an interest measure in their exploration. Holland's (1994) SDS is one measure that is both cost effective and efficient for counselors to use. From the results of the SDS, Ted could learn about his priorities regarding six personality dispositions of vocational significance—realistic, investigative, artistic, social, enterprising, and conventional. People with a realistic inclination like to use machines, tools, and things, while investigative types prefer exploring and understanding things or events. Artistic people like to read, write, and participate in musical or artistic activities, and people with a social preference enjoy teaching and therapeutic activities. The enterprising person enjoys persuading or directing others, and the conventional type prefers to follow orderly routines and have clear standards.

In the work world, occupations are characterized by some combination of these same six dimensions. Hence, with results from the SDS, it is possible to identify not only the client's interest priorities but the job titles characteristic of that particular combination of interest dimensions. This linking of personal and job profiles creates a wide range of occupational alternatives to explore. For example, based on his SDS results, Ted learned that he has an Enterprising–Social–Realistic (ESR) profile, which is consistent with that of barber and cosmetologist. Even though *E* (enterprising) was Ted's primary disposition, he continued to express little interest in sales positions, which are a part of the *enterprising* category. Results from the SDS also reinforced Ted's negative opinion about bookkeeping (Conventional–Realistic–Enterprising, CRE), which he was already questioning because he did not want to be confined to a desk working with numbers all day.

The counselor introduced Ted to the *Dictionary of Holland Occupational Codes* (Gottfredson & Holland, 1996) and its list of job titles falling into the ESR category. Using the *Dictionary*, Ted and the counselor considered at some length the following positions: coaching, hotel or motel manager, teacher, buyer, dispatcher, health club manager, and park ranger.

The *Occupational Outlook Handbook*

As revealed in the review of the DOT, the *Enhanced Guide*, and Ted's SDS results, Ted is both interested in and capable of a number of different jobs. To gather some very specific information about those jobs, the counselor may turn to another annually updated resource—the *Occupational Outlook Handbook* (Annual)—to learn about the educational demands, training needed, pay, and long-term outlook for each of those occupations. Of course, the counselor should already have considerable knowledge about many local jobs through personal contacts with employers and observation of work sites.

The counselor might first check those jobs for which Ted has expressed an interest—social worker, furniture upholsterer, recreation program services agent, camp counselor, and motorcycle mechanic. Combining information from both personal knowledge and the *Occupational Outlook Handbook* (Annual), the counselor's profile of each of the jobs is presented in Table 7.2 (Table 7.2 was compiled from information in the U.S. Department of Labor's *Occupational Outlook Handbook*, 1996–1997).

Of the jobs Ted mentioned, recreation specialist, social worker, and motorcycle mechanic seemed to have the best local possibilities and long-range outlook. The counselor should, however, keep several things in mind. First, Ted had some concerns about jobs requiring long and expensive educational preparation (e.g., social worker) because he needed to make money as soon as possible. Second, Ted does have family members in the upholstery business, which could be significant if he could eventually own his own shop and expand his services to include furniture refinishing. Third, Ted must keep in mind the relationship of his physical limitations and the physical requirements of mechanic and upholsterer. Should Ted express an interest in the other vocational alternatives suggested by the SDS analysis—for example, sales, coaching, buyer, dispatcher, or health club manager—the counselor might check the *Occupational Outlook Handbook* for additional information on employment projections, training, and salary or wage levels.

By using resources such as the DOT, *Enhanced Guide*, SDS, and *Occupational Outlook Handbook*, counselors can investigate the match between client and job characteristics in order to identify feasible vocational alternatives. If the counselor does not have sufficient understanding of some of these job titles, he or she can return to the DOT to examine the compatibility between the physical and intellectual demands of those jobs and the physical and intellectual capacities of a client.

TABLE 7.2
Job Profiles from *Occupational Outlook Handbook* (1996–97)

Social Worker

Education—Bachelor's degree minimum, Master's in Social Work (MSW) preferred

Training—Educational preparation plus on the job

Salary—$17,500 to mid $30,000

Outlook—Good

Local opportunities—Fair to good

Furniture Upholsterer

Education—High school graduate with vocational training

Training—On-the-job and vocational training

Salary—$18,000 to $24,000

Outlook—Limited

Local opportunities—Good

Recreation Program Services

Education—Associate degree or college degree preferred

Training—Postsecondary mostly

Salary—$10,600 to $30,000

Outlook—Good

Local opportunities—Improving

Camp Counselor

Education—High school graduate with some postsecondary training

Training—Educational preparation plus on-the-job

Salary—$10,600 to $15,500

Outlook—Fair

Local opportunities—Fair

Motorcycle Repair

Education—High school graduate with formal vocational training

Training—On-the-job training and vocational school program in motorcycle mechanics

Salary—$14,000 to $25,000

Outlook—Fair

Local opportunities—Good

GAINING A PERSPECTIVE

In closing the vocational analysis, the counselor must help Ted consolidate his thinking about his vocational options. To do so, the counselor helped Ted answer the questions from the Work Group Evaluation Chart in the *Guide for Occupational Exploration* (Harrington & O'Shea, 1984). To begin this process, Ted's counselor asked him to reconsider his preliminary choices in Table 7.2 in relation to each of the following questions (Harrington & O'Shea, 1984):

1. *Interest:* Would I like this kind of work well enough for a career?

2. *Values:* Would I be able to satisfy my work values?

3. *Skills and abilities:* Do I have the skills and abilities needed, or the potential to develop them?

4. *Physical capability:* Am I physically able to do this kind of work?

5. *Working conditions:* Could I tolerate the working conditions?

6. *Work setting:* Is this kind of work done in a setting I would like?

7. *Preparation:* Am I able and willing to obtain the education and training required? Can I afford the time, money, and possible relocation?

8. *Employment opportunity:* What are my chances of getting into this kind of work? Am I willing to compete for jobs?

9. *Opportunity for advancement:* What are my chances of getting higher-level jobs in this field?

10. *Licenses and certificates:* Am I willing to qualify for licenses and certificates required? (p. 23)

In discussing the five job possibilities in light of the 10 questions, Ted returned to some familiar themes. He maintained an interest in social work, but basically eliminated it from further consideration because of the extended and expensive preparation time (Question 7). He acknowledged the practicality of upholstery work, but questioned its capability of satisfying his interests and values (Questions 1 and 2). Recreation program services sounded very feasible to Ted; he responded positively to all 10 questions when he considered recreation work. Ted also reacted positively to the camp counselor position, but felt that employment opportunities and opportunities for advancement were poor in that field (Questions 8 and 9). Finally, Ted considered motorcycle repair, which led him to some serious reservations, particularly in regard to his capabilities to do the job, his concern about the working conditions, and his preference for a different type of work setting.

The occupational information resources and interest assessment results helped Ted carefully analyze his vocational options. First, information from these sources helped Ted expand his range of options. It also helped Ted delimit his options as when he decided that the persuading involved in sales was not for him. With the counselor's help, Ted directed his own vocational analysis to the point of having five potential goals. Further consideration of each of these goals in terms of the job–person match issues and employment prospects led Ted to a preliminary commitment to the field of recreation. Ted and his counselor are now ready to discuss the best ways to develop a rehabilitation program to prepare Ted for employment as a recreational specialist.

CONCLUDING STATEMENT

For several reasons, counselors must be prepared to guide their clients through a vocational analysis using existing occupational information resources and interest assessments. First, vocational evaluation units may not exist in the counselor's area. Second, because they have a positive work history and wish to return to a job consistent with their previous employment, some clients do not require intensive vocational evaluation, and yet these individuals may not be returning to their previous job. Therefore, the counselor may wish to initiate a brief vocational analysis with the client based on the concept of job–person match, enhanced by appropriate accommodations.

The vocational analysis process was demonstrated with the case of Ted Johnson. Because of diabetes-related circulatory problems and inflammation resulting from rheumatoid arthritis, Ted could no longer tolerate the standing involved in being a barber and needed to enter a new line of work. Because of Ted's positive work history and many transferable skills, his counselor opted for a briefer type of vocational analysis using the DOT, the *Enhanced Guide*, the SDS, and the *Occupational Outlook Handbook*.

Preparing and Planning for the Rehabilitation Program

A counselor's ability to identify potentially appropriate vocational alternatives for a client to consider is greatly dependent on the sufficiency of information from the intake interview, medical evaluation, and other necessary specialty evaluations (psychological and vocational). Therefore, prior to any serious consideration of vocational alternatives with a client, the counselor should be able to answer relevant questions in Table 1 in Chapter 2. Hence, the questions in Table 2.1 comprise a checklist that the counselor should study before proceeding to goal planning with the client.

Answers to questions in Table 2.1 are useful, not only in developing a list of potential vocational alternatives, but also in narrowing that list down to the most feasible vocational alternatives. Although identifying the most feasible vocational goals is a significant step, the counselor must remember that these options are simply reasonable suggestions for the client to consider. The process of identifying feasible vocational goals by the counselor, the diagnostic step preceding counselor–client joint development of the rehabilitation plan, is demonstrated in the case of Shirley Steed (see Case Study, Chapter 3).

PREPARING FOR THE REHABILITATION PROGRAM INTERVIEW

In preparing for program development with Shirley, the rehabilitation counselor should review the information gathered during the intake interview and the medical, psychological, and vocational evaluations. That review should allow the counselor to determine the potential feasibility of occupations previously identified for Shirley, given her personal characteristics and the characteristics of her environment.

During the intake interview, Shirley expressed an interest in office work. Information relevant to this interest developed during the different phases of her evaluation. For example, the physician ruled out heavy work because of her varicose veins and emphysema (see Table 4.2). Given proper medical treatment and self-care, however, Shirley could return to a sedentary job requiring little physical exertion. Although indicating the ability to succeed in an office setting, Shirley's psychological results revealed personal adjustment problems that must be resolved before she resumes work (see Table 5.2). According to the psychological report, Shirley also should avoid work that causes high levels of tension or pressure.

As the final step in Shirley's diagnostic program, vocational evaluation focused on translating Shirley's employment potential into specific vocational roles. Results indicated that Shirley is highly competitive for employment in clerical occupations. By updating her training in typing, word processing, office practices, and business machines, she could qualify for any of the following jobs: administrative secretary, accounting clerk, bookkeeping machine operator I, billing machine operator, and data entry clerk. If Shirley must seek employment immediately, she might complete a short-term course in typing, word processing, and use of the dictaphone and apply for a job as a driver's license examiner, insurance clerk, administrative clerk, hotel clerk, file clerk, or medical records clerk.

Knowing the local job market and Shirley's physical, psychosocial, educational, intellectual, and interest attributes, the counselor selected from the vocational evaluator's list the following vocational objectives to guide the information processing activity: billing machine operator (214.482-010), accounting clerk (216.482-010), and insurance clerk I (219.367-014). The counselor tentatively chose the first two jobs because of their advancement potential and local availability. Of course, Shirley must complete additional training to qualify for these jobs. In the event that she must return to work immediately, Shirley might wish to consider the insurance clerk position. To review the specific demands of each of these jobs, the counselor consulted the *Dictionary of Occupational Titles* (DOT, U.S. Department of Labor, 1991). DOT descriptions were as follows:

214.482-010 **BILLING MACHINE OPERATOR** (clerical). Bill clerk; biller; billing clerk; invoicing machine operator.

Operates billing machines with or without computing devices to prepare bills, statements, and invoices to be sent to customers, itemizing amounts customers owe. Inserts blank billing sheets in machine and sets carriage. Transcribes data from office records, such as customer's name, address, and items purchased or services rendered. Calculates totals, net amounts, and discounts by addition, subtraction, and multiplication, and records computations. May make computations on separate adding and calculating machines. May be designated according to type of bill prepared as DELINQUENT-NOTICE-MACHINE OPERATOR (clerical). (U.S. Dept. of Labor, 1991, p. 171)

216.482-010 **ACCOUNTING CLERK** (clerical)

Performs any combination of following calculating, posting, and verifying duties to obtain financial data for use in maintaining accounting records. Compiles and sorts documents, such as invoices and checks, substantiating business transactions. Verifies and posts details of business transactions, such as funds received and disbursed, and totals accounts, using calculator or computer. Computes and records charges, refunds, cost of lost or damaged goods, freight charges, rentals, and similar items. May type vouchers, invoices, checks, account statements, reports, and other records, using typewriter or computer. May reconcile bank statements. May be designated according to type of accounting performed, such as Accounts-Payable-Clerk (clerical); Accounts-Receivable Clerk (clerical); Bill-Recapitulation Clerk (utilities); Rent and Miscellaneous Remittance Clerk (insurance); Tax-Record Clerk (Utilities). (U.S. Dept. of Labor, 1991, p. 175)

219.367-014 **INSURANCE CLERK** (financial; insurance)

Orders insurance policies to ensure coverage for property owned by establishment and for property held as security for loan; Reviews premium notices from insurance companies for property owned by establishment. Types check or voucher requesting payment of premium. Reviews notification from insurance companies of lapse in premium paid by customer for loan collateral, such as real estate, automobile, aircraft, or boat. Orders payment of premium and notifies customer of delinquency in premium. Arranges for renewal, transfer or cancellation of insurance coverage. Records dates of insurance expiration and cancellation, using computer. (U.S. Dept. of Labor, 1991, p. 177)

In addition to the preceding options, the counselor also considered related job descriptions in the clerical area. Other job descriptions of potential interest for Shirley included *billing clerk* (214.362-042); *pricer—message and delivery service* (214.467-014); and *invoice-control clerk* (214.362-026).

To arrive at these feasible options for Shirley, the counselor processed considerable evaluation data. One scheme for this information processing in the counselor's mind is presented in Table 8.1. This table clarifies the type of supporting evidence necessary for developing a diagnostic rationale for a vocational goal. For example, Table 8.1 lists the potential assets and limitations in the physical, psychosocial, and educational–vocational areas that should be considered. It also draws attention to multiple special needs (housing, transportation, childcare, and finances) that affect vocational success. The end product of that information processing for the case of Shirley Steed can be observed in Table 8.2.

TABLE 8.1
Information Processing Summary Form

Vocational Goal: _____

1. Supporting Evaluation Data

    a. Physical strengths and limitations related to client's capacity to do the job, for example:

    Physical endurance
    Hand and finger dexterity
    Mobility

(continues)

TABLE 8.1 (*Continued*)

Upper body strength
Lower body strength
Speech, hearing, and/or sight

b. Psychosocial strengths and limitations related to client's capacity to do the job, for example:

Adjustment to disability
Evidence of secondary gain from disability
Psychosomatic tendencies
Excessive concern with health
Current emotional stability
Effects of family and social environment

c. Educational–vocational strengths and limitations related to client's capacity to do the job, for example:

Educational skills (basic reading skills, math skills)

Vocational skill level (current and potential)

Vocational interests:

Working with people or things
Amount of personal responsibilities
Type of work setting
Opportunities for creativity
Routine or variety
Work hours
Amount of earnings
Amount of physical energy expenditure
Opportunities for advancement

Vocational self-concept, that is, realistic perceptions of:

Strengths
Weaknesses
Vocational potential
Reasons for unemployment

Job acquisition or retention problems

d. Special considerations

Economic
Transportation
Housing
Childcare

(*continues*)

TABLE 8.1 (*Continued*)

Placement
Accessibility
On-the-job coping demands

2. Services Needed To Achieve Vocational Goal

	Necessary	Available in Community	Available Outside Community	Provider	Cost
a. Services needed to remove or reduce physical limitations for job in question:					
Prosthetics	☐	☐	☐	☐	☐
Orthoses	☐	☐	☐	☐	☐
Physical therapy	☐	☐	☐	☐	☐
Occupational therapy	☐	☐	☐	☐	☐
Bioengineering	☐	☐	☐	☐	☐
Surgery	☐	☐	☐	☐	☐
General medical	☐	☐	☐	☐	☐
Speech therapy	☐	☐	☐	☐	☐
b. Services needed to remove or reduce psychosocial limitations for job in question:					
Work adjustment training	☐	☐	☐	☐	☐
Personal adjustment training	☐	☐	☐	☐	☐
Individual psychotherapy	☐	☐	☐	☐	☐
Group therapy	☐	☐	☐	☐	☐
Family counseling	☐	☐	☐	☐	☐
c. Services needed to remove or reduce educational–vocational limitations for job in question:					
Remedial reading instruction	☐	☐	☐	☐	☐
Remedial math instruction	☐	☐	☐	☐	☐
Vocational training	☐	☐	☐	☐	☐
Job seeking skills training	☐	☐	☐	☐	☐
On-the-job training	☐	☐	☐	☐	☐

(*continues*)

TABLE 8.1 (*Continued*)

	Necessary	Available in Community	Available Outside Community	Provider	Cost
d. Services for special considerations					
Supported employment	☐	☐	☐	☐	☐
Financial maintenance	☐	☐	☐	☐	☐
Transportation (automobile or automobile adaptation)	☐	☐	☐	☐	☐
Housing	☐	☐	☐	☐	☐
Childcare needs	☐	☐	☐	☐	☐
Placement (job modifications, and accessibility)	☐	☐	☐	☐	☐

TABLE 8.2
Information Processing Summary Form

Name: Shirley Steed

1. Potential vocational goals suggested by consideration of evaluation data:

   a. Most optimal: Billing machine operator (already suggested by client ___Yes _X_No)

   Supporting evaluation data:

   Physical: Has physical endurance to satisfy work demands. Job basically sedentary but does allow for some standing (suitable for varicose vein condition). Work setting free of fumes, dust, and dyes. Must not work in an area where individuals smoke.

   Psychosocial: Has a history of coping with psychological demands of work, for example, print shop job. Currently must guard against self-defeating thoughts and expectations. No evidence of excessive or unrealistic concern with health. Both sons are a constant source of worry.

   Educational–vocational: Has some previous educational training in clerical and office work. Job consistent with vocational interests and ability levels. Mrs. Steed can seek work independently. May need initial support on the job from supervisor.

   Special considerations: Needs financial assistance.

   b. Second: Accounting clerk (already suggested by client ___Yes _X_No)

(continues)

TABLE 8.2 (*Continued*)

Supporting evaluation data:

Physical: See most optimal goal.

Psychosocial: See most optimal goal.

Educational–vocational: Demonstrated capability to use office machines. Has sufficient verbal, numerical, and clerical perception aptitudes for position. Vocational interests consistent with this job.

Special considerations: See most optimal goal.

c. Third: Insurance clerk I (already suggested by client ___Yes _X_No)

Supporting evaluation data:

Physical: See most optimal goal.

Psychosocial: See most optimal goal.

Educational–vocational: See most optimal and second most optimal goal descriptions.

Special considerations: More immediate employment would help her meet her need for financial support.

2. Services needed to achieve vocational goals:

a. Most optimal: Billing machine operator

Physical: Medical maintenance, support hose.

Psychosocial: Personal counseling, family therapy.

Educational–vocational: Business school training with emphasis on bookkeeping and office machines.

Special considerations: Financial counseling and financial assistance (low-cost housing, food stamps, welfare).

b. Second: Accounting clerk

Physical: See most optimal.

Psychosocial: See most optimal.

Educational–vocational: Business school training as above with additional emphasis on office practices and typing.

Special considerations: See most optimal.

c. Third: Insurance clerk I

Physical: See most optimal.

Psychosocial: See most optimal.

(continues)

TABLE 8.2 *(Continued)*

Educational–vocational: Short-term business school course on typing and office practices. On-the-job training.

Special considerations: See most optimal.

3. Vocational goals expressed by the client that appear to be inappropriate based on evaluation data. Discuss.

   Jobs requiring lengthy periods of sitting, for example, key punch operator, typing pool typist, should be viewed with caution. See medical results regarding varicose veins.

Thorough consideration of client assets and limitations provides a basis for identifying the services needed to remove or reduce physical, psychosocial, or educational–vocational limitations for the jobs in question. From a practical point of view, these rehabilitation services must be available either locally or within reasonable traveling distance. The counselor should also have a specific provider in mind and an idea of the cost of the services. Table 8.1 identifies relevant services in the physical, psychosocial, educational–vocational, and special consideration areas.

As indicated in Table 8.2, the three jobs discussed appear suitable for Shirley for several reasons. Their work demands would not negatively affect her emphysema or varicose veins. Second, each job is consistent with her measured vocational interests and ability level. Rehabilitation services are available to address any remaining physical, psychosocial, or vocational–educational barriers to successfully carrying out these jobs. Finally, these jobs are available in the community.

The purpose of the preceding material was to present a structure for the information processing phase of the counselor's work. Data to process originate from the answers to the questions in Table 2.1, as well as the questions generated and refined during the evaluation phase. Counselors then organize that information into a vocational perspective as they work through the Information Processing Summary Form (Table 8.2) in their minds. In so doing, counselors have completed the steps in the top half of the Crux Model (see Figure 2.1). For example, thinking through the various sections of the processing form leads to specific conclusions about (a) client assets for different jobs, (b) necessary rehabilitation services, and (c) vocational goals suggested by the client that do not appear feasible. Although they have much to recommend them, feasible vocational goals identified by the counselor should not be presented to Shirley as vocational imperatives. Shirley undoubtedly has other jobs in mind that she and the counselor should mutually explore by applying the same information processing steps.

Before proceeding, one point should be clarified. The intent of introducing the forms in this chapter is not to create new reporting and recording demands for the counselor. Rather, the purpose of the discussion is to concretize a diagnostic thinking process. In thinking through the demands on the Information Processing Summary

Form, rehabilitation counselors are involved in synthesizing information vital to their vocational counseling role. In other words, counselors must have the information called for in these forms if they are to involve people with disabilities in meaningful discussions of evaluation results, vocational alternatives, and, finally, the rehabilitation plan itself (bottom half of the Crux Model, Figure 2.1).

DEVELOPMENT OF THE REHABILITATION PROGRAM

The remainder of the chapter focuses on the process of involving the individual meaningfully in the development of the rehabilitation program. A problem-solving model of vocational planning is presented, followed by application of the concepts in the case of Shirley Steed.

Co-Management: A Prerequisite for Vocational Planning

Before discussing models of vocational planning, attention should be given to the concept of meaningful involvement of the client in planning. The most appropriate view of the counselor–client relationship may be summed up in terms such as "co-management" (Rubenfeld, 1988) or "client as colleague" (Heinssen, Levendusky, & Hunter, 1995). Eschewing the more hierarchical (expert) approach of the medical model, the co-management model stresses a team approach with the consumer playing an active role in processing information and making decisions. In describing their "client as colleague" approach in psychiatric rehabilitation, Heinssen et al. (1995) stressed that reconstruing the client's role is "a crucial step in creating a more efficacious, cost-effective clinical service system. Persons with serious mental illness represent an untapped resource in the existing health care network and will remain so until treatment programs recognize the client's affinity for self-initiated, goal-directed behavior" (p. 523).

Client involvement in goal planning results in improved therapeutic outcomes for a variety of reasons. It increases the client's knowledge of the service plan and creates multiple opportunities for client choice in developing the plan (Heinssen et al., 1995). It improves the precision of goals and strengthens personal motivation to achieve the goals (Fuhriman & Pappas, 1971). Engagement of the person's frame of reference encourages commitment of time and energy to the vocational exploration process (Dolliver & Nelson, 1975).

Evidence from the rehabilitation planning process supports these positive expectations regarding the effects of client involvement. People participating in rehabilitation who chose their own job goals, as opposed to accepting the counselor's choice, tended to spend more time in training and had greater personal earnings at closure. To the credit of many rehabilitation counselors, approximately 75% of the consumers in one study reported that their vocational choices were based on their own ambitions or experiences (Walls & Dowler, 1987). Choosing vocational goals consistent with one's interests is extremely important in the long run because congruence between preferred work activities and eventual job placement is related to higher levels of job satisfaction among rehabilitation clients (Jagger, Neukrug, & McAuliffe, 1992).

Understanding Vocational Planning

Vocational planning may be described simply as a problem-solving process (D'Zurilla, 1986; Heppner & Krauskopf, 1987; Nezu, 1987) that consists of the following stages: goal setting, information processing, decision making, planning, and action and self-evaluation. These five phases are defined as follows:

Goal setting: establishing a primary objective for counselor–client involvement (i.e., employment).

Information processing: considering all relevant data collected during the evaluation process.

Decision making: selecting a vocational goal to guide the development of the rehabilitation program.

Planning: identifying intermediate objectives and rehabilitation services pertinent to the vocational goal and developing the steps of an action plan.

Action and self-evaluation: following the action plan, using available data to evaluate progress, and making necessary course corrections when warranted by results.

Goal Setting

As Murphy (1988) noted, employment was the "sine qua non" for involvement in rehabilitation for people with disabilities he interviewed in an in-depth study of counselor and client expectations. Hence, the rehabilitation counseling process begins with the goal-setting activity that Glasser (1981) referred to as "focus your pictures," in which the client explores personal images and idealized images of self as worker. These images provide a context for discussing the relevance of evaluation data and potential vocational choices consistent with those data (Holmes & Karst, 1989).

Information Processing

In the co-management model, consumers and counselors participate jointly in exploring the significance of information in the following areas: (a) evaluation results pertinent to the vocational plan, (b) occupational information, and (c) client emotions. By presenting the information included on the Information Processing Summary Form (see Table 8.2), the counselor enables the person to consider the relationship of evaluation data (physical, psychosocial, educational–vocational, and economic) to multiple occupational alternatives. Joint discussion of the form's content in light of expressed or potential client vocational interests should stimulate establishment of realistic directions and objectives for the decision-making, planning, and placement stages (Jagger et al., 1992).

Occupational information is introduced to help the client understand the day-to-day demands, rewards, and frustrations of the work world. Specifically, this information should deal with the following factors regarding different occupations suggested by the individual and the counselor: (a) intrinsic reinforcers related to job satisfaction, (b) extrinsic reinforcers such as salary or wage level and fringe benefits, (c) skill demands of the job, (d) potential for advancement, and (e) local employment opportunities. The more detailed pictures of specific vocations allow people to better envision how they would function in a variety of job roles and, thus, how they would fit into different work environments (Dolliver & Nelson, 1975; Salomone, 1996).

Both the client and the counselor must consider other issues that affect the feasibility of various vocational choices. For example, the workplace may be a considerable distance from the person's home. These distance factors may be complicated by deficiencies in public transportation systems and other aspects of urban sprawl. People living in rural settings may find it even more difficult to commute daily to work.

Employment opportunities are closely tied to the state of the economy and to the natural resources or attributes of a given geographic area. Times of economic recession are synonymous with decreases in production and high unemployment rates, making it all the more difficult for people with disabilities to find employment. Certain areas of the country may be overly dependent on a few industries, thereby limiting the range of available vocational alternatives (e.g., Appalachia and coal mining and Detroit and automobile production). On the other hand, decreases in the birth rate result in eventual labor shortages that increase employment opportunities for individuals who traditionally have difficulty securing employment (Roessler, 1987).

The rehabilitation counselor must also be aware of the way the client's emotional reactions influence vocational choice. Helping people explore feelings of vocational significance calls for examination of the person's vocational self-concept. For example, the individual and counselor might discuss the following questions: (a) What are the chief reasons for your current unemployment? (b) How would you describe yourself as a person; as a worker? and (c) What types of work activities do you prefer? Other related issues worthy of discussion in order to clarify client feelings and perceptions include: (a) What are some of the things you want most from a job? (b) What personal accomplishments give you a sense of pride? (c) What are some activities that you are doing now that give you a sense of pride? and (d) What plans for the future give you a feeling of pride? To assist the person in making an appropriate vocational choice, the counselor must have a personal understanding of the way in which the client perceives self and world. Open discussion of emotions mobilizes the person for action and clarifies barriers that must be overcome if the individual is to secure work.

Throughout the information processing phase, the rehabilitation counselor must not lose sight of the realities that play a part in either increasing or decreasing the number of potential vocational choices for the client. For example, the individual's range of vocational choices is shaped by many historical factors. The person's social class background, as manifested in parental education, income, occupation, and place of residence influences vocational development. Goals of parents and siblings, personal role in the family, and acceptance of family values channel client aspirations. Likewise, school background in terms of values of peers and faculty and specialized training received shapes the person's vocational goals (Eigner & Jackson, 1978; Osipow & Fitzgerald, 1996; Roessler & Greenwood, 1987). Although these factors cannot be changed, they can be reexamined by the person in order to understand more clearly the factors influencing one's vocational preferences.

Decision Making

During the decision-making phase, the person determines options, makes preliminary choices, and evaluates the implications of these choices against information gained from the preceding phase. Choosing a specific vocational goal to pursue requires, therefore, an accurate understanding of (a) local job opportunities; (b) personal preferences for extrinsic and intrinsic reinforcers; (c) skills, self-images, and vocational interests; and (d) the impact of the choice on one's own lifestyle and the lifestyle of one's family. The eventual outcome of this decision making is a vocational goal that directs the development of the vocational plan.

Arriving at the choice of a feasible vocational goal to direct rehabilitation planning may be facilitated through the use of a "Balance Sheet" (Janis & Mann, 1977, p. 151). The first balance sheet step involves the individual in ranking vocational goals in order of desirability. The pros and cons for each of the top alternatives are then processed through the balance sheet in terms of the following four categories:

1. Gains and losses for self

2. Gains and losses for others

3. Approval or disapproval by others (social approval)

4. Self-approval or self-disapproval

The client and counselor should consider a number of issues when analyzing the impact of a vocational alternative in terms of gains and losses for self and others, social approval and disapproval, and self-approval and disapproval. Key considerations relevant to gains and losses for self include income, difficulty of work, client interest in work, freedom to select work tasks, chances for advancement, security, and time available for avocational pursuits. Gains and losses for others might be discussed in terms of income for family, status for family, time available for family, type of living environment for family, fringe benefits for family, and ability to help an organization or group. Social approval or disapproval can be estimated by considering how others would respond to the client if he or she were to choose a particular job; these "others" include parents, friends, wife or husband, colleagues or co-workers, community at large, and social, political, or religious groups. Finally, the person can consider his or her own reactions (self-approval or disapproval) to the job alternative (e.g., self-esteem from contributing to good causes; judgment that work tasks are ethically justifiable, or, to the contrary, involve compromising oneself; creativity or originality of work; and opportunity to fulfill long-range life goals).

With the counselor's assistance, the client discusses the implications of the various pros and cons for vocational decision making. If deemed a valuable exercise, the client writes the pros and cons for self and others for desirable vocational alternatives and rates each factor on a 5-point importance scale (5 = *very important*, 1 = *little or no importance*). Shirley's balance sheet is shown in Table 8.3. Upon completion of the balance sheet analysis and discussion of the rated pros and cons, the client and counselor consider the implications of the activity for selecting a vocational goal that will provide the nucleus for the rehabilitation plan.

Planning

The purpose of the planning phase is to develop a program for achieving the rehabilitation goal. The rehabilitation program is an example of a "top–down" plan to achieve higher level goals (Heppner & Krauskopf, 1987). In other words, the plan specifies a hierarchy of goals and objectives, coupled with the steps required to reach those objectives. The highest order goal refers to enhanced quality of life (QOL) for the client, which may be promoted by attainment of the vocational objective. However, achievement of the vocational objective is dependent on action in regard to certain intermediate objectives as defined in terms of physical, psychological, educational, and vocational targets.

The counselor can begin to involve the individual in program planning through use of goal analysis. Goal analysis is directed at determining what a client needs to do to achieve his or her vocational goal. During this analysis, the person identifies needs or concerns in each of the following areas (which require some type of attention in the rehabilitation process):

1. Physical functioning (medical condition)

2. Psychosocial functioning (personal problems)

3. Educational–vocational functioning

4. Special considerations

Each need or concern then becomes an intermediate objective that must be attained in order to reach the vocational rehabilitation goal.

In the physical functioning area (restoration), an individual might discuss some type of functional limitation requiring an operation, prosthesis, or orthosis. At a later stage in the program planning process, the counselor can demonstrate how this functional limitation such as "unable to stand very long due to pain in feet" can be stated

TABLE 8.3
Balance Sheet: Shirley Steed

Consideration	Alternative 1: Billing Machine Operator	Importance Rating	Alternative 2: Accounting Clerk	Importance Rating	Alternative 3: Insurance Clerk	Importance Rating
Gains for self	Good pay	4	Good pay	4	Feel like I can do the job	4
	Interested in job	4	Advancement chances	4	Get to work sooner	5
	Advancement chances	4	Best fringe benefits	4	Adequate pay	3
	Nice building to work in	4				
Losses for self	Worried I can't do the job	–4	Worried about pressure	–3	Little chance for advancement	–3
Gains for others	Regular money for family	4	Regular money for family	4	Regular money for family	3
Losses for others						
Social approval						
Social disapproval	Feel I should be working, not in training	–4	Want to work, not train	–4		
Self-approval	Feel good about working	4	Feel good about working	4	Feel good about working	4
Self-disapproval	Would never get over messing up accounts of customers	–4				
Sum-rated positive anticipation		24		20		19
Sum-rated negative anticipation		–12		–7		–3
Final score		12		13		16

as an intermediate objective for the program. After the concern has been stated as an intermediate objective, the counselor discusses the steps that both the counselor and the client must take if the individual's need is to be met. For example, if a person states, "I need to get my physical problems under control," he or she needs a physical goal statement that must be broken down into steps:

1. Make an appointment with Dr. Wanamaker

2. Ask doctor about the following:

   a. Insulin intake

   b. Diet

   c. Condition of hands and feet

   d. Another operation on hands

3. Make appointment for molded shoes with podiatrist

Additional needs in the educational–vocational (training) and psychosocial (counseling) areas can also be developed into intermediate objectives and then broken down into specific steps. Hence, goal analysis can help clients develop their own solutions. It helps them identify (a) their needs, (b) the relationship of those needs to intermediate objectives, (c) the steps that must be taken to meet those needs, and (d) the order in which the steps must be taken.

Using Shirley Steed as an example, Table 8.4 shows her goal analysis, which represents a response to the question, "What do you need to do to reach your vocational rehabilitation goal?" The goal analysis exercise helped Shirley state basic physical, psychosocial, educational–vocational, and economic needs. With the counselor's help, Shirley then explored the relationship of needs in a given area to the steps that must be taken to meet those needs.

TABLE 8.4
Goal Analysis: Shirley Steed

Medical condition	Personal Problems	Educational– Vocational	Special Considerations
Get emphysema under control	Get along better with son	Complete clerical work training	Money (while in training)
Ease pain of varicose veins	Help son graduate from high school and enroll in Seaman's School		
	Cope with stress better		

The goal analysis also provides the counselor with information appropriate for developing criteria to measure progress toward the intermediate objectives. These criteria should follow basic principles for behavioral objectives (Mager, 1984), for example:

1. Beware of stopping with abstract statements such as "to become self-sufficient, to be more active, and to be more effective." Abstract goal statements do not indicate what the person must do to accomplish the goal.

2. Emphasize the behavior, action, or performance the person must complete in order for others to see the client's progress toward the goal. For example, the person's need to be more effective might be met by setting an intermediate objective in the vocational training area such as "obtain a welding diploma from the trade school."

3. Two other considerations in stating intermediate objectives are:

    a. the extent, level, or amount of the desired behavior

    b. the date by which the client should attain the objective.

For example, a client might stabilize his or her level of blood sugar to a range of 120 to 150 mg per 100 ml of blood by October 15 to achieve a general goal of controlling diabetes.

Applying these principles to Shirley's situation, the counselor could develop a list of objectives for the rehabilitation program:

Vocational Goal and Intermediate Objectives for Shirley Steed

Vocational goal

To have an office job paying $1,400 a month by October 1.

Physical objective

To miss no more than 2 days of work as a result of health problems for a 60-day period beginning October 17.

Psychosocial objective

To have five or fewer arguments with son in 1 week's time by January 1.

To help son graduate from high school by May.

To help son enroll in Seaman's School by September.

To miss no days of work because of depression for a 60-day period beginning December 1.

Educational–vocational objective

To complete satisfactorily clerical and office work training at the business college by September 1.

On the basis of the Information Processing Summary Form, the Balance Sheet, the goal analysis, and the behavioral objectives, both the client and the counselor are in an excellent position to finalize the rehabilitation program (the solution). The process of drawing up a rehabilitation program can be termed program development and should cover several basic tasks: (a) select a feasible vocational goal; (b) select meaningful objectives in supporting areas; (c) describe the steps needed to achieve the goal and objectives; (d) set deadlines for accomplishing each step; (e) clarify responsibilities of each party, client and counselor, for program steps; and (f) specify expected outcomes of goal attainment efforts. Keeping the program development goals in mind, the counselor and client must integrate previously discussed and developed material into a plan that is congruent with the client's vocational objective.

Action and Self-Evaluation

During the action and monitoring phase, the individual completes the steps in the goal plan and determines the acceptability of outcomes. Research indicates that the probability of achieving a complex outcome such as a vocational goal is increased by the presence of concrete strategies and plans (Locke, Saari, Shaw, & Latham, 1981). By the same token, no plan is infallible, and the person must be flexible in adapting to psychological and environmental factors that negatively and positively influence intended outcomes.

Psychological factors or attributes of the person that are significant include expectations for success, belief in internal control of one's life, and the need for achievement (D'Zurilla, 1986; Locke et al., 1981; Roessler, 1980). Environmental factors have a bearing on plan outcomes as well, such as support of spouse and family, quality of vocational training, employer attitudes and expectations, availability of transportation, and accessibility of training and work sites (Anthony, 1980).

Both the client and the counselor must monitor the effects of psychological and environmental factors and incorporate remedial strategies in the plan when needed. If results are not consistent with expectations, then the client and counselor must identify the problems, recycle and repeat certain steps, or initiate new steps. Moreover, the person's goal-oriented performance is enhanced by periodic feedback regarding the outcomes resulting from the various steps of the plan (Locke et al., 1981). As a result of effective monitoring, the plan becomes even more comprehensive, thereby increasing the probability of success for the client.

Monitoring plan outcomes occurs during pursuit of the intermediate objectives in the physical, psychosocial, educational, and vocational areas. It also is important during the person's initial adjustment to the job, as well as at later stages of employment when job advancement becomes an issue (Salomone, 1996). Too often, possibilities of advancement are overlooked because all of the planning effort has been invested in identifying and preparing for an entry level job as the terminal goal. Looking forward toward career development, the counselor can also help the person select additional training experiences or job changes that will maximize the chances of increasing the remuneration and status derived from employment (Hagner, Fesko, Cadigan, Kiernan, & Butterworth, 1996; Pumpian, Fisher, Certo, & Smalley, 1997).

THE INDIVIDUALIZED WRITTEN REHABILITATION PROGRAM

Many private and public rehabilitation agencies provide vocational counseling services. In all of these settings, the ultimate outcome of the counseling process is some type of vocational plan. An example of a widely used vocational plan is the Individualized Written Rehabilitation Program (IWRP) that was implemented in state vocational rehabilitation agencies in 1973 and includes:

1. The rehabilitation goal (i.e., the vocational goal)

2. Intermediate rehabilitation objectives

3. Objective criteria, evaluation procedures, and schedules for determining whether the rehabilitation goal and intermediate objectives are being achieved

4. Jointly planned vocational rehabilitation services

5. The projected dates of initiating and completing services (i.e., the anticipated duration of services)

6. The client's views regarding the planned objectives and services

7. The date for a periodic review of the program

Other sections of the IWRP may contain counselor and client identifying information; DOT (1991) descriptors for the main vocational rehabilitation goal; a diagnostic rationale for the vocational objective; statements of the client's rights and responsibilities; the service providers; cost of the program assigned to vocational rehabilitation, client, or similar benefits; and actual service outcomes.

Rehabilitation Goal

As with any vocational plan, the vocational objective selected by the client guides the entire development of the IWRP. This rehabilitation goal becomes the standard by which the appropriateness of the intermediate objectives and the rehabilitation services is judged. Unless it contributes to the client's eventual attainment of the rehabilitation goal, an intermediate objective or service should not be included in the program. The rehabilitation goal can be classified generally in terms of such distinctions as competitive labor market, sheltered workshop, self-employment, state agency managed business enterprises (including home industries and farms), homemaker, unpaid family worker, and student. If it is possible to identify the exact job the individual is working toward, the nine-digit DOT (1991) code should be entered on the IWRP.

Whenever possible, the specific vocational objective of the program should be identified, followed by the expected rehabilitation date and a diagnostic rationale for selecting that job. This diagnostic rationale includes the client's strengths and limitations in the physical, educational–vocational, and psychosocial functioning areas that are pertinent to the feasibility of the chosen rehabilitation goal. In this same rationale, the counselor should include information regarding the person's vocational interests and the local economy, which is supportive of the vocational objective chosen for the program.

Intermediate Objectives

If the vocational objective is to be attained, major gains must be made in the physical, psychosocial, educational–vocational, and special considerations areas by the client. The rationale for selection of intermediate objectives emanates from the goal analysis. During the goal analysis, the counselor and client reiterate the needs identified by specialized evaluation sources. Major concerns or needs are then translated into appropriate intermediate objectives for the program. Appropriate objectives state the action or behavior the individual is expected to be capable of; the extent, level, or amount of the desired behavior; and the date by which the person should be able to perform the desired behavior. These objectives provide reasons for including the various rehabilitation services in the program.

Progress Evaluation

Well-written rehabilitation goals and intermediate objectives include the criteria by which progress toward the goal can be measured—that is, can the client perform the desired action at the proper level by the desired date? The procedure for obtaining this material requires identification of the source of outcome information regarding the person's progress. These sources might include a physical therapist, an occupational therapist, a psychologist, a physician, grade reports from a business college, paychecks from an employer, and the client's self-report. For example, to secure feedback on the physical intermediate objective "to increase ability to stand," the counselor might rely on information from the client, the physician, or the employer. Information regarding actual outcome of the service should be entered on the IWRP.

Because the planning process is somewhat complicated, counselors must approach the task logically. Special emphasis should be placed on the steps of (a) identification of a vocational objective, (b) specification of a diagnostic rationale, (c) development of key intermediate objectives, and (d) selection of rehabilitation services. At the same time, the counselor should not forget the importance of client commitment to the plan. In closing the planning phase, therefore, counselors should discuss any concerns the person might have about the program, the effects of the program on significant others, essential steps of the program, and the rewards the individual can expect from following the program. After discussing these issues, Shirley and her counselor developed the IWRP presented in Table 8.5.

TABLE 8.5
Division of Rehabilitation Services (DRS)
Individualized Written Rehabilitation Program (IWRP)

Name: Shirley Steed   **Case:** VR144   **SSN:** 494-522-5545

Address: Johnson, Arkansas

Plan type: Extended Evaluation   ☐ Original   ☐ Revision

Plan for Rehabilitation Services

1. Vocational objective: Insurance clerk   Code: 219.362-034

2. Plan justification

   a. *Vocational handicap*: Limited in ability to do strenuous activity by pulmonary emphysema. Must have reasonably easy access to job (e.g., avoid climbing flights of stairs). Requires variable schedule of sitting and standing because of varicose veins. Present physical and psychological disabilities will preclude a work or training schedule that exceeds 5 hours per day. Stress exacerbates anxiety and depression. Hence, job should have no sales or commissions aspects. Needs to work in area free of fumes, smoke, and allergens.

   b. *Vocational objective*: Insurance clerk. With counseling and medical services, she should achieve sufficient stamina and functional capacity for clerical work. Passed her high school equivalency exam 3 years ago. Functions at above average level on general intelligence on the *General Aptitude Test Battery*. Best score in the area of verbal performance. Interests are consistent with insurance clerk job, but she will need short-term vocational training to upgrade her skills.

   c. *Economic situation*: Will need maintenance during training.

	Responsibility for payment		
3. Services to be provided	**DRS**	**Client**	**Other**
a. *Diagnostic evaluation:*			
Medical examination by a specialist in internal medicine established physical disabilities.	X		
Psychological examination by a licensed psychologist established psychological disability.	X		
Vocational evaluation by Certified Vocational Evaluator.	X		
b. *Counseling and guidance:*			
Personal counseling—Larkspur Mental Health Center			
Objective:			
Decrease episodes of depression—work for 60 days with no absences because of depression (10/17–12/17).	X		

(continues)

TABLE 8.5 (*Continued*)

	Responsibility for payment		
	DRS	Client	Other
Counseling: Rehabilitation counselor			
Objective:			
Enable client to complete steps of IWRP and become successfully employed.	X		
Family counseling—Larkspur Mental Health Center			
Objectives:			
Decrease number of arguments (five or fewer per week) with 15-year-old son by 1/1.	X		
Help son graduate from high school (May) and enroll in Seaman's School (December).	X		
c. *Training*:			
Insurance clerk training—Metropolitan Business College			
Objective:			
Successfully complete insurance clerk training by 9/1.	X		
d. *Restoration*:			
Medical services—Hammond Rehabilitation Institute			
Objective:			
Treat and monitor client's emphysema and related bronchial conditions—work for 60 days with no more than two absences because of illness (10/17–12/17).	X		
e. *Training Materials*:			
Purchase textbooks and related training materials.			
Objective:			
Enable client to participate in vocational training.	X		
f. *Maintenance and Transportation*:			
Transportation to business college and rehabilitation institute, assistance with expenses while in training.			
Objective:			
Enable client to obtain training and medical services.	X		
g . *Tools, Equipment, and Licenses*:			
h. *Placement (job placement and follow-up)*			
i. *Other*:			

(*continues*)

TABLE 8.5 (*Continued*)

4. *Client responsibilities*:

Report to rehabilitation and training programs. Successfully complete insurance clerk program. Seek employment in office work.

5. Please place initials in the appropriate space.

_SS_ I am in essential agreement with the goals, objectives, and services as outlined in the IWRP, and I participated in planning them with my counselor.

_SS_ I participated in planning the services outlined, but disagree with this IWRP.

Comments:

Client's signature _____ Date _____

Counselor's signature _____ Date _____

CONCLUDING STATEMENT

Effective vocational planning is essentially a problem-solving process that meaningfully involves people with disabilities in goal-setting, information processing, decision making, planning, action, and self-evaluation. In preparation for the planning process, the counselor must have collected sufficient evaluation information to assess the appropriateness of potential vocational goals. Counselor preparation requires processing information collected through interviews with the person and through necessary medical, psychological, and vocational evaluation techniques (see the Crux Model in Figure 2.1).

Having developed a working understanding of evaluation data, the counselor involves the person with a disability in identifying an initial goal for the program (goal setting). In vocational rehabilitation, employment of people with disabilities is of foremost importance. This goal is developed in relation to the individual's self and vocational images and is further sharpened through joint consideration of pertinent information.

During information processing, the person identifies feasible vocational options, given his or her strengths and limitations in physical, psychosocial, and educational–vocational functioning. Consideration is given to special needs of the individual in the areas of transportation, childcare, housing, and financial support. Information processing on the client's part prepares him or her to move to the decision-making stage, the phase in which a vocational goal is selected to guide the development of the rehabilitation program. Appropriate vocational objectives are characterized by compatibility between the demands and reinforcers of the job and the skills and preferences of the individual. Of course, realistically speaking, the ultimate vocational choice often represents a compromise between some ideal and achievable alternatives, given existing opportunities for training and employment in the community.

In the planning phase, the counselor and client clarify not only the vocational goal, but also the pertinent physical, psychosocial, and educational–vocational intermediate objectives. Steps for achieving the goal and intermediate objectives are specified in terms of a variety of rehabilitation services. The counselor provides expert guidance in helping the individual select services that have the potential to increase the person's capability to fulfill demands of certain jobs and to lessen the likelihood that other problems will interfere with vocational success.

Finally, as co-managers of the rehabilitation program, the client and counselor take the actions necessary to achieve the goal and subobjectives as well as monitor the outcomes of their activities. Flexibility of all parties involved in the action phase is extremely important. Results may suggest that certain steps should be amended or deleted and that additional steps and services should be added. As noted in the chapter, monitoring of plan outcomes is recommended beyond placement of the person in an entry level position. Further assistance in terms of job modifications, accessibility concerns, vocational training, and job changes is often needed to increase the probability that the person will maintain and improve his or her employment status.

Chapter 8 provides a practical application of the problem-solving and client involvement process via the completion of the Individualized Written Rehabilitation Program (IWRP). Mandated in state and federal rehabilitation agencies, the IWRP is a prototype of the hierarchical (top down) vocational plan central to the primary role and function of vocational counselors in both public and private rehabilitation settings.

Job Placement

Previous chapters discussed the evaluation (Chapters 4 to 7) and planning (Chapter 8) components of the rehabilitation process. Based on evaluation results, the rehabilitation plan delineates the necessary services for enhancing the productivity and quality of life of the person with a disability. However, regardless of how effectively the person has been served during the pre-placement phases (evaluation, planning, and treatment) of the rehabilitation process, ineffective counselor performance during the placement phase can result in client underemployment or unemployment.

THE COUNSELOR'S ROLE IN PLACEMENT

Most rehabilitation professionals agree on the importance of placement services and that placement is, indeed, a proper function of the rehabilitation counselor (Leahy, Shapson, & Wright, 1987). Counselor commitment to the goal of full-time competitive employment for clients is shared by a great many consumers who view employment as their primary reason for seeking rehabilitation services (Murphy, 1988). It is also mandated by Public Law (P.L.) 102-569, the 1992 amendments to the Rehabilitation Act (Hagner, Fesko, Cadigan, Kiernan, & Butterworth, 1996). Although general agreement exists on the importance of the employment goal, different positions have been taken regarding the appropriate level and type of counselor placement activity.

While, on average, counselors estimate spending approximately 10% of their time carrying out placement activities, much variability exists among individual counselor reports of the time they devote to placement. Some counselors report spending as much as 20% to 30% of their time on placement (Leahy et al., 1987). This variability may signify more than differences in time spent on placement. It may also reflect philosophical differences regarding the type of placement assistance to provide. A timeless debate exists as to whether extensive counselor involvement with the employer on behalf of clients results in increased dependency of the job seeker on counselor assistance. It has been argued that dependency can be minimized by limiting placement assistance to enhancing the person's independent functioning in the job-seeking process via specialized services such as job-seeking skills training.

While preparation for independent job seeking has considerable appeal, it is not the only viable intervention strategy in the job placement process. Many individuals with severe disabilities cannot return to their previous jobs, lack other contacts in the job market, or are unaware of how to use a network of community connections to obtain job leads (Hagner et al., 1996). For these individuals, lack of active counselor placement assistance with employers could result in either underemployment or failure to obtain employment. In fact, if an attempt is made by counselors to build self-reliance via a "hands off attitude," such individuals could be disadvantaged compared to those without disabilities who have the ability to use the "hidden job market of personal and community contacts" to obtain employment (T. Jackson, 1991, cited in Hagner et al., 1996, p. 311). In taking a "hands on attitude," rehabilitation counselors should attempt to involve any of the client's natural sources of support for tapping into that "hidden job market." In a recent survey of vocational service agencies and secondary school transition programs in Massachusetts regarding their placement strategies, Hagner, Butterworth, and Keith (1995) found that the most frequent approach "was to ask a consumer's friend or family network to use their personal contacts to identify potential employers. For example, one individual reported that a consumer's parent made initial inquiries at a local supermarket, leading to a job for their son" (p. 113).

People with severe disabilities may also be at a distinct disadvantage if they are totally dependent on employment agencies for job placement. Survey studies of the sources of successful job leads for unemployed job seekers show that state employment service leads account for less than 15% of the jobs obtained (Zadny & James, 1976). Many employers may question the validity of the information received from employment agencies because of the brief relationship that such agencies have with their clients. That limited relationship also greatly restricts the information that the employment agency can provide about a given client. Fortunately, due to the thorough evaluation in vocational rehabilitation, the rehabilitation counselor is in a more credible position to intervene on the person's behalf with potential employers. Furthermore, by absorbing the costs of prescreening persons with a disability in regard to the match between their abilities, skills, and interests and the demands of specific types of positions in the labor market, the rehabilitation counselor takes on the role of an information intermediary or broker between clients (job seekers) and employers (Hagner et al., 1996). Because of the valuable cost saving services they provide and their ability to communicate comprehensive relevant knowledge on potential job applicants, rehabilitation counselors can be very effective employment advocates for their clients.

COUNSELOR KNOWLEDGE OF THE WORLD OF WORK

Personal contacts with employers also enable rehabilitation counselors to learn about the specific characteristics of many jobs in the local labor market. Such contacts can be even more important in ethnic communities where some unique jobs exist. For example, "Dim-Sum" cart pusher is a position that is found primarily in restaurants within urban Chinese communities. Without knowledge of the local labor market, rehabilitation counselors would have much difficulty effectively carrying out their evaluation and planning responsibilities with people with severe disabilities. For example, during the evaluation and planning phases of the rehabilitation process, counselor knowledge of the world of work is a prerequisite for effectively dealing with the "feasibility for what" issues. Resolving feasibility-related issues by helping the client identify appropriate job options requires the counselor to determine the degree of correspondence between client capabilities and the demands and environmental characteristics of local jobs.

Figure 9.1 illustrates the relationship of counselor activity in job development and placement and the amount of his or her knowledge of job characteristics and work opportunities in the community. The counselor uses this knowledge during the feasibility determination and vocational decision-making aspects of client evaluation and planning. Hence, a cycle is created in which activity in job development and placement for one person yields occupational information that the counselor uses throughout the rehabilitation process with countless other individuals in the future.

While the counselor may be tempted to learn about local jobs through printed resources—such as the *Dictionary of Occupational Titles* (DOT, U.S. Dept. of Labor, 1991), *Occupational Outlook Handbook* (U.S. Dept. of Labor, annual) or local newspapers—printed occupational materials yield only partial insights into actual work role demands. Partial insights can be misleading—for example, "Punch press operators need good dexterity" (Flannagan, 1977). Flannagan pointed out that if the objects being punched out are trash can lids or milk can covers, "stamina, strength and gross mobility" are needed (p. 118). Good dexterity may be somewhat irrelevant. Because tasks and work environments differ from site to site, information found in Department of Labor publications must often be supplemented with local knowledge. For example, production quotas could vary across job sites reflecting differences in psychological and physical stress factors. In one work unit, workers may stand most of the day, while workers in another unit sit most of the day. At one job site, the worker may have to retrieve the work from another part of the plant, whereas at another job site the work may be brought to him or her. Therefore, acquisition of comprehensive and accurate information on the characteristics of jobs in the local labor market often requires direct contact with employers and tours of their establishments. During such visits, rehabilitation counselors could also identify jobs that are difficult to fill or that have high turnover rates (Mund, 1981; Roessler & Hiett, 1983).

Acquiring relevant information about specific jobs in the community through job site visits does not require extensive training in job analysis. A visit to the work site informs the counselor about the physical setting itself, including the immediate work station, building accessibility, and transportation requirements to and from work.

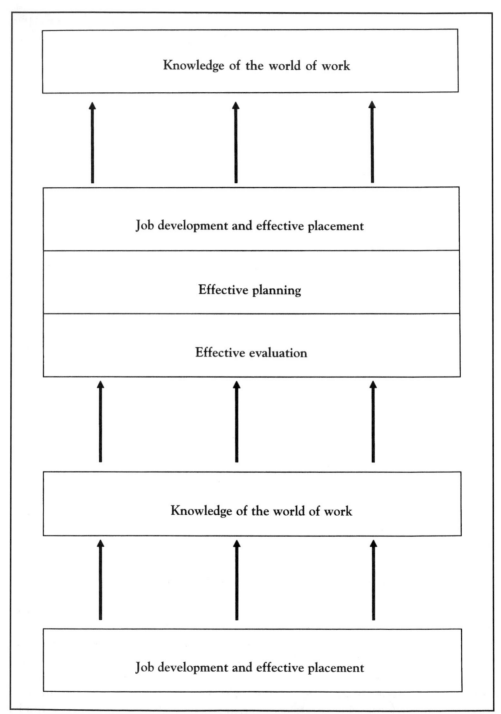

FIGURE 9.1. The central role of placement in the rehabilitation process.

Through direct observation of the job, most rehabilitation counselors should be capable of answering the following five questions (Minton, 1977):

1. What does the worker do?

2. How is it done?

3. Why is it done?

4. What skills are required?

5. Are there alternative methods of doing the job? (p. 146)

Having answered these questions, the job seeker and counselor might explore necessary accommodations in any of three possible areas: (a) environmental modifications through barrier removal, (b) equipment modifications via assistive devices and adapted tools, and (c) procedural modifications by altering tasks, work methods, or work schedules. People with physical disabilities tend to need assistance with equipment or environmental modifications. Individuals with cognitive disabilities such as mental retardation, learning disabilities, or head injuries often profit from procedural modifications.

During work site visitations, the counselor can also acquire a good picture of psychosocial factors in the work environment (Canelón, 1995). Minton (1977) saw these factors as being addressed via a focus on the following two aspects of the work environment:

1. The psychological environment—the amount of interaction with fellow employees, the extent and type of supervision, the amount of stress and pressure in the job, and the amount of routinized job procedures.

2. The social environment—the types of employees with whom the individual will come in contact, the number and scope of social activities on and off the job. (p. 147)

Psychosocial demands of work must be considered in determining the suitability of a particular job for a person.

TAILORING PLACEMENT SERVICES

Historically, people seeking rehabilitation services have fit several profiles. One profile of consumers in public and nonprofit rehabilitation programs dominated during the 1960s and 1970s. This group of rehabilitation clients tended to be older and have more severe disabilities. They were high school educated, had only moderate work experience, and were past recipients of vocational rehabilitation services. By most standards, those characteristics would not be conducive to placement success. In fact, these individuals were characterized as having "marginal labor market potential" (DeLoach & Greer, 1979; Matkin, 1980; Vandergoot & Swirsky, 1980).

Of course, rehabilitation counselors serve a number of individuals requiring considerable on-the-job support even after completion of evaluation, planning, and treatment services. People needing this support can be those with chronic psychiatric disabilities; individuals with moderate mental retardation; people with schizophrenia who also have a history of institutionalization; and older persons with severe physical disabilities, few vocational skills, and a poor job history. Training in skilled vocations is often not feasible for such individuals; however, through appropriate rehabilitation services (e.g., supported employment programs), these individuals can become more employable for entry-level unskilled positions such as "maintenance, kitchen aid, laundry worker, shoe repair, busboy, production worker, farm worker, grounds keeper, mail room clerk, mail delivery, and carpenter's helper" (Smith, 1981, p. 317). Still, acquisition of those jobs often requires the help of an aggressive rehabilitation counselor who can interest employers in establishing supported employment contracts and, eventually, assuming some of the job coaching responsibilities.

Recent trends in the type of people seeking rehabilitation services have brought two other groups to the fore. The first group comprises youth with severe disabilities who are in need of improved school-to-work transition services. According to statistics from the President's Committee on Employment of People with Disabilities, 650,000 students with disabilities either graduate from high school each year or leave school because they are too old to receive services. Employment outcomes for this group are typically poor, with only about 21% becoming fully employed (Johnson & Atkins, 1987). Placement assistance needed for this group begins with in-school programs focusing on career education and real work experiences through summer programs and work internships. Counselors must then consider each student's capabilities for independent job seeking when determining the extent of placement intervention needed following completion of school.

Bowe (1987) noted a trend in United States census data indicating a decrease in the number of 16- to 24-year-olds in the general population. Moreover, within this group, there is a lower proportion of youth with disabilities than has been the case in the past. During the mid 1980s, the number of youth with work disabilities represented only 8% to 9% of the working age population of persons with disabilities. In fact, the majority of people with disabilities was in the 25 to 54 age group, which includes people "neither young enough to benefit from transition services nor old enough to be eligible for early retirement" (Bowe, 1987, p. 19). The majority of these individuals did not acquire their disability until well into their working lives and found it particularly difficult to cope with the problems associated with the sudden imposition of disability. Research indicates that this clientele of vocational rehabilitation, particularly workers in their 30s and 40s, is less likely to seek services on their own initiative (Bowe, 1987; Olsheski & Growick, 1987). Adequate placement services for these mid-career individuals require interventions at the worksite in terms of job modifications (usually minor), retraining, transitional or light duty assignments, and flexible scheduling. The key to successful employment for this group is to return to the same job in the same industry as quickly as possible (Pimentel, 1995; Tate, Habeck, & Galvin, 1986).

An expanded clientele for vocational rehabilitation also calls for more creative thinking about employment opportunities, particularly for women with disabilities. According to Parent and Everson (1986), people with disabilities are often limited to stereotyped job placements due to the low expectations of employers and co-workers. Rehabilitation counselors can do much to shatter this unfortunate typecasting. One method for doing so involves communicating to employers the wide range of jobs held by people with disabilities (e.g., computer programmers and operators; electronics assemblers; professional, technical, and managerial personnel; jet engine assemblers; offset press operators; drafters; coding clerks; meteorological technicians; library assistants; and X-ray technicians [Parent & Everson, 1986]).

Regardless of the client group involved, the effectiveness of placement greatly depends on employer cooperation. Some employers may need to maintain a supported employment program. Other employers may need to offer rapid interventions via medical and retraining services at the worksite. Still others may need to raise their expectations about the capabilities of youth and women with disabilities. To encourage this cooperation, rehabilitation counselors must strive to place clients with a very high probability of success with each firm. The positive experiences for the employer should reduce reluctance to hire additional workers with disabilities. To assure that the experience retains its positive quality for the employer, the counselor must follow up periodically with both client and employer and help resolve any post-placement problems that arise (Greenwood & Johnson, 1985).

Dealing with Common Employer Concerns

The rehabilitation counselor can expect to be confronted with a number of employer concerns regarding employment of people with disabilities. For example, employers are concerned about the effect that hiring individuals with disabilities could have on their workers' compensation insurance rates. Fearing that their insurance costs will rise, they screen out job applicants with disabilities. Rehabilitation counselors can defuse this issue by providing prospective employers with accurate information. Workers' compensation insurance rates are based on two factors. First, they are based on the nature of the work performed by the insured organization (e.g., premium rates are influenced by the hazards associated with the performance of the job) (Analysis of Workers' Compensation Laws, 1981, p. 2). Second, rates are based on the previous accident rate of the firm and the amount of compensation and medical costs charged to the insurance carrier. Since research evidence shows that workers with disabilities do not have a higher accident rate than nondisabled workers, it is not surprising that a "study made by the United States Chamber of Commerce and National Association of Manufacturers found that 90% of 279 companies surveyed reported no effect on insurance costs" as a result of hiring people with disabilities (Sears, 1975).

In addition, most states have second injury laws that provide funds to cover the additional costs resulting from a second injury. Those laws allow injured employees to be compensated for their total disability while employers are liable only for injuries occurring while workers are in their employ.

> Second-injury funds (or like arrangements) were developed to meet problems arising when a pre-existing injury combines with a second to produce disability greater than that caused by the latter alone. The funds (1) encourage hiring of the physically handicapped and (2) more equitably allocate costs of providing benefits to such employees. Second injury employers pay compensation related primarily to the disability caused by the second injury alone—even though the employee receives a benefit relating to his combined disability; the difference is made up from a second injury fund. (Analysis of Workers' Compensation Laws, 1981, p. 26)

Employers often have questions about the productivity potential of the person with a disability. In fact, reviews of employer reactions to hiring people with disabilities stress that the primary concerns of the employer are the individual's job qualifications and productivity potential (Berven & Driscoll, 1981; Greenwood, Johnson, & Schriner, 1988; Zadny, 1980). Therefore, the rehabilitation counselor must inform the employer of the results of studies in which the performance of workers with disabilities compares favorably with that of workers without disabilities on production rate, turnover, and absenteeism. Favorable data are available from studies comparing the quantity and quality of work produced by workers with disabilities and workers without disabilities (Parent & Everson, 1986) and individuals with severe disabilities (cerebral palsy, epilepsy, blindness, deafness, and spinal cord injury) and employees without disabilities (Gade & Toutges, 1983; Goodyear & Stude, 1975). Over 90% of a sample of employers surveyed in San Francisco and Portland rated the performance of their employees with disabilities "as being average or above average as compared with other workers" (Zadny, 1980, p. 167). In a Harris survey (Louis Harris & Associates, 1987), managers summarized their experiences with workers who have disabilities.

> Overwhelming majorities of managers give disabled employees a good or excellent rating on their overall job performance. Only one in twenty managers say that disabled employees' job performance is only fair, and virtually no one says they do poor work. Eighty-eight percent of top managers rate the performance of disabled employees as excellent or good. . . . Nearly all disabled employees do their jobs as well or better than other employees in similar jobs. (p. 7)

By the same token, the literature suggests that employers may have special reservations about employees with mental, emotional, or communication disorders (Becker & Drake, 1994; Rojewski, 1992; Thomas, Thomas, & Jorner, 1993). Hence, the previous information on the work history of people with disabilities becomes doubly important in the placement of individuals from those three groups (Johnson, Greenwood, & Schriner, 1988).

Rehabilitation counselors should encourage employers to not underestimate the capability of persons with disabilities to perform many jobs with reasonable accommodations. Focusing totally on functional limitations typically associated with a disability—without observing the individual performing the actual job tasks with reasonable accommodations—can lead to erroneous assumptions about what the individual can or cannot do (Brodwin, Parker, & DeLaGarza, 1996). In making recommendations to employers for reasonable accommodations for a person with a disability, rehabilitation counselors should fully explain each of the following: (a) the functional limitations associated with the disability, (b) how the functional limitations will impede the individual's ability to perform the essential functions of the job(s) in question, and (c) how the reasonable accommodations can allow the individual to perform the essential job tasks in spite of the functional limitations associated with the disability. Advance preparation by the counselor should help to allay the employer's concerns about hiring the person with a disability since the individual will be seen as having strengths as well as limitations (Brodwin et al., 1996). Functional limitations, associated with different disabling conditions, have been sorted into the following 15 categories by Mueller (1990):

1. Difficulty in interpreting information

2. Limitations of sight and total blindness

3. Limitations of hearing and total deafness

4. Limitation of speech

5. Susceptibility to fainting, dizziness, and seizures

6. Incoordination

7. Limitation of stamina

8. Limitation of head movement

9. Limitation of sensation

10. Difficulty in lifting, reaching, and carrying

11. Difficulty in handling and fingering

12. Inability to use the upper extremities

13. Difficulty in sitting

14. Difficulty in using the lower extremities

15. Poor balance (cited in Brodwin et al., 1996, p. 175)

Reasonable accommodations can be made to allow individuals with any of the above functional limitations to perform many jobs. Brodwin et al. (1996) described workplace accommodations for persons with visual impairments who are not totally blind that "include adaptations in illumination, color and contrast, space and arrangement, and size and distance . . . The most common optical devices are magnifiers and telescopes . . . Typical nonoptical vision aids are closed-circuit televisions that enlarge print electronically and personal computers and peripherals with the capability of large print magnification, speech output, and optimal scanning" (p. 185).

Roessler and Rumrill (1995) described how limitations commonly associated with severe chronic illnesses such as multiple sclerosis affect vocational functioning. As depicted in Table 9.1, the researchers indicated how to accommodate those limitations using the reasonable accommodation strategies cited in the Americans with Disabilities Act of 1990 (ADA).

Rehabilitation counselors should also attempt to alleviate any unrealistic employer expectations regarding the cost of reasonable accommodations. Very minimal costs

TABLE 9.1
Accommodations for Limiting Factors of Multiple Sclerosis (MS) in Job Functions

Job Function	MS Factor	Possible Accommodation
Restructuring of Existing Facilities		
Entering place of business	Muscular weakness	Electronic door opener
Restructuring of the Job		
Supervising activities in the gymnasium	Loss of strength in lower extremities	Supervising study halls instead of activities in the gymnasium
Modification of Work Schedules		
Conducting medical examinations more than 8 hours a day	Fatigue	8-hour work day with breaks
Reassignment to Another Position		
Supervising farming operations and activities	Fatigue and coordination/ balance problems	Reassignment to sitting, indoor job as a business manager
Modification of Equipment		
Turning dictation machine off	Numbness of hands, problems with eye–hand coordination	Installation of foot pedal to control equipment
Installation of New Equipment		
Remembering details, setting priorities, and developing production schedules	Impact on cognitive skills and short-term memory	Portable computer with printer hook-up
Provision of Qualified Readers and Interpreters		
Reading reports and self-generated typing	Blurred vision	Reader or proofer in office when needed

have been found to be associated with a large percentage of reasonable accommodations provided by employers in the private sector (Brodwin et al., 1996). Nevertheless, in a recent report titled "ADA Watch Year One," the National Council on Disability (1993) reported that implementation of the ADA had proceeded smoothly with the exception of provision of reasonable accommodations. Citing results of a survey conducted by the United Cerebral Palsy Association, Douglas (1994) stated that 40% of the businesses sampled had not taken action to implement the ADA some 2 years after its implementation. Satcher (1992) quoted research that indicated that employers remained concerned about the cost of providing accommodations, particularly accommodations needed by job applicants.

Fortunately, the weight of Title I of the ADA is behind people's rights to reasonable accommodation. Reasonable accommodation is intended to "level the playing field" (O'Keeffe, 1994) so that employees with disabilities have an "equal opportunity to perform the essential functions of the job" (Satcher & Dooley-Dickey, 1992, p. 15). In "leveling the playing field," employers are not expected to provide the "best accommodation, but rather one that is effective in meeting the demands of the job, is acceptable to the employer and the employee, and does not constitute an undue hardship to the business" (O'Keeffe, p. 7). As indicated in Table 9.1, the ADA describes several remedies for barriers to on-the-job productivity, such as restructuring of existing facilities, restructuring of the job, modification of work schedules, reassignment to another position, modification of equipment, installation of new equipment, and provision of qualified readers or interpreters.

Another concern often expressed by some employers is the uncomfortable experience that they would face if the worker with a disability did not perform well and had to be fired (Louis Harris & Associates, 1987). Although unable to guarantee success, the rehabilitation counselor can point out to the employer that the person has been thoroughly evaluated for the position in regard to interests, abilities, and physical and psychological capacities (Berven & Driscoll, 1981). The rehabilitation counselor should also assure the employer of his or her intention to help resolve any postemployment difficulties that might arise through personal intervention or through the development of on-the-job support groups (Emener & McHargue, 1978; Gade & Toutges, 1983).

Even though counselors play the role of client advocate in the direct placement process, they are professionally obligated to be honest with the employer in respect to a client's readiness for placement. Failure to do so is unethical as well as self-defeating in regard to placing future clients with that employer. "It's the reputation that a counselor develops with local employers and personnel people that often dictates how successful placement efforts will be. If an employer knows that the counselor can be trusted to be honest in a presentation about a client who is being placed, then the employer will try to be helpful because it is in his own best interest" (Mund, 1981, p. 36).

Being honest does not mean, however, that clients should be described by general diagnostic labels such as "mentally retarded" or "schizophrenic." To do so places an unnecessary emphasis on the negative. It makes more sense to avoid such labels and focus directly on the person's work-related strengths and weaknesses as they relate to the specific job or jobs in question (Borgen, Amundson, & Biela, 1987).

The Law: The Ultimate Facilitator

Sections 501 and 503 of Title V of the Rehabilitation Act of 1973 and, most significantly, the ADA, particularly Title I, make the rehabilitation counselor's placement job easier. Section 501 mandates federal agencies to take affirmative action to hire people with disabilities. Section 503 established the same mandate for private businesses that are receiving federal contracts in excess of $10,000. According to a Harris poll (Louis Harris & Associates, 1987), Section 503 has had a significant impact. Businesses with federal contracts are more likely to hire people with disabilities and to have established hiring policies in that regard.

Passage of the ADA in 1990 added, however, the biggest gun to the legal arsenal (U.S. Department of Justice, 1996). The ADA is the most significant piece of civil rights legislation for people with disabilities. Addressing public accommodations and services as well as employment, the ADA has several key provisions that lend support to rehabilitation counselors.

1. Discrimination in employment against people with disabilities is specifically prohibited under the law. Moreover, companies employing more than 15 people are required to make "reasonable accommodations" for people with disabilities. Individuals with disabilities may file charges of employment discrimination with the Equal Employment Opportunity Commission (EEOC).

2. Public accommodations (hotels, restaurants, theaters, museums, schools, social service agencies, etc.) must be accessible to people with disabilities where that accessibility is "readily achievable." The Department of Justice handles complaints regarding accessibility of public accommodations.

3. Transportation services developed after passage of the ADA must be accessible (e.g., new public buses, rail facilities, and train cars). Problems with public transportation are filed with the Federal Transit Administration. Complaints regarding private transportation are filed with the Department of Justice.

4. Telecommunications must be available for people with hearing or speech impairments, and any complaints regarding telecommunications may be filed with the Federal Communications Commission.

Thanks to 501, 503, and the ADA, Weisenstein's (1979) assessment in the late 1970s rings truer than ever. It is now more than just "good business to hire the handicapped, it is the law for many businesses. The emphasis is now on the employer to consider ways in which the handicapped worker could fit in, rather than ways in which his or her handicap might prevent him or her from performing a task" (p. 62).

Rehabilitation counselors should also remain up-to-date with tax legislation that provides incentives for employers to hire people with disabilities. For example, a provision of the 1976 Tax Reform Act (Section 190 of the Internal Revenue Service code) enables employers to take tax deductions up to $35,000 per year for barrier removal. Architectural barrier removal efforts that qualify include modifications to "walks, parking lots, ramps, building entrances, doors and doorways, drinking fountains, public telephones, elevators, warning signals, curb ramps, and wheelchair lifts" (Eastern Paralyzed Veterans Association, 1989).

Replacing the Targeted Jobs Tax Credit program (TJTC; Tax Reduction and Simplification Act, P.L. 95-30; Barnow, 1996), the Work Opportunity Tax Credit (WOTC) provides employers a special tax credit when they hire individuals from targeted groups, such as individuals with disabilities, veterans, disadvantaged youth, and chronically unemployed individuals. Employers could receive a tax credit of up to $2,100 for each eligible individual hired. For the employer to receive the maximum tax credit, the eligible employee must earn at least $6,000 during the first year of employment (Salomone, 1996). In the past, the majority of employers were unaware of TJTC or of other related government or private job initiatives (Louis Harris & Associates, 1987). Hence, rehabilitation counselors must stay apprised of developments with targeted tax credits and communicate that information to employers, particularly small employers.

Employers who hire persons with disabilities who are less productive than those without disabilities in the same position can obtain special certificates to pay the workers with disabilities below minimum wage. This standard comes "from the Wage and Hour Division of the Department of Labor's Employment Standards Administration" (Barnow, 1996, p. 324). For example, if a worker with a disability is 75% as productive as the typical worker on that job, the former could be paid an hourly wage that is three-fourths of that paid the latter. "A Department of Labor official has estimated that approximately 7,000 employers have certificates and that about 200,000 workers are employed under the program. It is believed that the majority of those working under the program have mental retardation as their disability" (Barnow, 1996, p. 325).

The movement of some persons with severe disabilities into competitive employment can be facilitated by initially placing them in supported employment. Supported employment has been defined as

> "competitive work in integrated work settings for individuals with the most severe disabilities (i) (I) for whom competitive employment has not traditionally occurred, or (II) for whom competitive employment has been interrupted or intermittent as a result of a severe disability; and (ii) who because of the nature and severity of their disability, need intensive supported employment services." (Rehabilitation Act Amendments, 1986, cited in Hanley-Maxwell, Bordieri, & Merz, 1996, p. 343)

While initially funded in 1987 as a supplemental program for state rehabilitation agencies, supported employment was made a regular part of their scope of services by the

1992 Rehabilitation Act Amendments (Danek et al., 1996). This service program can provide ongoing support services for a person at the job site through an individual such as a job coach.

PREPARING EMPLOYERS TO COMPLY WITH THE ADA WHEN INTERVIEWING JOB APPLICANTS WITH DISABILITIES

Many employers with current or potential job openings may be less than optimally prepared to adhere to the ADA when screening job applicants with disabilities. By preparing employers to follow the law when interviewing job applicants with disabilities, rehabilitation counselors can strengthen their relationship with these employers. As a result, rehabilitation counselors can effectively advocate with these employers for hiring any of their qualified clients.

Using materials available from the Equal Employment Opportunity Commission (EEOC), rehabilitation counselors can educate employers on the "do's and don'ts" when interviewing job applicants with disabilities. In October 1995, the EEOC issued revised guidelines on the questions employers legally can ask applicants *prior to making a conditional job offer* (EEOC, 1995). Presented in Table 9.2, sample EEOC (1995) guidelines clarify the nature of permissible and impermissible questions in the interview. By following the guidelines, employers are assured of *not* violating the rights of job seekers with disabilities.

TABLE 9.2

Guidelines for Interviewing Job Applicants with Disabilities
(Equal Employment Opportunity Commission, 1995)

- Under the law, an employer may not ask disability-related questions and may not conduct medical examinations until after it makes a conditional job offer to the applicant. (p. 2)

- At the pre-offer stage, an employer cannot ask questions that are likely to elicit information about a disability. This includes directly asking whether an applicant has a particular disability. (p. 4)

- Employers *may* ask about an applicant's ability to perform specific job functions. For example, an employer may state the physical requirements of a job (such as the ability to lift a certain amount of weight, or the ability to climb ladders), and ask if an applicant can satisfy these requirements. (p. 2)

- Employers *may* ask about an applicant's non-medical qualifications and skills, such as the applicant's education, work history, and required certifications and licenses. (p. 2)

- Employers *may* ask applicants to describe or demonstrate how they would perform job tasks. (p. 2)

(continues)

TABLE 9.2 (*Continued*)

- When an employer could reasonably believe that an applicant will not be able to perform a job function because of a known disability, the employer may ask that particular applicant to describe or demonstrate how s/he would perform the function. An applicant's disability would be a "known disability" either because it is obvious (for example, the applicant uses a wheelchair), or because the applicant has voluntarily disclosed that s/he has a hidden disability. (p. 5)

- An employer may tell applicants what the hiring process involves (for example, an interview, timed written test, or job demonstration), and may ask applicants whether they will need a reasonable accommodation for this process. (p. 5)

- If the need for an accommodation is not obvious, an employer may ask an applicant for *reasonable* documentation about his/her disability if the applicant requests reasonable accommodation for the hiring process (such as a request for the employer to reformat an examination, or a request for an accommodation in connection with a job demonstration). The employer is entitled to know that the applicant has a covered disability and that s/he needs an accommodation. (p. 6)

- Questions about whether an applicant can perform major life activities are almost always disability-related because they are likely to elicit information about a disability. For example, if an applicant cannot stand or walk, it is likely to be a result of a disability. So, these questions are prohibited at the preoffer stage *unless* they are specifically about the ability to perform job functions. (p. 9)

- An employer may not ask applicants about job-related injuries or workers' compensation history. These questions relate directly to the *severity of an applicant's impairments*. Therefore, these questions are likely to elicit information about disability. (p. 10)

- Employers should know many questions about current or prior lawful drug use are likely to elicit information about a disability, and are therefore impermissible at the preoffer stage. For example, questions like, "What medications are you currently taking?" or "Have you ever taken AZT?" certainly elicit information about whether an applicant has a disability. (p. 10)

- An employer may not ask a third party (such as a service that provides information about worker's compensation claims, a state agency, or an applicant's friends, family or former employers) any questions that it could not directly ask the applicant. (p. 13)

- An employer may ask applicants about current illegal use of drugs . . . because an individual who currently illegally uses drugs is not protected under the ADA (when the employer acts on the basis of the drug use). (p. 10)

PREPARING CLIENTS FOR JOB INTERVIEWS

Even though they are responsible for preparing applicants for job seeking, some counselors do not provide adequate services in this area. In a survey of 200 young adults with disabilities, McCarthy (1986) reported that 75% of the respondents were dissatisfied with the job referrals and training in job search skills they had received through rehabilitation. Louis Harris (1986) survey results from a random sample of 1,000 people with disabilities corroborated McCarthy's findings. The majority of adults with disabilities who had contact with vocational rehabilitation were dissatisfied with the job finding help they received. To improve these evaluations from consumers, counselors should concentrate—at a minimum—on helping the prospective job seeker (a) develop an adequate and accurate picture of what to expect in the job interview, (b) learn how to effectively complete a job application form, and (c) practice appropriate job interviewing skills.

Informing the Client of What To Expect

When deemed necessary, rehabilitation counselors should help clients develop an accurate picture of what to expect during job interviews. For example, clients could be provided with a list of questions that they might be asked, such as, What do you consider a satisfactory salary? What skills do you have for the job? Were you ever fired? Why? Have you ever had any problems with other workers? Job seekers should understand that the typical job interview is likely to last about 20 to 35 minutes (Galassi & Galassi, 1978).

Instruction on Completing Job Application Forms

The rehabilitation counselor should be prepared to provide clients (when necessary) with instruction on completing the types of items found on most job application blanks, for example, personal information, educational history, work history, and references. Applicants should complete the job application in a manner that accurately emphasizes their ability to perform the work without providing information irrelevant to the job in question. Answers must be accurate, appropriate to the question, legible, spelled correctly, and written in the space provided (Mathews & Fawcett, 1984).

Research evidence suggests that responses on job application forms could greatly affect the job interviewer's decision to hire or not hire regardless of the effectiveness of the person's behavior during the job interview itself. Stone and Sawatzki (1980) conducted an experimental study that investigated the effect of pre-job interview information on disability and work history on MBA students' ratings of the interviewee's performance and a probability-of-hire rating. The results showed no significant effect of the preinformation on the MBA students' ratings of interviewee performance. On the other hand, type of work history and type of disability had a significant effect on probability-of-hire scores with the group. For example, people with psychiatric disabilities received significantly lower probability-of-hire scores than individuals with physical disabilities. Although not diminishing the importance of job interview training, Stone and Sawatzki (1980) emphasized that the contents of the application form (and resume when appropriate) can increase or decrease the probability of receiving a job offer.

Client Job Interviewing Skills

Rehabilitation counselors should help job seekers (when necessary) upgrade their job interviewing skills in several ways. For example, counselors should discuss the impact that attire, punctuality, and specific interview behaviors have on the job interviewer's decisions. Because employers decide whether or not to hire an individual within the first 4 minutes of the interview, first impressions created by one's dress and appearance are extremely important (Arvey & Campion, 1982). Guidelines for proper attire for women suggest that a dress with jacket or sweater or a skirted suit are usually appropriate. Men should wear slacks, shirt, and tie with a sport coat, or even a suit. Applicants might follow another general guideline for dress; dress like the employer's workers, but do not wear jeans unless applying for a labor position. Previous research (Galassi & Galassi, 1978) suggests that punctuality may even be more important than appearance in order to make a good first impression. The basic rule of thumb is to arrive about 10 minutes early for the interview. Employers quickly conclude that applicants who arrive late for interviews are likely to arrive late to work as well.

The job seeker should be prepared to discuss his or her skills and the relationship of personal skills to job demands. Presenting a neatly typed data sheet helps to answer many of these questions. During the remainder of the interview, the employer will ask for more detailed information from the applicant in the following areas: personal history; personal skills and abilities; interpersonal relations; educational background; work history; and vocational desires, aspirations, and plans. In practicing appropriate answers to such questions in mock interviews, job seekers must remember that both *what* they say and *how* they say it are important. What the applicant says communicates his or her special qualifications for the position. Answers to employer questions enable job seekers to portray themselves as productive, loyal, and dependable workers who have successfully overcome challenges such as disabilities. Of course, applicants may decide whether and how they wish to disclose their disabilities. Many people with disabilities recommend disclosure or being open with an employer if they have a disabling condition. Suggested strategies include:

1. Inform the potential employer of the disability before the first interview.

2. Mention the disability in the resume, on the job application, or both.

3. Tell the employer's secretary at the time the interview is scheduled.

4. Inform the interviewer early in the interview. Indicate reasons why the disability does not affect on-the-job performance.

Of course, applicants have no obligation to answer direct questions about their disabilities; they are required only to describe how they could perform essential job functions with or without accommodation. They need to mention disability only when they are discussing their needs for reasonable "post-offer" accommodations.

Counselors should remind clients that how they answer questions (i.e., their verbal and nonverbal behavior) is also important. Paralinguistic (style) variables affecting job interview outcomes include speech loudness, fluency of speech, speech disturbances, verbosity, and sentence complexity. In addition to grooming and personal appearance, important nonverbal behaviors include body posture, appropriateness of gestures, composure, eye contact, and smiling. Counselors can help individuals develop socially appropriate modes of paralinguistic and nonverbal behavior as well (Roessler & Johnson, 1987).

Rehabilitation clients are heterogeneous in regard to their skills for negotiating the job interview. Therefore, the rehabilitation counselor must assess the person's needs via a mock job interview in which the counselor plays the role of job interviewer, and the client the role of job applicant. Based on the assessment results, the rehabilitation counselor can ascertain the most effective service intervention strategy. That determination can result in the client being referred to a job seeking skills training group. However, if the rehabilitation counselor has the time, the equipment (e.g., videotape equipment), and the training skills and materials, he or she can work directly with the person on upgrading job interview skills.

REHABILITATION COUNSELORS' ATTITUDES TOWARD PLACEMENT

Although rehabilitation counselors consider placement counseling with clients to be a substantial part of their job, they do not report the same responsibility for direct involvement with employers (Emener & Rubin, 1980; Rubin et al., 1984; Thomas et al., 1993). The rehabilitation literature tends to suggest that the latter is the result of rehabilitation counselor preferences rather than the actual demands of their job role (Flannagan, 1977; Urban Institute, 1975). Their preference to avoid placement activities calling for direct contact with employers may stem from viewing those tasks as low-prestige activities (Starkey, 1969). The fact that placement has been perceived as a sales activity has not tended to elevate its prestige. Elaborating on this point, Granovetter (1979) stated:

> It conjures up the image of a vacuum cleaner peddler shoving his foot in the door and throwing dirt on the carpet to facilitate the demonstration of his wares . . . one's personality is on the line all the time, the results depend entirely on the others' decisions. . . . In Arthur Miller's well-known play "Death of a Salesman," the protagonist, Willy Loman, is even given a name—"low man"—that explicitly reflects this social status. (pp. 94–95)

Usdane (1976) suggested that rehabilitation counselor aversion to placement may have resulted from the failure of rehabilitation counselor training programs to place sufficient emphasis on the counselor's placement role. Total emphasis is placed on preparing the client for placement—that is, on being an effective counselor and case manager. To redress this imbalance in rehabilitation counselor education, Hershenson (1988) called for more coursework on the "social psychology of the workplace, work adjustment and readjustment, and job redesign" (p. 215). State rehabilitation agency administrators echoed Hershenson's recommendation. Agency administrators rated job placement, job development, and vocational assessment as three of their top priorities for counselors. At the same time, they rated counselor skill attainment in these areas lowest among eight different job functions (Herbert & Wright, 1985).

The alternative to the rehabilitation counselor becoming more involved in placement is the widespread use of placement specialists. Granovetter (1979) pointed out that such an alternative can create an information credibility problem in the eyes of the prospective employers:

> For employers, the most believable and reliable information about potential employees will come from those individuals who know the applicants best, that is, those who have planned and implemented their rehabilitation programs . . . insofar as placement specialists are used at all, they will be valuable to the degree that they are in personal touch with the individuals they will place. This argues strongly for a conception of such a specialist not as someone who comes in at the end of rehabilitation as part of a "mop-up" operation, but rather as someone whose skills have been made an integral part of the rehabilitation process from the beginning to end. (pp. 96–97)

ENCOURAGING COUNSELORS TO DEVELOP AND USE PLACEMENT SKILLS

It is not enough to inform rehabilitation counselors that placement is an important job function or even that they are legislatively mandated to become involved in placement. Concrete approaches for maintaining counselor activity in placement are needed. Salomone and Usdane (1977) suggested a reinforcement strategy for placement-related behaviors and outcomes that involves "end-of-year bonuses, sponsorship to . . . conventions, annual state-wide dinners and awards, and credit toward promotion" (p. 101). Punishment in the form of negative performance evaluations for too few successful closures at the end of the year remains a strong motivator too. Administrative mandates to counselors to increase their contacts with employers are valuable (i.e., the Michigan Division of Rehabilitation's advocacy of the employer account system [Molinaro, 1977]).

Increasing counselor commitment to the process of placement must begin at the graduate training level. Rehabilitation practitioners, educators, staff development specialists, state agency administrators, and facility specialists identified the university setting as the most appropriate location of training for job development and placement competencies (for academic credit), while allocating little responsibility for such training to in-service and on-the-job training localities (Sink, Porter, Rubin,

& Painter, 1979). Rubin (1979) examined the essential rehabilitation counselor competencies of Sink et al. (1979) and concluded that graduates of rehabilitation counselor education programs should have sufficient knowledge of the following:

1. Theories of career development

2. General employability behaviors

3. Major societal barriers to the job placement of people with disabilities

4. Sources of occupational information

5. Job modification and restructuring procedures

6. Affirmative action laws

They also should be able to

1. Use sources of occupational information

2. Develop a job placement file

3. Conduct a job analysis

4. Identify education and training requirements for specific occupations

5. Use occupational information for formulating training and job choice recommendations for clients

6. Counter employer concerns about hiring people with disabilities

7. Gain help of employers and organized labor in finding jobs for job seekers with disabilities

8. Conduct a follow-up interview with employers to assess the effectiveness of placement

Past research suggested that counselors were not masters of those placement skills, but that such mastery would lead to positive results for clients. Zadny and James (1977) found statistically significant (although weak) relationships between percentage of the counselor work week allocated to placement activities and client outcomes for a sample of 208 rehabilitation counselors located in seven Western states. As the amount of time spent on placement or job development activities increased, the percentage of rehabilitation counselor cases closed not rehabilitated decreased. They also found "increments in the amount of time spent on job development . . . associated with a greater number of rehabilitations of" clients with severe disabilities (Zadny & James, 1977, p. 33). The amount of travel devoted to placement and job development was significantly related to the percentage of the rehabilitation counselor's cases closed as rehabilitated.

CONCLUDING STATEMENT

Although most rehabilitation counselors underscore the value of placement activities, they do not all agree on the extent of counselor assistance needed. Some feel that the counselor's help should be limited to preparing the person for the job and for job seeking. Others advocate counselor intervention at the work site during the job seeking and early employment stages. In all, the appropriateness of a particular placement activity should be based on the needs of the individual. It is the responsibility of counselors to make such decisions as they conduct the placement process.

As a result of being involved in placement activities in which they have direct contact with employers, counselors gain much knowledge of the local world of work. This first-hand knowledge of work demands and work characteristics cannot be gained through any other occupational information resources. Given this knowledge of jobs in the community, the counselor can be much more effective in other aspects of the rehabilitation process, such as evaluation, information processing, vocational planning, and job accommodation.

As the rehabilitation plan so clearly illustrates, the end goal of the vocational rehabilitation process is the achievement of an occupational objective; yet, rehabilitation counselors report placement activity with employers as a less than substantial part of their job. Reasons for this relative lack of commitment to placement include insufficient professional training and a perception of the tasks involved as having low prestige.

Given the desires of clients and the mandates in rehabilitation legislation, rehabilitation counselors must begin to view placement with more than mild interest; they must see it as a logical conclusion of the rehabilitation process. Although this has not always been the case in the past, it will have to become the model rehabilitation counselor attitude of the future if individuals with severe disabilities are to be served effectively. Needed placement services extend beyond direct client services such as job seeking skills training and identification of reasonable accommodations. Counselors must educate employers on their responsibilities under the law to conduct nondiscriminatory job interviews and to provide reasonable job accommodations to otherwise qualified job applicants with disabilities.

Systematic Caseload Management

Reed Greenwood and Richard T. Roessler

Through a combination of counseling, case management, and caseload management skills, the rehabilitation counselor serves a variety of individuals who are dealing with a wide range of disabling conditions. The caseload management phase of the counselor's work is analogous to practice management in other professions. Although caseload management is a widely used term in rehabilitation counseling, it has various meanings within the profession, frequently linked to the setting in which the counseling takes place (see Goodwin, 1989; Matkin, 1983; and Riggar & Patrick, 1984, for discussions of practice settings). Most references to caseload management are addressed to rehabilitation counseling within the state–federal vocational rehabilitation system, particularly the state agency field counselor. However, caseload management principles and techniques apply to rehabilitation counseling, regardless of the setting.

Definitions of caseload management in the literature typically focus on practice management, as opposed to case management or counseling services. For example, Henke, Connolly, and Cox (1975) described caseload management as "how to work with more than one case at a time, how to select which case to work with, how to move from one case to another, how to establish a system to insure movement of all cases, how to meet objectives one has established" (p. 218). This definition coincides with the one this chapter uses that focuses on a more limited view of caseload management, as opposed to the more encompassing approach provided by Cassell and Mulkey (1985):

> Caseload management is a systematic process merging counseling and managerial concepts and skills through application of techniques from intuitive and researched methods, thereby advancing efficient and effective decision making for functional control of self, client, setting, and other relevant related factors for anchoring a proactive practice. (p. 11)

In their broader concept of caseload management, Cassell and Mulkey (1985) discussed topics such as the definition, rationale, and benefits of caseload management; management models; counselor control of the caseload management process; decision making; time management; case status classifications in the vocational rehabilitation process; management of caseflow; case recording and documentation; correlative dimensions (e.g., casefinding); and caseload management in transition. Used as the basis for a comprehensive training program by the Texas Rehabilitation Commission for the Blind (1993), the Cassell and Mulkey reference is recommended for the reader who is interested in a more in-depth exploration of caseload management and related rehabilitation counselor tasks.

Caseload management definitions usually emphasize planfulness, control, decision-making, efficiency, and goal attainment within a systematic context—that is, the achievement of one's purpose in the most effective manner. Although rehabilitation counselors are direct service providers who typically work with one person at a time, they are responsible concurrently for a caseload of many individuals who are progressing through a wide variety of counseling, restoration, and training services. Hence, the manner in which they manage their time and activities contributes significantly to the efficiency and effectiveness of the rehabilitation process (Cassell & Mulkey, 1985; Henke et al., 1975; Willey, 1979). Therefore, the counselor needs to develop caseload management practices that reflect effective allocation of time and services.

SYSTEMATIC CASELOAD MANAGEMENT

Systematic caseload management is based on the assumption that, in addition to having a caseload of clients, most rehabilitation counselors have multiple functions and tasks to perform. A function, according to Merriam-Webster (1984, p. 338), is "one of a group of related actions contributing to a larger action." Therefore, systematic caseload management requires *planning* for effective allocation of counselor functions and tasks; *managing* the plan making the best use of counselor time; and *evaluating* the achievement of goals established in the plans by monitoring, judging, and changing. This approach to systematic caseload management was developed within the larger context of the case management model of rehabilitation counseling that stresses rehabilitation of the whole person (Rubin & Roessler, 1995; Greenwood, Rubin, & Farley, 1980).

In the case management model, the counselor's role is focused on interviewing clients, counseling with clients and family, planning rehabilitation programs, coordinating services, interacting with other service providers, placing and following-up clients, monitoring progress, and solving problems. Additionally, the counselor is involved in business management activities, professional development, and related tasks.

PLANNING: GOALS, FUNCTIONS, AND TASKS

Effective planning requires the counselor to have the knowledge and tools to systematically scan a caseload to determine service goals and the actions necessary for achievement of the goals. This means that the counselor must understand rehabilitation counseling functions and tasks and have an established mechanism for goal set-ting for the caseload. Therefore, the counselor must regularly establish goals so that time is allocated to the functions and tasks that result in the greatest payoff for clients (Henke et al., 1975).

Goal-setting is a decision-making process that includes two primary steps: (a) select-ing the goals to be achieved and (b) determining the order in which the goals should be addressed. Goals are set in collaboration with clients and family members in re-gard to client services, with managers in regard to client services and practice man-agement procedures, and with external community service personnel for case coordi-nation. Effective caseload management requires the counselor to exercise good judgment in the balanced allocation of time to activities. It is beyond the scope of this chapter to provide a review of the factors that should be considered in decision-making relative to caseload management (see Cassell and Mulkey, 1985). However, because the overriding factor in selecting goals is the welfare of the client, priorities must be assigned to counselor services necessary to plan, initiate, and maintain reha-bilitation services. Examining the primary functions and tasks of the rehabilitation counselor helps to focus the counselor's goals and plans on the most important activities.

The case management model of rehabilitation counseling requires the counselor to emphasize five functions: *intake interviewing*—information collection and dissemi-nation tasks associated with initiating the client into the rehabilitation process; *coun-seling and rehabilitation planning*—identification of medical, psychological, and voca-tional evaluations, processing of information with the client, joint determination of the major rehabilitation goal, intermediate goals, and the goal attainment assessment plan; *arranging, coordinating, or purchasing rehabilitation services*—tasks through which the rehabilitation plan is implemented, including services such as training, physical restoration, transportation, and housing; *placement and follow-up*—tasks associated with the employment process (e.g., job development, job analysis, job placement, and follow-up after placement in employment or independent living); and *monitoring and problem solving*—collecting information on client service programs, and assisting in solving problems that occur in the process. In addition, effective caseload manage-ment requires attention to *business management*, the tasks associated with finances, personnel management, case recording and reporting, and case processing and related activities.

The counselor has to establish goals to be accomplished within the parameters of the practice setting, which may be in a public agency, a non-profit program, or a pri-vate for-profit organization. The practice setting affects the range of functions and tasks that are to be performed, and may include the management of financial resources to purchase services or the determination of eligibility for services, as in a public rehabil-itation agency, or the business management of a practice, as in the case of a private for-profit setting. The latter will require involvement with accounting, loans, and other factors that counselors are not concerned with in public and non-profit settings (see Goodwin, 1989, or Matkin, 1983, 1995, for discussions of private practice functions).

MANAGING: TIME ALLOCATIONS

Once counselors understand the planning process, functions, and tasks (what and how) in rehabilitation counseling practice, they can translate those responsibilities into personal action and time allocations (when), assuring that the functions and tasks are performed efficiently and effectively. Time is certainly the most limiting factor for the counselor in caseload management, and time considerations important to caseload management can be identified by the primary functions of the counselor. The following review by functions suggests some of the time parameters associated with key counselor functions.

Intake Interviewing

New referrals to the practice must be seen as soon as possible. Willey (1979) reviewed techniques for following-up referrals, emphasizing the importance of a rapid follow-up to ensure that rehabilitation services are initiated in a prompt fashion. His rationale is based in part on the continuing finding that early intervention in rehabilitation is related to greater positive outcomes of the rehabilitation process (Gardner, 1991). For most clients, the comprehensive intake interview will likely consume at least an hour.

Counseling and Planning

Once assessment information is obtained, the counselor should plan on at least an hour for processing the information, leading to review of the information with the client, which will also take a minimum of an hour of face-to-face counseling time. Depending on the needs of the client, additional sessions are likely to be required prior to the meeting in which the rehabilitation plan is finalized. Sessions with family members during this process are frequently essential to the overall success of the rehabilitation effort (see Chapters 12 and 13).

Arranging, Coordinating, and Purchasing Services

These services frequently accompany the more basic counseling services provided by the counselor. For example, it is estimated that the rehabilitation counselor will need to devote at least 30 minutes following the intake interview to making required arrangements. Prior to subsequent counseling sessions with clients to develop the rehabilitation plan, the counselor will have to devote time to processing client information in order to develop possibilities for the client to consider. Interaction with community service providers is often required as a part of the overall rehabilitation program, and the counselor frequently handles this casework activity. Finally, the purchase of rehabilitation services is arranged for by many counselors, including those in private settings who may serve clients receiving financial assistance through insurance.

Placement and Follow-up Services

Clients ready for employment require some form of placement assistance and monitoring. Although placement needs vary considerably across individuals, at a minimum the counselor should spend the time necessary for assessing placement readiness and suggesting possible employment opportunities to the client. These contacts and services typically require an average of 1 hour per client per month. The job search process is stressful; and the counselor will need to carefully assess the progress of the client in this effort, and provide essential support during this time. This period, and the time from intake to service initiation, are critical for counselor involvement in order to support the client and assist in dealing with difficult decision making and stressful situations. Thus, a proactive stance of weekly counselor contacts may be required. Clients in employment should receive at least one contact from the counselor for each 30 days of employment to follow-up and determine the success of the employment experience. Such contacts are estimated to require an average of 30 minutes per client.

Monitoring and Problem Solving

Once rehabilitation planning has been completed and services are initiated, a client monitoring system must be established. The intensity of this system varies, depending on the comprehensiveness of the client's service program and the level of support required by the client. However, a minimum of one contact per month should be the standard in order to assure orderly flow of rehabilitation services.

Counselors often find themselves responding to crises that arise in the provision of services (e.g., the client who suddenly has to be hospitalized, or the supervisor who requests a meeting during the day when everyone has a busy schedule). These contingencies call attention to the need to manage time to allow for unexpected events. One way to plan for such contingencies is to allow at least 1 hour each day for unscheduled activities. If the time is not claimed, it provides an opportunity to catch up on something else, such as a review of the latest employment information for the local area.

Problem-solving and monitoring interviews should be of sufficient length to cover the counseling needs of the client. Although it is not possible to anticipate the time required for any given interview, in many instances the difficulty encountered will require at least an hour of problem-solving activity.

Business Management

Personnel management tasks are an important part of the rehabilitation counselor's job. Counselors usually have clerical assistants or aides who handle many routine caseload and case management tasks delegated by the counselor (see Morgan & Bost, 1989, for a discussion of the importance of clerical assistance for rehabilitation counselors). Time must be allocated to this function in order to assure the viability and accountability of the practice. Although frequently spread throughout the day, interactions with clerical assistants, aides, and managers will likely consume at least 30 minutes per day. In addition, counselors must budget time for annual reviews of the performance of clerical assistants and technicians with whom they work.

Budget management is a required task for field counselors in the state–federal system who deal with significant sums of case service dollars and for private counselors who may manage not only case funds, but a business as well. The counselor will be required to regularly review cases and the overall budget to determine what purchases to make, to assess when encumbrances may need to be cancelled and funds reallocated to other needs, or to determine whether or not practice expenses are in keeping with planned budgets. The counselor will likely be required to spend a minimum of 30 minutes per week on budget management tasks.

Finally, case recording or reporting and case processing tasks are clearly placing greater demands on the counselor's time. Case recording is a requirement for the professional and serves a variety of functions (Holmes & Karst, 1989). The state agency field counselor has mandated case recording tasks, frequently originating from policies and regulations adopted at the federal level. Also, counselors report activities to other community service providers who are participating in the rehabilitation process (Crimando & Riggar, 1996). Regular reports to insurance carriers and other third-party payment sources are vital to the effectiveness of private practice counselors (see Isom, 1995). Case recording or reporting and case processing tasks will require significant amounts of counselor time, perhaps as much as 15 minutes for each client or community service provider contact.

Time Management Principles

Rehabilitation counselors devoted to professional services understand that the initiation of services to new clients generates a need to allocate significant time to face-to-face sessions with clients, accompanied by counselor planning activities prior to these sessions and follow-up activities after each session. One can readily determine the limiting size of a caseload when such principles as those above are articulated. Although counselors vary considerably in their styles and efficiency, and the estimates provided above are suggested minimums, it should be clearly recognized that the acceptance of a new client by the counselor requires continuing time allocations. The amount of time required to provide quality professional services is considerable, thus limiting the number of clients a counselor can effectively serve. Therefore, in addition to understanding the primary functions required of the rehabilitation counselor, and the associated tasks and their time requirements, the rehabilitation counselor can benefit from some personal organizing principles. There are nine that are particularly applicable to the rehabilitation counselor (Adcock & Lee, 1972): (a) analyze time allocations; (b) plan daily; (c) allow for the unexpected; (d) assess the uncontrollable; (e) delegate and minimize involvement in routine and repetitive tasks; (f) consolidate similar tasks;

(g) use prime time for important tasks; (h) avoid procrastination; and (i) identify and avoid the time wasters.

When asked to estimate how their time is spent, professionals frequently provide estimates that are considerably different from reality. To obtain a more accurate estimate of time use, counselors can conduct a time analysis by noting in a time log the amount of time actually consumed by the functions and tasks they perform. Although such a process may seem exceedingly cumbersome, it can be very instructive to the busy professional. Data in the log help to evaluate whether time allocations are in line with the differential importance of rehabilitation tasks.

Research has shown that professionals who plan daily and into the future are able to realize more important work goals than those who do not (Adcock & Lee, 1972; Mackenzie, 1990). A "to do" list that is reviewed and changed daily is frequently recommended as a caseload management tool (Henke et al., 1975; Texas Rehabilitation Commission for the Blind, 1993). Hence a calendar providing space for each significant task on a weekly basis over at least a year is a valuable tool. The best map allows the counselor to examine 1 full week's work activities at one time. All service goals and action plans necessary for clients can be recorded. In addition to identifying the time allocated for meeting counselor and practice goals, the time map can be shared with supervisors to indicate the implementation of work activity plans by the counselor. As indicated earlier, allowing time for unexpected events is an effective system for dealing with these inevitable events.

It is also important to gain an understanding of events and time that are outside the complete control of the counselor. For example, the counselor usually has time commitments programmed by managers. Within this limitation, the counselor can decide how much time is available for personal control and plan for the use of this discretionary time. Also, when the counselor can show a clearly developed itinerary and time map, and what an interruption in that will do to client services, there is an increased possibility of minimizing disruptions in important client services.

Another important time management strategy is to delegate and minimize involvement in routine and repetitive tasks. Fortunately, many rehabilitation agencies are providing counselors with personal computers and caseload management software, as well as with rehabilitation technicians so that much of the clerical, reporting, and contacting work could be done by others or machines. The delegation of paperwork, scheduling of client interviews, arrangements for services, and routine requests from clients can free significant amounts of counselor time. This can be done by instructing the clerical assistant about the type of requests to be handled and techniques for responding. Concurrent with the emphasis on delegation is a need for task consolidation. Grouping similar tasks assists in making effective use of time. Reviewing the mail and answering correspondence, making telephone calls, dictating case narratives, and clustering interviews are examples of tasks that can be consolidated into one block of time.

In addressing the above time commitments, the counselor should keep in mind the concept of personal prime time—that is, the time in which a person is most effective. Some counselors find they are at their peak early in the day, while others discover that midday or afternoon are their peak times. If there is a period when effectiveness is greatest, that time should be used for the most important work tasks. In rehabilitation counseling, it would be hard to imagine a counselor not reserving prime time for client interviews and related tasks.

One of the more difficult problems in time management is procrastination—deferring difficult, unpleasant, uninteresting, or what appear to be overwhelming tasks (Mackenzie, 1990). Rehabilitation counselors are frequently faced with such tasks, including the difficult client, the complicated report, the overly critical manager or supervisor, or the rejecting employer. Techniques for dealing with procrastination include a nagging reminder, such as a note in the middle of the desk; talking with someone about the task to explore the problems and procedures for getting started, a technique that often results in ideas that make the task seem less formidable; and breaking the job down into components and working on one component at a time so that the job does not seem as difficult. Time wasters, such as the extended visitor in the office, should be avoided or dealt with effectively. Setting up availability hours, keeping the door closed for part of the day, and other strategies have proven useful for this problem.

EVALUATION: MONITORING, JUDGING, AND CHANGING

The rehabilitation counselor has a professional obligation to monitor and review services to clients. Moreover, counselors are evaluated by their managers in terms of accomplishment of important case service goals for clients and compliance with policies and practices. Therefore, evaluation activities are essential to understanding whether goals have been achieved as a result of the counselor's work plans and actions.

Occurring preferably on a weekly basis, evaluation activities involve monitoring, judging, and changing strategies. Reference to a time map (monitoring) allows the counselor to determine whether the goals listed on the map have been attained. In addition, the case record is an important tool for evaluating client progress (Holmes & Karst, 1989). Unmet goals should be analyzed (judged) to determine what should be done (changed) to accomplish the goals. The counselor can also identify the chief problem with goal attainment (i.e., is the source of the problem the client, counselor, some third party, or a combination of several individuals?). In this review, counselors should look for patterns that may call for an in-depth assessment of their skills. If done thoroughly, such a review can easily consume an hour per week of counselor time. Additionally, a brief review at the end of the day, or during the day, is necessary when directions in plans must be changed. The weekly evaluation, however, should be a longer term examination of the types of goals achieved, the problems encountered, and the professional development needed for the counselor to become more effective.

The counselor should also analyze available resources in the practice setting to assist in evaluative activities. The use of supervisors, colleagues, and staff development personnel for additional feedback on performance can be very helpful. By presenting a problem situation to a supervisor, the counselor can initiate a discussion of ways to analyze and resolve the problem. This places the counselor in the position of seeking help for difficult problems in case management and counseling, rather than reacting to negative assessment by management. Additionally, when the counselor seeks assistance from management, an opportunity is created to understand management's perspective on counselor performance. Emener (1979) and Payne (1989) have reviewed the importance of feedback and other caseload management practices for the prevention of counselor burnout.

In summary, evaluation addresses three aspects of the counselor's work: monitoring, judging, and changing based on a review of work plans and accomplishments. The counselor can use internal consultants to help to understand and seek solutions to difficult problems or unmet goals.

COMPUTERS, COMPUTER SIMULATIONS, AND CASELOAD MANAGEMENT

Caseload management requires the use of significant amounts of information about clients, business management procedures, and case coordination. The development of low-cost, readily available personal computers has made information storage, retrieval, and analysis much more efficient. Crimando and Sawyer (1983) described the utility of the personal computer for tasks such as the storage of job analysis data, the production and editing of documents, and networking with other professionals. One computer-assisted caseload management program (Chan, McCollum, & Pool, 1985) is designed for state agency use and includes four modules: general utility—policy reminder, form writer, and calendar programs; expert consultant—disability-based and other variables; feasibility determination—clinical and statistical outcome predictors and interventions; and vocational planning and placement—job matching and analysis. Isom (1995) developed a computer-based system for recording and retrieving client data in private rehabilitation settings for purposes of report and invoice writing. Computer-assisted counseling programs are also available as are widely marketed computer-assisted career guidance and exploration programs (Burkhead, 1992; Issacson & Brown, 1997; Schmitt & Growick, 1985).

Computer case management simulations, with single and multiple case versions, are used to assess and train rehabilitation counselors in caseload management skills (Burkhead, 1992; Chan, Berven, & Lam, 1990; Chan, Rosen, Wong, & Kaplan, 1993). In an application of a computer-based caseload management simulation, Chan et al. (1993) assessed the performance of rehabilitation students (undergraduate and master's levels) and practicing rehabilitation counselors on eight simulated cases (taking about 1 hour to complete). Representing clients with different types of disabilities and socioeconomic backgrounds, the cases included information from the case record and diagnostic evaluations, as well as on outcomes from services and placement activities. Based on results of a multivariate analysis (discriminant function analysis), the authors demonstrated that the performance of the two groups differed significantly in several crucial ways. Experienced rehabilitation counselors were more likely to complete preferred actions for the cases, as well as to make proper use of the rehabilitation status system in working with clients. Wheaton and Berven (1994) reported similarly encouraging findings regarding the positive effects of training and experience, specifically regarding one's level of professional education, on caseload management outcomes of rehabilitation counselors.

Commenting on the need for more training in caseload management in their programs, the students participating in the Chan et al. (1993) study recommended that undergraduate and graduate rehabilitation programs include comprehensive computer-assisted simulations in caseload management that mirror the typical demands faced by counselors. Although unsure about the number of cases to include in a more complex caseload simulation, Chan et al. concluded that more than 8 cases (with a wider range of possible case service options) were needed to adequately simulate the diversity of most counselors' caseloads. To improve the educational value of the simulation, they also recommended that the software program provide participants with immediate feedback regarding the appropriateness of their caseload management actions.

CONCLUDING STATEMENT

Throughout this book, emphasis is placed on the diagnosis, evaluation, treatment, and follow-up of the individual client. This chapter examined the broader issues of caseload management, placing emphasis on planning, managing, and evaluating the counselor's practice. Planning involves the determination of the counselor's goals, based on an understanding of the functions and tasks performed on behalf of clients. Effective planning requires knowledge and skills related to (a) counselor functions and tasks for clients; (b) counselor tasks with significant others; (c) recording, reporting, and decision-making demands of a practice; (d) ability demands of the functions and tasks; (e) the rehabilitation process; (f) the relationship between counselor tasks and the rehabilitation process; (g) the use of a systematic process to monitor service goals and develop action plans; (h) practice and personal needs; and (i) priority assignment and the ability to adjust plans as needed.

Once plans are determined, the counselor has to manage effectively by allocating time to the most critical functions and tasks. The time demands required to carry out counseling, case management, and practice management functions and tasks must be recognized. Given an understanding of these demands, the counselor can determine the upper limits of caseload size. In addition, general time management principles can help to increase effectiveness. These principles include (a) analyzing time allocations; (b) planning daily; (c) allowing for the unexpected; (d) assessing the uncontrollable; (e) delegating and minimizing involvement in routine and repetitive tasks; (f) consolidating similar tasks; (g) using prime time for important tasks; (h) avoiding procrastination; and (i) identifying and avoiding time wasters.

Evaluation requires the counselor to monitor, judge, and change. The goals, time allocation plans, and case records of the counselor are the resources to be used in monitoring activities. With these aids and other information received by the counselor, judgments about progress can be made, and changes based on these judgments can be initiated. The computer is a powerful tool that can be used in storing, retrieving, and analyzing caseload management data for the counselor, thus fostering more efficient caseload management. Affordable software programs to assist with different aspects of caseload management are now available and they can greatly streamline the work of the counselor in both public and private settings. Software applications exist also for assessment and training of counselors in the use of caseload management skills.

In conclusion, effective caseload management requires a systematic process for planning, managing, and evaluating the entire spectrum of counseling functions and tasks. The process advocated in this chapter requires that the counselor have the prerequisite knowledge and skills in counseling, case management, and business management, in addition to the knowledge and skills required to plan for, serve, and evaluate a caseload of clients. Time is indeed a limiting factor, and the time requirements for quality counseling services should be clearly recognized and honored in all practice settings. Finally, it should be noted that effective caseload management becomes even more important in view of developments in rehabilitation and other disability-related services (e.g., supported employment, transition initiatives, and community integration) that have increased the scope of the rehabilitation counselor's role.

Ethical Considerations in Case Management Decision Making

Richard P. Millard and Stanford E. Rubin

The writings on professional ethics have tended to be so theoretical and general that their utility for guiding everyday professional practice has been limited (Haas & Malouf, 1989). In response to this limitation, this chapter shows both how rehabilitation counselors can draw upon rules found in the Code of Professional Ethics for Rehabilitation Counselors (American Rehabilitation Counseling Association [ARCA], Commission on Rehabilitation Counselor Certification [CRCC], & National Rehabilitation Counseling Association [NRCA], 1987) to address ethical problems in the case management process, as well as use an ethical decision-making model for resolving ethical dilemmas confronted. The goal of the chapter is to increase rehabilitation counselor awareness that case management decisions should take ethical principles into consideration, should be justified through a reasoning process, and should be consistent with the law.

Ethical case management practices are expected of rehabilitation counselors. The American public expects rehabilitation counselors to act toward their clients in a manner that (a) respects their freedom of choice, (b) protects them from harm, (c) maximizes their benefits, (d) is fair, and (e) demonstrates an honoring of commitments made. These expectations of professional conduct are consistent with five ethical principles (i.e., autonomy, nonmaleficence, beneficence, justice, and fidelity) that can provide a guide for service delivery actions, a structure for decision making in human services (Kitchener, 1984), and a basis for rehabilitation practice (Welfel, 1987).

THE ETHICAL PRINCIPLES DEFINED

Autonomy

Autonomy refers to freedom of choice (Beauchamp & Childress, 1983). An example of a service delivery action that is consistent with the principle of autonomy is a rehabilitation counselor's supporting the decision of a 40-year-old woman with quadriplegia to stop using her parents as personal care attendants and hire someone outside the family to provide personal care.

Nonmaleficence

Nonmaleficence stresses the obligation of doing no harm to others. Nonmaleficence involves both avoiding and removing conditions that could be harmful to a person's liberty, property, reputation, and physical or psychological well-being (Beauchamp & Childress, 1983). Rehabilitation counselors who do not support a move to a less restrictive, but probably more dangerous, living situation because of concern for the safety of the client are acting in a manner that is consistent with the principle of nonmaleficence.

Beneficence

Beneficence refers to the duty to assist others. This duty encompasses actions that are beneficial, contribute to the welfare of others, confer benefits, and promote good (Beauchamp & Childress, 1983). Arranging for a job to be modified in order to allow an individual with a recent spinal cord injury to return to her old position provides an example of a service delivery action that would be consistent with the principle of beneficence.

Justice

Fairness is fundamental to the principle of justice (Rawls, 1958). In rehabilitation, justice pertains to the fair allocation of limited resources (e.g., who will receive limited rehabilitation funds). The principle of justice dictates that people should be treated equally unless a reason for unequal treatment can be provided. For example, unequal treatment can be considered to be fair (just) if based on the differences in likelihood of benefit or need. An example of a service delivery action that is consistent with the principle of justice is providing a person with quadriplegia a $6,800 motorized wheelchair and a person with paraplegia a $1,700 manual wheelchair to enable each to obtain independent mobility. While the action depicts unequal treatment, it can be considered just based on differing need and likelihood of benefit.

Fidelity

Fidelity refers to faithfulness and duty to keep promises. Fidelity is especially pertinent for rehabilitation counselors. The job role of rehabilitation counselors, as well as their ethical code, requires that they maintain loyalty to numerous publics (e.g., clients, employers, agency supervisors, and colleagues). An example of a service delivery action that is consistent with the principle of fidelity is adhering to the agreements contained in the Individualized Written Rehabilitation Program (IWRP).

ETHICAL CASE MANAGEMENT DECISIONS

Not all case management decisions contain ethical considerations. Some decisions are strictly technical decisions (Haas & Malouf, 1989). For example, deciding which interest inventory to administer to a client is not an ethical problem; it is a technical problem. On the other hand, deciding between (a) supporting a client's choice of a low-probability of success vocational goal and (b) helping the client to achieve only "realistic" vocational goals can be viewed as an ethical dilemma that contains a conflict between the ethical principles of autonomy and beneficence.

Rehabilitation counselors are expected to provide services and place clients in positions where they are most likely to succeed. They are also expected to involve clients in the service delivery decision-making process and respect the rights of clients to make autonomous choices. While meeting those expectations, counselors are also expected to adhere to agency policy. However, in attempting to simultaneously meet all three expectations, counselors are likely to encounter a variety of ethical dilemmas (Wong, 1990). To deal effectively with such ethical dilemmas inherent in their work and to have the skills necessary for developing defensible resolutions for those dilemmas, rehabilitation counselors need to be capable of recognizing the ethical dilemmas inherent in their work and to have skills necessary for developing defensible resolutions for those dilemmas.

CHARACTERISTICS OF ETHICAL DILEMMAS

The ethical principles of autonomy, nonmaleficence, beneficence, justice, and fidelity provide guidance for ethical case management action. However, rehabilitation counselors encounter case management situations in which they must choose between conflicting courses of action, each supported by an ethical principle. In these situations, an ethical dilemma may be present (Wong, 1990).

Ethical dilemmas occur when four characteristics are present in a case management situation:

1. A choice must be made between two courses of action.

2. There are significant consequences associated with taking either course of action.

3. Each of the two courses of action can be supported by one or more ethical principles.

4. The ethical principles supporting the unchosen course of action will be compromised (Rubin, Millard, Wong, & Wilson, 1990).

In a recent survey by Wong (1990, pp. 135–138), rehabilitation counselors reported frequently encountering the following types of ethical dilemmas:

1. Rehabilitating a SSDI client into competitive employment (*autonomy*) conflicts with maximizing the client's financial security (*beneficence*).

2. Supporting a client's selection of a particular vocational objective (*autonomy*) conflicts with channeling a client toward a more realistic vocational objective (*beneficence*).

3. Providing support for a specific type of training requested by the client (*autonomy*) conflicts with supporting the type of training recommended in the client's evaluation report (*beneficence*).

4. Encouraging a client to take responsibility for securing necessary medical services (*autonomy*) conflicts with action in accordance with an overly dependent client's request to obtain necessary medical services for him or her (*beneficence*).

5. Supporting a client's own choice of services (*autonomy*) conflicts with providing services that can increase the client's potential (*beneficence*).

6. Providing clients with case file information they request (*autonomy*) conflicts with withholding distressing information from clients (*nonmaleficence*).

7. Maintaining client confidentiality regarding a poor work history to increase employment opportunities (*fidelity*) conflicts with providing an employer with the necessary information for making an informed hiring decision (*justice*).

8. Providing an employer with all relevant requested client information (*justice*) conflicts with serving as an advocate for the client in the job placement process (*beneficence*).

9. Adhering to agency case movement guidelines (*fidelity*) conflicts with providing an optimal package of rehabilitation services to a client (*beneficence*).

10. Keeping client records up-to-date to promote timely delivery of services (*fidelity*) conflicts with providing essential counseling services to clients that will reduce their anxiety (*nonmaleficence*).

11. Providing comprehensive services to clients with the most severe disabilities (*beneficence*) conflicts with providing adequate and timely services to large numbers of clients with less severe disabilities (*justice*).

Given the many types of ethical dilemmas identified above that rehabilitation counselors frequently encounter, guidance in responding to these difficult case management decision-making situations is needed. A logical potential source of such guidance is the *Code of Professional Ethics for Rehabilitation Counselors* (ARCA, CRCC, NRCA, 1987). The ability of the Code to provide such guidance is discussed in subsequent parts of this chapter.

PROFESSIONAL CODE OF ETHICS

Since the early 1970s, the rehabilitation profession has developed a variety of ethical codes. Ethical standards were developed and accepted by the National Rehabilitation

Counseling Association (NCRA) in 1972 (Cottone, Simmons, & Wilfley, 1983; NRCA, 1972). The National Association of Rehabilitation Professions in the Private Sector (NARPPS) adopted their code of ethics in 1981 (NARPPS, no date). The Vocational Evaluation and Work Adjustment Association (VEWAA) published their code of ethics in 1980 (VEWAA,1980). The Code of Ethics of the National Rehabilitation Administration Association (NRAA) was published in their newsletter in 1979 and again in 1983 (NRAA, 1983). Most recently a Code of Professional Ethics for Rehabilitation Counselors has been jointly adopted by the American Rehabilitation Counseling Association (ARCA), the Commission on Rehabilitation Counselor Certification (CRCC), and the National Rehabilitation Counseling Association (NRCA) (ARCA, CRCC, NRCA, 1987).

The Code of Professional Ethics for Rehabilitation Counselors comprises 10 Canons and numerous Rules. The Canons are general standards for rehabilitation counselor behavior. The Rules are specific standards that can be used as a basis for determining if a rehabilitation counselor is behaving in a manner consistent with the Canon. The drafters of the Code of Professional Ethics for Rehabilitation Counselors have stated that, unlike the general directions provided by the Canons, the Rules represent specific standards that will provide guidance in particular situations. (The complete Code of Professional Ethics for Rehabilitation Counselors is provided in Appendix B.)

To illustrate the strengths and weaknesses of the Code for case management decision making, selected Rules of Canons 2, 4, and 6 will be focused on in the next section. These Canons address the counselor–client relationship, professional relationships, and confidentiality, respectively.

The Ethical Decision-Making Process

When faced with an ethical problem in the case management process, the rehabilitation counselor should first determine if a rule is present in the professional code of ethics that can be drawn upon for guidance in dealing with the situation (Haas & Malouf, 1989). If a rule is present, the rehabilitation counselor must have a good reason for not adhering to that rule. The examples that follow demonstrate the ability of the rules in the Code of Professional Ethics for Rehabilitation Counselors to provide adequate guidance for case management decision making.

▶ Example 1

At the beach on the weekend, a rehabilitation counselor runs into one of his clients who has been receiving vocational services. After talking a while, the client confides being attracted to him. The counselor is flattered and wrestles with whether or not to ask the client out on a date (Rubin, Millard, & Wong, 1989).

In this situation, the counselor must choose between asking and not asking the client out on a date. The rehabilitation counselor can turn to Rule 2.3, which states,

Rehabilitation counselors will be continually cognizant of their own needs, values, and of their potentially influential position, vis-a-vis clients, students, and subordinates. They avoid exploiting the trust and dependency of such persons. Rehabilitation counselors make every effort to avoid dual relationships that could impair their professional judgments or increase the risk of exploitation. Examples of dual relationships include, but are not limited to, research with and treatment of employees, students, supervisors, close friends, or relatives. Sexual intimacies with clients are unethical. (ARCA, CRCC, NRCA, 1987)

As can be observed, Rule 2.3 provides clear guidance in this situation. Rule 2.3 is based on the ethical principle of nonmaleficence. It is likely that establishing a dating relationship with a client can cause harm to either the client, the counselor, or both. In addition, if the fact that a counselor was dating a client became public knowledge, it could damage the reputation of the agency and reduce the credibility of the profession (Rubin et al., 1989).

▶ **Example 2**

A rehabilitation counselor is providing vocational placement services to Sally, a 23-year-old woman with cerebral palsy (CP). Sally has an associate degree in business. She is unemployed and lives with her parents. Sally wants to take a job she has been offered working as an expediter in a manufacturing company located in a large metropolitan area 200 miles away. If Sally takes the job, she must start work in 3 weeks. Sally indicates that she can care for herself, doesn't mind moving, and can hire a housekeeper for her apartment. Her parents call, requesting that the counselor not support Sally's taking the job. Her parents state that she has never lived on her own before, and still relies on them to do her shopping, laundry, and housecleaning. The counselor must decide whether to support Sally's wishes or support her parent's request (adapted from Rubin, Millard, & Wong, 1989).

In this situation, the counselor must choose between supporting Sally's wishes and supporting her parent's request. Rule 2.8 states,

Rehabilitation counselors and their clients will work jointly in devising an integrated, individualized rehabilitation plan that offers reasonable promise of success and is consistent with the abilities and circumstances of clients. Rehabilitation counselors will persistently monitor rehabilitation plans to ensure their continued viability and effectiveness, remembering that clients have the right to make choices. (ARCA, CRCC, NRCA, 1987)

Sally qualifies for the position and wants to take the job. In addition, she indicates that she can care for herself and can hire a housekeeper to assist her with her apartment. Although Sally's parents have asked the counselor to not support her moving, the reasons they have provided for this request do not indicate that harm will likely come to Sally if she moves. Therefore, the principle of nonmaleficence does not support their request. However, both the principles of autonomy and beneficence support Sally's moving because she will obtain employment in accordance with her wishes (Rubin et al., 1989). Given the absence of any major concern over violating the principle of nonmaleficence by supporting Sally's wishes, the content of Rule 2.8 clearly supports that alternative.

▶ **Example 3**

Jason, a 25-year-old client with asthma, has been on a rehabilitation counselor's caseload for 2 years. Jason calls the counselor and indicates that a local cotton mill is hiring. Although he realizes that this environment is not the best for him considering his asthma, he really wants this work. Jason asks the counselor to assist him in applying for work in the cotton mill. The counselor must decide whether or not to provide Jason with assistance (Millard, 1990).

In this situation, the counselor must choose between assisting and not assisting Jason in applying for the job at the cotton mill. Rule 2.9 states,

Rehabilitation counselors will work with their clients in considering employment for clients in only jobs and circumstances that are consistent with the clients' overall abilities, vocational limitations, physical restrictions, general temperament, interest and aptitude patterns, social skills, education, general qualifications and other relevant characteristics and needs. Rehabilitation counselors will neither place nor participate in placing clients in positions that will result in damaging the interest and welfare of either clients or employers. (ARCA, CRCC, NRCA, 1987)

Assisting Jason to obtain employment in the cotton mill would likely place him in a situation that would be harmful to his health. Therefore, in this situation, Rule 2.9—which rests on the principle of nonmaleficence—clearly supports not assisting Jason in applying for the job at the cotton mill.

▶ **Example 4**

A friend (Peter) of a rehabilitation counselor is a client of one of her colleagues. Peter stops by the counselor's office to see her and indicates he is not sure that his counselor really knows what he is doing, and asks if his counselor is competent. The counselor personally believes that Peter's counselor does not have the experience necessary to develop an adequate IWRP for a person with Peter's complex rehabilitation needs. The counselor must decide whether or not to share her beliefs about her colleague's ability to develop Peter's IWRP (Millard, 1990).

In this situation, the counselor must choose between sharing and not sharing her beliefs about the colleague's ability with Peter. Rule 4.7 states,

Rehabilitation counselors will not discuss in a disparaging way with clients the competency of other counselors or agencies, or the judgements made, the methods used, or the quality of rehabilitation plans. (ARCA, CRCC, NRCA, 1987)

Sharing her beliefs regarding Peter's counselor's ability to develop an adequate IWRP for him would likely result in a decrease in Peter's confidence that rehabilitation services will be helpful to him. Consequently, he may discontinue needed rehabilitation services. Therefore, in this situation, Rule 4.7—which rests on the principle of nonmaleficence—clearly supports not sharing her beliefs about her colleague's ability with Peter. A rehabilitation counselor confronted by this situation can talk with Peter's counselor directly regarding his ability to develop an adequate IWRP and suggest that Peter's case be transferred to another counselor with more experience.

▶ Example 5

A rehabilitation counselor receives a call from an employer with whom she has worked in the past. He indicates that one of the counselor's clients (Marsha) has applied for a sales job. The employer states that he has interviewed the client and is interested in offering her a job, but needs more information about Marsha. He states that she indicated she has epilepsy but has been seizure-free for 2 years. The employer asks the counselor to verify that she has been seizure-free for 2 years. The counselor tells the employer that she needs to call Marsha to get permission to release information from her file. He replies that he must make a decision today and has three other qualified candidates for the job. The counselor pulls Marsha's file and attempts to call her. Her roommate answers and tells the counselor that she left to go camping for the week. Upon reviewing her file, the counselor discovers that Marsha has been seizure-free for 20 months. The counselor must decide whether or not to give the information to the employer (adapted from Rubin et al., 1989).

In this situation, the counselor must choose between providing or not providing the information regarding Marsha's seizure history to the employer. Rule 6.3 states,

> Rehabilitation counselors will not forward to another person, agency, or potential employer, any confidential information without the written permission of clients or their legal guardians. (ARCA, CRCC, NRCA, 1987)

Sharing the information regarding Marsha's seizure history with the employer without her permission would violate her autonomy. In this situation, Rule 6.3—which rests on the principle of autonomy—clearly directs counselors not to share the information with the employer.

Many times, a rehabilitation counselor will be faced with an ethical problem for which the rules in the Code provide insufficient guidance. In such cases, the ethical issue present should be sufficiently clarified. In many of these situations, an ethical dilemma is present that contains a conflict between two potential actions, each supported by an ethical principle (e.g., autonomy and nonmaleficence) with the course of action to take for resolving the dilemma not being readily apparent. Example 6 depicts such a situation.

► **Example 6**

Susan is a 25-year-old woman with quadriplegia receiving SSDI funds of $850 per month. Prior to her injury, Susan worked for 5 years as a file clerk. Susan applied for rehabilitation services and indicated that she would like to obtain work in order to improve the quality of her everyday life by reducing her social isolation. Given her 10th-grade education and physical capabilities, Susan will need vocational training to enable her to obtain suitable employment. The jobs that are feasible via training for Susan all tend to pay about $800 per month. Therefore, by being vocationally rehabilitated, Susan's monthly income will slightly decrease. After learning the results of her vocational evaluation, Susan indicates that she is very confused. Through effective counseling, the rehabilitation counselor attempts to help her sort out the pros and cons of each alternative. However, all it does is raise her anxiety. Susan asks the counselor to tell her what to do. The counselor suggests that she take a week to think about it and return. She returns more confused than ever and again asks the counselor to tell her what he thinks she should do. Although the counselor thinks there are some financial risks involved, he thinks that Susan would be better off working. The counselor must decide whether to give an opinion (Rubin et al., 1989).

In this situation, the rehabilitation counselor must choose between providing Susan with an opinion (supported by the principle of beneficence) and not providing her with an opinion (supported by the principle of autonomy).

The Code of Professional Ethics for Rehabilitation Counselors provides conflicting guidance in this situation. Rule 2.8 (see Appendix B) supports providing Susan with an opinion (based on the principle of beneficence), and Rule 2.8 supports not providing Susan with an opinion (based on the principle of autonomy). If the rehabilitation counselor provides an opinion, it is likely that the client will opt to take the employment option. Therefore, the rehabilitation counselor would be facilitating the client's selection of a rehabilitation goal he considered to be viable. However, in doing so, an important life decision is made for the client (violating autonomy). If the rehabilitation counselor does not provide an opinion, it is likely that the client will remain on SSDI. By increasing the likelihood of this outcome as a result of not offering an opinion that has been strongly and persistently sought by the client, the rehabilitation counselor will be inhibiting, rather than facilitating, the client's selection of a rehabilitation goal that he considers to be viable (violating beneficence). Therefore, guidance for resolving the ethical dilemma in this situation, which contains a conflict between promoting the client's autonomy and the need to facilitate development of a viable rehabilitation plan (adhering to beneficence), cannot be obtained from the Code of Professional Ethics for Rehabilitation Counselors.

Although ethical codes are designed to provide guidance for professionals facing ethical issues, as can be seen above, they are limited when ethical dilemmas are present (Tymchuk et al., 1982). They provide unclear and contradictory guidance in some instances (Kitchener, 1986; Mabe & Rollin, 1986).

Ethical codes teach the importance of honesty, respecting the dignity of clients, maintaining confidentiality, upholding fidelity to colleagues, and practicing non-maleficence. However, familiarity with ethical codes does not prepare rehabilitation counselors to make ethical decisions when faced with situations containing conflicting ethical principles (e.g., when adhering to the ethical principle of beneficence compromises the ethical principle of autonomy). Therefore, familiarity with ethical codes does not necessarily enable rehabilitation practitioners to act in an ethical manner when confronted by dilemmas (Kitchener, 1986; Pape & Klein, 1986; Welfel & Lipsitz, 1984). Because ethical codes provide limited guidance to counseling professionals for resolving ethical dilemmas, counselors need to be equipped with critical–analytical decision-making skills to resolve many of the ethical dilemmas encountered in the course of their work (Corey, Corey, & Callahan, 1979; Kitchener, 1986; Welfel & Lipsitz, 1984).

When the Code Fails, Ethical Reasoning Must Prevail

Tymchuk (1981, 1982) and Tymchuk et al. (1982) stressed that practitioners facing ethical dilemmas should be equipped with a critical–analytical problem-solving method. Tymchuk (1982) delineated the following critical–analytical decision-making model for addressing ethical dilemmas:

Step 1. Describe the parameters of the situation.

Step 2. Describe the potential issues involved.

Step 3. Describe the guidelines already available that might affect each issue (e.g., values, laws, codes, practice, and research).

Step 4. Enumerate the alternative decisions for each issue.

Step 5. Enumerate the short-term, ongoing, and long-term consequences for each alternative.

Step 6. Present evidence (or the lack thereof) for those consequences, as well as the probability of their occurrence.

Step 7. Rank order and vote on a decision. (p. 170)

A six-step ethical decision-making model for addressing ethical dilemmas has been recently developed for rehabilitation counselors. The steps of this model are as follows:

1. Review the case situation and determine the two courses of action from which one must choose.

2. List the factually based reasons supporting each course of action. These reasons will often be important consequences.

3. Given the reasons supporting each course of action, identify the ethical principles that support each action.

4. List the factually based reasons for not supporting each course of action. These reasons will often be important consequences.

5. Given the reasons for not supporting each course of action, identify the ethical principles that would be compromised if each action were taken.

6. Formulate a justification for the superiority of one of the two courses of action by processing all information from the previous five steps. This means that an effective justification provides an analysis of the dilemma that includes:

   a. Factually based reason(s) supporting each of the actions. These reasons will often be important consequences.

   b. The ethical principle(s) supporting each of the actions, given the reasons in *a*.

   c. The selected course of action and the reasons why precedence should be given, in that situation, to the ethical principles supporting the selected course of action. (Rubin, Millard, Wong & Wilson, 1990)

The application of the model case can be demonstrated via the case of Nancy.

 ## CASE STUDY: NANCY

A rehabilitation counselor is providing services to Nancy, a 24-year-old client with spina bifida who has mild mental retardation. Nancy has been working in a sheltered workshop for the past 6 years. She is legally competent, acting as her own guardian. The workshop director contacts the rehabilitation counselor, indicating that Nancy might do well in competitive employment. However, Nancy has told the workshop director that she wants to keep working at the workshop because all her friends are there. Although the workshop director thinks that Nancy would be better off in competitive employment, she is not sure if she should respect Nancy's wishes to remain at the workshop. The director asks the rehabilitation counselor's opinion. The director's decision will likely be strongly influenced by the rehabilitation counselor's response. The rehabilitation counselor must decide whether to support the director's inclination to place Nancy in competitive employment or to suggest that she respect Nancy's wishes.

In Step 1, the rehabilitation counselor reviewed the case situation and determined the following two courses of action from which to choose:

A. Support the director's inclination to place Nancy in competitive employment.

B. Suggest that the workshop director honor Nancy's request.

In Steps 2 and 3, the rehabilitation counselor listed the following factually based reasons for supporting each course of action and the ethical principles that support each:

Course of Action A (Pros)	Course of Action B (Pros)
Nancy will have increased contact with people in the community (adhering to beneficence).	Nancy's wishes will be respected, and she will be able to continue working with her friends (adhering to autonomy).

In Steps 4 and 5, the rehabilitation counselor listed the following factually based reasons for not supporting each course of action and the ethical principles that would be compromised by each action:

Course of Action A (Cons)	Course of Action B (Cons)
Nancy will not be working in the position she desires (compromising autonomy).	Nancy will be working in a position in which she is unnecessarily segregated from nondisabled persons.
	Nancy will not be able to take advantage of increased opportunity to participate in community life that will likely result in competitive employment (compromising beneficence).

In Step 6, the rehabilitation counselor formulated the following justification for the superiority of Course of Action B:

The alternative course of action, *Support the director's inclination to place Nancy in competitive employment,* can be supported by the ethical principle of beneficence, and the following reasons can be provided for choosing that course of action:

1. Working in competitive employment will provide Nancy with an opportunity to have increased contact with people in the community, as well as increased opportunity to participate in community life.

2. It is likely that Nancy has the ability to succeed in competitive employment.

3. She will not be unnecessarily segregated from persons without disabilities in employment.

However, Course of Action A is contrary to Nancy's expressed wish to continue working at the workshop with her friends, and, therefore, compromises her autonomy. The counselor chose to support Nancy's wish to continue working at the workshop, giving precedence to the principle of autonomy for the following reasons:

1. Remaining at the workshop is her wish.

2. She has indicated a desire to continue working with her friends.

3. If pushed into competitive employment at this time, Nancy will likely not succeed because she does not want to leave the workshop.

4. If she does not succeed, it will be less likely that she will become interested in competitive employment in the future.

5. If she does not succeed, it will be harder to place her in competitive employment in the future.

6. Given that she is likely capable of competitive employment, this option can remain open for her in the future.

Although the Course of Action A could benefit Nancy in terms of increased community involvement, and she is capable of competitive employment, it is likely that she will not succeed in a competitive employment situation she does not want. Therefore, the beneficence attributed to working in competitive employment will probably not materialize. In addition, she has provided a valid reason for wanting to remain at the workshop; she wants to work with her friends. Those reasons strongly support giving precedence to the ethical principle of autonomy, even though the ethical principle of beneficence may be compromised (adapted from Rubin et al., 1990).

While decision-making models for addressing ethical dilemmas are based on identifying the most rationally defensible and ethical actions, these models do not "thoroughly take into account legal considerations" (Haas & Malouf, 1989, p. 14). Therefore, in addition to ethical considerations, legal considerations should be sufficiently considered in the case management decision-making process.

CONCLUDING STATEMENT

Rehabilitation counselors frequently encounter case management situations containing ethical issues. Some of those ethical issues can be resolved by referring to the Code of Professional Ethics for Rehabilitation Counselors (ARCA, CRCC, NRCA, 1987). However, when an ethical dilemma is present, the Code may not provide sufficient guidance for resolving the ethical conflict. When such situations are present, rehabilitation counselors need to be able to systematically analyze the situation, taking into consideration the ethical principles involved to choose the best possible course of action. The six-step ethical decision-making model presented in this chapter provides a mechanism for doing so.

Regardless of where the guidance for addressing ethical issues in the case management decision-making process is obtained, the decision should be made "in a way that is consistent with what we would want for ourselves, our loved ones, and all people under the same conditions" (Kitchener, 1984, p. 53). Finally, universalizability is an important characteristic of an ethical action. Therefore, a criterion for an ethical action is the likelihood that the rehabilitation counselor will recommend the "same course of action to every other person essentially similar to . . . [him or her] . . . who is operating in essentially the same circumstances" (Haas & Malouf, 1989, p. 12).

Multicultural Considerations in the Rehabilitation Counseling Process

Stanford E. Rubin, Walter Chung, and Weihe Huang

As products of the White middle class, many rehabilitation counselors have been culturally encapsulated and therefore culturally biased in their responses to ethnic minority clients (Casas & Vasquez, 1989; Richardson & Molinaro, 1996). The following examples of that core set of White middle-class values have been identified by Althen (1988):

1. Importance of individualism and privacy

2. Belief in the equality of all individuals

3. Informality in interactions with others

4. Emphasis on the future, change, and progress

5. Belief in the general goodness of humanity

6. Emphasis on the importance of time and punctuality

7. High regard for achievement, action, work, and materialism

8. Pride in interactional styles that are direct and assertive (cited in Lynch, 1992, p. 38)

When unaware of their cultural bias, White middle-class rehabilitation counselors may perceive these as universal values (Casas & Vasquez, 1989). However, clients from specific minority cultures in U.S. society may not ascribe similar levels of importance to each of those values. For example, in contrast to the valuing of individualism, the Japanese have the concept of *amae*, which has been described "as technically referring to the relationship between a mother and her eldest son. While the son is young and dependent he is being prepared for a time when his mother will be old and dependent. . . . Significantly this concept of amae is widely used as the criteria for evaluating . . . many other relationships in society in which dependency is considered a healthy and normal aspect of relationships" (Pederson, 1987, p. 20).

It has been suggested that when the counselor's behavior in cross-cultural counseling manifests his or her cultural bias, counseling outcomes are affected negatively (Richardson & Molinaro, 1996; Rubin, Pusch, Fogarty, & McGinn, 1995; Sue & Zane, 1987) and that rehabilitation counselors whose professional practices reflect such biases are incompetent in cross-cultural settings (Green, 1995). Sue and Zane (1987) have attributed much of the cause for cross-cultural service delivery ineffectiveness to lack of counselor familiarity "with the cultural backgrounds and lifestyles of various ethnic-minority groups" and professional training for counselors primarily developed to prepare them to serve "Anglo, or mainstream Americans" (p. 37). Therefore, to avoid such ineffectiveness, rehabilitation counselors must "not only strive to learn techniques for how to work with culturally diverse clients, but also strive to understand the underlying core value structure of diverse cultures" (Richardson & Molinaro, 1996, p. 238).

The enculturated biases of the counselor from the White majority, when paired with a lack of knowledge about an ethnic minority culture, can sometimes result in an incorrect attribution (misinterpretation) of the cause of the behaviors of clients from that cultural group in cross-cultural counseling situations (Salzman, 1995). For example, a rehabilitation counselor who has been enculturated to believe that adults should desire independence may misinterpret "an ethnic minority client's reluctance to pursue independence as a result of disability related functional limitations rather than to cultural values such as family interdependence" (Rubin et al., 1995, p. 257). A counselor's inaccurate interpretations of the reasons for the client's behavior can result in undermining the credibility of the counselor in the eyes of the client.

Lack of awareness by rehabilitation counselors of the relevant cultural differences in regard to attitudes, values, and behaviors between them and their ethnic minority clients can promote misdiagnosis of the presenting problem, culturally inappropriate recommended means of problem resolution, and unacceptable service outcome goals, thereby inhibiting rapport development and possibly driving ethnic minority clients away from much needed rehabilitation services (Rubin et al., 1995; Sue & Zane, 1987). This can be seen in the following hypothetical example.

 ## CASE STUDY: LI

Li, a 27-year-old Chinese woman with asthma and allergies, sought services from a local rehabilitation counselor to acquire training as a computer programmer at a local junior college. She currently lives with her extended family, which includes her parents who came to the United States from Hong Kong 15 years ago, her paternal grandparents who were brought to the United States by her parents 5 years ago, and two younger sisters. Li and her two younger sisters were brought to the United States 10 years ago by her parents. The family owns a Chinese take-out restaurant where Li has worked full time for 5 years. Li tells the rehabilitation counselor that working in the restaurant has become difficult for her due to her

medical conditions. Her father has been very critical of her during the last few years because she has not been very helpful in the restaurant.

After assessing Li's aptitudes, the rehabilitation counselor advised Li to apply for admission to a computer science bachelor's degree program at a university 100 miles from her family's home. He also encouraged Li to acquire assertiveness training in order to confront her father in regard to his frequent criticism of her and to assert her independence about leaving home to go to college. The rehabilitation counselor saw Li's employment as a computer software specialist, as well as living independently in her own apartment, as optimal rehabilitation service outcome goals. He felt that continuing to both live at home with her family and work in the family restaurant would aggravate her asthma and allergies.

Li was very uncomfortable with what the rehabilitation counselor was encouraging her to do. Some of his advice was simply incompatible with her cultural values. For example, family intimacy and interdependency are important values in the Chinese culture. Li has been taught to stay with her parents until she gets married. Being the eldest child in the family, she is even expected to live close to her family after marriage so that she can support other family members—that is, her grandparents, parents, and two younger sisters. Going to a university 100 miles away from home would make it difficult for Li to fulfill her responsibility to her family.

In addition, harmony among family members is central in the Chinese family value system. Harmony within the context of Chinese culture presumes complying with a hierarchical relationship among family members. For example, children are expected to respect and obey the will of their parents. Learning assertiveness, as proposed by the counselor, will create a conflict with that cultural value.

Culturally appropriate solutions may involve advising Li to enroll in the computer programmer training program in the local junior college. Efforts should be made to avoid potential conflict between Li's going to college and her obligations to the family business. For example, she may begin her education as a part-time student to allow time to help in the family business. Also, instead of sending her to an assertiveness training program, the counselor could help Li find a mediator between her and her father. For example, the counselor could involve Li's mother or grandparents so that the conflict could be solved in a non-confrontational manner.

While the counselor was correct in encouraging Li to acquire training for an occupation that would be more compatible with her medical conditions, he failed to take into consideration the incompatibility of his recommendations with her cultural values. As a result, he rapidly lost credibility in Li's eyes, and she failed to return after her second appointment.

Pederson (1987) would likely see the rehabilitation counselor's ineffectiveness with Li as resulting primarily from the counselor's cultural bias of valuing individualism more than the integrity of the family unit. As Pedersen pointed out, this bias manifests itself in the presumption in the United States

> that counseling is primarily directed toward the development of individuals rather than units of individuals or groups such as the family, organizations, or society. If one examines the jargon used in counseling, the preference of Western counselors for the welfare of individuals becomes quickly evident. The criteria of self-awareness, self-fulfillment, and self-discovery are important measures of success in most counseling in Western society.
>
> In Chinese culture it would be normal and natural to put the welfare of the family before the welfare of any individual member of the family. To speak of an individual's health and welfare independent of the health and welfare of the family unit would not make sense in that context. (p. 18)

Cultural sensitivity can be acquired via an ongoing process of discovery directed at learning about cultures within U.S. society that differ from one's own. The ultimate outcome of that process of discovery is "a systematically learned and tested awareness of the prescribed and proscribed values of a specific community, and an ability to carry out professional activities consistent with that awareness" (Green, 1995, p. 90). The operations of the process of discovery are comparative in nature, requiring rehabilitation counselors to contrast their "own views of situations with those of others to find the patterns and values in them both" (p. 84). Questions for that process of discovery can focus on how clients from specific ethnic minority groups perceive the counseling relationship and what they expect from rehabilitation counselors. Green (1995) stated:

> At a minimum, that means that the . . . [service provider] . . . ought to have a sense of how the social artifact called the "counseling relationship" fits into a client's normative expectations. Do clients perceive as normal or acceptable a deeply personal conversation with a near stranger, one who has a great deal of authority and who is a representative of another, possibly threatening, ethnic group? Is the . . . [service provider] . . . expected to give something of value—advice, goods, or an eligibility rating—in return for a proper show of deference or need? What is the agenda, and how is action begun? (p. 93)

Questions for that process of discovery can also relate to culturally dependent interpretations of nonverbal behaviors such as eye contact and personal space orientation. Lack of counselor awareness of such different interpretations can undermine the development of client–counselor rapport in cross-cultural rehabilitation counseling situations. Sue (1990) has elaborated as follows regarding personal space:

> Different cultures dictate different distances in personal space. For Latin Americans, Africans, Black Americans, Indonesians, Arabs, South Americans, and French, conversing with a person dictates a much closer stance than normally comfortable for Northwest Europeans. . . . A Latin American client may cause the counselor to back away because of the closeness taken. The client may interpret the counselor's behav-

ior as indicative of aloofness, coldness, or a desire not to communicate. In some cross-cultural encounters, it may even be perceived as a sign of haughtiness and superiority. On the other hand, the counselor may misinterpret the client's behavior as an attempt to become inappropriately intimate, or as a sign of pushiness or aggressiveness. Both the counselor and the culturally different client may benefit from understanding that their reactions and behaviors are attempts to create the spatial dimension to which they are culturally conditioned. (p. 425)

Eye contact or lack thereof is interpreted differently across cultures. Intermittent eye contact is expected in interpersonal interactions among White middle-class Americans. Sincerity and trustworthiness are associated with such eye contact in the majority American culture. Therefore, client avoidance of eye contact can be attributed by White Anglo Saxon counselors to negative traits such as "shy, unassertive, sneaky, or depressed" (Sue, 1990, p. 426). This would not tend to be the case for many traditional Navajos who would consider a direct stare as a hostile act and who, therefore, would tend to "use much more peripheral vision and avoid eye contact if possible" (p. 426). Lynch (1992) further elaborates on how eye contact is interpreted differently across cultures, stating that

among African Americans, making eye contact with someone in authority is viewed as disrespectful. Among Asian groups, eye contact between strangers may be considered shameful; and prolonged eye contact may be interpreted as disrespectful in Latino cultures. (p. 46)

Therefore, rehabilitation counselors must be careful about attaching diagnostic significance to lack of client eye contact in some cross-cultural counseling situations.

IMPORTANCE OF WITHIN-GROUP DIFFERENCES: THE NEED FOR THE INDIVIDUAL FOCUS

The culturally sensitive rehabilitation counselor is not one who tends to totally identify an individual with the characteristics of a single cultural group. The tendency to do so allows one to view the identity of an individual from a subgroup culture (e.g., Hispanics) (a) as being totally unaffected by exposure to members of other subgroup cultures (e.g., White Anglo Saxons) in society or (b) as totally metamorphasized by such exposure (e.g., acculturated into the majority culture). Neither tends to be the case for most members of ethnic minority groups.

The tendency to view a person as part of a single homogeneous subculture often results from a failure to sufficiently recognize individual differences within a culture. Such individual differences, which typically result from exposure to other cultures and environmental variations within the culture, are inevitable. Drawing upon Hispanic clients as an example, Casas and Vasquez (1989) spoke to the individual differences within the culture as follows:

Hispanic clients are not solely products of their sociocultural background, nor are they mere reflections or extrapolations of the statistically derived "average" Hispanic found in the literature. Just as there are specific sociohistorical factors that distinguish Hispanic subgroups, there are also unique sociohistorical life factors that differentiate Hispanics regardless of subgroup. These life factors play major roles in the psychosocial development and adjustment of each and every Hispanic as they do for the general populace. Such life factors can be as mundane and "normal" as family size, birth order, childhood illnesses, family mobility, family deaths, authoritarian parenting, and family overprotectiveness; they can also be as dramatic and sociopolitically generated as racism, segregation, unequal opportunities for education, unequal accessibility on health and social services, unfair employment (or unemployment) practices, and political disenfranchisement. (p. 166)

The tendency to view all persons from a single culture as products of the exact same sociocultural background also tends to ignore personal choice factors in regard to differences both in what individuals identify as significant within their environment and in how they respond to those environmental factors. Consequently, individuals are often able to consciously choose the extent to which they expose themselves to cultural influences, as well as adopt behaviors compatible with those influences. For example, "a Mexican-American adult can 'choose' whether or not to acculturate into the mainstream Anglo society in the sense of adopting or rejecting Anglo cultural perspectives" (Garza & Gallegos, 1995, p. 7). Therefore, within-group variability is contributed to by individual choices that reflect differential levels of acculturation and assimilation. In fact, within-group differences tend to increase as the cultural group becomes more identified as bicultural (e.g., Mexican American). This is the result of the addition of many "unique, hybrid characteristics atypical of either parent culture" (Garza & Gallegos, 1995, p. 13).

In essence, the counselor must adopt Hays's (1996) more particularistic perspective on multiculturalism by "adressing [sic]" the individual and his or her specific life experiences. In her "adressing" model, Hays sensitizes counselors to the need to understand how age, disability, religion, ethnicity and race, social status, sexual orientation, indigenous heritage, natural origin, and gender affect the values, beliefs, attitudes, and behaviors of people receiving counseling services. With an awareness of the multiple factors that shape not only clients but also counselors, counselors are better prepared to function in cross-cultural counseling roles. They understand the potential for and source of personal bias. They are also able to explore through counseling the salience of different background factors in the client's life and use that knowledge in working with the person in a culturally sensitive manner.

SPECIFIC CULTURES

As one proceeds through the subsequent parts of this chapter on African Americans, Hispanic Americans, Asian Americans, and Native Americans, it will become apparent that, as pointed out by Sue and Zane (1987), "when working with ethnic-minority groups, no knowledge of their culture is detrimental" (p. 39). However, information on the most salient characteristics of a particular ethnic group cannot always be assumed to be helpful for understanding a given member of that group because of individual differences among the members of the ethnic group.

In the following sections, salient characteristics of some minority groups such as African American, Hispanic American, Asian American, and Native American will be described. It is important for rehabilitation counselors to be aware of and sensitive to the characteristics associated with each minority group. Theoretically, different ethnic minority groups can be considered as representing different categories and their salient characteristics as the defining features of each of these categories. The way that these characteristics or features are selected and organized is a process of idealization, and the outcome of the process is an idealized model of a particular minority group. Such models are "idealized" in that they contain all characteristics that are practically significant for purposes of differentiating the member of a category (group) from the members of other categories (groups). For example, the salient characteristics presented below capture features that are hypothesized to be important to rehabilitation counselors to take into consideration in formulating their responses to clients from different minorities.

Usually, these idealized models work well for the most representative cases, which can be briefly defined as members of "best fit" for a certain category. Unacculturated members of certain minority groups (those who have had little exposure to cultures other than their own or who deliberately refuse to be assimilated into other cultures) could be examples of this kind of prototypical case. Thus, in the case of cross-cultural rehabilitation counseling, the usefulness of knowledge of the salient characteristics of a minority group is mainly relative to how closely the characteristics of a client correspond to those of the most typical members of that minority group.

Idealized models have their intrinsic limitations in that they are necessarily simplified models and may not fit every particular case exactly (Johnson, 1993). Some members of the category possess more defining features of the category, and they are more stable in possessing these features over a period of time. Therefore, they are more representative of best fits in the category. Others possess fewer defining features, and they are less representative cases. Therefore, within any minority group, within-group differences exist. Consequently, while the salient characteristics of minority groups described below may explain some behaviors of some members, they are not sufficient to explain the behavior of all members of a particular group.

Applying idealized models of categories without realizing the limitations of these models and the importance of within-group differences constitutes a theoretical foundation for stereotyping. Stereotyping has negative implications for cross-cultural counseling in general and cross-cultural rehabilitation counseling in particular. Using African Americans as an example, Smith (1977) has revealed that some helping professionals have created stereotypes of African American clients by overgeneralizing some cultural characteristics of this group, thereby using this overgeneralized model to explain and predict their African American clients' behaviors. Such stereotypes can include the concepts of cultural disadvantage, weak family structure, negative self-esteem, and nonverbal communication style. These stereotypes can negatively affect the practice of rehabilitation counseling with African Americans by inhibiting the counselor's recognition of the individual characteristics of each client.

Salient characteristics discussed in this chapter can be useful for rehabilitation counselors if such descriptions help them better understand their minority clients. Overgeneralizing these characteristics and overlooking other factors such as within-group differences, however, can only do a disservice to the process of multicultural rehabilitation counseling.

African Americans

According to the 1990 U.S. census, the 33 million African Americans in the United States make up approximately 12% of the population (Dana, 1993). By 2050, African Americans are expected to account for 16% of the population (Feist-Price & Ford-Harris, 1994). Due to long-standing social and attitudinal barriers, major inequities in education, income, and health exist today between African Americans and Anglo Americans. For example, 11.5% of African American adults have completed 4 or more years of college compared to 22.2% of Anglo American adults (McDavis, Parker, & Parker, 1995). The poverty ratio for African Americans and Anglo Americans is 3 to 1 (Dana, 1993). With high unemployment, low-income jobs, and poor benefits, African Americans are less likely than Anglo Americans to have adequate health care (McDavis et al., 1995).

About 14% of African Americans have a disability, while the disability rate for Caucasian Americans is 8.4% (Alston & Turner, 1994). African American adults with disabilities are faced with the "double whammy" of discrimination against racial minorities and people with disabilities (Feist-Price & Ford-Harris, 1994; Wright, 1988). Some authors have even described African American females with disabilities as facing a "triple whammy" resulting from discrimination against African Americans, women, and people with disabilities (Hanna & Rogovsky, 1992).

Different models have been proposed to explain the problems confronting the African American population (Littlejohn-Blake & Darling, 1993; Wilson & Stith, 1991). One of the more popularly embraced has been the deficit model that "attributes the social ills afflicting minority and low-income groups to internal rather than external factors" (Hill, 1993). Historically, the deficit model has led to a *blaming the victim* orientation for the failure of human service interventions. Fortunately, efforts have been made in recent years to attribute less responsibility to the client and more to the counselor for undesirable outcomes, a change stimulated by the identification of functional strengths within the African American culture (Billingsley, 1992; Hill, 1993). For example, Hill (1971) indicated that strong kinship bonds, strong work orientation, adaptability of family roles, strong achievement orientation, and strong religious orientation are responsible for the survival and advancement of many members of the African American community. The change has also been contributed to by efforts focused on changing the value judgments of human service professionals from negative to neutral regarding some characteristics of individuals in the African American culture. For example, Sue (1990) has maintained that African American clients have their unique communication styles and that counselors should be willing to accept communication styles different from their own.

In the discussions to follow, salient characteristics of African Americans will be highlighted. The implications of these characteristics for rehabilitation counseling will also be addressed.

Salient Characteristics

Religion is highly valued by the great majority of African Americans. According to a review by Billingsley and Caldwell (1991), 84% of African American adults consider themselves to be religious, 80% consider it very important to send their children to church, and 77% report that the church is still very important. Of African American adults, 78% indicate that they pray daily, 71% indicate that they attend church at least once a month, and 68% listen to weekly religious broadcasts (Billingsley, 1992). Having reviewed several large-scale surveys, Hill (1993) reported the following comparative data. Three fourths of African American adults belong to a church, while two thirds of Caucasian adults do. Eight out of 10 African American adults think that Black churches have helped them in their lives. Two thirds of the church members have belonged to their churches for over 10 years, while less than one tenth have been members less than 1 year.

In addition to its American influences, African American religion has its roots in African culture (Hill, 1993; Willis, 1992). Willis described the religious origins of African Americans as follows:

> Early African religion was centered on the concept of a supreme God who created the Earth, and that this Creator had a life force that was present in all things. The worship of ancestors and the spirits of nature existed simultaneously. . . . These spirituals, in their purity and intensity, continue to be the foundation of African American worship and a dynamic part of African Americans' proud heritage. (pp. 126–127)

Some authors (e.g., White, 1984) perceive the world view of African religion as a holistic conception, characterized by the concept of interrelatedness with an emphasis on the tribe and cooperation rather than on the individual and competition. The influence of this world view is also evident in contemporary African American culture (Rogers-Dulan & Blacker, 1995).

While the primary role of Black churches is to influence the spiritual life of African Americans, they also serve several important social functions (Lyles, 1992; Rogers-Dulan & Blacker, 1995). One distinctive function of the Black church is its tendency to serve as a center of community services (Billingsley & Caldwell, 1991). For example, in an interview study in North Carolina, Baptist pastors reported that provision of social services was a central responsibility for Black churches. Those social services included counseling on marital, financial, family, medical condition, employment, unwanted pregnancy, alcohol, legal, relational, and sexual matters. Billingsley (1992) reported that Black churches in the Northeastern region "engage in a wide range of outreach activities, including programs for children and youth, adults and families, and the elderly, as well as broadly based community development projects" (p. 375). Finally, based on data from several national surveys, Hill (1993) concluded that a wide variety of social services are provided currently by Black churches "directed toward strengthening families and enhancing positive development of children and youth" (p. 87).

The high level of religiosity among African Americans and the services available from Black churches, in general, serve positive functions for African Americans in the process of adapting to a disability. For example, the high level of religiousness might be a contributing factor to the finding that African American mothers of children with disabilities reported less difficulty psychologically adjusting to the situation than did Caucasian mothers of children with disabilities (Mary, 1990). The religious beliefs of African Americans can also facilitate the acceptance of people with disabilities by other members of the family and community because many African Americans believe that all people are God's children, including people with disabilities (Rogers-Dulan & Blacker, 1995). This may help explain the results of research (Grand & Strohmer, 1983; Pickett, Vraniak, Cook, & Cohler, 1993) that suggest that African Americans are likely to be more accepting of people with disabilities than are Anglo Americans. The high degree of religiosity among African Americans may also explain why some African Americans with disabilities turn away from human service agencies. For example, Dungee-Anderson and Beckett (1992) found that African American families with a person with a disability (e.g., Alzheimer's disease) were more likely than Anglo American families to turn to religion to obtain relief from caregiver stress.

Another salient characteristic of the African American community is its family values and practices. One perspective holds that African Americans lack a distinctive family value and practice because the slavery system in America has destroyed all elements of African culture (Frazier, 1939). Another perspective is that many aspects of African culture have survived the experience of American slavery and continue to influence contemporary African Americans (Herskovits, 1941). Historically, the first perspective has been pervasive. Recently, however, the latter perspective is being supported by more and more empirical evidence (Billingsley, 1992; Hill, 1993).

To understand contemporary African American families, it is necessary to be cognizant of relevant traces of African culture. In African society, primacy was given to extended families rather than to nuclear families. Extended families include blood kin groupings, husband–wife relations, sibling bonds, grandparent–grandchild relationships, and extension of kinship to elders throughout the community. During slavery, the African family value that emphasized the extended family was sustained. The extended family tradition remained strong in America because it provided a support system for African Americans within the context of the slavery (White, 1984).

The extended family tradition was passed on to subsequent generations in the African American community through oral education and real life modeling. For example, the majority of contemporary African Americans live in close proximity to their kin network. Eighty-five percent "of all Blacks have relatives that live in the same city but in separate households" (Hill, 1993, p. 105). The extended family has also served valuable functions for middle-class African Americans. For example, in a study of middle-class African Americans, McAdoo (1981) found that

> the education and achievement of the individuals were often impossible without the support of the extended family. . . . [T]he kin support network is still as essential now as it was in earlier generations, for it involves cultural patterns that were created and retained from earlier times that are still functional and supportive of Black family life. (p. 167)

This cultural carryover (i.e., the value and practice of the extended family) cuts across socioeconomic classes among the majority of contemporary African Americans.

In African families, roles of family members are flexible. As Billingsley (1993) pointed out, in African society, "while there was women's work, men's work, and children's work, there was a great deal of flexibility and interchange and no stigma attached to men doing women's work and vice versa" (p. 94). Furthermore, in African society, grandparents often share child-rearing and other responsibilities. Accordingly, the elderly are more respected by other family members in the African community.

Numerous studies have found that role flexibility has been sustained in contemporary African American families (Billingsley, 1992; Hill, 1993; Rogers-Dulan & Blacker, 1995). African American women are more likely than Caucasian women to be breadwinners, and African American men are more likely than Caucasian men to perform household chores. In reviewing published literature on this topic, Smith (1981) reported that about 87% of African American men agreed that a wife should work according to her needs and desires while only 48% of Caucasian men agreed with this position. Hill (1993) noted the role flexibility in African American households and reported that more elderly African American women than Caucasian women help rear children: "Only one out of ten white families headed by women 65 years and over are rearing children today, compared to one out of three Black families headed by elderly women" (p. 111). Alston, McCowan, and Turner (1994) pointed out that this role flexibility within the family, with its members being willing "to assume nontraditional or additional roles," facilitates the successful adjustment of African Americans with disabilities (Alston et al., 1994, p. 285). Furthermore, simply being a member of the family results in being unconditionally accepted by the other members whether the family member has a disability or not (Taylor & Bogdan, 1989).

The communication style used by many African Americans represents another salient characteristic of their culture. According to Hall (1976a), a culture can have either low or high context communication. Low context communication emphasizes general rules for governing interpersonal behaviors. It stresses that the verbal part of communication is more important than the nonverbal part. In contrast, high context communication puts emphasis on personalized interaction and nonverbal behaviors. Anglo American communication is generally low in context. The U.S. courts can be seen as an example of the low context system. The communication style of grass-roots African Americans generally is higher in context than that of Anglo Americans. For example, in conversations, African Americans, compared to Anglo Americans, can use fewer words to convey the same content (Sue, 1990). The difference sometimes leads to misunderstandings between African Americans and Anglo Americans (Hall, 1976b). For example, if an African American client in a counseling session has maintained a close conversing distance and displayed many bodily movements, a Caucasian counselor might see this style as communicating hostility (Sue, 1990). This interpretation is, of course, incorrect.

African Americans do not necessarily maintain eye contact at all times when conversing with others (Smith, 1981). It is not unusual for African Americans to speak to another person while continuing to do other things. When experiencing this with an African American client, a culturally naive counselor might interpret it as disinterest or shyness.

The institution of slavery, as well as the racism experienced by Blacks since the abolishment of slavery, have influenced their expectations of and trust in human service agencies. African American clients tend to have lower expectations of, and less trust in, human services agencies, especially when encountering a Caucasian counselor (White, 1984). As a result, African American clients are more likely to drop out of counseling after the first interview (Sue & Sue, 1990). Reasons have been offered to explain this phenomenon. For example, Nickerson, Helms, and Terrell (1994) have found that some African Americans' mistrust of Caucasians can predict their negative attitudes about seeking counseling help and their low expectation of counseling outcomes. Also, many African Americans see counseling as an instrument of control and oppression because, oftentimes, the outcome of the process is the client's adoption of the counselor's value system (Smith, 1981). Finally, in the past, some African American clients were diagnosed as retarded or psychotic because of their different learning experiences and belief systems. As a result of this type of misdiagnosis, some African American clients are reluctant to take psychometric tests or share personal information with their counselors (White, 1984). Smith (1981) succinctly summed up the roots of mistrust that pose a frequent challenge to the cross-cultural counseling relationships as follows:

> It has become increasingly clear that the crises observed between Blacks and whites . . . in . . . American society are reenacted daily in the counseling interview. The forces that have historically estranged Blacks and whites; that is, the lack of trust, the prejudices surrounding cultural differences, the subtle and the not-so-subtle forms of

racial discrimination have infiltrated the counseling relationship. . . . In America, prejudice runs deep and dies hard. It is nurtured by generations of "hand-me-down" hatreds. (p. 141)

Guidelines for Rehabilitation Counselors Working with African American Clients

Given the centrality of the church in the lives of many African Americans, some authors (Alston, McCowan, & Turner, 1994; Lyles; 1992) have suggested that the client's minister can be of assistance in the rehabilitation counseling process by providing the counselor with relevant information on the client and by helping the client understand the nature of counseling services. Therefore, Lyles (1992) suggested that interaction between helping professionals and ministers be increased. Alston and Turner (1994) warned that rehabilitation counselors must avoid discouraging clients from using religious activities as a coping mechanism because such actions may be interpreted by African Americans as lack of counselor respect for their religion, a client perception that can undermine the development of rapport. On the other hand, the ability of a rehabilitation counselor to genuinely appreciate and accept the acquisition of assistance from a church or other religious organization by the African American client can increase his or her credibility in that client's eyes and thereby promote rapport development.

Due to the fact that most African Americans value the importance of family and community, rehabilitation counselors should encourage their African American clients to use supports available from family and community. Smith (1981) proposed a stress-resistant delivery (SRD) model for counseling African Americans, which encourages the use of those supports. The SRD model contains three steps: (a) identifying a stressor for the client, such as making a decision about the final goals to include in a vocational rehabilitation plan; (b) identifying sources of support within the African American culture, such as the extended family kinship system or a minister to help the client deal with the stressor (i.e., make the decision); and (c) deciding on a service delivery strategy (e.g., possibly a paraprofessional such as a job coach will be needed to assist the client in an on-the-job training placement). White (1984) reinforced Smith's approach by pointing out that collective survival and interdependence are a vital part of the African American experience and that the maintenance of support systems and interdependent relationships with others should be acknowledged rather than discouraged. Atkins (1988) and Feist-Price and Ford-Harris (1994) have maintained that African American clients tend to function best in the community. African Americans with disabilities usually value the input, opinion, and support of family members and significant others. Therefore, the process of rehabilitation counseling should involve members of the nuclear family, extended family, even the larger community. Turner and Alston (1994) suggested that rehabilitation counselors, with the client's permission, should interview nuclear and extended family members to ascertain how they can help meet the needs of the person with disability.

Many African Americans tend to place a greater reliance on the nonverbal part of communication. Nonverbal behaviors are seen as more accurately reflecting what Caucasians believe about African Americans than what they verbalize (Sue, 1990). When working with African American clients, rehabilitation counselors should be aware that not only what they say, but the way they say it, will have an important effect on their clients. For example, an African American client can quickly sense whether a rehabilitation counselor has racial prejudices by reading nonverbal cues as well as by listening to the words of the counselor. Therefore, rehabilitation counselors need to adequately deal with their own racial prejudices and attend to the impact of both their verbal and nonverbal communications.

Rehabilitation counselors should also be cautious in interpreting the nonverbal behaviors of their African American clients. For example, African Americans in the lower socioeconomic strata of society "do not nod their heads or make little noises to show that they are listening to a person in the manner which Whites do" (Smith, 1981, p. 155). In a rehabilitation counseling session, therefore, an African American client's failure to give the "uh-hum" sound should not be automatically interpreted as a lack of interest.

While many African Americans emphasize the nonverbal part of communication, it does not follow that they tend to be nonverbal and to have limited ability to express themselves verbally when compared to Caucasians (Smith, 1977). However, by embracing the myth that African Americans tend to be nonverbal in cross-cultural counseling situations, rehabilitation counselors can attribute blame for the lack of rapport and progress with their African American clients to lack of client verbal communication skills. While this may be somewhat comforting to many rehabilitation counselors, it is often inaccurate and fails to motivate counselors to upgrade their cross-cultural counseling competencies. The experience of Smith (1977), who had never met a "normal" African American who is nonverbal, tends to clearly undermine the myth. She stated,

> I have encountered those who have refused to talk and those who have communicated in a manner that some would consider inappropriate. I have also found that on their own grounds, clients whom some would label as nonverbal do in fact open up and become eloquent speakers—displaying an insight into life that some who consider themselves to be educated do not.
>
> Yet, there is a difference between labeling a client nonverbal and recognizing that the person refuses to talk for some reason or that the person does not communicate in the manner we expect and desire. (p. 393)

In order to build a trusting relationship and to work effectively with African American clients, rehabilitation counselors should understand that African Americans are living in the context of American society in which enculturated racism remains prevalent. Most African Americans have experienced racial discrimination. They can remember how unfairly their parents were treated and they can see their children's future being affected negatively by the same racial barriers. As a result, many

African American clients have some psychological reactions to the Caucasian majority culture; such reactions can include disappointment, distrust, depression, and rage (White, 1984).

Viewing society, not the individual, as the locus of the problem, several authors (e.g., G. Jackson, 1991; Smith, 1981) stress the need to avoid blaming the victims of institutionalized racism. Rehabilitation counselors should be especially cautious in this regard if they hold a traditional notion of responsibility, according to which an individual is free to make a choice and is responsible for any subsequent consequences. In reality, many African American clients have very limited power when it comes to making decisions about their lives. Cheatham (1990) and Sue (1990) suggested that by overemphasizing the responsibility of individuals for their situations or behaviors and by oversimplifying responsibilities of the social system, a counselor can create barriers to rapport building with African American clients. Therefore, rehabilitation counselors might alienate African American clients if they lose touch with the oppressive reality of racism and its effects.

Rehabilitation counselors should also help their African American clients better understand the rehabilitation process. Many African American clients either have had no previous experiences or have had negative experiences interacting with counseling professionals. Rehabilitation counselors should spend time with African American clients discussing the rehabilitation counseling process and the rights and responsibilities of both the client and the counselor.

Smith (1981) has pointed out that when race appears to be a factor in the cross-cultural counseling relationship, rather than be avoided, it should be dealt with forthrightly. The Caucasian rehabilitation counselor's ability to do so lets the African American client "know that . . . the counselor is aware of the difference in their ethnic backgrounds and . . . is not afraid or hesitant to talk about the client's feelings concerning race—even if such feelings are hostile" (Smith, 1981, p. 174).

To avoid misdiagnosing African American clients in the assessment process, rehabilitation counselors must take cultural influences into consideration. Many professional standards for conducting tests for minority populations have been published. *Multicultural Assessment Standards: A Compilation for Counselors* (Prediger, 1993), recommended by the Association for Assessment in Counseling in 1993, classified 34 published standards into four categories. The first category is named "Selection of Assessment Instruments: Content Considerations." It requires helping professionals, when selecting the types of tests, to consider their contents in relation to the cultural backgrounds of test takers, and to determine the performance limitations of test takers on these tests due to ethnic background. The second category addresses the issues in "Selection of Assessment Instruments: Norming, Reliability and Validity Considerations." For example, when selecting an assessment instrument, helping professionals should be certain that norm groups available for a standardized test are appropriate for interpreting the raw scores of test takers from a minority group. The third category focuses on issues associated with "Administration and Scoring of Assessment Instruments." For example, in the process of assessment, professionals are expected to "consider potential effects of examiner–examinee differences in ethnic and cultural background, attitudes, and values" (Blackwell, Martin, & Scalia, 1994, p. 435). "Use/Interpretation of Assessment Results" is the fourth category. Helping professionals should take into consideration any major relevant differences between the characteristics of those individuals who have been used to develop the norms for interpreting new test scores and the characteristics of the actual test takers as well as any differences in "familiarity with the specific questions on the test" (Blackwell et al., 1994, p. 436).

It was reported that, when taking intelligence or aptitude tests, African Americans usually score about 15 points lower than Anglo Americans (Baker & Taylor, 1995). Hinkle (1994) pointed out that the deviation is probably caused by the cultural bias in the testing instruments. Failure to take this factor into consideration in rehabilitation planning may lead to lack of optimal vocational placement for African American clients. As Baker and Taylor stated,

> The General Aptitude Test Battery (GATB) was used by the U.S. Employment Service (USES) in selecting persons for referral to job openings. As with other measures of ability, the GATB showed significant differences in mean scores across Blacks, Hispanics, and Whites (Hartigan & Wigdor, 1989). Since determination of appropriate jobs for individuals is figured on aptitude measures, a disproportionate number of Blacks and Hispanics were slotted for lower level, lower pay jobs. (p. 49)

In order to increase the effectiveness of the cross-cultural rehabilitation process, rehabilitation counselors should be familiar with various theoretical approaches, be aware of strengths and weaknesses of these theories, and selectively use components of these theories within certain cultural contexts. Some theories that work well with certain populations may be less than optimal for solving problems faced by African American clients.

African American clients usually respond better to a more active, intervention-oriented approach. Smith (1981) suggested that counselors help African Americans develop good survival behaviors, such as how to present themselves to majority individuals. Cheatham (1990) recognized the usefulness of the modeling technique associated with social learning theory and the importance of real life role modeling in the development process of African American clients. Being relatively realistic and objective, behavioral therapy has demonstrated some promising treatment outcomes with African American clients (Messer & Winokur, 1980). However, some authors (e.g., Calhoun & Wilson, 1974) have warned that professionals should be cautious using this approach if they are not familiar with the African American culture. Some authors (e.g., Todisco & Salomone, 1991) have indicated that a group approach will be more effective in counseling African American clients because the group approach "is more compatible with Afrocentric values than are other counseling strategies" (p. 153).

Rehabilitation counselors should be aware that the value systems of people are affected and shaped by general human conditions, cultural traditions, and individual experiences. Early formulations of fair treatment advocated a doctrine of color-blindness, which claimed that helping professionals should not consider skin color differences in their professional work (G. Jackson, 1991). However, it has been revealed that statements such as "We are all alike under our skins" or "I treat every one the same way—be they Black, blue or green" represent simplistic thinking and may lead to ineffective practice (Smith, 1981). Although people share certain common values due to some similarities among them such as similar genetic makeups, people from different ethnic groups are indeed different from one another in some significant ways (i.e., in beliefs and values as we have discussed).

Furthermore, since individual experiences vary across members of a certain ethnic group, the value systems of these individuals also differ to a considerable extent. Smith (1977) warned against the danger of stereotyping ethnic groups:

> Whenever any body of research focuses primarily upon one race of people, there is the potential danger of stereotyping. In an effort to sensitize others to the situations of members of a particular racial group, we sometimes ignore individual differences—defeating in part the very goals we set out to accomplish. (p. 390)

Therefore, rehabilitation counselors cannot automatically assume that all their African American clients share the same value system (Hays, 1996). Rehabilitation counselors should make efforts to be cognizant and respectful of the value system variability among their clients (Atkins, 1988). Freeman (1990) suggested that rehabilitation counselors ask their African American clients some subtle but non-judgmental questions to help understand their values and beliefs. For example, if a client tells the counselor that he goes to predominantly African American churches, that client is more likely to embrace the traditional values of the African American community than those who belong to predominantly Caucasian churches. Rehabilitation counselors can also attempt to understand the value system of their African American clients through direct observation (McRoy, 1990). For example, African American clients speaking Black English are more likely to reside in a predominantly African American community and to embrace the traditional values of that community than other English speakers. Having identified the value system of his or her client, a rehabilitation counselor can take its influence into consideration in the rehabilitation counseling service delivery process (Wilson & Stith, 1991).

Hispanic Americans

According to the 1990 U.S. census, the Hispanic population numbers 22.4 million persons, or 9% of the U.S. population. It is expected to become the largest ethnic minority group in the United States by 2020, numbering 47 million persons (or 15% of the population) (Altarriba & Santiago-Rivera, 1994; Dana, 1993). In selected parts of the country, such as Texas, California, Arizona, Florida, New York, and Illinois, Hispanics currently constitute up to 25% of the population (Marin, 1994). Compared to the general U.S. population, Hispanics tend to be "younger, poorer, less educated and more likely to live in the inner city" (Garzon & Tan, 1992, p. 378).

The term Hispanic is used in the United States to refer to a heterogeneous population of persons of Spanish descent. This population includes those individuals who migrated to this country from Mexico, Puerto Rico, Cuba, Central America, and South America (Dana, 1993; Wodarski, 1992). The great majority of the Hispanic American population is made up of Mexican Americans (about 9 million), Puerto Ricans (about 3 million), and Cubans (about 1 million) (James & Hastings, 1993). Because it covers a heterogeneous group of "persons from a variety of ethnic, racial, national, and cultural backgrounds, who differ markedly in education, income, and social class, as well as immigrants and 'Hispanos,' or 'Californios,' who trace their ancestry to Spanish colonists and Southwest Indians" (Dana, 1993, p. 66), the term 'Hispanic' can create an inaccurate expectation in non-Hispanic individuals regarding the attitudes, values, or behaviors of a particular Hispanic individual. As Wodarski (1992a) cautioned, one should not automatically generalize the cultural characteristics of any of its subgroups to any other of its subgroups:

> Puerto Ricans, Chicanos, Peruvians, Guatemalans and all other Latin cultures have distinctive backgrounds. An Argentinean is as different from a Puerto Rican as an English person is from a Jamaican. The first two speak Spanish; the second pair use English as a native tongue; but all of them have a separate historical tradition. (p. 71)

However, Dana (1993) pointed out that, in spite of the heterogeneity noted above,

> there is a consistency in the cultures of these Hispanic populations that includes their identities, values, beliefs, perceptions, and language. . . . All of them originally came from Spanish-speaking nations, and about 85 percent are nominally Roman Catholic. . . . that approximately 90 percent of them continue to speak Spanish with some degree of fluency, in spite of a national opposition to bilingualism that has been crystallized in an English-only movement. (pp. 66–67)

Still, given the number of subcultures covered by the term 'Hispanic,' any generalizations suggested in the discussion of salient characteristics below should be seen as tentative hypotheses for any one Hispanic client, to be refuted or confirmed by the rehabilitation counselor's experiences with that individual. Properly used, the information on salient characteristics can help orient the rehabilitation counselor to culturally related issues that may affect the efficacy of the rehabilitation counseling process with Hispanic clients (Garzon & Tan, 1992).

Salient Characteristics

Hispanic people tend to manifest a strong loyalty to and solidarity with family members (Locke, 1992; Marin, 1994; Wodarski, 1992a). The Hispanic family is a kinship group including those in the nuclear family, grandparents, aunts and uncles, cousins, and some surrogate relatives, such as close friends of the family who tend to participate in important family activities and decisions (Dana, 1993; Wodarski, 1992). Constituting an informal network of persons who feel a level of mutual trust that allows them to become personally involved in each other's lives, the extended family is a source of emotional and material support (Dana, 1993; Marin, 1994). When a crisis arises in the nuclear family, it is frequently mediated by the extended family network (Garzon & Tan, 1992). For Hispanic Americans, self-interest often takes second place to the interests of the family (Dana, 1993; Locke, 1992). Wodarski (1992a) described these strong family ties in the Hispanic community by contrasting Anglo American and Hispanic family values as follows:

> . . . in the mainstream culture, a young adult displays his maturity and responsibility by physically separating from the family and establishing an independent living situation. In the Hispanic community, such behavior would be viewed as a selfish disregard of familial responsibility. Instead, maturity and responsibility would be demonstrated by the young adult remaining at home and contributing to the support of the family. (p. 92)

The Hispanic family tends to be patriarchal with the mother showing deference to the father as the autocratic head of the household (Locke, 1992; Wodarski, 1992a). The father's roles include providing economic support and disciplining the children. The father has little involvement in the daily care of the children (Garzon & Tan, 1992). The mother's role is to take care of the home and children as well as to "serve the needs of her husband" and "support his actions and decisions" (Locke, 1992, p. 139).

In Hispanic families, members with a disability tend to be responded to in an overprotective and paternalistic manner. This is especially the case for those with congenital disabilities. Mexican Americans view hardships and suffering as a normal part of life or as a punishment sent from a higher being or God that should be endured with courage and dignity. In the case of hardships resulting from disability, individuals and their families may adopt a fatalistic attitude of resignation and acceptance by the individual and his or her family and a belief that the situation cannot be changed (Smart & Smart, 1991).

The Hispanic family is not a static entity. The extent of the subordination of the Hispanic individual to the preferences of his or her family is somewhat dependent on the level of his or her acculturation to Anglo society. The more highly acculturated Hispanics are, the more likely they are to be egocentrically oriented in their decisions and actions (Dana, 1993). Influences such as one's generation of being an American (first, second, third, etc.); upward socioeconomic mobility; level of acculturation; and intermarriage can create variations in family structures and values that make it difficult to determine what a typical Hispanic family is like. Still, even when heavily exposed to these influences, Hispanics value family centeredness and loyalty, commitments which by and large appear to be immune to the effects of acculturation and assimilation (Zuniga, 1992).

Another defining characteristic of Hispanics is their strong need for harmony and conflict avoidance in interpersonal relations. Consistent with this characteristic is the tendency of Hispanics to place greater importance on smooth interpersonal relationships than on task achievements (Marin, 1994; Wodarski, 1992a). For example, Locke (1992) has pointed out that Mexican Americans consider directly arguing with or contradicting another person to be rude and disrespectful. Unless they know the person well and have the time to express their disagreement tactfully, Mexican Americans will not typically reveal genuinely felt disagreement. This appearance of agreement in order to be courteous "often causes misunderstandings between Anglos and Mexican Americans" (Locke, 1992, pp. 140–141). It is also suggested that in order to show respect, Hispanics may be less self-assertive in communicating with someone who is regarded as having authority. Therefore, the rehabilitation counselor may find the Hispanic client to be quiet, compliant, and lacking eye contact in the counseling session (Baruth & Manning, 1992; Casas & Vasquez, 1989).

In interacting with others, Hispanics often maintain little physical distance (Baruth & Manning, 1992) and manifest acceptance and affection frequently via touching. Grossman (1995) points out that it is not unusual for Hispanics "to hold others by the arm or place their hands on their shoulders when conversing" (p. 120). It is also not unusual for Hispanics to kiss their friends when they meet. "Males are likely to hug each other or pat each other on the back as well as shake hands" when they meet (Grossman, 1995, p. 120).

Religion plays a prominent role in the Hispanic culture, with most Hispanics adhering to Catholicism (Ruiz & Padilla, 1977; Zuniga, 1992). Hispanics tend to see God's role in their lives as being major, to the point of accepting "the hardships of life as the will of God" (Wodarski, 1992a, p. 74). Therefore, it is not unusual for Hispanics who are Catholic to initially place more faith in the power of traditional Catholic rituals (such as praying "to Saint Jude to do the impossible") than in human service professionals for changing an undesirable situation (Wodarski, 1992a, p. 75). Zuniga provides the following examples of the prominent place that religious beliefs and rituals have in the lives of Mexican Americans who are Catholic:

> It is not uncommon for a parent to implore the Virgin Mary to intercede for him or her to cure a child of a disease or disability. The use of *mandas* (a promise or offering in return for God's intervention) is another aspect of this intercession. For instance, a parent commits to carry out a tradition or ritual in return for the intercession of a saint or the Virgin Mary. . . . Sometimes parents feel that the disability is the cross that has been sent to them as part of God's will and thus must be borne as part of the pain of the human condition. Others will respond with less acceptance, may feel they are being treated unjustly, or feel that they are being punished for a previous wrongdoing. (p. 155)

In the Hispanic culture, religion plays a definite role in how a disability is perceived, especially in regard to causation and motivation for rehabilitation. Disability may be viewed as punishment by God for sin. It is not unusual for the sin to be attributed to "the parents of the individual with a disability" (Smart & Smart, 1991,

p. 361). This interpretation of disability can inhibit interest in rehabilitation since any "conscious attempts to change the course of life events . . . may be interpreted as thwarting God's will or, in the extreme, playing the role of God" (Smart & Smart, p. 361).

In the Hispanic culture, folk healers such as curandero, herbalist, santiquador, spiritist, and santero are seen as significant sources of help in overcoming illness and disability. They "use unique culture-specific methods to diagnose and treat ailments" (Wodarski, 1992a, p. 97). Taking a person with a disability to a folk healer for a second opinion would not be unusual in the Hispanic community (Zuniga, 1992). To some extent, the practices of folk healers are directed at acquiring the assistance of God in ameliorating an illness or disability. One can acquire a "flavor" of the theory and practice of folk healers found in the Hispanic culture from the following descriptions of the santiquador and the curandero provided by Wodarski (1992a):

> Santiquadores specialize in treating chronic and intestinal diseases, as well as in setting dislocated bones and curing various forms of muscle and body aches. The beliefs of the santiquadores have a naturalistic foundation, although they also consider the possibility that supernatural forces may be involved in the individual's problems. A cure must enlist the will of God. Santiquadores use various methods of treatment. These may include the laying on of hands, as well as massages, herbs, prayers, changes in daily routine, and various dietary recommendations.
>
> Curanderismo is based on the premise that illness and bad luck are brought about by weakening ties with the Roman Catholic church, the family, and culture. The theme of Christ permeates much of the curandero's thinking about illness and misfortune. Curanderos see their work as harmonious with orthodox religion and do not view themselves as being in conflict with Catholicism. . . . Culturally, symbolic techniques are used by curanderos to return individuals to harmony with culture and with God. (p. 98)

Hispanics with less education tend to be present rather than future oriented. Rather than wanting to focus on abstract future problems, they are more interested in addressing current problems in a concrete manner (Casas & Vasquez, 1989). Hence, their more immediate time orientation and concrete outlook may result in an underuse of human services. While Hispanics use human services, they do not use them with the frequency that Anglo Americans do, and they tend to drop out of the service process earlier than Anglo Americans (Flaskerund, 1986; Lopez, 1981).

Efforts have been made to identify factors that account for the underuse of human services by Hispanics. One reason involves misdiagnoses in the evaluation process. Due to cultural bias in assessment instruments, Hispanics, like other minorities, are sometimes misdiagnosed as having intellectual and psychological problems. Such misdiagnosis has tended to create the impression of severe cognitive disabilities among Hispanics (Cheung & Snowden, 1990). Some customary behaviors and feelings among Hispanics might be seen as indicative of pathology on the *Minnesota Multiphasic Personality Inventory* (Malgady & Rogler, 1987). As a result of this kind of misdiagnosis, some Hispanics are reluctant to contact professionals.

Guidelines for Rehabilitation Counselors Working with Hispanic Clients

When working with Hispanic clients and their families, it is important for the rehabilitation counselor to initially use a very interpersonal, rather than task-oriented, style (Zuniga, 1992). Zuniga has described this initial interaction as involving "friendly, informal, and leisurely chatting that establishes the . . . atmosphere in which the work will take place" (p. 164). The importance of the rehabilitation counselor being personable with Hispanic clients and their families cannot be overstressed. In this regard, Locke (1992) has recommended that the counselor use first names when addressing Mexican American clients and also introduce him- or herself by first name. Ruiz and Padilla (1977) have reinforced this point by indicating that a counselor who is sensitive to Hispanic culture, will immediately introduce him- or herself to a new Hispanic client by extending his or her hand and using his or her first name rather than a formal title. The counselor also should be tactful in handling the physical proximity during contact with his or her Hispanic client. An apparent backing away from the client may be interpreted as rejection, indifference, and dislike (Sue, 1990). In some situations, it may be necessary to allow the client to determine the physical distance for conversing to facilitate his or her comfort in the counseling interaction (Grossman, 1995). However, rehabilitation counselors must be aware that being too personal without sensitivity may cause the Hispanic client to feel disrespected. For example, some clients may regard it as impolite when the counselor uses the informal Spanish word *tu* rather than *usted* to address the client as "you." Therefore, the rehabilitation counselor must be alert to the feelings of every individual Hispanic client. As one non-Hispanic counselor suggested, "When counseling the Hispanics I have learned to let them lead. If they tu me, I tu them. Until they do I use the usted form and maintain as formal a relationship with them as they do with me" (Grossman, p. 1995, 152).

When working with Hispanic clients, the rehabilitation counselor must understand and not underestimate the significance of involving the family in the rehabilitation counseling process. Acknowledging that including family members in the rehabilitation counseling process may be cumbersome, Smart and Smart (1991) advocate that families be involved since their roles as family members can be affected by the presence of a family member with a disability and by the outcome of the rehabilitation service process. According to Smart and Smart, involving family members:

> may mean increased home visits to become more acquainted with families in . . . home settings. Understanding of well-defined gender roles may also be best accomplished by working with the entire family because these roles are most clearly expressed in the family setting. When disability forces a modification of such traditional gender roles, a healthy adaptation may be best accomplished when the family understands and is supportive of such changes. (pp. 363–364)

Rehabilitation counselors, therefore, should be aware that more time for counseling sessions may be needed for the Hispanic client (Grossman, 1995). In addition, since

Hispanics are often present-time oriented, families may perceive rehabilitation goals that are short term as being more desirable, and therefore be more willing to promote the accomplishment of these goals (Locke, 1992).

Given the prominent role that religion plays in Hispanic culture, at times rehabilitation counselors may find it useful to refer Hispanic clients for pastoral counseling services. James and Hastings (1993) provided an excellent example of a timely referral of a Hispanic client to a priest for pastoral counseling:

> A 35-year old Mexican American man was complaining of extreme anxiety attacks because his impending marriage would reduce the amount of money he could send to his parents in Mexico. He felt that this would be a sin and sought counseling to deal with his anxiety and feelings of guilt, remorse, and shame. The counselor who was aware of the influence of religious and cultural factors, suggested that he talk with his priest about these feelings. Over time, his priest convinced him that it would not be a sin to reduce the amount of money he sent to his parents and to discuss the matter with his parents. He was ultimately convinced that he was not an ungrateful son, could continue his marriage plans, and continue sending a reduced amount of money to his parents. With this information and support from his priest, he was able to deal with his feelings of anxiety. (p. 330)

Rehabilitation counselors should avoid being outwardly critical of a Hispanic client's positive impressions of folk healers. However, when the person with a disability is involved with folk healers, the rehabilitation counselor should attempt to solicit information from the individual with a disability regarding the practices of the individual to determine if medications or interventions that are contraindicated by the client's condition are being used. Such inquiry should be posed in a positive manner to avoid putting the client or his or her family on the defensive (Zuniga, 1992).

When working with some Hispanic clients, rehabilitation counselors must be prepared to deal with language barriers. It is often important for rehabilitation counselors to obtain an accurate assessment of the English language proficiency of their Hispanic clients. Altarriba and Santiago-Rivera (1994) suggested that

> language proficiency and fluency be measured through the use of writing, reading, and oral tests. Both conversational and listening skills should be assessed given that in a typical counseling setting, most of the interaction is verbal. Proficiency tests can be acquired at institutions that provide programs in English as a Second Language (ESL) and intensive English programs for newly arrived immigrants. (p. 393)

The following checklist is useful for the rehabilitation counselor to identify the possible language problems or bias of his or her Hispanic clients (adapted from Murdick, Gartin, & Arnold, 1994): (a) Is English the primary language spoken in the home? (p. 86), (b) Is the client more proficient in another language? (p. 86), and (c) Is the client unable to communicate in the language spoken by the counselor? If "yes" is the answer to any of the above questions, then the rehabilitation counseling session may need to be conducted in the client's primary language.

Rehabilitation counselors should realize that the current situation and needs of Hispanic clients who speak English, but whose dominant language is Spanish, could be misunderstood by the counselor. Misunderstanding can occur if the client becomes more concerned about his or her correct pronunciation of words and phrases than with accurately describing his or her problems and needs (Altarriba & Santiago-Rivera, 1994). It has also been contended that when some Spanish dominant clients speak in English about emotionally charged experiences they may "not necessarily display the corresponding emotion. This lack of emotional expression makes sense given that emotions are tied to the first language learned as a child" (Altarriba & Santiago-Rivera, 1994, p. 389). However, it can lead to the misdiagnosis of client psychological problems. For example, in one study, Hispanic clients were interviewed in English and in Spanish. When interviewed in English they "often spoke slowly and paused frequently, exhibiting characteristics attributed to depressed moods or denoting a defensive reluctance to communicate" (Altarriba & Santiago-Rivera). It was hypothesized that the style of communication in their nondominant language could have resulted in their counselor rating them higher on dimensions of psychopathology such as depressed mood, anxiety, and emotional withdrawal than when they were interviewed in Spanish (Altarriba & Santiago-Rivera, 1994).

A number of methods can be used by human service providers to help overcome language barriers to effective communication when their Hispanic clients have limited facility with English. Paraprofessionals from the same neighborhood as the client can be "trained in the nomenclature and key concepts" of the rehabilitation counseling process and used as translators by the non-Spanish speaking rehabilitation counselor (Garzon & Tan, 1992). Of course, problems can occur with the use of translators. For example, misperceptions of the client's problems can result if the translator attempts to interpret, rather than literally translate, the client's verbal responses. Garzon and Tan (1992) pointed out that in the case of clients with psychiatric disabilities, "if the interpreter is a family member, he or she may deliberately attempt to minimize the psychopathology present in the client" (p. 380). Altarriba and Santiago-Rivera (1994) stressed that when "relatives are used, they often answer questions for the client rather than communicate the necessary questions to them" (p. 390).

For rehabilitation planning purposes, it is important to have a clear picture of the Hispanic client's acculturation level in regard to language preference, as well as adherence to "traditional cultural values, customs and beliefs" (Altarriba & Santiago-Rivera, 1994, p. 394). Such diagnostic information is highly relevant for determining the probability of client adjustment and success in specific vocational training situations and job placements. Knowing the acculturation level of the Hispanic client is also important in motivating the client to actively participate in testing for rehabilitation planning. According to Smart and Smart (1993), many Hispanics do not come from a culture that is pervaded by test taking and in which its members realize the potential impact of the results of standardized tests on their lives. As a result, they may not be sufficiently attentive during testing. In order to have valid assessment results for rehabilitation planning, the rehabilitation counselor should motivate the less acculturated Hispanic client to cooperate and actively participate in the evaluation. Of course, it would be naive to assume that lower levels of acculturation always decrease the probability of achieving successful vocational rehabilitation. For example, certain jobs in which repair services are provided primarily to Hispanic consumers might be more effectively filled with less acculturated Hispanic rehabilitants.

When working with Hispanics, rehabilitation counselors must make efforts to facilitate the active participation of their clients in the assessment process. For example, to reduce assessment errors, counselors should encourage Hispanic clients to define their problems in their own words (Sue & Sue, 1990). Then counselors can attempt to rephrase the client's description of his or her problem for purposes of verification. Counselors also should encourage Hispanic clients to express any of their concerns about the assessment process (Grossman, 1995). Such counselor actions should both increase client involvement in the assessment process and increase diagnostic accuracy. When such is the case, Hispanic clients are more likely to accept and use human services.

Asian Americans

Of people living in the United States whose origins are in Asia, many have ancestors who were the first to migrate from China, settling in California in the 1820s. The number of Asian Americans remained small until the late 1840s, when many Chinese came to Hawaii and the continental United States as fortune-seekers and cheap laborers (Kim, 1994). They were employed in the gold mines on the West Coast, as well as on Hawaiian sugar plantations and western railroads. However, their willingness to work for low wages and thereby undercut the wages of European American workers stimulated the emergence of an anti-Chinese movement (Fong, 1992). That movement lead to the Chinese Exclusion Act of 1882, which suspended the immigration of Chinese laborers (Kitano & Daniels, 1995). After 1882, a sizable number of Japanese and some Koreans came to the United States to fill jobs previously held by Chinese immigrants (Fong, 1992; Kitano & Daniels, 1995). These new immigrants also became a target for the hostility of organized European American workers. The continuing negative attitudes toward Asian laborers led to Congress passing the Immigration Act of 1924, which terminated all Asian immigration to the United States (Toupin, 1980).

Filipinos were the only Asian American ethnic group exempted by Congress from the exclusion provisions of the Immigration Act of 1924 (Fong, 1992). Until the Philippines was granted independence in 1934 by the United States, Filipinos were regarded as legal American nationals (Kitano & Daniels, 1995).

The Chinese Exclusion Act of 1882 was repealed by Congress in 1943 in response to the wartime alliance between the United States and China. As a result, the

U.S. government established an annual quota of 105 Chinese immigrants (Kim, 1994). The McCarran-Walter Act of 1952 removed all absolute exclusions of racial and ethnic groups in U.S. immigration policy. However, the law granted only small quotas to Asian immigrants (Fong, 1992). Large numbers of Asian immigrants were not permitted to enter the United States until the Immigration Act of 1965 abolished the restrictive Asian quotas allowing 170,000 immigrants from the Eastern Hemisphere annually (Fong, 1992; Kitano & Daniels, 1995). As a result of the Immigration Act of 1965, the Asian American population expanded to nearly 3.5 million by 1980 (U.S. Bureau of the Census, 1988). Between 1980 and 1990, the total number of Asian Americans doubled, reaching almost 7 million in 1990 (U.S. Bureau of the Census, 1993).

There are currently 28 nationalities represented in the Asian American community, in which Chinese (1,648,696), Filipinos (1,419,711), Japanese (866,160), Korean (797,304), Asian Indian (786,694), and Vietnamese (593,213) constitute the largest subgroups (U.S. Bureau of the Census, 1988, 1993). Based on the 1990 U.S. Census (Kitano & Daniels, 1995), the states with the largest number of Asian Americans are California (2,735,060), New York (689,303), Hawaii (522,967), Texas (311,918), Illinois (282,569), New Jersey (270,839), and Washington (195,918). It is estimated that the size of the Asian American population will reach 16.5 million in 2010 and 38.8 million in 2050. Therefore, by 2050, 1 in 10 Americans will be an Asian American (Pollard, 1993).

In the next section, cultural factors to consider when working with Asian Americans are addressed. However, due to the differences among Asian American cultures, the discussion will mainly refer to Asian Americans who originate from countries influenced by traditional Chinese values that reflect a mixture of the teachings of Confucianism, Buddhism, and Taoism. Originating in ancient China, traditional Chinese values later spread to countries such as Japan, Korea, Vietnam, Laos, Cambodia, and Singapore through educational, economic, and political influences (Lassiter, 1995; Li, 1965).

Salient Characteristics

Traditional Chinese values emphasize harmonious relationships with nature, society, and family. Having harmony with nature means having balance between the yin and yang, two opposing aspects in nature. Sickness will occur if the yin and yang are imbalanced in the human body (Lassiter, 1995). To have harmony with society and family, individuals must fulfill their roles in the social structure. These roles are mainly defined by the five Cardinal Relations of Confucianism, which are the relations "between superior and subordinate, between parent and child, between husband and wife, between brothers, and between friends" (Chung, 1992, p. 30). For example, in terms of the power hierarchy within a marriage, the husband has absolute authority over his wife while she is expected to serve her husband and take care of children and household matters (Chan, 1992).

Confucianism teaches people how to interact and maintain harmony within their natural, social, and familial environments. Some examples of these virtues are sacrificing self for the group, protecting family members, submitting to parents and authority, cooperating with the group, being shameful about making mistakes, valuing interdependence among family members, fulfilling obligations to family, reciprocating kindness of others, being in control of one's emotions and impulses, and avoiding arguments (Chan, Lam, Wong, Leung, & Fang, 1988; Chung, 1992; Marsella, 1993; Uba, 1994). Similarly, filial piety is a very significant value in the Asian American culture. Traditional parent–child relationships among Asian Americans require the unquestioning loyalty and devotion "of children to their parents with the parents' . . . role being to define the law and the child's role . . . to obey it" (Wodarski, 1992b, p. 49).

Achievement is highly valued by Asian Americans in part because it elevates "the status of the person and the family and partially fulfills obligations to the family. By the same token, failure by an individual is believed to shame the entire family" (Uba, 1994, p. 18). Traditionally, Asian American values also include respect for people of status and for academic and occupational achievements.

In order to uphold the family's reputation, Asian Americans tend to be secretive about family and private problems and are unwilling to discuss personal matters with outsiders. In fact, a proverb among Asian cultures is *Don't let others know your family's shame* (Oka, 1994; Sue & Sue, 1995; Wong & Chang, 1994).

The socialization process in Asian culture somewhat inhibits the development of verbal expression. For instance, European Americans regard verbal self-expression as important, whereas the Japanese prefer quieter modes such as comprehension and insight. In addition, the Japanese consider proficiency in listening, reading, and writing as being more important than oratory competence (Oka, 1994).

Only a few studies have explored the attitudes of Asian Americans toward disability, and most of these studies involved the Chinese population (e.g., Chan, Hedl, et al., 1988; Chan, Hua, Ju, & Lam, 1984; Jacques, Burleigh, & Lee, 1973; Shokoohi-Yekta & Retish, 1991). Using an adaptation of the *Attitudes Toward Disabled Persons Scale*, Chan, Hedl, et al. (1988) studied the attitudes of 338 Chinese students toward people in three major disability groups (physical, emotional, or intellectual disabilities). The Chinese students expressed similar attitudes toward persons who were mentally retarded and those who were emotionally disturbed, which were less positive than those they expressed toward people with physical disabilities.

Shokoohi-Yekta and Retish (1991) compared attitudes of Americans and Chinese toward mental illness. Eighty-three male college students (41 Americans and 42 Chinese) completed the *Opinion About Mental Illness Scale*. Compared to the Americans, the Chinese were more authoritarian, more socially restrictive, and less benevolent toward people with mental illness. Chinese students were more likely to view persons with mental illness as an inferior class and as a threat to society requiring coercive handling, restrictions in their functioning, and authoritarian treatment. Chinese students who had a longer period of residence in the United States expressed less authoritative and socially restrictive attitudes toward people with mental illness than did those who had a shorter period of residence.

The results of these studies generally suggest that the attitude of Asian Americans toward persons with disabilities is more negative than the attitude of Americans, particularly toward people who suffer from mental disability. However, these differences tend to decrease as Asian Americans become more acculturated. Acculturation refers to the "degree to which Asian Americans are identified with and integrated into the white majority culture" (Leong, 1986). Studies have found differences in the degree of acculturation between earlier and later generations of Asian Americans, with more internalization of American culture among later Asian American generations (Leong, 1986).

Recent research has revealed the multitude of social problems and inferior economic situations of Asian Americans. Many Asian Americans are experiencing poverty, unemployment, educational deficiencies, physical illness, and mental health problems such as alcoholism, drug abuse, depression, and schizophrenia (Kim, 1995; Nishio & Bilmes, 1987). Given the presence of these problems and the expanding Asian American population, rehabilitation counselors will increasingly encounter rehabilitation service consumers who are Asian American.

The urgent and growing need for rehabilitation services among Asian Americans becomes more evident given the more than 700,000 refugees who have been admitted to the United States from such Southeast Asian countries as Vietnam, Laos, and Cambodia since 1975 (Kitano & Daniels, 1995; U.S. Bureau of the Census, 1993). Studies of these new immigrants revealed a higher rate of psychiatric symptomatology and distress, and more emotional, psychological, and physical complaints than the general population (Cheung, 1995; Pernice & Brook, 1994; Sue & Sue, 1987).

While the needs of Asian Americans for physical and mental health rehabilitation services have been growing, such services have been underused by them (Cheung & Snowden, 1990; Loo, Tong, & True, 1989; Uba, 1992; Uba & Sue, 1991). For example, it was reported that only 10% of Vietnamese refugees in Denver used medical services when ill (Uba, 1992). Loo et al. (1989) interviewed 108 Chinese American adults living in San Francisco's Chinatown regarding their use of mental health services. Only 5% of the subjects sought such services, a proportion equivalent to Americans overall who sought mental health services before the 1960s.

Research has also indicated that when Asian Americans use health care services, they usually terminate treatment prematurely. For example, among the group of Vietnamese refugees in Denver who sought health care services, 73% dropped out before their follow-up session (Uba, 1992). In a large-scale study conducted by Sue and McKinney (1975), out of 13,198 patients served by 17 community mental health centers in the greater Seattle area, the researchers found that 30% of White Americans did not return for treatment after the initial session, whereas 52% of Asian Americans dropped out.

Reviewing statistics on ethnic minority use of mental health services reported in the *Inventory of Mental Health Organizations* for 1983, Cheung and Snowden (1990) found that, when compared to that of other ethnic groups, the rate of use for all mental health services among Asian Americans and Pacific Islanders was the lowest in relation to their proportions in the general population. These mental health services included inpatient care, residential treatment, residential support, outpatient care, and partial care. The low Asian American use rates for mental health services support "the premise that cross-cultural counseling has failed to meet the needs of this client population" (Wodarski, 1992b, p. 56).

Several cultural factors explain Asian Americans' underuse of health care services. One such factor is the incompatibility between the Western world view of mental health services and the values, needs, and expectations of Asian American clients (Uba & Sue, 1991, pp. 6–8). For example, the view of Asian Americans toward life—in particular, the necessity of suffering in life—contributes to their hesitation to seek health services. As such, they tend to endure difficulties and suffering by themselves (Marsella, 1993; Uba, 1992; Wong & Chan, 1994). Rather than seeking help from outside systems, their immediate response tends to be turning to family members and friends for help unless the problem is too severe. Even for extremely severe cases, it was reported that in Hong Kong, nearly 20% sought help only after a year or more had elapsed from the discovery of the problem (Sue & Sue, 1987).

Stigma and shame associated with disabilities exist for both the Asian American with a disability and the family. Asian Americans who suffer from disabilities, especially mental illness, often feel shame about their condition because of the myths associated with illness in the Asian culture. The perceived causes of disability are punishment for the sins of the individual or his or her ancestors, demon possession, or the imbalance of yin and yang that results from the irresponsible care of one's health (Lassiter, 1995; Wong & Chan, 1994). Social stigma causes the person with disability and his or her family members to view the disability as a failure for both the individual and the family (Morrow, 1987; Wong & Chan, 1994). In fact, the stigma can be perceived as being so strong that the disability is kept secret even to the third and fourth generations of Asian Americans (Sue & Sue, 1987). Therefore, many Asian Americans may be concerned about seeking social services for fear of bringing disgrace to their family (Liem, 1993; Uba & Sue, 1991).

The provision of rehabilitation services to Asian Americans is not only impeded by the attitudes of Asian Americans toward suffering and the stigma and shame associated with disabilities, but also by language barriers and lack of knowledge about available services. Smith and Ryan (1987) interviewed 59 Chinese parents of children with developmental disabilities to investigate how language differences and cultural perspectives affected their understanding of the developmental disability and use of rehabilitation services. Results indicated that language and cultural barriers interfered with both the parents and the children with disabilities receiving appropriate information about the disability and rehabilitation services. Sixty percent of the parents said the professionals involved in the diagnosis could not speak Chinese. The parents simply could not communicate with the professionals. The language and communication problems experienced by these families were compounded by their lack of understanding of systems in the United States, especially the medical and educational systems. For example, a mother experienced trouble with school authorities because she was unaware that education was mandatory for children. The language and cultural barriers not only restricted the parents' access to programs, but also discouraged them from pursuing services.

Language barriers in service delivery can reduce the likelihood that some Asian Americans with disabilities will acquire needed rehabilitation services. Difficulties with English could impede their acquiring knowledge of available rehabilitation services, their ability to complete forms, and their ability to interact with counselors (Uba & Sue, 1991). The need for an interpreter to facilitate communication between the rehabilitation counselor and the Asian American client can sometimes discourage Asian Americans from continuing to seek services. Uba and Sue speak to this point as follows:

> . . . when non-English-speaking client's seek services, they are often told to come back at another time with a neighbor or a child who can translate. . . . This acts as a deterrent to the delivery of services since the clients are often reluctant to disclose private information in front of their neighbors or children. The non-English-speaking client is, in effect, denied confidentiality and is embarrassed. (p. 11)

In addition, Asian Americans often lack knowledge about available services. Chan, Lam, et al. (1988) mentioned that although Chinese Americans can effectively use their network of family members and friends, they can be easily intimidated by bureaucracy. As a consequence, they tend to be less effective in using social service networks such as vocational rehabilitation services for which they may be feasible candidates. As a result, the help perceived as available by many Chinese Americans with disabilities is often limited to that which is available from extended family members.

Guidelines for Rehabilitation Counselors Working with Asian Americans

Since not all rehabilitation needs of Asian Americans can be exclusively addressed by Asian rehabilitation practitioners, non-Asian rehabilitation professionals are needed to work with this population, particularly in major metropolitan areas such as Los Angeles, New York City, San Francisco, Houston, and Seattle (Leung & Sakata, 1988; Nishio & Bilmes, 1987). These individuals must be culturally sensitive if they are to provide effective rehabilitation services to Asian Americans.

Because of the fear and confusion in many Asian Americans associated with accepting outside help, rehabilitation counselors should positively reinforce those with a disability and their family members for seeking services, as well as emphasize the positive benefits of receiving rehabilitation services. In addition, the rehabilitation counselor should assure the individual with a disability and the family of his or her concern and desire to help. In the Asian culture, concrete actions such as providing help in translating documents or facilitating placement in vocational training programs provide greater assurance than mere words (Huang, 1991). Rehabilitation counselors also need to respect the intense need of Asian Americans for confidentiality without feeling that they are being distrusted (Liem, 1993).

Rehabilitation counselors must be sensitive to the stigma-related psychological and social pressures Asian Americans with disabilities, especially those with mental and emotional disorders, experience. Due to the sensitivity of Asian Americans to the concept of mental health, it is important for rehabilitation counselors to be cautious in referring the client for psychological evaluation. Many Asian Americans have had no previous contact with mental health service providers, especially with psychologists. Therefore, they may not understand the need to see a psychologist. Detailed explanation must be offered to avoid stimulating any uncomfortable feelings of shame or stigma in the client that may lead to premature termination of rehabilitation services.

Problems in using standardized psychological measures with Asian Americans should also be considered. For example, because of cultural and language bias, positive virtues of Asian Americans such as modesty and filial piety are usually reflected and interpreted as negative traits in personality inventories (Chan, Lam, et al., 1988; Leong, 1986; Sue & Sue, 1987).

In the rehabilitation counseling process, the counselor should be cautious in interpreting the inhibited verbal and nonverbal communication of Asian Americans. Based on Western standards that stress open-mindedness, psychological mindedness, and assertiveness, their inhibition may be easily and wrongly interpreted as lack of cooperation. For example, when working with Asian American clients, the rehabilitation counselor should not automatically interpret infrequent client verbal initiatives during the interview as lack of interest in or resistance to rehabilitation services. Quite possibly, the client expects the rehabilitation counselor to take an active information-providing role. Being quiet is a way to show respect for the counselor (Uba & Sue, 1991). In addition, many Asian Americans consider eye contact as rude, especially with people of higher social status such as the counselor. Therefore, lack of eye contact may not indicate insecurity and untrustworthiness (Chung, 1992; Marsella, 1993).

The counselor also needs to be sensitive to the tendency of Asian Americans to attribute mental problems to somatic causes due to the stigma and shame they associate with mental illness (Nishio & Bilmes, 1987; Sue & Sue, 1995). Rather than immediately and directly discrediting their etiology of illness, the counselor should maximize the function of medical evaluation in the process of rehabilitation counseling. During this phase of evaluation, counselors can work with physicians to help clients distinguish between organic and nonorganic causes of their problems and understand how treatment solutions relate to each cause. This can minimize the possibility of premature termination by the client (Sue & Sue, 1995).

In a review of the literature on the counseling expectations of Asian Americans, Leong (1986) found that Asian Americans usually believe that counseling should be direct, paternal, authoritative, and basically an advice-and-information-giving process by an experienced person. They also expect counselors to be considerate, sensitive, supportive, and less demanding of them in regard to responsibility, openness, and motivation. Since the Asian American client typically expects the counselor to be an authority figure capable of "fixing" his or her problem (Wodarski, 1992b), it is recommended that the counselor provide much information about the rehabilitation service delivery system, process, and goals in the initial interview. Due to the lack of knowledge and misunderstandings of some Asian Americans about disabilities and rehabilitation services, special care must be exercised in the initial session to explain available services and clarify any misconceptions or incorrect expectations (Ryan & Smith, 1989). Because Asian Americans tend to expect concrete direction, the rehabilitation counselor should provide specific details on the structure and process of rehabilitation services.

Rehabilitation counselors should avoid excessive use of direct questions about their clients and family during the initial interview. To make this possible, the rehabilitation counselor should attempt to acquire much relevant information about the Asian American client and the client's family prior to the initial interview (Wodarski, 1992b).

Since Asian Americans expect a counselor to be an expert, the counselor should clearly explain his or her professional position and credentials. For example, professional diplomas, awards, and accreditation should be displayed in the office (Fugita, Ito, Abe, & Takeuchi, 1991; Huang, 1991).

The counselor must be cautious about opposite gender counselor relationships. For example, because of the power hierarchy within an Asian American marriage, the male client may have difficulty accepting a directive or authoritative approach by a female counselor. Therefore, "gender matching" of counselor and client may be necessary for the Asian American male who is greatly influenced by traditional values (Fugita et al., 1991). In terms of counseling approach, a more structured, directive, assertive, and solution-oriented procedure has been recommended (Atkinson & Matsushita, 1991; Leong, 1986; Murase, 1992). The treatment should first of all be targeted at relieving immediate needs within a reasonably short period. Further treatment can be discussed later as necessary (Murase, 1992).

Encouraging Asian Americans to be more independent of their family may "conflict with a cultural system in which individualism is equated with selfishness" (Wodarski, 1992b, p. 49). In fact, if vocational rehabilitation services are viewed as a threat to family unity, failure to rehabilitate the client is likely to result (Wodarski, 1992b). The prominent influence of the family on the lives of Asian Americans suggests that family members should be involved in the rehabilitation counseling process, and the client should not be expected to act independently of his or her family (Liem, 1993; Murase, 1992; Nishio & Bilmes, 1987). Because Asian Americans are obligated to respect the opinion of parents and family members, family members are expected to be an influencing factor in the process of counseling (Liem, 1993; Wong & Chang, 1994). To effectively involve the family in the rehabilitation process, the counselor must understand the traditional family roles in the Asian American culture and show appropriate respect for them. For example, Wodarski (1992b) pointed out that the father "may be easily offended if any aspects of treatment or decision making fail to involve him" (p. 59). Reinforcing his family-based role in the rehabilitation counseling process is necessary for maintaining the counseling relationship.

Another advantage of involving the family is the opportunity for the counselor to educate family members. This education can help reduce the stigma associated with the disability of the client, as well as clarify any confusion or bias against receiving rehabilitation services. Involvement of parental and family members, therefore, can potentially contribute greatly to client cooperation and the achievement of desired service outcomes. For example, family members can be involved in determining vocational goals with the client. By doing this, the individual client may function within the expectations of the family such as pursuing higher academic or occupational goals. In addition, the possibility of family members forcing the client to withdraw from services because the goals contradict their expectations is minimized.

The challenge of counseling Asian Americans encompasses more than general cultural issues. In the process of providing rehabilitation services, the counselor should always be aware of the influence of social–environmental factors on Asian American clients, such as acculturation and individual subculture differences. These factors can significantly affect the accuracy of diagnoses and the effectiveness of services provided. Awareness of level of acculturation can help the counselor to be sensitive to the needs and the responses of Asian American clients. For example, the nature of problems encountered by Asian American clients varies according to level of acculturation (Hong, 1993). People who are less acculturated experience a higher rate of mental health problems (Cheung, 1995). The degree of acculturation also affects the client's response to the counseling process and outcome. Asian Americans who are more acculturated may respond better to a nondirective, nonjudgmental, and less-structured counseling approach (Chan et al., 1988; Leong, 1986). Therefore, it is important for the rehabilitation counselor to know how to assess the acculturation level of a client. This can be done based on several factors, including the age the client migrated to the United States, the length of stay in this country, the individual's background, and the environment of the country from which he or she migrated (Sue & Sue, 1995). Asian Americans are likely to be more acculturated if migration occurred at a younger age, the period of residence in the United States is longer, and greater consistency is found between the background of the individual and the country of origin and the environment in the United States. However, the rehabilitation counselor still needs to take into consideration individual differences in order to avoid overgeneralizing.

Although the macro-cultural view of the client is important in offering a broad understanding of the individual's cultural values and social attitudes, the counselor must be aware of the micro-view of the client, taking into consideration his or her unique personal experiences. Consideration of those experiences in the individual's life minimizes the likelihood of attributing general cultural stereotypes to the client.

Native Americans

Before the arrival of Europeans in 1492, an estimated 9 million indigenous people, now called Native Americans, lived on the North American continent (Trimble & Fleming, 1989, p. 181). As more and more European settlers migrated to this continent, conflicts over land led to years of intense warfare between the Europeans and the Native Americans. The Europeans seized the land through annihilation or coercive displacement of resisting tribes. Many Native Americans were killed. Native Americans who were willing to reside peacefully with the Europeans were compelled to formally assimilate into the European culture and to reject their own traditions (Dana, 1993; Joe & Malach, 1992). By the late 19th century, the European domination in North America was complete. At that time, Native Americans were forced to migrate to reservations in remote and barren areas of the country, leaving many in poor and difficult conditions until this day (Joe & Malach, 1992). That involuntary migration was still occurring in the 1930s, when "over 125,000 Indians from different tribes were forced from their homes in many different states to a reservation in Oklahoma" (Sue & Sue, 1990, p. 175).

Arrival of the Europeans adversely affected the economic well-being of Native Americans and greatly reduced their population through warfare, displacement, and the introduction of new infectious diseases (Young, 1994). By the early 1800s, the size of the Native American population had decreased to about 600,000, and by the mid-19th century, the count declined to approximately 250,000 (Trimble & Fleming, 1989). However, the trend was reversed in the 20th century when the Native American population increased in every decade, numbering about 1.9 million by 1990 (Saravanabhavan & Marshall, 1994; Young, 1994). Much of the increase in the Native American population occurred between 1970 and 1990 when, as a result of a birthrate twice that of the general population, it doubled in size (Blount, Thyer, & Frye, 1992; Sue & Sue, 1990).

The 1985 U.S. Census indicated that over half of the Native American population lived in urban areas, while the rest resided on reservations with a small minority living on farms (Saravanabhavan & Marshall, 1994; Stock, 1987). According to the U.S. Bureau of the Census in 1990, the 10 states with the largest Native American population in 1990 were Oklahoma (252,132), California (243,736), Arizona (204,150), New Mexico (133,816), North Carolina (82,428), Washington (79,353), Texas (68,565), Michigan (58,667), New York (57,425), and South Dakota (50,294). Therefore, almost half of the Native American population currently resides in Oklahoma, California, Arizona, New Mexico, and North Carolina (U.S. Department of Commerce, 1994). There are approximately 500 American Indian tribes in the United States (Blount et al., 1992; Sue & Sue, 1990). One can find "approximately 200 different dialects and languages spoken" among these tribes (Blount et al., 1992, p. 112).

Native Americans tend to strongly identify with their tribe. When residing on or near the reservation, their "sense of self, security, and belonging are centered in their affiliation with the tribe" (Blount et al., 1992, p. 113). In such locations, Native Americans "judge themselves in terms of whether or not their behaviors are of benefit to the tribe" (Sue & Sue, 1990, p. 177). However, movement of Native Americans away from the reservation and into urban areas for economic reasons often weakens their tribal ties and identity. This is especially the case when frequent visits are impossible due to transportation costs (Blount, et al., 1992).

Native Americans vary greatly in regard to identification with traditional Native American values and customs. LaFromboise, Trimble, and Mohatt (1990) placed the Native American population in four groups on the basis of level of commitment:

1. Traditional—those who generally speak and think in their native language; they practice only traditional beliefs and values.

2. Transitional—those who generally speak both native language and English; they do not fully accept the cultural heritage of their tribal group nor identify completely with mainstream culture.

3. Bicultural—those who are generally accepted by dominant society; they are simultaneously able to know, accept, and practice both mainstream values and traditional values and beliefs.

4. Assimilated—those who are generally accepted by dominant society; they embrace only mainstream culture. (Adapted from LaFromboise et al., 1990, p. 638, by Garrett & Garrett, 1994, and cited in Garrett & Garrett, 1994, p. 140)

Understanding the Native American culture is necessary to provide culturally sensitive rehabilitation counseling services to Native Americans with disabilities. In the following discussions, salient characteristics of Native Americans are described with particular emphasis on implications of these characteristics for rehabilitation counseling.

Salient Characteristics

Poverty, high unemployment, and limited education are major problems in the Native American culture. Blount et al. (1992) elaborated as follows:

> The unemployment rate for Native American reservations is almost four times that of the national average. Poverty and extended periods of unemployment or underemployment have resulted in substandard housing, malnutrition, inadequate health care, and a shortened life expectancy as well as less formal education. Native Americans 25 years of age and older have an average education of 9.6 years. This is the lowest of any major ethnic group in the United States. Nearly one third of all Native Americans are classified as illiterate and only one in five have a high school education. (p. 118)

Such conditions have prevented and continue to hinder successful career development among Native Americans. For example, lack of employment opportunities and education significantly limit the Native Americans' knowledge of the world of work, resulting in the making of poor and ineffective vocational decisions (Martin, 1991).

Compared to the general population, the overall health of Native Americans is poorer in spite of the fact that a higher percentage of the Native American population is younger (Stock, 1987). Therefore, it is not surprising to find that the onset of health problems tends to occur at an earlier age among Native Americans than is the case for the general population (Marshall, Martin, Thomason, & Johnson, 1991).

There is a high incidence of diabetes-related health problems within the Native American population. Aston (cited in Orr, 1993) reported that vision impairment caused by diabetic retinopathy occurred in 13.5% of 55- to 64-year-old American Indians and in 8.2% of those 65 to 71 years old. In addition, the probability of endstage renal disease (ESRD) in Native Americans is eight times higher than in Caucasians, with the number of ESRD cases increasing 18% yearly (Ponchillia, 1993). Health and rehabilitation professionals expect the rate of blindness associated with diabetes among Native Americans to increase in the future because of factors like "poverty, isolation, the lack of education, or the lack of access to basic health care" (Ponchillia, 1993).

The incidence of mental disorders in the Native American population is higher than for most other ethnic groups. Contributing factors include lack of education and employment opportunities, financial difficulties, racial rejection and prejudice, and isolation (Nelson, McCoy, Stetter, & Vanderwagen, 1992). The leading mental health problem experienced by both adults and children is depression (Marshall et al., 1991; Nelson et al., 1992). The incidence of suicide among Native American adults is double that of the general population (Marshall et al., 1991). In addition, antisocial behaviors such as assault and homicide are on the rise (Nelson et al., 1992).

Alcoholism is also a significant problem in the Native American population (Rhodes, Mason, Eddy, Smith, & Bums, 1988). Since the U.S. government legalized drinking for Native Americans in 1953, Native Americans have led the nation (on a per capita basis) in alcohol-related diabetes, cirrhoses, and fetal abnormalities (May, 1982). Of the 10 major causes of death among Native Americans, 5 "are directly related to alcohol in some way, for example, alcohol related accidents, cirrhosis of the liver, alcohol dependency, suicide and homicide" (Blount et al., 1992).

Determining the attitudes of Native Americans toward disability is difficult because such attitudes can vary among the tribes (Ponchillia, 1993). Many Native Americans express no negative attitudes toward people with disabilities, due somewhat to their belief that a person's circumstances are self-determined. Therefore, one is seen as having a disability by choice (Orlansky & Trap, 1987). Furthermore, disability is seen as just another characteristic of the individual, and Native Americans feel little need to judge it as desirable or undesirable (Connors & Donnellan, 1993).

However, not all tribes are equally accepting of people with disability. According to Joe and Malach (1992), Native Americans usually perceive two possible causes of disability: the supernatural and the natural. Supernatural causes of disability include "witchcraft, spirit loss, spirit intrusion, spells, and various unnatural forces" (p. 106). Natural causes of disability include certain human behaviors considered irresponsible.

The fact that the Dogrib Dene (Indian) community in Canada's Northwest Territories consider the blindness of an individual to be a consequence of "a forbearer carelessly neglecting to pierce the eyes of a lynx before skinning it or failing to pierce the eyes of a caribou before cooking it" is an example of attributing a disability to natural causes (Garber-Conrad, 1987, pp. 164–165). Knowing the Native Americans' various views of the causes of disability can help the counselor to understand the basis of certain types of responses by Native American clients toward their disability and toward the sufficiency of rehabilitation services offered. For instance, even when the Native American client and family respond positively to the rehabilitation counselor's service recommendations, they may also seek services from traditional healers whom they also consider to be potentially helpful, either concurrently with or prior to receiving rehabilitation services (Joe & Malach, 1992).

Based on the U.S. Bureau of the Census in 1980, the rate of work disability among Native Americans is 1.5 times higher than that of the general population. However, the rate of Native Americans seeking state–federal rehabilitation services is disproportionately low (Marshall et al., 1991). Many contributing factors have been suggested for such underrepresentation of Native Americans in rehabilitation services. One factor is the non-Native counselors' insufficient understanding of Native American culture, which leads to ineffective rehabilitation services (Clark & Kelley, 1992). Another factor is the Native Americans' lack of awareness of available rehabilitation services for which they are eligible (Orr, 1993). Distrust of Caucasian counselors is also a factor that contributes to their underuse of rehabilitation services.

Another major determinant of the level of use of rehabilitation services is the Native Americans' cultural commitment. Price and McNeill (1992) examined the relationship between Native Americans's cultural commitment and their attitudes towards seeking counseling services among 74 Native American subjects. Their results indicated that the stronger the subjects' commitment to the Native American culture, the lower their (a) preference for counseling services, (b) perceived need for counseling, and (c) trust in counselors. About half of the Native American population in the United States live off the reservation. The strength of identification with the Native American culture and commitment to its values have been found to differ considerably among these Native Americans (Heinrich, Corbine, & Thomas, 1990).

Religion is a central element in Native American culture. As Joe and Malach (1992) stated, "Religion was never a separate institution for Native Americans. . . . Religion or the spiritual side of man is perceived to be an integral part of every living thing. Thus, religion or spiritual beliefs are an integral part of every tribal culture" (p. 97). One concept that is foundational to Native American spirituality is holism, which suggests that all things and all people are interrelated, with each entity having its specific place in the universe. As long as this natural order is respected and not disturbed, life will be harmonious. However, violation of this harmony will lead to physical and mental disorders (Garrett & Garrett, 1994; Heinrich et al., 1990).

Since the etiology of illness is seen as intricately related to this natural order, healing is therefore seen as dependent on the restoration of harmony. Traditional treatment of illness is obtained by visiting a medicine man who will uncover the disruptions of harmony in the patient's life and prescribe methods for restoring harmony. These methods may include herbs, religious services, or rites (Garrett & Garrett, 1994; Ponchillia, 1993). In handling illness, many Native Americans turn to this trusted practice (Nelson et al., 1992). When they visit the traditional healer, they expect the problem to be diagnosed and resolved quickly without any lengthy inquiry regarding personal information (Thomason, 1991).

The Native American definition of family encompasses both immediate and extended family members and sometimes includes the community. Consistent with the Native American concept of holism, family members are viewed as interconnected, and therefore the needs and responsibilities of each person are shared by the family. For instance, children are often not primarily raised by the parents, but rather by grandparents, aunts, and uncles (Garrett & Garrett, 1994; Joe & Malach, 1992; McWhirter & Ryan, 1991; Ponchillia, 1993).

A characteristic of the Native American family is the high esteem for older people because of their rich experience and authoritative status. The elderly usually assume the leadership role in the family as well as the community. Their advice is respected and sought after on important issues of life. High regard for the elderly is a value that has been transmitted from generation to generation (Garrett & Garrett, 1994; McWhirter & Ryan, 1991).

Even though consisting of approximately 500 tribes, the Native American population possesses some common values that differ from the Anglo American culture (Heinrich et al., 1990). The following is a summary of comparisons between the values that dominate Anglo American and Native American cultures (adapted from Joe & Malach, 1992, p. 100; Heinrich et al., 1990, p. 129):

Native American Values	Anglo American Values
Harmony with nature	Mastery over nature
Cooperation (conscious submission of self to the welfare of the tribe)	Competition (each person maximizing own welfare will maximize the general welfare)
Anonymity, humility	Individuality, fame
Submissiveness	Aggressiveness
Work for present needs	Work to "get ahead"
Sharing wealth	Private property, acquisition of wealth
Time is flexible	Time is not flexible
Reliance on extended family	Reliance on experts
Present-time orientation	Future-time orientation

Using the present-time orientation as an example, Sue and Sue (1990) noted that Native Americans tend to emphasize living in the here and now instead of planning for the future. Many Native Americans consider long-term planning to be an egotistical behavior that attempts to disrupt the natural order of things (Sue & Sue, 1990).

A salient characteristic of Native American interaction is the proclivity for humor, which serves to reduce tension, impart messages that are otherwise unacceptable if expressed directly, and bring about a sense of bonding. Exaggeration, clowning, and teasing are common means of creating laughter (Garrett & Garrett, 1994; Herring, 1994).

Another important characteristic of Native American interaction is the use of silence to promote thinking and an atmosphere of bonding. Pondering in silence before replying is the appropriate style of response after a Native American has spoken (Orlansky & Trap, 1987; Ponchillia, 1993). Value is placed on taking turns to speak and waiting in silence for one's turn while another is speaking (McWhirter & Ryan, 1991). Those who respond immediately without pausing in silence, talk unceasingly, or interrupt others are considered childish and unwise (Orlansky & Trap, 1987; Ponchillia, 1993). Those who use direct confrontation are considered to be rude and inappropriate (Blount et al., 1992).

For Native Americans, avoiding eye contact and a high speech tone, as well as refraining from asking direct questions, are means of conveying respect (Joe & Malach, 1992; McWhirter & Ryan, 1991; Orlansky & Trap, 1987; Sue, 1990; Thomason, 1991). For example, direct eye contact is considered a sign of aggression by some Native Americans (Blount et al., 1992).

The indirect, subtle, and slower pace communication style of Native Americans is the opposite of the direct, confrontative, and assertive style of Caucasians. For example, in the Caucasian culture, being candid and outspoken, raising direct questions, and making eye contact are regarded as important communication skills. Silence may bring discomfort instead of respect (Sue, 1990).

It is not unusual for Native Americans to distrust Caucasians. That distrust has been shaped, to a great extent, by the way the U.S. government has treated American Indians throughout American history. For example, the federal government repeatedly violated the treaties with American Indian tribes with the result being American Indians forced from their homes and involuntarily moved to reservations (Joe & Malach, 1992). Native Americans' mistrust of Caucasians may have been further fueled by failure to value the achievements and contributions of Native Americans to American history. Achievements of Native Americans not only have been overlooked in the teachings of most American history books, but have been specifically denied (Vogel, 1987). Therefore, it is important for rehabilitation counselors to be aware of how their Native American clients perceive their trustworthiness. Counselors should spend time developing rapport and building a strong relationship with Native American clients to merit their trust, rather than to automatically assume its presence (Thomason, 1991).

In general, rehabilitation services received by Native Americans have been less effective than those received by the general U.S. population. For example, an analysis of the Rehabilitation Services Administration data between 1980 and 1982 revealed that "almost 50 percent of those Native Americans who applied for rehabilitation services were closed from statuses 02 (applicant) and 06 (extended evaluation) compared to 42 percent of those who applied from the general population" and that only "52.7 percent of Native Americans who were accepted . . . [for services] . . . were successfully rehabilitated compared to 62.7 percent of the general caseload client's" (cited in Tanner & Martin, 1986, p. 118).

Clark and Kelley (1992) have attributed the discrepancy in the effectiveness of rehabilitation services for persons in general with disabilities and Native Americans with disabilities to the lack of understanding of Native American cultures by service providers. The researchers also assert that lack of understanding by rehabilitation service providers contributes to the relatively low use of rehabilitation services by Native Americans with disabilities.

The following example highlights the way in which ignorance of the Native American culture can result in negative consequences of rehabilitation services for Native Americans:

> Because of the lack of services in the Navajo Nation, blind and visually impaired children are generally taken to residential training schools at five or six years to receive specialized training. In such schools, they may forget the Navajo language and other more subtle ways of communicating with their family and culture. Although their home may have no indoor plumbing and heating and cooking may be done with wood, they were taught daily living and mobility skills that are relevant to life in a middle-class urban community. As adults, many find it impossible to return to their homes because they have not been prepared for life on a reservation and have become far too dependent on such urban services as public transportation, electricity, and running water. Major retraining is often needed but seldom available for those who wish to return to their home communities. (Lowrey, 1987)

Guidelines for Rehabilitation Counselors Working with Native Americans

In order to provide culturally sensitive rehabilitation counseling services, the rehabilitation counselor must be flexible enough attitudinally to respect the cultural values and beliefs of his or her Native American clients (Marshall et al., 1991). This is particularly important because, as Nelson et al. (1992) pointed out, "many of the 500 Native American tribes have maintained much of their traditional culture" (p. 257). These traditional cultural values and beliefs of Native Americans differ sharply from those of the mainstream culture.

Underuse of counseling services by Native Americans will probably continue unless human service professionals play a primary role in improving the situation (Trimble & Fleming, 1989). For example, the counselor must build a trusting relationship with the client as early as possible in the process of counseling in order to eliminate fear and negative perceptions of White counselors. Several methods are proposed to enhance the client's trust in the counselor, such as showing interest and sensitivity to the client, demonstrating respect for the Native American culture, providing concrete guidance, and refraining from showing prejudice and making disdainful remarks (Garrett & Garrett, 1994; Orlansky & Trap, 1987). The counselor is also urged to be flexible in working with Native Americans. For example, being flexible in regard to the length of interviews and not adhering to a rigid appointment system can promote rehabilitation counselor–client rapport (Heinrich et al., 1990).

Since Native American clients usually expect their problems to be resolved quickly, counselors should conduct the initial interview in both a diagnostic and therapeutic manner. Counselors should avoid the appearance of interrogating the client by asking too many personal questions. Rather, they "can use self-disclosure as a way to prompt self-disclosure" by the client (Thomason, 1991, p. 323).

Counselors can also enhance the Native Americans' use of rehabilitation services by using a counseling style that is compatible with the client's level of acculturation. For example, it has been suggested that a directive counseling approach is more appropriate for Native Americans, particularly for those strongly committed to the traditional culture (Trimble & Fleming, 1989). Perhaps this is related to the Native American's value of respecting authority and seeking advice from older people who have more life experience and wisdom.

Therefore, it is important for the rehabilitation counselor to accurately assess the client's level of acculturation. When working with Native Americans, rehabilitation counselors should determine the following: (a) degree of cultural commitment; (b) whether the person comes from a reservation, rural, or urban setting; and (c) tribal structure, customs, and beliefs that are relevant to the situation (Garrett & Garrett, 1994). The counselor must be creative and sensitive in determining the acculturation level of the client (Heinrich et al., 1990; McWhirter & Ryan, 1991). Having an accurate evaluation of the client's acculturation level facilitates the counselor's selection of appropriate counseling goals and procedures, as well as roles for and responsibilities of the client.

In regard to attitudes toward disability, rehabilitation counselors need to be sensitive to the unique culture of every tribe from which they have clients. The fact that persons in the Native American culture in general do not tend to discriminate against people with disabilities does not mean that a need for rehabilitation services does not exist. Because the family and community by tradition initially assume the responsibilities of caring for people with disabilities, those with disabilities and their family members may not see any need for rehabilitation services. Therefore, rehabilitation service programs need to actively promote their services and educate Native Americans on the importance and benefits of rehabilitation services. However, this must be done sensitively within the context of the Native American culture.

Based on the Native Americans' supernatural view of the causation of disability, rehabilitation counselors should not be surprised when some of their clients turn to traditional healers, often referred to by titles such as shaman, medicine maker, or sakim (Blount et al., 1992), in conjunction with seeking rehabilitation services.

Several suggestions can be found in the literature for dealing with this type of situation. For example, it has been recommended that rehabilitation counselors not be afraid to acknowledge their lack of understanding about traditional healing. Without being overly intrusive, the rehabilitation counselor should attempt to determine if the client plans to use traditional healers in order to better coordinate all services in the rehabilitation plan. If the need arises to discourage the use of traditional healing approaches that contradict rehabilitation procedures, the counselor should first obtain family consensus before taking any action (Joe & Malach, 1992). When the client and family members insist on using traditional healing rather than the recommended rehabilitation services, a written statement of intent to do so should be signed by them (Garrett & Garrett, 1994).

Given the significance of the family in the Native American culture, the rehabilitation counselor should obtain a clear picture of how family attitudes can affect the determination of feasible rehabilitation goals. For example, the counselor should know if, as is often expected, other members in a traditional Native American family take over the pre-disability onset roles of a family member with a disability. Lack of such awareness can result in inaccurate counselor diagnosis of the client's situation (Ponchillia, 1993). Ponchillia (1993) elaborated via the following example regard- ing a client from the Dogrib Dene (Indian) community in Canada's Northwest Territories:

> . . . when a visually impaired person was asked, "Do you have any problems cooking your food?" the answer was no, and the conclusion could have been that the person's vision or skills were sufficient to perform the task. The real reason why the person had "no problems cooking" was that since people with vision loss are not expected to be able to cook, other family members had taken over this person's chores."
>
> [A] . . . second problem arises if the person with vision loss desires instruction to regain skills necessary to cook, shop for groceries, and so on, but members of his or her circle perceive it as their duty to relieve the person of such "aggravations." Again, interaction with others besides the individual would be indicated, so a group consensus could be reached and mutually agreed-on goals could be achieved and supported by the circle of people around the individual with visual impairment. (p. 334)

Thus, the counselor should be aware of the impact of Native American family dynamics on the rehabilitation counseling process. In addition, because of the family orientation, instead of counseling the client alone, the counselor may seek to involve family members in rehabilitation counseling sessions and decision making (McWhirter & Ryan, 1991; Orlansky & Trap, 1987). In a survey conducted by Martin, Frank, Minkler, and Johnson (1988), more than 70% of the 332 vocational rehabilitation counselors agreed that it is important to work with the family members of Native American clients. However, less than 30% of the vocational rehabilitation counselors surveyed reported that they were able to gain support from the family members in the process of rehabilitation.

The following behavioral guidelines should prove useful for effectively involving family members in the rehabilitation counseling process:

1. Ask parents whom they want to include in meetings. Do not assume that all Indian parents want to include extended family members or that those family members will want to attend all the meetings. Explain to the parents that all family and nonblood relatives whom they choose to include are welcome. Some families may want to include extended family in meetings while other families will meet with the professionals and then go back to talk to other family members. During home visits, family members may actively participate, while in other homes they may watch or listen from another room.

2. When extended family members participate in a meeting, communication should be directed to the entire group, not just to the parents, interpreter, or spokesperson for the family. This shows respect for the entire family.

3. Always show respect and provide emotional support to the family. That is done by listening to the family's ideas, acknowledging their concerns and feelings, and including interested family members. This approach allows the family to be an integral part of the intervention plans. (Joe & Malach, 1992, p. 111)

Rehabilitation counselors should be sensitive to any language difficulties found among Native American clients stemming from their use of both English and their native language in their daily interactions. When that bilingualism has resulted in the client having low proficiency in English, any evaluations of the client done solely in English can result in the client's capabilities and potentials being underestimated. Therefore, "[a]dministrative policies and practices must encourage language-fair appraisal techniques and rehabilitation modalities to improve services to Native Americans" (Tanner & Martin, 1986, p. 120). Being aware of the language problems and deficiencies of Native American clients will help the rehabilitation counselor not only to gain a more accurate assessment, but also to provide more effective rehabilitation services.

Rehabilitation counselors should also consider both cultural and environmental factors in the job development and placement process with their Native American clients. For example, studies have reported that the vocational interests of Native and non-Native Americans are different because of different developmental experiences (Marshall et al., 1991). Lack of employment opportunities on the reservation not only limits the concept of the world of work among Native Americans, but also implies that employment requires the person to move to places outside the reservation.

When working with Native American clients, rehabilitation counselors should carefully interpret their results on standardized tests. Studies have indicated that Native Americans usually score higher on performance measures than on verbal measures in the *Wechsler Intelligence Scale For Children–Revised* (Wechsler, 1974), and perform better on spatial aptitude measures than on verbal aptitude measures in the *General Aptitude Test Battery* (Martin, 1991).

The rehabilitation counselor needs to interact with Native American clients in a manner that is appropriate to their style of communication. Rather than interpreting their lack of eye contact and their silent pauses as passivity, disinterest, sullenness, or lack of cooperation, the rehabilitation counselor should realize that those responses are often culturally determined and adapt to that style of communication. For example, rather than striving to eliminate awkward periods of silence by persistent talk (Orlansky & Trap, 1987), the rehabilitation counselor should attempt to be relaxed during those moments (Heinrich et al., 1990). In addition, instead of responding immediately to a client's words, the counselor might learn to ponder in silence before answering (Ponchillia, 1993), a manner that could put the client and the family at ease (Joe & Malach, 1992). Caution should be exercised to avoid making the client and family feel imposed upon by intrusive questioning (Orlansky & Trap, 1987). When extensive questioning is necessary, it is advisable to inform family members about its purpose and nature, and also to grant them permission to ask for clarification of a question or to have more time to consider a question (Joe & Malach, 1992). Counselors also should not hesitate when necessary to show humility by expressing gaps of knowledge about the client's culture (Heinrich et al., 1990).

A nonaggressive approach is important when interacting with Native American clients. For example, counselors should avoid strong handshakes and a loud tone of voice (Heinrich et al., 1990; Orlansky & Trap, 1987). The majority of Native Americans do not use a hearty, firm grasp when shaking hands. Native Americans view the handshake "as a feeling or touch of the other person and thus is to be done in a sensitive and gentle way" (Blount et al., 1992, p. 126).

CONCLUDING STATEMENT

This chapter examined the issues of cross-cultural rehabilitation counseling with an emphasis on understanding the salient characteristics of African, Hispanic, Asian, and Native Americans. Guidelines for culturally sensitive responding have also been presented to help rehabilitation counselors work more effectively with clients from specific minority cultures. Many rehabilitation counselors have lacked a sufficient knowledge of the salient characteristics of minority cultures. The cultural insensitivity that results contributes to the problem of the underuse of rehabilitation services by, as well as poorer service outcomes for, persons with disabilities from minority cultures.

As noted in the chapter, many individuals from minority groups mistrust helping professionals, especially Caucasian counselors. For example, rehabilitation counselors can be seen as agents of the majority society using their services to make the thoughts and behaviors of minority clients compatible with the ideas, beliefs, and conduct of the dominant society (Sue, 1990). Each minority group mentioned in this chapter has had its unique "trust undermining" historical interactions with Anglo-European Americans. Therefore, the rehabilitation counselor should understand how historical factors may affect the relationship with his or her ethnic minority clients so that necessary actions can be taken to facilitate the development of more trusting cross-cultural counselor–client relationships.

Factors other than mistrust also likely contribute to the underuse of human services by members of ethnic minority groups. For example, many African Americans do not use such services because they usually turn to the church for needed assistance. In the Hispanic culture, people view folk healers such as spiritualists or herbalists as an important source of help in coping with health-related problems. In the Asian culture, some people avoid using services because of the stigma and shame associated with disabilities, especially with mental disabilities. In any event, the underuse of human services contributes to a continued unfamiliarity with these services among many members of ethnic minority groups.

The Caucasian majority U.S. culture is individualistic in nature. In this type of culture, the model for the ideal personality is to become self-sufficient and independent of the family. Nearly any dependency is perceived negatively (Rubin & Roessler, 1995). On the other hand, many minority cultures such as the African American culture, the Hispanic culture, the Asian American culture, and the Native American culture are very family oriented. In all these cultures, the psychological and functional unit tends to be the family that is often defined as the extended family rather than the nuclear family (Sue & Sue, 1990). Therefore, in these cultures, mutual supports among family members can be perceived as crucial for the mental and physical well-being of individuals. Such individuals are more likely to have major difficulties functioning effectively apart from their family. This can be especially evident in regard to critical decision making. For example, many Asian American clients are reluctant to make their own personal and vocational decisions without consulting with their family members first.

Religion plays an important role in all four minority groups described in this chapter. For example, a common characteristic of these four minority groups is the tendency to seek alternative treatment or help for their needs in addition to the formal rehabilitation services available. These alternative treatments may be religious services or rites, as well as those provided by folk healers. Rehabilitation counselors should be aware of all these alternative resources and their effects in the process of rehabilitation counseling.

In the process of rehabilitation counseling, many counselors expect or would like their clients to be verbal and able to express their thoughts and feelings openly and clearly. However, verbalization is not as highly valued in many minority cultures as in the Caucasian majority culture. For example, African Americans usually believe that nonverbal behaviors are more important than verbal behaviors in communication because the former is a more accurate reflection of what a person is thinking than the latter (Sue, 1990). Many Asian Americans believe that doing is more important than talking and that the uncontrolled expression of emotions in public settings is rude.

Persons from ethnic racial minority groups tend to prefer active, directive, and structured counseling approaches in which counselors are less guarded about revealing their thoughts and feelings to their clients (Sue, 1990). Sue (1990) at least partially attributes this preference for more active counseling approaches to distrust of Caucasian counselors that stems from a belief that they harbor either conscious or unconscious racist attitudes, such as the White culture is superior to all others. Sue delineates this client feeling of distrust that is often present in cross-cultural counseling via the following example of thoughts of minority clients in regard to their counselor in that situation:

> "What makes you any different from all the Whites out there who have oppressed me?" "What makes you immune from inheriting the racial biases of your forebears?" "Before I open up to you, I want to know where you are coming from." "How open and honest are you about your own racism, and will it interfere with our relationship?" "Can you really understand what it is like to be Asian, Black, Hispanic, American Indian, or of any other race?" (p. 430)

Consequently, ethnic–racial minority clients are less likely to self-disclose personal information until they feel they can trust the counselor. This establishment of trust is less likely to occur until the counselor begins to allow the client to get to know him or her, which tends to occur more naturally in an active–directive counseling approach. "To give advice or suggestions, to interpret, and to tell the client how you, the counselor, feel may" be perceived as acts of counselor self-disclosure by the client (Sue, 1990, p. 430).

While all four of these minority groups share some common characteristics in regard to communication style, they have different preferred conversational distances, interpretations of physical contact, and body movements in the process of communication. For example, while African and Hispanic Americans tend to be comfortable with hugging, back-slapping, and elaborate handshaking, many Asian Americans feel embarrassed by such interactions. Asian Americans also require greater conversational distance than African and Hispanic Americans.

Knowledge of the characteristics of other cultures provides a foundation for the rehabilitation counselor to understand his or her ethnic minority clients. However, any cultural knowledge-based presuppositions for cross-cultural rehabilitation counseling with a given client cannot be assumed to be valid until the counselor goes a step further to examine the unique personal experiences of each client. Therefore, successful cross-cultural rehabilitation counseling relies on the awareness of both intergroup and intragroup differences.

Family-Centered Rehabilitation Case Management

Richard T. Roessler, Walter Chung, and Stanford E. Rubin

The importance of involving the family in the rehabilitation process has been well recognized and documented in rehabilitation literature during the last two decades (e.g., Bray, 1977; Kosciulek, 1994; Marsh, 1992; Power & Dell Orto, 1980a; Smith & Godfrey, 1995). For example, studies have found that involving family members in the rehabilitation process facilitates their adjustment to having a family member with a disability (Dumas & Sadowsky, 1984; Marsh, 1992; Vargo, 1983), enhances the probability of vocational placement and success (Gerhardt, 1990; Herbert, 1989; Moore, 1984), increases satisfaction with rehabilitation services (Smith & Godfrey, 1995), and promotes adaptation to the disability as well as treatment compliance by the individual with a disability (Arnold & Orozco, 1988; Evans et al., 1987; Jamison & Virts, 1989). Successfully involving the family in the rehabilitation process also reduces family fear and suspicion of rehabilitation goals, with the end result being increased effectiveness of the rehabilitation process (Westin & Reiss, 1979).

Although the need to involve the family in the rehabilitation program has been strongly advocated in the rehabilitation literature, family involvement has never been a common occurrence (Dew, Phillips, & Reiss, 1989; Herbert, 1989; Power, Hershenson, & Fabian, 1991). After analyzing the Rehabilitation Service Administration national case closure data of 1981, Cook and Ferritor (1985) reported that family services were provided in less than 2% of the closed cases. Bernheim and Suitalki (as cited in Cohen & Lavach, 1995) also found that most staff members in a state-operated mental health facility failed to initiate contact with families of clients. One critical factor that contributes to the discrepancy between actual and advocated rehabilitation practice is that many rehabilitation counselors continue to hold on to the traditional focus of rehabilitation in which family involvement is not emphasized (Herbert, 1989; Lindenberg, 1980). The traditional focus of rehabilitation can be described as "adhering to the myopic view of planning and delivering case services to one person" (Herbert, 1989, p. 45). Scott (as cited in Cottone, Handelsman, & Walters, 1986) further commented about this traditional focus of rehabilitation:

The focus of rehabilitation is on the individual. The problem of disability is thought to be like a trait or need, that is, something inhering in the individual. The process of rehabilitation is not usually thought of as part of a complex social system involving family, friends, and community. (p. 37)

The traditional rehabilitation approach also fails to meet the needs of future rehabilitation clients because of growing diversity in the U.S. population. By 2050, it is expected that 45% of the total population will be Black, Hispanic, Asian, and Native American (Pollard, 1993). One salient characteristic of these four ethnic groups (see Chapter 12) is their family orientation, implying that involving the family in the rehabilitation program is necessary for these groups of clients. Therefore, to provide optimal rehabilitative services to both current and future rehabilitation service consumers, the larger social–cultural context of individuals with disabilities (e.g., the family and community) that affects their rehabilitation must be considered (Dew et al., 1989; Marsh, 1992).

The purpose of this chapter is to discuss a family-centered rehabilitation case management approach that focuses on the family and the community as well as on the client. The basic premises of this type of rehabilitation case management approach are that effective rehabilitation services for people with disabilities result from (a) involving interdependent family members in the rehabilitation process and (b) drawing upon the strengths of the family, the rehabilitation agency, and the community to meet the disability-related needs of clients and their families. In family-centered rehabilitation case management, the family is defined as the person with a disability and all of his or her relatives in the nuclear or extended family who can be considered members of an interdependent constellation. Just as is the case for the individual rehabilitation client, any of these family members can be affected by the presence of disability in the family constellation.

THE NECESSITY OF INVOLVING THE FAMILY AND COMMUNITY IN REHABILITATION

When an individual acquires a disability, every member in his or her family is affected because of the interdependency within the family unit (Hornby & Seligman, 1991). Turnbull, Summers, and Brotherson (1986) elaborated on the impact of disability on family members via the following example regarding a family with a child who has severe retardation:

While the mother is working with the child on feeding, her dinner conversation with her husband and other children is substantially limited. After the other family members finish dinner, the father cleans the kitchen and siblings proceed to their homework, all feeling that some of their needs have been overlooked. Meanwhile, the mother is feeling isolated from the rest of her family and frustrated about all the tasks to which she must attend before midnight. (p. 50)

Involving families in rehabilitation is necessary because the unmet needs and unresolved problems among family members may hinder a client's adaptation to the disability and accomplishment of optimal vocational outcomes (Bray, 1980). To properly involve family members in rehabilitation, counselors must understand that disability affects all family members (Drotar, Crawford, & Bush, 1984) in a multitude of ways. For example, studies have indicated that disability can have economic, social, and psychological effects on the family of the individual with a disability (Bray, 1977; Hornby & Seligman, 1991; Kosciulek & Pichette, 1996; Marsh, 1992; Smith & Godfrey, 1995; Sutton, 1985).

Economic

An important family issue is the generation of income for household expenses (Marshak & Seligman, 1993). Disability causes stress for the client and family members by threatening their economic well-being (Falvo, 1991) and, thus, achievement of goals such as home or car purchase, retirement planning, and maintenance of education funds for children (Sutton, 1985). Arnold and Case (1993) assessed the needs of families with members with disabilities and found that 70% of the families had a household income of less that $15,000 per year. Financial assistance, medical care, and job placement were reported by participants as the most urgent needs. Disability of a family member usually brings financial pressure to bear on the family because of the costs and expenses involved in hospitalization and rehabilitation (Smith & Godfrey, 1995). For example, it was estimated that the average cost of hospitalization for a head injury in 1985 was $115,300 (Kosciulek, 1994), which is, of course, far below what the cost would be in today's dollars. McMordie and Barker (as cited in Kosciulek, 1995) examined the medical, legal, and rehabilitation costs of 150 families with a member suffering from a head injury. The researchers found that the total expense for a family could reach $1 million. Because certain costly treatments such as blood plasma used for hemophilia are usually not covered by insurance (Power & Dell Orto, 1980b), the high treatment costs of disability may create an enormous financial burden on the family.

Under the current health care system, the person with a disability is usually discharged after a brief period of inpatient treatment and returns home for extended aftercare. Family members of the person with a disability now "can no longer go on with their lives unencumbered by the burden of ongoing caregiving responsibilities" (Marsh, 1992, p. 10). Therefore, the economic burden on the family is further compounded by loss of income when the client and family members who provide care are unable to work during the process of recovery (Sutton, 1985). If the client and the caregiving family members are the primary breadwinners, the family will be vulnerable to great financial debt (Sutton, 1985).

Social

Disability also causes social changes within the family. One significant social change is the shift in customary roles among family members when disability affects the client's physical, mental, and social capabilities (Almagor, 1991; Kosciulek, 1995). As Hornby and Seligman (1991) pointed out,

> Disability requires family members to shift roles from ones they have grown accustomed to and which support the family's sense of predictability and equilibrium, to other roles that feel strange and awkward and that they would not choose to assume. Breadwinners need to become supports at home and persons choosing a domestic lifestyle may become more housebound or may need to share in a breadwinner capacity to help finance costly aids and services. When roles fail to shift in response to a major change in the family, problems erupt. (p. 268)

Role changes in the family are often difficult to accept because of the values people have been socialized to attach to certain family roles. For example, the husband of a woman with a physical disability may need to assume the homemaker role. But the new role may be in conflict with his enculturated value that a male should not be the primary homemaker. Therefore, role changes can result in conflict, confusion, anger, and frustration among family members (Jongbloed, 1994; Sutton, 1985).

As Jongbloed (1994) noted, role changes do not typically involve shifts from independence to dependence. Indeed, no family members maintain independent relationships prior to disability. Rather, they maintain patterns of interdependence that now change with the advent of disability. Shifts in interdependent roles for the person with a disability are frequently accompanied by the need to ask for help from one's spouse or children, an undesirable state for adult family members with strokes in the Jongbloed study. Two reasons for not wishing to request help were given: People with a disability felt less in control and as though they were more of a burden to others.

Another social change to which families of rehabilitation clients must often adjust is greater isolation (Kosciulek, 1994). In a 10- to 15-year follow-up study, Thomsen (as cited in Kosciulek, 1995) reported that only one third of the families in the study had interactions with people other than their immediate family members. Many factors contribute to the social isolation of the families of rehabilitation clients. For example, when family members spend most of their time and effort to take care of the person with a disability, the family may become a closed system that isolates itself from society (Sutton, 1985). Family isolation is also stimulated by crisis situations encountered by the family or when family members are being overwhelmed by their grief over the disability of one of its members (Almagor, 1991; Smith & Godfrey, 1995). Other reasons that cause families to isolate themselves include the lack of people who are able to empathize with their situations or feelings of embarrassment about the disability of the family member (Kosciulek, 1995).

Disability brings changes to the family relationship as well. In terms of the marital relationship, studies indicated that disability has both negative and positive effects on the relationship. Several researchers reported that the presence of disability results in decreased marital adjustment, ineffective communication patterns, and difficulty in sexual functioning (Bayer, 1996; Jongbloed, 1994; Smith & Godfrey, 1995; Sutton, 1985). Poor marital adjustment may be caused by role and lifestyle changes such as added work and domestic responsibilities (Marshak & Seligman, 1993). Tension arises when the spouse of the person with a disability fails to adjust to his or her new expectations, roles, and daily experiences.

Difficulty in sexual functioning due to disability also negatively affects the spousal relationship. Marshak and Seligman (1993) identified that there are three causes of sexual dysfunction: organic, psychogenic, and mixed. One example of organic sexual dysfunction is the side effects of medications. Psychogenic sexual dysfunction is associated with the couple's anxieties about sexual activities. For example, in the case of cardiac-related disability, the couple may have difficulty in enjoying their sexual relationship because of the fear of death (Falvo, 1991). Both organic and psychogenic sexual dysfunctions may occur simultaneously in some situations, thereby causing difficulty in sexual functioning between the client and his or her spouse. However, disability does not always have a negative impact on the marital relationship. Almagor (1991) assessed the degree of marital satisfaction among 40 couples with spouses who have disabilities. Couples with spouses with a disability reported a more cohesive marital relationship than did members of the control group, indicating that disability sometimes affects the spousal relationship positively.

Disability affects not only the marital relationship but other aspects of family relationships as well. As Marshak and Seligman (1993) noted, disability in the family will increase older children's responsibility and cause them to be more independent of their parents. When a parent acquires a disability, children may experience feelings of fear about the loss of physical and emotional support from parents whose energies are exhausted by the process of coping with the crisis. For families with a child who has acquired a disability, research indicates that the siblings of the child with a disability may experience feelings of parental abandonment, bitterness toward additional responsibilities, low self-esteem, and anxiety and anger toward the child with a disability (Simeonsson & Bailey, 1986).

Psychological

Many families undergo a series of emotional reactions as they are exposed to the effects of disability on one of their members. Power (1988) outlined a sequence of such family reactions as follows:

1. shock (feelings of helplessness, being overwhelmed, and inability to plan),

2. denial (denying the implication of the event for work, family life, and physical/mental functioning), and

3. acknowledgment/search for meaning (angry about family disruptions; realizing that disability will not go away; aware of family losses; anxiety over what future will bring; looking for understanding; grief. [p. 250])

Other documented emotional reactions within families to onset of disability in one of its members include disbelief, fear, stress, grief, numbness, guilt, shame, hopelessness, withdrawal, depression, and self-doubt (Bray, 1977; Hyde & Goldman, 1993; Kosciulek, 1994; Marsh, 1992; Munro, 1985; Sutton, 1985). After her extensive review of the literature, Marsh (1992) concluded that the salient emotional reactions of family members of the rehabilitation client with a disability include anger, guilt, depression, withdrawal, and empathic suffering.

Anger

Anger is a common reaction expressed by family members of the rehabilitation client in their process of adjustment to the disability (Bray, 1977). Family members may feel angry at the devastating reality of disability, the injustice of fate or God, and the family member with a disability who is believed to be responsible for the occurrence of the disability (Bray, 1977; Falvo, 1991; Marsh, 1992). Family members will also be angry at the insensitivity of the rehabilitation system and counselors (Marsh, 1992). One prominent example of a counselor's insensitivity toward families is blaming them for the disability of the client. The parent of a child with a disability is extremely vulnerable to such blaming (Cohen & Lavach, 1995; Wright, 1960). As Cohen and Lavach (1993) noted, blaming mothers for their children's need for psychotherapy has contributed to the conflict between parents and professionals. Cohen and Lavach further pointed out that even though there are no research studies to support the theory that a child's disability is caused by his or her parents, the parent blaming attitude is still common among counselors.

Guilt

Guilt is usually a result of internalized anger involving self-blame, shame, and self-recrimination (Livneh, 1986). Family members experience feelings of guilt when they assume the responsibility for the onset of disability in one of the members (Steinhaur, Mushin, & Rae-Grant, 1980). For instance, due to the congenital nature of their child's disability, the parents of a child with mental retardation may have difficulty forgiving themselves. Frequently, the guilty feelings of a parent are intensified when negative attitudes of other people are encountered:

> One of the psychiatrists up at the hospital said that I needed to grow up, that the child had no problem, it was the mother with the problem. And then I felt like a failure. I'm a single parent. Maybe if my son had had another mother he would have been all right. All kinds of guilt went through my mind. What did I do wrong? What did I do to this child? My most precious possession in life, and I've done something wrong. I've ruined him. (Marsh, 1992, p. 87)

Depression

Depression is regarded as "an affective reaction whose main features include feelings of sadness, worthlessness, helplessness, hopelessness, futility, despair, self-depreciation or aversion, inadequacy, insecurity, dejection, desolation, devastation, despondency, distress, discouragement, and self-pity" (Livneh, 1986). Steinhaur et al. (1980) considered depression as a natural response when family members accept the reality of disability and its effect on the family:

> When [the tears] come, they come hard. I remember one time when my son was in the hospital and I'm watching a story on television about some little child that was treated poorly. I'm sitting there folding clothes. I cried and cried. And I knew I was not crying over that. I finally allowed myself to cry, and it did feel better. (Marsh, 1992, p. 87)

Withdrawal

Withdrawal is associated with depression and characterized by "turning away from others, resignation (to fate), passivity and dependency" (Livneh, 1986). The following two excerpts illustrate the feelings of withdrawal experienced by the family members of an individual with a disability:

> I just want to be by myself most of the time. I just don't want to be bothered. I just don't sleep. I can't eat. I get headaches. I can't associate with people. (Marsh, 1992, p. 87)

> When she was hospitalized in the beginning, I felt like I was falling apart. And I was crying a lot and I was withdrawing from everyone. The whole family was going through that process. (Marsh, 1992, p. 87)

Empathic Suffering

Empathic suffering experienced by family members refers to their awareness of the negative consequences of disability and "of the discrepancy between the promise of the past and the impoverishment of the present" (Marsh, 1992, p. 88). Empathic suffering is painful and tearful:

> I've lost a child to death. This is worse, because death is final [and with] this I have to continue to see him suffer. To see a handsome, young, bright life destroyed. (Marsh, 1992, p. 88)

In the life of the individual and his or her family, disability is clearly a significant event that has economic, social, and psychological ramifications. For this reason, the rehabilitation counselor's perspective must be broader than simply an individual focus.

Counselors must act on the understanding that their role includes identifying and addressing the extent disability affects family functioning. Otherwise, unmet needs and unresolved problems within families will negatively affect rehabilitation outcomes of people with disabilities. The challenge for counselors is how to provide family-centered case management so that the concerns of rehabilitation clients and their families can be met.

FAMILY-CENTERED REHABILITATION CASE MANAGEMENT

Underscoring the need for family-centered case management, Nochi (1996) discussed evidence documenting the ways family relationships can enhance or impede the rehabilitation process. In an extensive review of literature on family dynamics and disability, Kelley and Lambert (1992) reported that family-centered interventions resulted in increased client participation in rehabilitation programs. They also commented on the wealth of clinical experience that indicates the value of providing "family-centered" services within a person's rehabilitation program. Hence, the essential message of this chapter is that clients and their families constitute a constellation of interdependent individuals that counselors must articulate with available community resources. This articulation is needed in order to maintain or restore equilibrium in the family, which is the primary support system for most persons experiencing disability. As Nochi (1996) noted, one of the most important factors affecting the ability of people and their families to overcome crisis situations (i.e., return to a state of equilibrium) is the level and quality of agency services and other community resources available at times of stress. Effective rehabilitation programs depend, in part, on the extent resources available from churches, neighborhood networks, and other formal or informal agencies in the local community are coordinated to meet the needs of rehabilitation clients and their families (Adams & Nelson, 1995).

Chubon (1992) stressed that rehabilitation counselors should mediate among parties (e.g., the client, his or her family, the rehabilitation agency, and community agencies) in order to maximize the rehabilitation gains of their clients. The purpose of the counselor's mediation is to help meet the disability-produced needs experienced by clients and their families. This mediation or family-centered rehabilitation case management is consistent with the "family support movement," which has its roots in the caregiving literature for families with children with developmental disabilities (Singer & Powers, 1993). Successful family-centered rehabilitation case management is characterized by the following: (a) an available database of information on formal and informal service resources, (b) "rapid response" to multiple family needs, (c) active listening and family empowerment, and (d) long-term time commitments to the client and family (Singer et al., 1993).

Family-centered case management promotes the involvement of clients and their families in service planning. It is very important, therefore, that counselors explain to the client and other family members the steps they must take to receive agency and community services and how those services will help the household meet its pressing needs (Chubon, 1992; Schwab, 1989). Working together, the client, his or her family, and the rehabilitation counselor identify needs of both the family and the person with a disability, as well as the types of referrals required to meet those needs. Barriers (e.g., transportation, childcare, and inability to take time off from work) to receiving services and family resistance to potential agency referrals should be discussed in order to reduce or remove any impediments to delivery of the service program.

Effective provision of family-centered case management by the counselor involves the following:

1. *needs analysis*—counselor ability to assess a broad range of individual and household needs and the way in which agency and community services might respond to those needs

2. *respect for client and family autonomy*—counselor ability to be a "clearinghouse" for service information for clients and their families and to ensure that family participation is based on informed consent

3. *advocacy*—the counselor as a third party who is there to help clients and their households secure coordinated services

4. *support*—the counselor as a warm, concerned person to whom the client can look for support and assistance

In the needs analysis process, counselors enable clients and their families to discuss and clarify their needs (i.e., household needs) and their perceptions of how external resources can assist in meeting those needs. Respect for client and family autonomy, advocacy, and support come into play as the counselor fosters a "united front" among family members to support the person with a disability in his or her rehabilitation. Hence, rehabilitation counselors must adopt a "total household" perspective in the case management process. The key functions of family-centered case management required to implement this "total household" outlook are described in Table 13.1.

The counselor's role as a family-centered rehabilitation case manager begins with problem identification early in the service planning process and ends with the counselor monitoring the outcomes of different services for clients and their families. As always, case management occurs in the context of a sound counseling relationship. The primary purpose of counseling in the family-centered case management approach is to provide understanding, support, and empowerment to rehabilitation clients and their families (Power & Dell Orto, 1980c; Smith & Godfrey, 1995).

TABLE 13.1

Key Functions of Family-Centered Case Management with Clients and Families

1. During the service planning process, rehabilitation counselors help individuals identify pressing needs affecting them and their families. Needs identification may be facilitated by an intake form that directs both counselor and client toward potential need areas and pertinent community resources.

2. Completing an actual household intake form or simply following the logic of such a form, the counselor and client identify client and household needs.

3. Needs of client and household members are identified, ranked, and translated into referrals.

4. Client and counselor discuss the referrals and what the client and household members must do to apply for agency services. The counselor clearly explains the purpose and process of service to the client and his or her family in order to promote their *informed* consent.

5. Barriers to receiving services (e.g., lack of transportation, the need to take time off from work) are identified and ways to overcome them are discussed.

6. The rehabilitation counselor notifies agencies of the client's and household's potential eligibilities. With the client's permission, the counselor shares relevant case data with involved agencies in referral letters.

7. The counselor checks on client and household contacts with the agencies and follows up with the client regarding lack of contact.

8. As new information regarding the person or the household becomes available, the counselor routes it to appropriate agencies.

9. The counselor monitors case progress.

10. The rehabilitation counselor notes either closure of individual agencies or continued service where appropriate.

11. The counselor, at a later date, follows up with clients and their family members to determine how well the original needs identified during the intake process have been and are being met. Additional services may be instituted as a result of the long-term follow-up.

Marshak and Seligman (1993) noted that the intervention of rehabilitation counselors with families can occur at any of the following five levels:

Level 1—Focus on the individual client (Emphasis on the needs of the client, especially his or her problems. No involvement with the client's family).

Level 2—Provide information for the family (Minimum involvement with the client's family, restricted to "fact" or "information" communication).

Level 3—Provide emotional support for the family (Encourage family members to disclose their feelings. Seek to show sympathy and emotional support to family members).

Level 4—Provide structured assessment and intervention (Provide well-planned support in reducing family stress and tension. Empower the family through changing the family patterns associated with the disability).

Level 5—Provide family therapy (Professional intervention for families that become dysfunctional due to disability).

Family-centered rehabilitation case management encompasses counselor functioning at Level 4 (i.e., constructing a structured assessment and planning procedure to provide information, support, and empowerment to clients and their families). To implement this procedure, the counselor must have both structural and relationship skills (Herbert, 1989; Ivey, 1988). Structural skills refer to the counselor's ability to identify problems or needs, define outcomes and alternatives, and confront family members' resistance. Relationship skills include the capacities to build rapport with and express empathic understanding to families.

Bray (1980) differentiated between the family intervention role of the counselor at the acute and extended phases of adjustment to disability. During the acute phase, the rehabilitation client and his or her family encounter and cope with the onset of the impact of disability. During this initial phase, client and family are experiencing tremendous stress, fear, shock, and distress. The role of the counselor at this stage is congruent with crisis intervention, with an emphasis on listening, understanding, observing, supporting, and encouraging (Bray, 1980; Power & Dell Orto, 1980c). According to Power and Dell Orto (1980c), counseling objectives during the acute phase include:

1. Establishing a trusting relationship with the family.

2. Learning early in family intervention the meaning of the disability to the family members, their expectations for the patient and for each other, and family goals.

3. Attempting to build self-esteem among the family members.

4. Observing the communication patterns among the family members. (p. 356)

During the extended phase of counseling, the rehabilitation client and his or her family members are in the process of gradually adapting to the disability. The roles of the counselor are to be an advocate and resource person (Power & Dell Orto, 1980c), emphasizing a proactive intervention approach (Bray, 1980). Counseling objectives in the extended phase include (a) improving family interaction, (b) providing information, (c) identifying and prioritizing treatment problems, and (d) developing and implementing treatment plans (Power & Dell Orto, 1980c).

Building a sound working relationship with the family is crucial in family-centered rehabilitation case management. One characteristic of such a good relationship is that the family members feel that the counselor is not working against them, but helping them seek solutions to their problems (Wright, 1960). Therefore, counselors should be aware of any personal bias that results in judgmental feelings toward the family. To have full cooperation from the family in the process of treatment, counselors must bring non-blaming attitudes into the counseling relationship (Cohen & Lavach, 1995). For example, when a counselor counsels the parents of a child with disability, Wright (1960) had the following suggestion:

> The counselor has to reach the point where, though recognizing parental shortcomings, he (she) can still respect the positives which are there if one looks for them. . . . He (she) must appreciate that the shortcomings of the parent have their own origins, and the effort to understand and cope with them must supplant derision of them. (p. 290)

The remainder of this chapter discusses how to operationalize a family-centered rehabilitation case management approach that encompasses individuals seeking rehabilitation services, their families, and available agency and community resources. Strategies are described for (a) doing a comprehensive needs analysis for people with disabilities and their families; (b) linking people with disabilities and their families to agency and community resources; and (c) implementing, monitoring, and evaluating the rehabilitation plan. In addition to their foundation in current literature, the steps of the family-centered case management approach have their roots in a services coordination project conducted in a co-located agency setting (Roessler, Mack, & Statler, 1975).

NEEDS ANALYSIS

The purpose of the needs analysis interaction is to delineate clearly the problems faced by the person and his or her family members. To do so, the rehabilitation counselor helps the individual answer the following questions in detail: (a) What is the problem? (b) Why is it a problem? and (c) How can the goals for resolving the problem be stated so that one can easily determine if it has been ameliorated or can be eliminated in the future? (Shank & Turnbull, 1993).

Developing Skills as a Needs Analyst

"Learning by doing" is a bit of folk wisdom that has considerable application for developing skill as a needs analyst. From experience working with people with disabilities and their families, rehabilitation counselors sharpen their ability to identify individual and household needs and then match those needs with services from other federal, state, and community programs. The key to a successful problem or need analysis is a sensitivity to both the individual and total household perspective, as well as to the spectrum of needs presented by the person and the household. In addition, the counselor must translate identified personal and household needs into agency referrals. Typical problems faced by people with disabilities and their families can be clustered into the following six need areas, which correspond to the range of health and human service agencies available in many communities:

1. *Physical Maintenance (PM)*—refers to health needs that are not disabling. It is primarily concerned with the services provided by Public Health and Social Services (e.g., immunization, family planning, and other health care monitoring and follow-up services).

2. *Physical Disabilities (PD)*—refers to physical problems that interfere with everyday functioning. The range of possible agencies that can help is broad, including Children's Clinic, Social Services, Mental Retardation and Developmental Disabilities, and Rehabilitation Services for people with visual or hearing impairments. Alcohol and drug abuse problems are included in the physical disability need area and may require referral to Alcoholics Anonymous, Narcotics Anonymous, and a variety of support groups for spouses and family members of individuals with substance abuse problems (e.g., ALANON).

3. *Psychological Adjustment (PA)*—refers to psychological problems that are not included under physical disability that indicate the need for referrals to mental health centers, psychologists, or psychiatrists.

4. *Counseling (C)*—refers to problems between and among household members that may best be alleviated by counseling and family therapy, although treatment is not indicated. There is a need for help from outside the household from resources such as community programs, schools, and churches.

5. *Training/Education (T/E)*—refers to problems related to insufficient academic or vocational preparation for all family members. Referrals to programs such as Department of Labor vocational training projects, Mental Retardation and Developmental Disabilities programs, Economic Opportunity Agency programs, local vocational and trade schools, postsecondary institutions, and youth services offered by community agencies and public schools may be in order.

6. *Finance (F)*—refers to needs stemming from lack of money. Food stamps, aid to families with dependent children, rent subsidies, and emergency payments represent specific responses to financial needs.

Table 13.2 presents examples of problem statements that rehabilitation clients might make to express both personal and household needs. In addition, each entry in Table 13.2 includes suggested responses consistent with the variety of health and human services previously described. Naturally, the problem statements reflect only a sampling of the types of issues that people with disabilities and their families face. Moreover, the potential range of responses offered reflect certain "generic" services offered by typical health and human services in most communities. Rehabilitation counselors must become experts on the range of services available in their own communities that supplement or exceed the referral options mentioned in Table 13.2.

TABLE 13.2
Client and Family Need Statements

1. #1 recently injured his back (ruptured disk) and is extremely anxious about his ability to work. He requires surgery and physical therapy. #2 lost her baby 3 weeks ago, and she may have physical complications as a result. The family has no income at the present time. #1 has had mental health group therapy in another state and thinks he needs to see a mental health counselor.

    Primary individual (#1) needs: PD, PA
    Family needs: PM, PD, F

2. #1 is a 43-year-old female single parent with chronic asthma and allergies. #2 has a learning disability and is enrolled in special education and her grades have improved in the past year. #3 dropped out of school because he did not like to go.

    Primary individual needs: PD
    Family needs: PD, T/E

3. #1 is a 28-year-old male with severe depression and alcoholism. He has worked as a farmer, but would like a job in auto mechanics even though he has no training in that area. #2 feels inadequate to cope with #1's depression. #3 may have to repeat first grade and is in poor health.

    Primary individual needs: PA, PD
    Family needs: C, PM

4. #1 is a 28-year-old female who received a brain injury in a recent automobile accident. She has worked as an optical lens grinder. Her husband (#2) is unemployed and has worked at unskilled jobs. There is no current source of income, and financial assistance is needed. #3 and #4 need their tonsils removed; however, funds are not available. #4 has a severe hearing problem which, according to #1, has resulted in learning problems in school. #1 doesn't remember her children's immunization status.

    Primary individual needs: PD
    Family needs: PM, PD, F, T/E

5. #1 is a 39-year-old female with severe Reiter's syndrome that causes pain in her joints, especially her feet. Since she cannot stand long periods of time, she wants training for a job in which she can sit or rest at times. #1 desires and is receiving family planning and immunizations for her child (#3). #2 has a drinking problem and has received treatment at a state hospital. Though she believes he needs further treatment, #1 does not feel #2 would accept it. #3 has juvenile diabetes and requires treatment.

    Primary individual needs: PM, PD, T/E
    Family needs: PM, PD, C

Note. #1 refers to the client; all other numbers refer to respective family members. PM = Physical Maintenance; PD = Physical Disabilities; PA = Psychological Adjustment; C = Counseling; T/E = Training/Education; and F = Finance.

In most cases, the statements in Table 13.2 include several problems and needs. The client (i.e., the primary person [#1]), may have more than one problem or need; likewise, the client's family members (#2, #3, and #4) may have one or more problems or needs suggesting eligibility for a variety of other services. Each problem statement in Table 13.2 ends with a coding of the need areas involved.

Organizing the Needs Analysis Data: A Sample Intake Form

The Program Development Form, modeled from a sample intake form addressing personal and household needs used in a family services project (Roessler et al., 1975), is presented in Table 13.3. Counselors may choose to complete the Program Development Form for the family or simply follow the logic of the form in their case planning.

Initially, counselors record family background information such as household member names and code numbers, sex, race, date of birth, relation to client, education level, and existing physical, emotional, or intellectual disabilities. The discussion then turns to the needs of the client and individual household members (see Table 13.4 for a list of needs analysis questions) and whether the presenting person wishes to pursue assistance for self and other family members. Specification of needs for each member of the family allows the rehabilitation counselor to identify possible referral sources and seek the person's reactions to beginning a program of household services.

In addition to presenting the rehabilitation process and services, the counselor describes the type of assistance he or she can provide to the family. Counselors can explain that they will work with their clients to

1. Help the person and other household members contact a variety of agencies that can assist them.

2. Clarify what the client and family members must do to apply for services.

3. Explain how the services will help each household member.

4. Monitor the progress of the household in meeting its needs.

Of course, counselors must secure the consent of their clients for the referrals, and, in some instances, people will reject services offered for themselves or their family members.

Barriers are also identified that might deter the client and other household members from contacting agencies and completing services. Important questions to ask about these barriers include (a) What can be done about the barrier? and (b) Who can do it? Counselors must explain carefully the solutions to barriers as well as who is responsible for removing different aspects of the barrier (the client, the household member, the counselor, the referring agency, or the individual referred to the agency). Barriers are clarified by questions such as (a) Do client and other household members know where to acquire services? (b) Do they have adequate transportation? and (c) Are they free to go for services or do they need childcare assistance or arranged time off from school or work? At this point, the role of counselors is to encourage and support the client and other family members to commit to and cooperate with the rehabilitation goals.

TABLE 13.3
Program Development Form

Family History

Family Member #	Name	Sex	Race	Date of Birth	Relation to #1	Education	Physical, Emotional, Intellectual Disabilities
1	Smith, John	1	1	1-8-48		12	Spinal cord injury; substance abuse
2	Smith, Jean	2	1	12-3-50	Wife	12	Carpal tunnel syndrome; depression
3	Jones, Michael	1	1	10-19-81	Stepson	11	None
4	Jones, Sara	2	1	5-7-83	Stepdaughter	7	Behavior or learning problem
5	Smith, Tom	1	1	12-20-86	Son	5	None
6	Smith, Toby	1	1	12-20-86	Son	5	None
7	Smith, Cindy	2	1	7-15-90	Daughter	2	None

Family Needs and Service Responses

Family Member #	Needs	Referral Agencies	Barriers	Progress Notes
1	Physical disability; finances	Alcoholics Anonymous; Income Maintenance		Attending AA; receiving income support and food stamps
2	Physical disability, psychological adjustment	Rehabilitation Mental Health Center	Transportation	Completed application; Using Ozark Transit
3				
4	Psychological adjustment Training/education	Children's Therapy Center School psychologist	Transportation	Using school transportation
5	Physical maintenance	Public Health		Receiving immunizations
6	Physical maintenance	Public Health		Receiving immunizations
7	Physical maintenance	Public Health		Receiving immunizations

TABLE 13.4
Establishing Family Need Status

Physical Maintenance

- What health problems do you or other members of your family have?
- Do you or your family have needs for family planning, medical checkups, or immunizations?

Physical Disabilities

- Do you or any of your family members have any serious physical, emotional, or learning problems?
- Are you or any other family member having problems with drugs or alcohol?

Psychological Adjustment

- Do you or anyone else in your family need to see a psychological professional?

Counseling

- Are there family problems that counseling might help resolve (e.g., fights, arguments, or conflicts)?

Training/Education

- What vocational interests do you or other family members have?
- Will you or any of the rest of your family need additional education or training to pursue those interests?

Finance

- Do you need money right now for food, rent, childcare, or transportation?
- Are there any other pressing personal or family needs for money?

Linking People with Disabilities and Their Families to Agency and Community Resources

Crimando and Riggar (1996) argued convincingly for the need to involve multiple service providers in rehabilitation programs. Even though rehabilitation counselors assume responsibility for the entire person, they cannot provide all of the services that any individual needs. They are even less able to provide comprehensive services when the family is taken into consideration. Crimando and Riggar also stressed that limited funding for social agencies is the prospect for the foreseeable future. Therefore, rehabilitation counselors must efficiently involve a host of "paid for" (i.e., by a third party such as churches) and "no-cost" services from community programs if they are to create comprehensive responses to the needs of individuals and their families.

Involving multiple agencies in service programs requires rehabilitation counselors to know the "what, where, how, and why of a broad range of community services" (Crimando & Riggar, 1996). They must share this information with clients and their families as well as teach them how to use these agencies in solving problems occurring at a later date. Thereby, counselors inculcate an independent problem-solving approach that will serve people well when they encounter similar problems in the future.

Consistent with information presented elsewhere in Chapter 13, the process of using community resources for clients and their families involves three steps. First, the counselor assesses the service needs of both clients and their families across broad categories such as health maintenance, intensive disability-related interventions, psychological adjustment, family counseling, education and vocational training, and financial support for basic living requirements (e.g., food, shelter, and clothing). Next, counselors identify resources and agencies that can provide the services needed to return the client and family system to a stable state. To be skillful in coordinating family-centered service plans, rehabilitation counselors must educate themselves thoroughly about community service providers. They must know the agencies' purposes, eligibility requirements, services, staff qualifications, referral procedures, timelines of service delivery, type of follow-up services, cost factors, and reputation among consumers (Crimando & Riggar, 1996). A list of services potentially available for incorporation into rehabilitation programs is provided in Table 13.5.

To use community resources effectively, it is also important for counselors to explore no-cost services in the community to meet the needs of clients and their families. Studies have indicated that many churches or para-church organizations offer successful programs in charitable giving, substance abuse treatment, recidivism prevention, and job training and placement (Shapiro & Wright, 1996; Walters & Neugeboren, 1995). According to Walters and Neugeboren (1995), churches and para-church organizations can supplement rehabilitation services in many ways. For example, benefits from such programs include (a) helping the client be independent from counselors, (b) expanding the client's social network in the community, (c) reducing the social stigma that the client encounters as he or she returns to the community, (d) offering nonclinical interventions to improve the client's social functioning (e.g., social interaction, mutual respect), and (e) exchanging valuable resources between the church or para-church organization and the rehabilitation agency. Walters and Neugeboren (1995) also suggested that counselors can search the potential church or para-church community resources by using the following methods:

1. Check to see if any agency staff, volunteers, or board members are active in religious organizations that might be receptive to linkage.

2. See if clients are involved in any religious organizations, or if relatives of clients are active in the religious community.

TABLE 13.5
The Array of Resources and Services

Health and Diagnostic Services

Home Health Services—Health care and social services designed to enable the person to remain in the home rather than receive institutional care.

Community Mental Health—Comprehensive, community-based mental health services including medication; medication management; and group, family, and individual therapy.

Pain Clinics—Multimodal treatment for chronic pain with the end goals of reduced consumption of pain medication and increased daily functioning.

Alcohol–Drug Programs—Programs including self-help, detoxification, psychological services, and family services to help individuals resume family and vocational roles without reliance on alcohol or drugs.

Social Services

Social Security Administration—Source of Social Security Disability Insurance (SSDI) and Supplemental Security Income (SSI), which provide income assistance for people with disabilities who are no longer able to work and their families. Also provides Medicare and Medicaid, which constitute major medical insurance programs for people with disabilities.

Children and Family Services—Divisions of state social services that provide adoption, foster care, and child-protection assistance.

Women's Centers—Community-based facilities offering emergency shelter, rape crisis, supportive counseling, and advocacy services.

Family Planning—Programs such as Planned Parenthood Federation of America, which offers family planning, pre- and post-natal consultation, and medical counseling and screening.

Related Rehabilitation Sources

Rehabilitation Facilities—Community-based programs delivering work evaluation, work adjustment services, and contractual production work on a fee-for-services basis.

Work Hardening Programs—Programs evaluating the work-related impact of disability and enhancing the person's productivity through graded work activities.

Rehabilitation Engineering/Technology Services—Programs or consultants capable of (a) identifying barriers to access and productivity for people with disabilities and (b) prescribing assistive technology or job and environmental modification strategies.

Supported Employment—Programs offering on-the-job training and job coaching to increase the employment success of people with severe disabilities.

Centers for Independent Living—Programs offering information and referral services, counseling, advocacy, and independent living skill training.

(continues)

TABLE 13.5 (*Continued*)

Vocational and Employment Services

Employment Security Job Service—U.S. Department of Labor sponsored programs offering vocational assessment, vocational counseling, and job placement services for people who are unemployed.

Private Employment Services—Employment agencies that (a) provide workers for a limited type of service (i.e., temporary employment) or (b) screen potential employees for employers and help job seekers secure or upgrade employment. Typically, these agencies charge for their placement assistance.

Legal Aid and Advocacy

Legal Aid and Public Interest Advocacy—Organizations offering legal consultation and representation for individuals from low-income groups.

Civil Rights and Equal Employment—Federal and state programs with the explicit purpose of mediating complaints regarding discrimination in employment (Equal Employment Opportunity Commission), transportation claims (U.S. Department of Transportation), public accommodation claims (State Attorney General), and telecommunication claims (Federal Communication Commission).

Client Assistance Programs—Programs offering "ombudsmen" support (i.e., advice regarding service programs and conflicts regarding service provision) for people with disabilities receiving services from state vocational rehabilitation agencies.

---

3. Visit area churches.

4. Exchange newsletters, invite clergy or significant lay leaders to agency open houses, share brochures, and offer to speak to church committees and groups about rehabilitation services. (p. 54)

Having developed an in-depth understanding of programs available in the community, rehabilitation counselors can begin the process of resource selection. As Crimando and Riggar (1996) stressed, resource selection necessarily follows a "satisficing" strategy (i.e., "do the best one can with the resources that are available"). Once agencies are selected that can meet the needs of the individual and the family, the counselor makes referrals to the programs via both telephone contacts and formal letters of referral. These letters of referral should provide sufficient background information about clients and their families for the agency to determine eligibility for services. In addition, the counselor should clarify service needs in the referral letter as well as list any questions that the agency could answer to aid the counselor in working with the person and family members. The referral letter documents that a contact was made, the purpose of the contact, and projected timelines for eligibility determination and service delivery. It can also clarify the types of support services the person needs to initiate and maintain contact (i.e., childcare, transportation, and housing).

Implementing, Monitoring, and Evaluating the Service Plan

With the identification of needs, referral agencies, community resources, and solutions to barriers, counselors are ready to help families implement their service plans. At this point, counselors should explain their intention to follow the client's and the family's progress by periodically checking to determine if their needs have changed or if they are having difficulty receiving quality service. Counselors should request permission to contact involved agencies for monitoring information. They should also encourage clients and their household members to follow through on the referrals as soon as possible. The counselor may choose to give the client a copy of the plan or simply review the next steps in the plan to be taken by the family. Examples of important steps include the following: make appointments, obtain birth certificates or Social Security numbers, keep scheduled appointments, and follow recommendations regarding medication and exercise regimens.

After specifying what the client and household members need, and providing referral contacts with a variety of agencies (telephone or referral letter), counselors monitor subsequent client and household activity. Did the person contact the agency? Did the agency accept or reject the applicant? What service plans and goals exist for the person? What behavioral steps are required for the client or household member to start, continue, and complete services? What are the estimated beginning and ending dates for agency services?

During long-term monitoring, the final phase of the household referral process, the counselor gathers information on the client's perceptions and on the referral agencies' experiences. Counselors can explore whether clients believe that their needs are being met. For example, "In the past, we identified several needs for you and your family. How do you feel about those needs now? Compared to when you and your family started your program, are your problems much greater, greater, no different, less, or much less?" Counselors can contact involved agencies to determine whether clients and family members are maintaining contact, making satisfactory progress, and following through on recommendations.

If people report no progress in resolving personal or household problems, counselors may wish to inquire about the following: (a) Are clients and household members doing what they said they would do? (b) Are individuals on schedule in making and keeping appointments, taking specified actions, and following the prescribed regimen? (c) Are results consistent with client and counselor expectations? (d) Are planned programs still what individuals and household members want and need? and (e) Are personal and household needs still realistic? If individuals respond negatively to any of these questions, they may require additional help from rehabilitation counselors and personnel or referral agencies.

Counselors may also need to check with individual referral agencies to determine whether adjustments are needed. Agency personnel are good sources of information about program adjustments needed, additional problems that have occurred, and unresolved barriers to service delivery. Counselors should maintain contact with their clients and any involved family members in order to determine the types of closures achieved with referred agencies and the effects of those closures on the client's rehabilitation program. The range of closure statuses include successful, unsuccessful, service dropout, and continuing services.

CONCLUDING STATEMENT

Critics of rehabilitation have stressed the dangers of an overly individualistic focus that views the person with the disability as the sole point of intervention. Recognizing the significant impact that disability has on the individual, these observers have pointed out that disability also affects all those in the person's circle of family members and friends. Indeed, disability imposes a toll on families that is experienced in economic, social, and psychological terms. Hence, rehabilitation counselors must adopt a family-centered rehabilitation case management approach.

No one agency or counselor can, however, meet the variety of needs experienced by any one individual or his or her family. Hence, a family-centered rehabilitation case management perspective is warranted that involves available federal, state, and community resources in closing the gap between the current and desired lifestyles of individuals with disabilities and their households. In the process of helping families cope with disability-related and personal problems and enhance their quality of life (QOL), rehabilitation counselors provide needs assessment, counseling, and coordinated services.

Needs analysis may be done formally through the completion of a comprehensive intake form (Program Development Form) or informally through the discussion of personal and household needs in relation to community resources. Once identified, the needs may dictate services emphasizing health and physical maintenance, amelioration of physical and substance abuse problems, psychological adjustment, family counseling and therapy, educational or vocational training, financial assistance, or any combination of these. Barriers to receiving the services, such as lack of transportation, childcare, or time off from work, must be resolved so that clients and their household members can pursue service plans.

Along with effective needs analysis abilities, counselors must possess the skills of active listening, clarification, problem solving, and planning. Competent counselors help people clarify not only what their needs are but also how they feel about these situations and the various agencies that might assist them and their households. The coordination aspect of family-centered case management begins with the phase of initiating services and ends with the phase of terminating services. Initially, individuals with disabilities and their family members need to know how to contact agencies and apply for services, and counselors must monitor client and household progress in scheduling and meeting appointments, following through on recommended programs and plans, and terminating agency services. Together, the client and the counselor determine whether needs have been met or whether additional services are required.

From the family-centered rehabilitation case management perspective, successful completion of services or satisfactory continued involvement is synonymous with need fulfillment—that is, enabling the individual and the family to develop, maintain, or restore a satisfactory state of equilibrium. This state of equilibrium provides a positive overall context for the client's rehabilitation program. As a result, the probability increases that family dynamics are supportive of positive rehabilitation participation and outcomes on the client's part.

Rehabilitation Case Management and Managed Care

Richard J. Beck

Case management has always been the modus operandi and forte of the field of rehabilitation. Unlike other, more traditional fields, rehabilitation has striven in the last 25 years to train persons to adopt the concept that rehabilitationists must be skilled in both human communication (counseling and negotiating) and coordination of community resources. This training, and the knowledge base that this profession has established through research, seems particularly well suited to a managed-care environment. This point will be demonstrated by (a) defining managed care and its history, (b) describing case management in rehabilitation in ways that seek to demonstrate its effectiveness in responding to the mandates of managed care, and (c) suggesting ways in which the match between the requirements of managed care and the strengths of the traditional rehabilitation model may be marketed. Managed care has created a vast change in the environments in which rehabilitation case management is practiced (i.e., in the private for-profit, private non-profit, and public sectors).

MANAGED CARE

Managed care has struck the community of health and human service providers like a major hurricane. As a result, providers are scurrying to understand this phenomenon and adapt to its effects on the service delivery environment. In order to ensure their inclusion in the group of approved providers eligible to receive reimbursements and contracts from funding sources, rehabilitation service providers and other types of human service agents are banding together into "provider alliances."

Concurrent with this consolidation move, providers are adapting the design of services in response to the coverage policies of the managed care organizations. Adjustments include changing the ways in which providers account for their actions and modifying their services according to the preferences of the funding source. For example, substance abuse centers are abandoning the 28-day inpatient treatment model in favor of outpatient treatments, and mental health centers are abandoning open-ended therapeutic treatment for the more problem-specific brief therapy.

According to Hampton (1993), managed care is "a method of organizing care that emphasizes communication and coordination of care among health team members . . . the essence is the organization of unit-based care so that specific patient outcomes can be achieved within fiscally responsible time frames (lengths of stay) while utilizing resources appropriate (in amount and sequence) to the specific case type and the individual patient" (p. 21). In other words, managed care is a system that takes into account the processes required to deliver appropriate services, the costs expected for such services, and the client outcomes desired within a specific time period and diagnostic category. It usually implies prepaid financing, comprehensive service, an organized delivery system, and a specifically defined population (Hale & Hunter, 1988). For example, the prepaid financing might be a capitation (i.e., a per-head fee for persons in the same category). The emphasis on comprehensive service relates to effective, holistic treatment, rather than fragmented, unconnected, and inchoate services. An organized delivery system might bring all of the formerly disjointed elements of the health-delivery system together in a team approach (in which administration and financing have as much input into service delivery as professional diagnosis and treatment). Finally, the specifically defined population refers to a more accurate diagnosis of recipients of service in order to make titration of resources (i.e., differential allocation according to severity of the problem) possible.

The principal objective inherent in managed care is cost control, and any insurance or funding scheme that adopts cost control measures is usually referred to as a managed care plan. Hale and Hunter (1988) provide three criteria for a managed care organization: (a) it offers one or more products which integrate financing and management with the delivery of health care services to an enrolled population; (b) it employs or contracts with an organized provider network which undertakes the responsibility to deliver services and which (as a network or as individual providers) either shares financial risk and/or has some incentive to deliver efficient services; and (c) it uses an information system capable of monitoring and evaluating patterns of utilization and financial outlays" (p. 18).

Addressing the impact of managed care plans in the health care industry, Hale and Hunter (1988) observed that providers find it necessary to forge alliances and to comply with service mandates. Those that remain independent may attempt to enhance their marketing programs, increase their specialization, or discount fees. In 1 year, 1996, in Illinois, three affiliations (i.e., protective associations) emerged whose mission is to bond providers together in order to respond to the perception by providers that the future would bring changes in the way of funding plans that are a type of managed care. Affiliated Network Plus is basically a response by the Illinois Association of Rehabilitation Facilities whose concern is mostly working with persons with developmental disabilities, while the Midwest Behavioral Association and the River-to-River Association are concerned with mental health and substance abuse. These associations offer a myriad of shared services from marketing to practice management. The size of these associations also provides a feeling of safety for their members.

Managed care will have many other significant effects on providers and clients alike. For example, contracted providers are subject to review by the managed care organization (MCO), and thus need to maintain a system for evaluating the effectiveness of their services. Cost effectiveness is a particular issue for preventive care services among contractors that may be approved in managed care plans only to the extent that they demonstrably save money. Consumers of managed care services may have to pay for an increasing share of their treatment, especially when seeking services outside of the system of preferred providers. Finally, managed care funding sources will increasingly look to the credentialing of providers in order to ensure that professional services are of a high quality (Hale & Hunter, 1988).

An example of the effect of managed care on rehabilitation programs recently appeared in a popular news periodical. Elizabeth Gleick wrote in an article in the February 5, 1996, issue of *Time* that substance abuse clinics were "retooling" for managed care. She reported that the 30-day inpatient programs were no longer being funded by managed care programs when these payers became aware that treatment usually ended when insurance coverage limits were reached. She reported that rehabilitation facilities now must offer a range of treatment options, with insurance companies playing a major role in deciding who receives *what* for *how long*. In Gleick's report, treatment personnel express concern about quality of care when the insurer makes treatment decisions, such as the fear that chronic conditions are being treated like acute ones.

History of Managed Care

The first attempt to contain mushrooming national health care expenditures (from $19 billion in 1960 to $275 billion in 1980, due to the enactment of Medicare) was Medicare's system of Diagnosis-Related Groups (DRGs) (Taylor & Taylor, 1994). For the first time, hospitals went from a cost-based to a price-based system in which they shared risk (i.e., profits are reduced as price of service increases) in rising costs. In 1983, with the assistance of Yale University, Medicare developed a methodology in which 468 DRGs established reimbursement rates for hospitals. Based on average historical costs related to medical diagnoses, Medicare paid the hospital a specific fee for each DRG at discharge. This change had the net effect of making the hospitals more responsive in lowering their own costs and hence ensuring a profit. Subsequently, many state Medicaid programs followed the lead of Medicare and used DRG-based payments (Taylor & Taylor, 1994).

Learning from the success of DRGs in cost containment, Health Maintenance Organizations (HMOs) and Preferred Provider Organizations (PPOs) experimented with similar pricing strategies. PPOs contract with providers at favorable rates and set up strict criteria for patient access to services, while HMOs use capitation agreements to realize cost containment. Under capitation, primary-care providers become gatekeepers who are paid a per-member fee each month. Profit occurs to the extent that outpatient services and preventive services are emphasized, and where more expensive services, such as surgery and hospitalization, are limited. This type of plan naturally rewards physicians who practice in general internal medicine and family care and punishes surgical and procedure-oriented specialists. The movement from charge-based systems, such as indemnity insurance, where there is complete freedom to choose physicians and for physicians to prescribe, to managed-care–type cost-containment plans, has vastly increased the importance and complexity of the finance departments of funding organizations such as insurers (Hale & Hunter, 1988; Taylor & Taylor, 1994).

Consequently, fee guidelines created by managed care funders have caused providers to respond with care maps (Hampton, 1993) in which the multidisciplinary team's actions are compared to a timeline, which is so detailed that it contains an outcome index specifying interventions required to produce desired outcomes. The net effect is the creation of treatment protocols for specific patient needs, which also spell out the negative consequences for lack of timely delivery of specific services (Hampton, 1993). For example, the patient with open heart surgery is compared to a care map that describes patient problems and needs on a daily basis for an expected 6 days of hospitalization, and charting becomes a *check and initial* system on the care map. Accountability for evaluations at variance with protocol standards (patients who vary from expectations) lies with the nurse, who charts the variance and analyzes it. Data regarding variances are then used by quality assurance teams to modify the optimal treatment protocols for meeting specific patient needs (Hampton, 1993).

Many states have responded with enthusiasm to managed care in the way they deliver increasingly expensive services to people with mental illness or substance addiction. States such as Washington and Tennessee have obtained Medicaid waivers in order to expand and control behavioral health services to high need (as well as uninsured) populations, to assure service intensity commensurate with recipient need, to provide individualized care requiring ongoing community support, and to reduce inappropriate use of acute care services. Allowing states to experiment with managed care alternatives to the traditional Medicaid system (Manderscheid & Henderson, 1995), waivers modify the Medicaid provisions that services be available on a statewide basis; that the amount, duration, or scope of services be the same for all recipients; or that recipients have freedom in their choice of providers.

Managed Care and Persons with Disabilities

Growing rapidly in the last 10 years, managed care affects persons with specific types of disabilities, particularly those with chronic problems, including cancer, mental illness, substance addiction, and mental retardation. In a feature article in *Time* (January 22, 1996), Erik Larsen wrote about the problems that a cancer patient experienced with her managed care organization, Health Net. He documented that Health Net had obstructed a cancer patient in obtaining payment for a bone marrow transplant that was, in her physician's opinion, essential. Health Net argued that the oft-used procedure was "experimental" and hence not covered. The article also cited an arbitration panel's decision that Health Net "crossed the line in interfering with the doctor–patient relationship" when company officials attempted to intimidate physician providers (p. 52). The cancer patient's surviving spouse was awarded $1.02 million in damages for the intentional infliction of emotional stress. The *Time* article intensively described abuses on the part of managed care funding organizations that have resulted in a paradigm shift—physicians are no longer accountable to patients, but rather to the managed care organization. Cancer patients seem to be the most vulnerable due to the fact that many cancer treatments are defined by insurers as investigational.

Anthony (1993) quotes Santiago (1992) in the *Psychosocial Rehabilitation Journal* as follows: ". . . the debate in health care, as well as in mental health care, is not whether rationing is acceptable or even exists, but how to ration and which form is tolerable" (p. 1097). Using the conceptual foundation of the Community Support System of service and the psychiatric rehabilitation model, Anthony (1993) advocates "more than symptom alleviating treatment; wanting such things as a suitable place to live, appropriate work and educational opportunities, and friends" as treatment goals (pp. 121–122). "From a managed care perspective, the value of an expanded constellation of comprehensive services lies not only in providing people with the services they want, but also in their potential to reduce more costly inpatient treatment services" (Anthony, 1993, pp. 121–122). Anthony sees case managed interventions as capable of actually decreasing more costly inpatient stays. He predicts optimistically that managed care will result in more comprehensive but less costly services for people, with a reduction in the cost of services, settings, and professionals.

In their chapter on managed mental health and substance abuse services, Anderson and Berlant (1995) acknowledge the factors that make these populations unique. These factors include more demand for enhanced managed care services to help people with these disabilities cope with social systems such as the family, increased societal stress, and the chronicity inherent in these conditions. These authors also acknowledge the "proliferation of private hospitals as a result of high profit margins, cheap capital investment, lifting of certificate of need laws in several large states, and exemption from diagnosis-related groups (and) aggressive advertising campaigns paid for by private hospital chains, often masquerading as public service announcements" (p. 150).

Managed care for mental illness and substance abuse (MH/SA) involves three principles of treatment: alternatives to hospitalization (psychiatric or substance abuse), goal-directed (i.e., brief) therapy, and crisis intervention. Partial hospitalization (such as day, evening, or weekend nonresidential) proved itself in several research studies (Schene & Gersens, 1986) to the satisfaction of managed care organizations. Inpatient care in substance abuse has not been found to be superior to outpatient care (Saxe & Goodman, 1988). Managed care organizations have also been influenced by research studies that support the effectiveness of brief therapy, which emphasizes problem solving rather than personality change oriented therapy (Husby et al., 1985). Finally, research has provided support for the belief that crisis intervention may obviate inappropriate psychiatric care, as well as diminish the incidence of future crises (Whittington, 1992). MCOs have used this information to justify (a) setting day or dollar limits on specific services (favoring brief therapy over long-term therapy, for example) and (b) using a gatekeeper to channel clients to a network provider approved by the MCO. Tangentially, MCOs use a broader range of professionals than traditional insurance indemnity plans (which use more traditional licensed professionals such as psychologists), in which a variety of professionals with master's degrees can be providers, thus assuring lower cost services (Anderson & Berlant, 1995).

In addition to shaping treatment choices, MCOs have used case management "for promoting cost-effective, quality MH/SA care" (Anderson & Berlant, 1995, p. 154). Anderson and Berlant point out that case management strives for four objectives: (a) promoting correct diagnosis and effective treatment; (b) promoting efficient use of resources; (c) preventing recidivism; and (d) monitoring for and avoiding substandard care. These authors state that MCOs use systems of triage (the amount of services or dollars are proportioned according to severity of disability) and quality screens (diagnosis-based protocols) to channel the patient into the correct network. They describe case management as "practiced optimally by qualified front-line case management staff with a minimum of 5 to 10 years of relevant clinical experience who are thoroughly trained in case management techniques, backed up by readily available doctoral-level advisors with relevant clinical experience" (p. 155). The gatekeeper role is assumed by a variety of professionals including Employee Assistance Program (EAP) counselors, case managers, and primary care physicians. Although widely used for assessment and treatment, matching client and services by gatekeepers in MCO systems is rarely based on theoretical or usable criteria. Anderson and Berlant (1995) listed examples of such criteria—geographic accessibility, comprehensive services, willingness to negotiate favorable rates, cooperation with MCO standards, credentialed staff, and a practice philosophy deemed desirable by MCOs. New associations are springing up to ensure that MH/SA providers have inside information to guide their access to MCOs.

In the area of developmental disabilities, the National Association of State Directors of Developmental Disabilities Services collaborated on a *Guidebook* on managed care (Smith & Ashbaugh, 1995). Smith and Ashbaugh (1995) have indicated that "this collaboration grew out of real concerns that service systems would be turned over lock, stock and barrel to for-profit managed care companies that would put their own economic interest ahead of those of people with developmental disabilities and their families" (p. i). However, the authors of the *Guidebook* offer a more positive note—that managed care might transform the "old–older" developmental disabilities service systems (program-driven, categorical services) into consumer-driven, person-centered systems of support. Consequently, the *Guidebook* was created to provide a blueprint on how that might be accomplished.

A number of guidelines for managed care for persons with disabilities have been provided (Smith & Ashbaugh, 1995). First, many people with developmental disabilities do not fit the primary care mold that is inherent in managed care. For example, these persons and their chronic conditions are better addressed by specialists in specialized centers than by general practitioners. Gatekeeping functions could be performed by these specialists. Second, varying capitation rates could be employed based on "risk adjustment," in which certain classes of persons are likely to consume more health care resources than others. Third, persons with special needs could avoid the mismatch with "patient averaging" by being exempted from mandatory enrollment in MCOs, or by creating "boutique" or "specialty" managed care plans that limit enrollment to persons with certain defined conditions. For example, Wisconsin's "I-Care" managed care plan was created to serve Medicaid recipients with disabilities exclusively. The plan operates through a partnership of the Wisconsin Health organization and the Milwaukee Center for Independence (National Association of State Directors of Developmental Disabilities Services, 1995; Smith & Ashbaugh, 1995).

CASE MANAGEMENT AND MANAGED CARE: A RESEARCH REVIEW

Ryan, Sherman, and Judd (1994) documented that in mental health services, habilitation–rehabilitation and community support services were more effective than traditional psychiatric services, lending legitimacy to the approach used in managed care (in which comprehensive, mainstreamed services are emphasized over institutional, inpatient, traditional services). Scarnulis (1989) has indicated that the following factors may affect the effectiveness of case management:

1. degree of independence of the person served;

2. disability served and severity;

3. family strengths (income, extended family involvement, ability of family to provide support, etc.);

4. agency resources;

5. case manager skill, experience, and education;

6. availability of community resources;

7. duration of the disability;

8. intensity of involvement, e.g. critical periods; and

9. role expectations. (p. 143)

McDonald (1989) has cited additional factors that may be detrimental to the case manager's ability to manage, such as lack of concern, time, skills, or authority.

Rapp (1995) comprehensively reviewed the literature regarding use of case management in the field of mental health, the field in which managed care has had the most impact. He cited four prominent models that have been addressed in the research literature: (a) the broker model; (b) the rehabilitation model; (c) the Assertive Community Treatment (ACT) model; and (d) the strengths model. In the broker model, the case manager assesses the needs of a person for services and identifies whether those services are available. The emphasis is placed on formal mental health services, though responsibility for carrying through with those services is primarily located with the client and the client's family. The results of six studies that evaluated the broker model of case management suggest that, for most clients, the model produces little positive effect. Clients served with the broker model tended to use more, rather than less, hospitalization, and showed no increase in quality of life (QOL) (Rapp, 1995).

The second model is the *rehabilitation model* that, according to Rapp (1995), emphasizes identifying and enriching client strengths, with planning programs and evaluating skill deficits playing significant roles. Roughly equivalent to the "Berven assessment model of case management" (discussed later in this chapter) the rehabilitation model is client-centered, placing significant emphasis on client preferences. Rapp noted that this model has only been evaluated in one study, and the results were inconclusive.

The third model, the *ACT model*, is based on Project ACT in Madison, Wisconsin (Stein & Test, 1980). This model requires the active involvement of an interdisciplinary team of professionals led by a case manager. It combines clinical and case management services and provides symptom management, as well as direct intervention, in the client's environment in order to meet client needs. The clinical aspect involves family counseling, coping-skill teaching, and assertive outreach. Citing 17 studies, Rapp (1995) noted that this is the most well-researched model in mental health. The results indicated a consistent decrease in hospital use, although other outcomes were consistently *not* influenced by ACT, such as occupational functioning, arrests and other contacts with the criminal justice system, and extent of family burden. Outcome criteria on which mixed results were found included social functioning, leisure time activities, behavioral symptomatology, medication compliance, emergency room contacts, and QOL. Rapp noted that the lack of fidelity in these studies to the original model makes conclusions tentative. Even the finding about a decrease in hospitalization is questionable, however, because some programs simply shifted people from hospitalization to residential living, which Rapp (1995) terms "*trans*institutionalization" rather than deinstitutionalization.

The last model, the *strengths model*, rests on several principles. First, counselors identify a person's strengths and actively create situations (environmental or personal) in which success can be achieved and the level of personal strength enhanced. Second, human behavior is largely a function of the resources available to individuals, and a pluralistic society values equal access to resources. Third, people who are mentally ill may need help in securing resources in important life domains essential for human growth and development (Rapp, 1995, p. 8). This model has been the subject of six studies (two experimental) with consistently positive outcomes. Improved social functioning was found in both experimental studies, and the other studies noted improvements in QOL, occupational functioning, leisure time activities, behavioral symptomatology, client satisfaction, and family burden. Decreased hospital use was found in some studies. However, one study showed an increase in hospital use. Rapp (1995) concluded that this model is promising because positive results are consistent across many studies, the quality of the research is high, and the model has produced positive outcomes in areas that were not obtained in research on the ACT model.

Based on an overview of all four case management models, Rapp (1995) attempted to define effective principles of practice. First, the use of teams is essential, though Rapp warns that the team is needed for backup, support, and service planning, and that other activities may be left to the direction of a single case manager. Second, quality staffing is critical. Experienced and trained professionals should act as case managers, though professional specialty is less of an issue. The presence of a nurse on the team seems to be critical to good outcomes, but the team can be staffed by psychiatrists, social workers, and rehabilitation counselors. Successful staffing ratios did not exceed 1 case manager to 10 clients (or 1:12 in the strengths model). Third, in-person, in-community contacts are far more efficacious than in-office visits or telephone contacts. This factor alone may account for the iatrogenic (counselor-caused) findings in the broker model. And fourth, the case manager as the primary deliverer of services, with a deemphasis on referral, is a more powerful predictor of client success over a variety of outcomes (such as hospitalization, employment, independent living, and goal achievement). The importance of the emphasis on the clinical and teaching role of the case manager was stressed by Rapp. As in traditional rehabilitation counseling, the relationship is pivotal.

Factors important in case management that were not included in empirical research were the fact that these services should be lifelong (time unlimited) and that client autonomy (self-determination) be present in all successful models (Rapp, 1995). Clients who are mentally ill or addicted have predictable relapses. Furthermore, because it obviates tension between the client and the case manager, the respect for the autonomy of the client protects clients from excessive or inappropriate direction by the case manager.

In regard to the characteristics of effective case management models in the field of mental health, some additional management suggestions of Rapp (1995) included (pp. 29–31):

1. Team leaders should be experienced mental health professionals.

2. Case managers can be paraprofessional (e.g. BA level), but need access to specialists; involvement of nurses seems particularly important.

3. Caseload sizes can vary based on client severity, geography, etc., but should never exceed 20:1. The average caseload size across program clients should probably be 12:1 to 15:1.

4. Clients need 24 hour, 7 days a week access to crisis and emergency services. That service should require access to staff who have familiarity and a relationship with the client (can be and perhaps should be the case manager).

5. Length of case management service should be indeterminate and expected to be on-going (although intensity at any point in time would vary).

6. The use of naturally occurring community resources (landlords, employers, coaches, neighbors, churches, friends, clubs, junior colleges, etc.) should be encouraged.

7. Case managers should have ultimate responsibility for client services (with the exception of medication).

8. They retain authority even in referral situations.

9. Clients should be given equal or greater authority than case managers or other professionals in treatment and life decisions with the exception of hospitalization decisions.

Case management models also differ along other dimensions, such as "aggressive" or "problem-focused" case management (Corrigan & Kayton-Weinberg, 1993). In the aggressive model, case managers actively assist patients in attaining service goals such as financial aid on the assumption that case managers are more skilled in navigating service agencies. The "down side" is that the patient assumes a passive role and learns little about self-advocacy. In problem-focused case management, "clinical" case managers (i.e., case managers who are also counselors, such as in the rehabilitation model) see each need situation as an opportunity to empower the patient through teaching problem-solving skills. The down side to this method is that some patients lack the cognitive skills to use a multistep decision-making method. Corrigan and Kayton-Weinberg (1993) have suggested that the solution to this problem is to differentiate the appropriateness of the two types of case management by phase of illness. In the acute phase of illness, patients should be provided aggressive case management. As they proceed toward relative remission, they should be involved in problem solving to enhance independence of functioning.

On a cautionary note, Dozier, Lee, Kleir, Toprac, and Mason (1993) found that adults with psychiatric disorders randomly assigned to case management were hospitalized *more* in the first year of treatment than those assigned to "standard care." These researchers opined that "the effectiveness of case management is limited by the resources available in the community as well as by the size of case managers' caseloads . . . If community-based services are inadequate, then case managers will be limited in their abilities to help clients access services . . . and if [they] are overextended with unwieldy caseloads, they will be unable to develop the relationship needed to avert crises" (pp. 187–188).

In a study on the importance of social recreational programs in case management with people with mental illnesses, Pyke and Atcheson (1993) pointed out that these programs are not only pleasurable and educational, but provide an opportunity to develop supports beyond formal caregivers and family members. In this study, case managers identified the following barriers to service delivery: (a) problems in accessibility of the service; (b) problems in the accommodation and acceptability (mainly having to do with the attitudes, values, and beliefs of staff members) of the service; (c) availability of the service (many persons with mental illness cannot use the YMCA unless support staff are available); and (d) affordability. The authors proposed lowering user fees, providing transportation subsidies, meeting with service providers to discuss activities and supports, providing consultation, identifying people who might assist with supporting clients in the use of social recreational activities, and maintaining an inventory of accessible activities.

Case management has demonstrated its usefulness and validity in both managed care organizations and rehabilitation service provisions. In their review of the research literature, Novak-Amado, McAnally, and Hubbard-Linz (1989) noted that the content of most literature on case management is conceptual rather than empirical, though some empirical studies document that case manager linkages "led to increases in the accessibility, comprehensiveness, and volume of services provided to clients" (p. 8).

The professional literature provides a testimonial to the wide variety of approaches to specific populations and situations in rehabilitation. Siegel et al. (1995) provide an example of how the strengths model of case management can be used effectively as an alternative approach to the more costly, and narrower, traditional disease model of alcoholism and substance abuse treatment. Noting problems with the traditional, but widely accepted, disease model approach such as creating resistance and noncompliance, emphasizing past failings by concentrating on pathology, treating everyone in hospitals or professional offices, and surrendering one's control to a more knowing professional, the case management approach instead focuses treatment on a patient's *strengths* rather than limitations. The case management approach is seen by the authors as a way to neutralize the problems with the disease model and to empower patients by encouraging their ownership and involvement. The authors state that the strengths perspective approach to case management is based on five principles:

1. Facilitating the use of clients' strengths, abilities, and assets.

2. Encouraging client control over the search for needed resources.

3. Promoting the client and case manager/advocate relationship as primary.

4. Viewing the community as a resource and not a barrier.

5. Advancing case management/advocacy as an active, assertive endeavor. (p. 69)

The authors tested the model with patients at the Dayton, Ohio, Department of Veterans Affairs Medical Center, with a sample of inpatients and outpatients with (a) a variety of drug and alcohol problems, plus employment problems (27%); (b) multiple problems such as health complications, inconsistent employment, and substance abuse (23%); (c) family problems (30%); and (d) primarily medical and psychiatric problems (20%). While traditional substance abuse counselors concentrated on the traditional disease model concept, half the group was assigned a case manager. The case manager employed a specific protocol that included providing some tangible service to the patient early in the process, and having patients rate themselves in nine domains: life skills, finance, leisure, relationships, living arrangements, occupation or education, health, internal resources, and recovery. Patients then rated themselves on their strengths using the *ETP Progress Evaluation Scale* (PES), which makes patients aware of their strengths and assets. Discussion of past failures was avoided. Patients established treatment goals, such as where they wished to be in 90 days, which were reviewed periodically. Given guidance, support, and advocacy of the case managers, two thirds of patient goals were completed.

Mowbray et al. (1994) describe the integration of the vocational rehabilitation component into a case management system for people with chronic mental illness. Called WINS (Work Interests and Needs Study), this project was added to the Kent County Michigan Community Mental Health board (CMH). In this project, clients prepare an intervention plan with their case manager that contains a vocational history, a problem statement summarizing the types of assistance needed, a goal statement, and projected services. Staff and clients specify their commitments to the intervention plans, and monitoring is provided by the vocational specialist and the case management team throughout the implementation of the plan. At times, the plan is amended after an assessment of feedback, and some persons require development of personal skills prior to the implementation of the vocational objectives. Trained peer support specialists (PSS) provide services such as job support groups, with instruction in job interview skills, coping with job hunting, and anger control (once the client is on the job). In a follow-along phase, much cognitive–behavioral training in the skills required to maintain employment is provided, through one-on-one counseling, involvement of the PSS, or a referral to a support group. In this phase, clients learn that failure experiences can teach them much needed skills in getting and keeping future employment. The project reported that 62 of 116 open cases were working in supported or competitive employment, while 6 were job seeking. Five clients were involved with school, 8 were in day-care programs, 5 were working as volunteers, and 10 were receiving services through traditional vocational agencies.

THE REHABILITATION CASE MANAGEMENT MODEL

Case management has often been referred to in the field of rehabilitation as "case coordination" (Wright, 1980). However, case management has been researched and written about in a wide variety of human services occupations, including psychology, nursing, and social work. An interesting comparison might shed light on how these differing professions perceive case management. In nursing, several authors have attempted to define case management (Faherty, 1990; Lyon, 1993; Wadas, 1993); however, the American Nurses Association definition probably covers the tone of them all: "health assessment and planning, procurement, delivery, coordination, and monitoring to ensure that the multiple needs of the client are met . . . The components of case management are based on the nursing process and include entry, assessment, nursing diagnosis, goal setting, service planning, implementation, and evaluation" (Goodwin, 1994, p. 30). In his book *Total Rehabilitation* (1980), Wright defines case management in rehabilitation thusly:

> The counselor's managerial activities that facilitate the movement of each rehabilitant though the service process. The counselor as a "manager" of the case process of each individual is responsible for effective activity at each step: case-finding, intake, eligibility determination, assessment, counseling, plan development and implementation, service provision and supervision, job placement and follow-up, and postemployment services. This responsibility depends on the rehabilitationist's professional abilities coupled with planning, coordinating, and managing skills. (p. 170)

Consistent with the definition used in this text, Wright (1980) refers to "Case*load* Management" as "the responsibility of the counselor for the progress of the whole group of clients who constitute the counselor's caseload. It is actually the collective result of the counselor's work with individual clients. Caseload management requires such administrative talents as observation, evaluation, decision-making, monitoring, and recording" (p. 170).

As can be observed above, the nursing and rehabilitation definitions contain the same components, although the two models define the components differently because of their unique services. The point is that case managers ought to have a background not only in case management, but also in the specialty area that addresses the needs of a specific population of consumers (Smith & Ashbaugh, 1995). Whereas nurses act as gatekeepers regarding medical care involving regular insurance plans (e.g., Intercorp contracts with Equicorp in Illinois to provide gatekeeping services for the medical service networks), rehabilitation counselors can provide specialty expertise in the areas of life planning and vocational development of persons with disabilities.

Case management is a well-developed area of study and research in rehabilitation. Besides the present text, other works are strictly devoted to that subject (e.g., Cassell & Mulkey, 1985). Chan, Berven, and Lam (1990) pointed out that, in their review of computer-based, case management simulations among the counseling specialties, such computer simulations have been developed only for rehabilitation counseling. Szymanski, Linkowski, Leahy, Diamond, and Thoreson (1993) identified training in *case management and services* as the training need second only to *vocational services* as reported by the rehabilitation counselors they surveyed.

Three principles provide the bases for case management in rehabilitation: (a) ongoing assessment is necessary to ascertain those critical needs in persons we are helping, through the scientific process of analysis–hypothesis–plan–feedback–synthesis;

(b) case management varies in intensity depending on type and severity of disability; and (c) case management should emphasize client strengths rather than deficits (this last point being critical in the managed care environment). Assessment in rehabilitation is more than collecting data for diagnostic purposes. In fact, assessment is different from diagnosis in that the latter is rather a static picture of the client (a "one-shot deal"), whereas the former is dynamic and ongoing. A rehabilitation counselor is continuously gathering information about the client, reviewing that data, and making service plan decisions with the client based on those evaluations. Critical to the success of any rehabilitation service plan, assessment continues until the day that the casefile is closed.

If the service plan developed by the counselor and client does not lead to the attainment of client goals, the counselor may have failed to use assessment information to develop a clear picture of the client. It is this picture that should emerge from the assessment process. McArthur (1954) found that the most important factor contributing to accurate clinical prediction about a client was the development of a systematically constructed model or conceptualization of a client. Therefore, it is crucial for the counselor to use an organized approach to collect and process assessment data in order to develop an accurate conceptualization of the client.

Rehabilitation counselors work with people who present varied and complex issues and needs. How a counselor approaches these issues will determine the success of the rehabilitation process. Berven (1984) suggested an approach that evaluates assessment data using three values: (a) assets, (b) limitations, and (c) preferences. Berven defined *assets* as those characteristics of the client that may facilitate the attainment of desired goals. *Limitations* are those characteristics that may present barriers to the achievement of the goals. *Preferences* are those likes, dislikes, interests, and needs that shape the goals toward a satisfying outcome for the client. By organizing assessment data into categories (e.g., medical, social, financial, Activities of Daily Living, psychological, and vocational), then placing a value on each datum (evaluating whether the datum is a strength, limitation, or preference), the counselor can provide an accurate representation of the client's issues and needs. This process is rightly called *analysis,* because in analysis one breaks things down into their component parts, assigns meaning to each part, then interprets the whole *in terms of the meaning of each part for rehabilitation*. The interpretation of the entire body of data, in its meaning for the rehabilitation effort, constitutes the synthesis. The synthesis of the assessment data is the foundation for the plan, in the logical flow from the *why* in the analysis–synthesis, to the *what* and *how* of the recommendations that constitute the plan. Feedback from implementing the plan (finding out what worked and what did not, and why) provides new data for a revised analysis, and the process starts anew each month. Goldman (1971) described this process as using inductive–deductive reasoning. The inductive part refers to analysis–evaluation, and the deductive part to interpretation–synthesis–plan. The counselor's accuracy of clinical predictions should increase using this approach. Consequently, the potential for the client to attain his or her goals will also increase. However, no matter how well the information is organized, it is useless if the counselor cannot interpret what the information means in relation to the client.

In his article on assessment practices in rehabilitation counseling, Berven (1984) outlined the essential steps of the assessment process. The following is a model of the assessment process that incorporates Berven's steps:

I. Sources of Assessment Data

    A. Interview or self-report

    B. Tests

    C. Inventories

    D. Simulated and real work

    E. Job try-outs

    F. Functional assessment scales

    G. Medical and psychological reports

    H. Family interviews

II. Interpretation of Assessment Data

    A. Organize or categorize (classify) data

        1. Group data into medical, social, psychological, and vocational–educational categories

        2. Assets (+)

        3. Limitations (−)

        4. Preferences (p)

    B. Inductive reasoning

        1. Draw inferences from data

        2. Make hypothesis

III. Synthesis of Assessment Data

    A. Test hypothesis

        1. Interpret new data

        2. Compare inferences to hypothesis

    B. Revise hypothesis

Note that the process of how to classify a datum is a judgment call by the counselor. For example, is addiction a medical or psychological problem—or a social problem, for that matter? Additionally, whether to consider a particular client attribute as an asset or a limitation is a judgment by the counselor based on his or her perception. This judgment is certainly influenced by the counselor's training, beliefs, values, attitudes, cultural background, and years of experience.

In order for the rehabilitation counselor to effectively use the assessment model, action is required. Not only does the counselor collect, organize, and interpret assessment data, he or she makes decisions based on the assessment process. The importance of these decisions cannot be overstated, since they will directly impact the client's life. Just as the counselor requires a systematic approach to organize and interpret data, so does the counselor require a systematic approach to decision making.

Various models for decision making have been developed over the years. The approach one selects will depend on the theoretical perspective of the counselor. The following decision-making model by Drucker (1967) as cited in Cassell and Mulkey (1985) provides a framework from which to work:

1. *Classify the problem*—is it generic or unique?

2. *Define the problem*—what situation(s) must be addressed?

3. *Specify the answers to the problem*—what are the short and long term objectives/goals?

4. *Specify the "best alternative"*—what is the preferred scenario by the client?

5. *Specify the action that must be taken*—what must be done and who is responsible to carry it out?

6. *Obtain feedback regarding the validity of the decisions*—how is the decision being carried out? Do the outcomes reflect the objectives and goals? (pp. 92–93)

The number of decisions a counselor may make when using the assessment process can be enormous. Information regarding a client's physical, social, psychological, educational, and vocational histories must be incorporated into the assessment model in relation to assets, limitations, and preferences. Continuous evaluation and synthesis are required throughout the rehabilitation process and the delivery of the service plan. The amount of assessment data may appear unmanageable. However, if the counselor can categorize the types of situations in which he or she may make decisions, the task of decision making may not appear insurmountable. Cassell and Mulkey (1985) cite Miller and Starr (1967), who classify situations for decision making into five essential categories:

1. *Certainty*—routine or familiar problem situations (e.g., to obtain a general medical examination).

2. *Risk*—nonroutine or unfamiliar problem situations (all decisions involve a degree of risk, such as placing a client with a valued employer).

3. *Uncertainty*—limitations/restrictions that create unpredictable situations (such as validity problems with test instruments leading to erroneous conclusions about clients' abilities).

4. *Partial Information*—decisions made on best available data (no situation will provide all possible information regarding a client).

5. *Conflict*—situations which may present differing interests between client and counselor and/or discrepancies between expressed and obtainable goals. (p. 124)

The rehabilitation counselor must learn to approach the assessment process with a global framework. Assessment is an ongoing activity involving organizing, evaluating, and decision making in order to develop an accurate picture of the client. Below is a case study with a case analysis (Table 14.1), which demonstrates (a) the classification of data into vocational, social, medical, and psychological categories; (b) the placing of a value (or evaluation) on these data; and (c) the interpretation of the data once evaluated.

 # CASE STUDY: MR. X

Mr. X was an over-the-road truck driver until his accident on a busy interstate highway. His injuries included a spinal cord injury resulting in quadriplegia. His physical rehabilitation brought him to the point at which he was able to live semi-independently with his family. He could feed himself with some devices created by occupational therapists at the hospital, he could occupy himself with reading and watching television, and he could go out with the family to restaurants and social gatherings. He was an intelligent man whose driving record was exceptional due to his reputation for reliability, good judgment, and trustworthiness. He managed his job with the same serious ideals that would typify a successful and ethical business manager. In high school, he had been an honor student and the manager of the football and basketball teams.

However, his reaction to his disability was remarkably negative. For example, he was angry at his doctors and rehabilitation workers. There were many reasons why he was angry—for example, a physical therapist was late or a nurse wouldn't give him a pain pill. He interpreted all inconveniences as a personal affront. His hostile outlook also extended to his family. He seemed to constantly test them by remaining dependent and overreacting when the family attempted to help him. This added fuel for his unyielding anger. In spite of all this, his confused and bewildered family loved him very much and continued to try and help him all that they could.

His former employer, who valued Mr. X highly, was convinced that he could be a terminal manager and offered to make any and all accommodations so that Mr. X could return to work. But Mr. X would have no part of it. Even though a job was being handed to him with little effort on his part, Mr. X became angry at a single mention of even discussing it with his former boss. Mr. X had no problems financially, since his long-term disability policy took care of his family's income needs, and his bills were all paid off by insurance, including all of his loans, credit accounts, and house mortgage.

TABLE 14.1
Analysis of Strengths, Limitations, and Preferences

Strengths	Limitations	Preferences
Vocational		
Excellent work record	Mobility restriction	Likes outdoor sports
Excellent managerial skills	Strength restrictions	Likes to stay current with sports
Highly regarded by boss	Motor restrictions—all extremities	
Intelligence	Cannot return to previous work	Does not want to return to previous work
Good judgment		
Reliability	Limited education and experience	
Transferable skills for sedentary work, including knowledge of Interstate Commerce Commission regulations and traffic routes		
Good reading, writing, and math skills		
Social		
The significant persons in his life, including family and ex-boss, are willing to accommodate him. He has no financial debt. He is secure in his home and can satisfy other living needs. He has a rock-solid support system in a family that is devoted to him.	Social isolation. His family is absorbing the consequences of his anger and demands without letting him know it affects them. He is isolating himself from others who may be able to give him important feedback. He feels stigmatized, since he is no longer able to do things he used to do.	
Medical		
He has excellent insurance. Good medical team.	Need for ongoing chronic care.	
Psychological		
Good premorbid adjustment.	Seems to be stuck in a hostility and anger rut.	He only wants to hang on to his way of seeing things.

*When his rehabilitation counselor asked him what he wanted for himself, he
stated that he wanted to stay at home and read his hunting and fishing magazines.
He also preferred to isolate himself from his former friends with whom he used to
hunt and fish because he no longer felt like a man.*

In the case study and Table 14.1, one sees an interaction between Mr. X's
preferences in reacting to his disability experience and the family's limitation in not
giving him feedback with regard to the consequences for them in those preferences.
The implication for Mr. X's rehabilitation is that he is stuck in a rut in which he will
remain until the family comes to realize that they are living for Mr. X and neglecting
their own needs. He needs to understand his own situation, and the rehabilitation
counselor can honestly confront him with the reality of it and let Mr. X and his family
determine how long this state will continue. Continuing this data-collecting,
analyzing, interpreting, planning, and feedback incorporation model throughout the
rehabilitation process ensures, then, increasing clarity of client issues and focus upon
critical, rather than tangential, problem areas.

Since rehabilitation has a well-defined case management approach, and since it
seems to be so compatible with the emerging managed care environment, attention in
the field must necessarily turn to how the approach can be marketed.

MARKETING CONSIDERATIONS

To market rehabilitation services in the future, rehabilitation professionals must
educate themselves about funding demands in MCOs. Their capacity to respond to
this managed care environment depends on specific and concrete responses to
emerging issues identified by Martha Hodges and Martha Knisley (1995), two consultants to managed care organizations. These issues include (a) a clearer definition of
case management; (b) differential benefit packages; (c) case management for priority
populations; (d) relationships with other systems; (e) collaboration with private
providers; (f) community integration; (g) titration of support; (h) recovery and peer
support; and (i) crisis prevention and support. Each of these issues is elaborated in the
sections to follow.

A clear definition of case management is critical as that role is taking on
increasing importance. Not only is the case manager at the core of managed care in
behavior health, but it is that professional who has the explicit responsibility to help
people acquire the assistance they need to live in the community. The Berven (1984)
model of assessment/case management provides an example of a clear definition of
case management. In this model, those elements that have been found in the literature
to be most efficacious in rehabilitating clients—a strengths emphasis, community
networking, the concept that a good case manager can handle only so many cases

(usually mediated by the number of clients with severe disabilities, or the rurality of a caseload)—have direct application to managed care priorities.

Differential insurance benefit packages have been prescribed in several states that have experimented with Medicaid waivers for people with mental illnesses (e.g., Washington). These packages provide varying capitation rates based on levels of severity of disability. In Washington, for example, Tier 1 patients (adjustment problems primarily) receive a capitation rate of $1.50 per member per month (pmpm), Tier 2 patients (chronic mental illness) receive $6.00 pmpm, while Tier 3 patients (severe and persistent mental illness) receive $1,000.00 pmpm. These rates are allocated for all members in that tier, whether they receive services or not.

Priority populations such as those with severe behavior disorders will receive special treatment from managed care organizations in the future, not only in terms of special capitation rates, but also in terms of special interventions. Those populations include persons of minority status, homeless people, people with coexisting disorders (e.g., developmental disability, hearing impairment, chemical dependence, medical fragility, or HIV positivity), people in state hospitals, and people with involvement in the criminal and juvenile justice systems.

Providers of behavioral health services will need to establish relationships and agreements with other service providers in the areas of vocational rehabilitation, housing, senior services, and others. According to Hodges and Knisley (1995), laws that govern accessibility to services, such as the Americans with Disabilities Act of 1990 (ADA), will need to be taken into account in the future as these relationships mature. With their knowledge of rehabilitation legislation such as the ADA, those in the rehabilitation field seem particularly well positioned to offer their services in this combined effort.

Case managers will need to educate themselves in state-of-the-art approaches to treatment. These professionals are responsible for contracting with provider organizations (many of whom are private) to deliver services to those with a serious mental illness. To prevent these persons from showing up on the doorstep of the state hospital after their insurance benefits have been exhausted, future case managers must be able to discern what is truly effective with this population.

Case managers will need to look increasingly at the community-at-large for support for persons with behavior disorders. Not only will they need to develop relationships with community organizations, but they will need to find ways of reducing stigma associated with mental illness.

Titration of services will mean a more just distribution of increasingly scarce resources. As Hodges and Knisley (1995) stated, "In the managed care environment, we really try to give the right amount of the right service at the right time" (p. 86). This means giving more supports and services when things are going poorly, and withdrawing from the person's life as the situation improves. Some of this support can come from peer and recovery groups, which are essential resources for people with mental illness. Case managers must educate themselves about these valuable resources and support their development.

Outcome assessment, according to Hodges and Knisley (1995), is the hottest topic in managed care (p. 87). The authors mention several program evaluation areas that will become particularly important. These include adequacy of staffing patterns, access to clinical staff (within 5 minutes for 95% of emergencies), timely appointments (within 4 to 7 days), satisfaction with services, and service quality.

Finally, crisis intervention takes on increased importance in the managed care environment. It is the best alternative to expensive hospitalizations.

Service providers planning for the future in disability areas such as developmental disability, mental health, and substance abuse are joining together to influence the direction of managed care plans that affect their specialties. Based on a remarkable broad-based cooperative effort, the National Association of State Directors of Developmental Disabilities Services (1995), anticipating the application of managed care strategies in the funding of state services to their clients, established several principles to guide managed care efforts, such as the following:

1. All key stakeholders, including individuals with developmental disabilities, family members, support agencies, advocates, and others, must be enlisted in designing, implementing and overseeing the operation of a managed care system.

2. Managed care should expand—not diminish—opportunities for people with developmental disabilities and their families to choose services and supports that will improve the quality of their lives.

3. Managed care strategies must provide for the effective coordination of specialized developmental disabilities services with other systems upon which people with developmental disabilities rely.

4. Managed care approaches must be premised on reprogramming any resulting savings to the provision of services and supports for individuals who are on service waiting lists.

5. The criteria used in authorizing services and supports under a managed care system must be spelled out prior to implementation.

6. Appeal and grievance rights/procedures must be specified in advance.

7. Managed care organizations, as well as provider agencies through which services are delivered, should not be permitted to profit at the expense of people with developmental disabilities.

8. The impact of managed care arrangements on existing community support agencies must be scrutinized carefully.

9. A managed care system must be structured in a manner that decentralizes decision making and promotes innovation.

10. Responsibility and accountability for overseeing the performance of a managed care system must be clearly fixed with, and vigorously exercised by, a designated agency within the executive branch of state government. (pp. 3–6)

CONCLUDING STATEMENT

Managed care is rushing through human service fields with the speed and dynamic force of a hurricane, breaking down old ways of delivering services and forcing human service and rehabilitation professionals to adapt to the requirements of a new way of looking at funding services to people. Nevertheless, the changes being forced by managed care provides those in the field of rehabilitation with a new opportunity if they do not succumb to fears about change.

First, managed care is concerned about expertise. It puts a premium on experienced professionals with credentials to deliver quality-controlled and well-conceived services. That can mean opportunies for rehabilitation professionals to gain entry to third-party payment systems to which access has not existed previously. It also means that rehabilitation professionals are now in a position to compete favorably with those in the more traditional professions, such as psychology and psychiatry, for managed care dollars. Thus, it behooves the field of rehabilitation to concern itself even more with state licensure for rehabilitation professionals where none exists currently.

Second, managed care requires case management approaches tailored to specific disability populations, because "standard case" criteria are not appropriate due to differing characteristics of client populations. Case management is a well-developed approach in the field of rehabilitation. Indeed, it is one of the two roles most often cited in the occupation of the rehabilitation counselor. Since managed care puts a premium on experienced case managers, rehabilitation counselors need to emphasize that role in their marketing.

Finally, managed care requires providers to be accountable for their case management decisions. Therefore, rehabilitation service providers must become expert in formative and summative evaluation systems.

Managed care provides rehabilitation with a golden opportunity to maximize professional gains and hence be of substantially more assistance to persons with disabilities. But the field must follow the collaborative example of the National Association of State Directors of Developmental Disabilities Services so that rehabilitation professionals can take the initiative in setting standards for managed care, developing professional procedures for delivering managed care, and marketing rehabilitation services to managed care organizations.

Appendix A: Practice in the Use of Case Management Principles

THE CASE OF JED PIERCE

Appendix A contains a series of exercises that reinforce principles in the earlier chapters of the book. Read the instructions for each step and complete each of the activities.

▶ **Step 1: Becoming Familiar with Jed**

Instructions: Read the synopsis of the case of Jed Pierce.

Synopsis: Jed Pierce is a 27-year-old male with a history of hypoglycemia, epilepsy, schizophrenia, and alcohol and drug abuse. At referral, Jed reported that he had been married six times and was currently separated from his sixth wife. Because of his deteriorating health and emotional condition, Jed has worked sporadically over the past 5-year period. His work experience includes jobs as an ambulance driver, supervisor of an ambulance service, ambulance attendant, and a used car salesman. Even though he did not persist in these jobs, he was able to fulfill job demands adequately. Jed's vocational handicaps are related both to his medical and his psychological problems. Because the pressure of working as an ambulance driver caused his medical problems to worsen, he often sought escape from stress through protracted bouts of alcohol or drug abuse.

▶ **Step 2: Attraction**

Instructions: Mr. Pierce has been referred by his physician to vocational rehabilitation. You have received the referral and want to increase the probability that Jed will come for an intake interview. Write a notification of an appointment that will attract Jed to vocational rehabilitation. Compare your invitation with the following one that was written by Jed's counselor.

Example Invitation

Mr. Jed Pierce   March 29

Type of appointment: Initial eligibility interview

Purpose: To discuss how vocational rehabilitation might be of help to you.

Appointment date: Wednesday, April 15

Time: 2:30 p.m.

With: Charles Gregson, Rehabilitation Counselor

Location: Rehabilitation Services, 1510 Morriss Ave., Middletown, LA, phone: 871-1415. Jan Kirk, the receptionist, will direct you to my office. Enclosed is a map to 1510 Morriss Ave.

Note: I am looking forward to seeing you. Dr. Grayburn has told me of your interest in vocational training. I certainly hope that we can assist you.

▶ **Step 3: Planning the Intake Interview**

Instructions: Review the following general and specific objectives for Jed. What would you add?

General Objectives

1. Communicate purpose of the agency and my interest in helping.

2. Determine appropriateness of referral.

3. Identify Jed's expectations and needs.

4. Complete intake forms.

5. _____

6. _____

Specific Objectives

1. Explore Jed's medical history regarding epilepsy.

2. Determine effect of psychiatric disability on past employment.

3. Plan for appropriate medical and psychological evaluation.

4. _____

5. _____

▶ **Step 4: Collecting Intake Interview Information**

Instructions: Read the summary of Jed's intake interview and identify information gaps. Use Table 3.1 and the vocational goal questions (see Chapter 3) to complete this activity.

 # CASE STUDY: JED PIERCE

Intake Interview Summary

Jed Pierce is a 27-year-old male who has been married six times. He has one son by a previous marriage and is currently separated from his sixth wife and her 2-year-old son by another marriage. Jed was referred to the state rehabilitation agency by his physician for assistance in dealing with medical and psychological problems, financial difficulties, and inability to work steadily.

Although Jed quit high school at the age of 16, he attained a GED while receiving services from the Veterans Administration (VA). He attended a junior college briefly.

Jed has a long history of serious medical and psychological problems. As a child he received several severe blows to the head. According to Jed, several doctors have speculated that there may have been some permanent brain damage from these accidents. In addition, Jed has had two bouts of encephalitis and a mild case of polio. He also has had periodic problems with high fevers and severe headaches. At the age of 14, he had an ulcerated stomach. According to Jed, this series of childhood illnesses not only caused him to become dependent on "Demerol, pep pills, and pain pills," but also taught him that he could get the attention of others by feigning illness. Jed now identifies his major medical problems as reactive hypoglycemia and epilepsy.

As a child, Jed felt rejected by his father. Jed's father and one of Jed's brothers have severe problems with alcoholism. His father dominated the family, and his mother passively accepted his drinking and domineering behavior. Jed was not particularly close to any of his brothers or sisters and, in fact, resented several of them because they were continually being held up to him as examples. At the present time, the only family member that Jed is close to is his mother. He can talk to her about some of his problems. His brothers and sisters still think of him as a "bum" who is unable to hold a job and support a family. Because they are unable to pay their rent, utilities, and medical bills, Jed and his wife are under extreme financial pressure. Jed is currently not working because of problems related to hypoglycemia, a condition that is exaggerated by pressures on the job.

Jed is seeking rehabilitation services for (a) the control of his medical and psychological conditions, (b) vocational training, (c) financial maintenance, and (d) alcoholism. He wants to be trained as an emergency medical technician and continue to work with an ambulance service. He apparently has a good relationship with an existing ambulance service in his home community and, if capable of controlling his other problems, could return to work with them. Jed is also in need of counseling assistance to resolve marital problems. In part, many of these problems might resolve themselves if financial pressures were eased. Steady employment would enable him to pay for his medical and family necessities.

After reviewing Table 3.1 and the vocational goal issues in Chapter 3, list the questions that were not answered in Jed's intake interview.

I. Physical Factors

1. _____
2. _____
3. _____
4. _____
5. _____

II. Psychosocial Factors

1. _____
2. _____
3. _____
4. _____

III. Educational–Vocational Factors

1. _____
2. _____
3. _____
4. _____

IV. Economic Factors

1. _____
2. _____
3. _____

V. Vocational Goals

1. _____
2. _____
3. _____

Information that the counselor should have gathered: _____

_____

I. Physical Factors

A. Questions that should have been answered

1. How long has Jed had some of his medical problems?

2. What types of treatment has Jed received?

3. Is Jed's condition worsening?

4. Is Jed currently taking any medication? What is the effect of the medication?

5. How do Jed's medical problems hamper daily functioning?

B. *Physical Profile*. Jed's history of seizures, polio, and ulcerated stomach began in childhood. Brain scans during adolescence and in the last 2 years revealed a mild seizure tendency. Jed currently is being treated for hypoglycemia with medication and dietary management. He is taking vitamins and Valium or Elavil on a sporadic basis. Claiming that the pressures of his work cause him to abuse alcohol and drugs, Jed has missed a great deal of work lately.

II. Psychosocial Factors

A. Questions that should have been answered

1. Do recent psychological test results exist for Jed? What are the implications of these results for Jed?

2. Is Jed currently receiving psychological services?

3. What is Jed's past history of psychological treatment—for example, therapy, medication, or both?

4. Will Jed's wife be supportive of his rehabilitation program?

B. *Psychosocial Profile*. Jed has recently received psychological evaluation and treatment from the VA. He has also received counseling from a rehabilitation center and has lived in a rehabilitation halfway house. Jed has taken Valium or Elavil as part of his treatment. He claims that the therapy and medication have done little to relieve the "anxiety and pressure" he feels. Jed reports that his current wife "couldn't care less" about what he does.

III. Educational–Vocational Factors

A. Questions that should have been answered

1. What did Jed like or dislike about school?

2. Why did Jed leave school?

3. What were Jed's last three jobs? In each of those jobs:

   a. What were his weekly earnings?

   b. What was his length of employment?

   c. What did he like and dislike?

   d. What parts of the job did he do well and poorly?

   e. What were his reasons for changing from one job to the other?

4. Is Jed currently employed?

B. *Educational–Vocational Profile*. Even though he had good grades in junior high school, Jed did not like the regimentation of school. He decided to drop out and join the service. Subsequently, he earned his GED through the VA. Mathematics was the only school subject that Jed enjoyed. Until recently, he worked as an ambulance driver with Quick Ambulance service. Before that he worked as a supervisor of an ambulance team and as an ambulance attendant. He also worked as a new and used car salesman. Jed was unable to retain his position as an ambulance supervisor due to frequent absences from work. Jed expressed problems with the pressures of ambulance work but noted that he can't live with it, and he can't live without it. Jed is currently unemployed.

IV. Economic Factors

A. Questions that should have been answered

1. What is Jed's primary source of support?

2. Does Jed have other sources of support?

3. Does Jed have any unpaid debts of significance?

B. *Economic Profile.* Jed is currently under tremendous financial pressure. He has no financial support, with the exception of food stamps and a small benefit check from the VA. Jed has some child support payments due and, of course, is continually behind in payments for rent, utilities, and medication.

V. Vocational Goals

A. Questions that should have been answered

1. Does Jed have more than one potential vocational goal?

2. How optimistic or pessimistic is Jed about his ability to achieve each vocational goal?

B. *Vocational Goals Profile.* Jed is currently interested in receiving additional training to become an emergency medical technician. The counselor does not know what other vocational goals Jed might view positively or whether Jed would be open to vocational training in other areas. Because he mentioned only one vocational goal, one might assume that Jed believes that goal to be feasible. The counselor gathered no information, however, about Jed's expectations for employment as a medical technician. Jed has worked successfully as a new and used car salesman.

▶ **Step 5: Identifying Questions Requiring Further Evaluation Data**

Instructions: Information from the intake interview suggests that Jed is severely handicapped. He has a seizure disorder that appears controllable, hypoglycemia, a history of substance abuse, and tendencies toward antisocial behavior. Given medical and psychological confirmation of these problems, Jed will qualify for rehabilitation services. Medical, psychological, and vocational evaluations, however, must help the counselor answer a great many more specific questions about Jed before the planning interview can be initiated. Consult Table 2.1 and identify some of the more important questions that the counselor must answer before involving Jed in goal setting. List some of the important questions under each of the following headings:

I. Physical Factors

1. _____

2. _____

II. Psychosocial Factors

1. _____

2. _____

3. _____

III. Educational–Vocational Factors

1. _____

2. _____

   _____

3. _____

4. _____

Additional questions and brief evaluation profiles for Jed: _____

I. Physical Factors

A. Questions that should have been answered

1. Are the disabilities progressive or stable?

2. What medical services are required?

B. *Additional Information.* Jed's seizures appear controllable with Dilantin. Episodes of hypoglycemia can be decreased through medication and a regular rest and dietary program (high protein, low carbohydrate meals). He must discontinue use of alcohol. Jed may be able to operate an automobile for private use, but should not work in high-stress jobs involving driving, using machinery, or working at heights.

II. Psychosocial Factors

A. Questions that should have been answered

1. To what degree has the client adjusted to the handicapping aspects of the disability?

2. Does the client have the emotional stability to engage in a vocational rehabilitation program at the present time?

3. Which personal counseling or family counseling services are necessary?

B. *Additional Information.* Psychological evaluation revealed a history of tension and depression as well as antisocial behavior (physical aggression). To avoid further abuse of drugs and alcohol, Jed must not reenter high-stress occupations such as ambulance work. In addition to a program of psychotherapy, Jed should join Alcoholics Anonymous (AA). With the control of his seizures and hypoglycemia and psychological support services, Jed should be able to return to work. Nevertheless, Jed's adjustment to his handicaps and current vocational readiness remain significant concerns for the counselor to deal with during the service and follow-up phases of the program.

III. Educational–Vocational Factors

A. Questions that should have been answered

1. What vocational skills does the client currently possess?

2. Are client vocational goals consistent with current vocational interests?

3. Does the client have a realistic perception of current strengths and weaknesses as a worker, potential for vocational skill development, and reasons for being unemployed?

4. Can the client satisfactorily meet the demands of competitive work— for example, accepting supervision and maintaining an adequate production rate?

B. *Additional Information.* Evaluation results do not support Jed's desire to be an emergency medical technician. There is evidence, however, that Jed could succeed in sales or clerical work—for example, he possesses the necessary general, verbal, and numerical intelligence, as well as clerical perception abilities. His vocational interests are also consistent with those of automobile sales personnel. Hence, Jed might pursue vocational alternatives in sales, clerical work, and even some skilled trade areas, presuming that he has the coordination and dexterity to meet the performance demands of the job and that the jobs do not involve the use of machinery.

▶ **Step 6: Vocational Hypothesizing**

Instructions: To initiate information processing with Jed's case, the counselor must first select some feasible vocational alternatives. Feasible jobs for Jed must be consistent with his strengths and limitations in the physical, psychosocial, and educational–vocational areas. Review the following 36 occupations that are available in Jed's community and select 3 that would be appropriate for Jed to consider. List these jobs in order of suitability. Provide a brief diagnostic rationale for each of your choices.

1. Auto mechanic
2. Armed services
3. Mail carrier
4. Laundry worker
5. Brick layer
6. Telephone operator
7. Electrician
8. Inspector
9. College student
10. Sales clerk
11. Printer
12. Woodworker
13. Body and fender repair
14. Auto parts salesperson
15. Key punch operator
16. Data processing operator
17. Social worker
18. Bookkeeper
19. Dispatcher
20. Diesel mechanic
21. Draftsperson
22. Building maintenance worker
23. Television repair
24. Scheduler

25. Welder
26. Teller
27. Exterminator
28. New and used car salesperson
29. Sewing or tailoring
30. Industrial services worker
31. Assembly line worker
32. Nursery worker
33. Taxi driver
34. Cook
35. Painter
36. Plumber

First choice _____

Rationale:

Second choice _____

Rationale:

Third choice _____

Rationale:

Review the following list to see how your choices match those of a group of practicing counselors.

First Choice Vocational Alternatives for Jed Pierce as Selected
by Practicing Rehabilitation Counselors ($N = 38$)

Job	Percentage
Auto mechanic	21
Mail carrier	5
Sales clerk	5
Body and fender repair	5
Auto parts salesperson	13
Bookkeeper	5
Dispatcher	3
Diesel mechanic	3
Television repair	3

(continues)

Job	Percentage
Welder	3
Exterminator	3
New and used car salesperson	11
Industrial services worker	3
Taxi driver	8
Cook	3

What problems might Jed encounter as an auto mechanic? How would Jed do in auto sales or auto parts sales? Review the list of 36 jobs again. Select the two worst jobs for Jed and provide a brief diagnostic rationale for why those jobs are inappropriate for Jed.

Most inappropriate choice _____

Rationale:

Second most inappropriate choice _____

Rationale:

Review the following list to determine whether your selections are consistent with those made by a group of practicing rehabilitation counselors.

Most Inappropriate Vocational Alternatives for Jed Pierce as Selected by Vocational Rehabilitation Counselors (N=38)

Job	Percentage
Armed services	5
Electrician	5
College student	5
Social worker	17
Taxi driver	37

▶ **Step 7: Information Processing**

Instructions: Review the work of Jed's counselor as reflected in the Information Processing Summary Form.

(*text continues on page 290*)

Information Processing Summary Form

Name: Jed Pierce

1. Potential vocational goals suggested by consideration of evaluation data.

   a. Most optimal: New and used car salesperson (already suggested by client __ Yes _X_ No)

   ### Supporting evaluation data:

   Physical. Jed's physical disabilities would not preclude his returning to work in automobile sales. However, the pace and stress of the work may pose some problems. For example, he must keep on a regular schedule with meals and medication.

   Psychosocial. This job may impair Jed's emotional functioning, particularly if the schedule is stressful and irregular. Jed's reaction to job and family tensions should be monitored to be sure that he does not return to drug and alcohol use.

   Educational–Vocational. Jed demonstrates good clerical and computational skills. He exceeds the cutoff for retail sales work on the *General Aptitude Test Battery* (GATB). Jed's interest profile resembles that of an automobile salesperson. In particular, auto sales provides him with an outlet for ability use, achievement, and compensation. At the same time, he would not have to supervise the work of others.

   Special considerations: None

   b. Second: Auto parts salesperson (already suggested by client __ Yes _X_ No)

   ### Supporting evaluation data:

   Physical. Jed possesses the physical capacity to do this job. The level of stress and work schedules are appropriate. Jed can use the business machines involved in the job.

   Psychosocial. With ongoing counseling services, Jed should learn how to cope with family and nonwork tensions so that they do not affect his performance on the job.

   Educational–Vocational. Jed is average in intelligence with adequate skills in the areas of verbal intelligence, clerical perception, and computation. Jed is interested in achievement, ability use, and compensation in his work. Because he has both a sales and a customer service position in this job, he should be provided with these preferred vocational reinforcers.
   Special considerations: None

   c. Third: Exterminator (already suggested by client __Yes _X_ No)

(*continues*)

Information Processing Summary Form (*Continued*)

Physical. Jed could follow a schedule of instructions for mixing pesticides and applying them at various commercial and residential sites. There would be no physical aspects of this position that Jed could not perform.

Psychosocial. Again, this work would be steady and well structured with less stress than other work Jed has done. This will enhance his ability to cope with nonvocational problems.

Educational–Vocational. According to Jed's GATB results, he exceeds the cutoff score on all aptitudes pertinent to this job. This job is suggested, in part, because of its availability in the local community. Jed also might enjoy the variety in work settings as well as the regularity of the hours and earnings. There is some question as to whether this job would provide Jed with the opportunities for the ability use and achievement that he desires.

Special considerations: None

2. Services needed to achieve vocational goals:

   a. Most optimal: New and used car salesperson

      Physical. Medical services including instructions as to dietary maintenance for hypoglycemia and specific medication to control seizures.

      Psychosocial. Individual psychotherapy and family counseling. Financial counseling and Alcoholics Anonymous.

      Educational–Vocational. On-the-job training.

      Special considerations: None

   b. Second: Auto parts salesperson

      Physical. See most optimal.

      Psychosocial. See most optimal.

      Educational–Vocational. See most optimal.

      Special considerations: None

   c. Third: Exterminator

      Physical. See most optimal.

      Psychosocial. See most optimal.

      Educational–Vocational. See most optimal.

      Special considerations: None

3. Vocational goals expressed by the client that appear to be inappropriate based on evaluation data. Discuss.

(continues)

Information Processing Summary Form (*Continued*)

Jed's interest in becoming an emergency medical technician appears to be inappropriate for several reasons. Initially, his GATB scores do not suggest that he has the intellectual capacity to deal with the demands of such a job. In addition, this is a high-stress job that would put increased pressure on Jed's ability to maintain some type of psychological equilibrium. In the past, his tolerance for stress has been limited and, when exceeded, stress has caused him to seek relief through alcohol or drugs. Stress on this job would also lead to a deterioration in his relations with spouse and family.

▶ **Step 8: Involving Jed in the Planning Interview**

Instructions: The counselor now must review the results of the evaluation phase with Jed. As has been suggested, one format for doing so follows the logic of the Information Processing Summary Form. Counselor and client discuss the evaluation data, paying particular attention to the significance of it for various vocational roles. As a part of this discussion, Jed completed the Balance Sheet (see Balance Sheet: Jed Pierce, Table A.1). After consideration of several alternatives, Jed decided to return to car sales. The remainder of the planning process would be devoted to completing the goal analysis (see Tab;e A.2) and selecting a series of intermediate objectives for the plan.

With the help of his counselor, Jed set the following objectives for his program:

▶ **Vocational Goal**

Auto sales job earning $2,500 a month by 10/10.

Physical Objectives: Go 90 days without a seizure beginning 7/1. Get on a schedule of eating three high-protein, low-carbohydrate meals per day by 7/11.

Psychosocial Objective: Miss work no more than 4 days per 60 days because of depression beginning 8/10. Say that marital problems are tolerable and that divorce is not contemplated by 10/10.

Educational–Vocational Objective: Complete auto sales on-the-job training by 8/10.

TABLE A.1
Balance Sheet: Jed Pierce

Consideration	Alternative 1		Alternative 2		Alternative 3	
	New and Used Car Salesperson	*Importance Rating*	*Auto Parts Salesperson*	*Importance Rating*	*Exterminator*	*Importance Rating*
Gains for self	Chance for commissions Interesting work Meet new people	5 5 4	Steady work Good pay	4 4	Steady work Regular pay	4 3
Losses for self	Stressful work Irregular schedule	−3 −3	Work behind counter	−2	Work does not vary	−4
Gains for others	Chance for more money Serving customers	5 4	Money for family Regular schedule Providing personal service	4 4 4	Money for family Regular schedule Providing personal service	4 4 3
Losses for others	—		—		—	
Social approval	Not a "bum"	5	Not a "bum"	5	Not a "bum"	4
Social disapproval	—		—		—	
Self-approval	Want to work	4	Want to work	4	Want to work	4
Self-disapproval			Want to sell cars, not just parts	−3	Work not "important"	−4
Sum rated positive anticipation:		32		29		26
Sum rated negative anticipation:		−6		−5		−8
Final score		**26**		**24**		**18**

TABLE A.2
Goal Analysis: Jed Pierce

Employment Goal: Auto Sales			
Medical Condition (Physical)	**Personal Problems (Psychosocial)**	**Educational–Vocational**	**Special Considerations**
Keep blood sugar stable	Work on problems with wife	Get on-the-job training	None
Control fainting spells	Do not go back to alcohol and drugs (stay with AA)		
	Get help with feelings of anxiety and depression		

Appendix B: Code of Professional Ethics for Rehabilitation Counselors

The Commission on Rehabilitation Counselor Certification has adopted the Code of Professional Ethics for Certified Rehabilitation Counselors, and the following professional organizations have adopted the Code for their memberships: American Rehabilitation Counseling Association, National Rehabilitation Counseling Association, and the National Council on Rehabilitation Education. Also, portions of the Code are derived from the American Psychological Association Ethical Principles of Psychologists.

PREAMBLE

Rehabilitation counselors are committed to facilitating personal, social, and economic independence of individuals with disabilities. In fulfilling this commitment, rehabilitation counselors work with people, programs, institutions, and service delivery systems. Rehabilitation counselors recognize that both action and inaction can be facilitating or debilitating. Rehabilitation counselors may be called upon to provide counseling; vocational exploration; psychological and vocational assessment; evaluation of social, medical, vocational, and psychiatric information; job placement and job development services; and other rehabilitation services, and so on in a manner that is consistent with their education and experience. Moreover, rehabilitation counselors also must demonstrate adherence to ethical standards and must ensure that the standards are enforced vigorously. The Code of Professional Ethics, henceforth referred to as the Code, is designed to facilitate the accomplishment of these goals.

The primary obligation of rehabilitation counselors is to their clients, defined in this Code as people with disabilities who are receiving services from rehabilitation counselors. The basic objective of the Code is to promote the public welfare by specifying and

Note. Appendix B is from American Rehabilitation Counseling Association, Commission on Rehabilitation Counselor Certification, and National Rehabilitation Counseling Association, 1987, *Journal of Applied Rehabilitation Counseling,* 18(4) pp. 28–32. Reprinted with permission of the Commission on Rehabilitation Counselor Certification.

enforcing ethical behavior expected of rehabilitation counselors. Accordingly, the Code consists of two kinds of standards, Canons and Rules of Professional Conduct.

The Canons are general standards of an aspirational and inspirational nature reflecting the fundamental spirit of caring and respect which professionals share. They are maxims which serve as models of exemplary professional conduct. The Canons also express general concepts and principles from which more specific Rules are derived. Unlike the Canons, the Rules are more exacting standards that provide guidance in specific circumstances.

Rehabilitation counselors who violate the Code are subject to disciplinary action. A Rule violation is interpreted as a violation of the applicable Canon and the general principles embodied thereof. Since the use of the Certified Rehabilitation Counselor (CRC) designation is a privilege granted by the Commission on Rehabilitation Counselor Certification (CRCC), the CRCC reserves unto itself the power to suspend or to revoke the privilege or to approve other penalties for a Rule violation. Disciplinary penalties are imposed as warranted by the severity of the offense and its attendant circumstances. All disciplinary actions are undertaken in accordance with published procedures and penalties of the offense designed to assure the proper enforcement of the Code within the framework of due process and equal protection of the laws.

When there is reason to question the ethical propriety of specific behaviors, persons are encouraged to refrain from engaging in such behaviors until the matter has been clarified. Certified Rehabilitation Counselors who need assistance in interpreting the Code should request in writing an advisory opinion from the Commission on Rehabilitation Counselor Certification. Rehabilitation counselors who are not certified and require assistance in interpreting the Code should request in writing an advisory opinion from their appropriate professional organization.

Canon 1—Moral and Legal Standards

Rehabilitation counselors shall behave in a legal, ethical, and moral manner in the conduct of their profession, maintaining the integrity of the Code and avoid any behavior which would cause harm to others.

Rules of Professional Conduct

R1.1   Rehabilitation counselors will obey the laws and statutes in the legal jurisdiction in which they practice and are subject to disciplinary action for any violation to the extent that such violation suggests the likelihood of professional misconduct.

R1.2   Rehabilitation counselors will be thoroughly familiar with, will observe, and will discuss with their clients the legal limitations of their services, or benefits offered to clients so as to facilitate honest and open communication and realistic expectations.

R1.3   Rehabilitation counselors will be alert to legal parameters relevant to their practices and to disparities between legally mandated ethical and professional standards and the Code. Where such disparities exist, rehabilitation counselors will follow the legal mandates and will formally communicate any disparities to the appropriate committee on professional ethics. In the absence of legal guidelines, the Code is ethically binding.

R1.4   Rehabilitation counselors will not engage in any act or omission of a dishonest, deceitful, or fraudulent nature in the conduct of their professional activities. They will not allow the pursuit of financial gain or other personal benefit to interfere with the exercise of sound professional judgment and skills, nor will rehabilitation counselors abuse their relationships with clients to promote personal or financial gain or the financial gain of their employing agencies.

R1.5   Rehabilitation counselors will understand and abide by the Canons and Rules of Professional Conduct which are prescribed in the Code.

R1.6   Rehabilitation counselors will not advocate, sanction, participate in, cause to be accomplished, otherwise carry out through another, or condone any act which rehabilitation counselors are prohibited from performing by the Code.

R1.7   Rehabilitation counselors' moral and ethical standards of behavior are a personal matter to the same degree as they are for any other citizen, except as these may compromise the fulfillment of their professional responsibilities or reduce the public trust in rehabilitation counselors. To protect public confidence, rehabilitation counselors will avoid public behavior that clearly is in violation of accepted moral and ethical standards.

R1.8   Rehabilitation counselors will respect the rights and reputation of any institution, organization, or firm with which they are associated when making oral or written statements. In those instances where they are critical of policies, they attempt to effect change by constructive action within organizations.

R1.9   Rehabilitation counselors will refuse to participate in employment practices which are inconsistent with the moral or legal standards regarding the treatment of employees or the public. Rehabilitation counselors will not condone practices which result in illegal or otherwise unjustifiable discrimination on any basis in hiring, promotion, or training.

Canon 2—Counselor–Client Relationship

Rehabilitation counselors shall respect the integrity and protect the welfare of people and groups with whom they work. The primary obligation of rehabilitation counselors is to their clients, defined as people with disabilities who are receiving services from rehabilitation counselors. Rehabilitation counselors shall endeavor at all times to place their clients' interests above their own.

Rules of Professional Conduct

R2.1 Rehabilitation counselors will make clear to clients, the purposes, goals, and limitations that may affect the counseling relationship.

R2.2 Rehabilitation counselors will not misrepresent their role or competence to clients. Rehabilitation counselors will provide information about their credentials, if requested, and will refer clients to other specialists as the needs of clients dictate.

R2.3 Rehabilitation counselors will be continually cognizant of their own needs, values, and of their potentially influential position, vis-a-vis clients, students, and subordinates. They avoid exploiting the trust and dependency of such persons. Rehabilitation counselors make every effort to avoid dual relationships that could impair their professional judgments or increase the risk of exploitation. Examples of dual relationships include, but are not limited to, research with and treatment of employees, students, supervisors, close friends, or relatives. Sexual intimacies with clients are unethical.

R2.4 Rehabilitation counselors who provide services at the request of a third party will clarify the nature of their relationships to all involved parties. They will inform all parties of their ethical responsibilities and take appropriate action. Rehabilitation counselors employed by third parties as case consultants or expert witnesses, where there is no pretense or intent to provide rehabilitation counseling services directly to clients, beyond file review, initial interview and/or assessment, will clearly define, through written or oral means, the limits of their relationship, particularly in the areas of informed consent and legally privileged communications, to involved individuals. As case consultants or expert witnesses, rehabilitation counselors have an obligation to provide unbiased, objective opinions.

R2.5 Rehabilitation counselors will honor the right of clients to consent to participate in rehabilitation services. Rehabilitation counselors will inform clients or the clients' legal guardians of factors that may affect clients' decisions to participate in rehabilitation services, and they will obtain written consent after clients or their legal guardians are fully informed of such factors. Rehabilitation counselors who work with minors or other persons who are unable to give voluntary, informed consent, will take special care to protect the best interests of clients.

R2.6 Rehabilitation counselors will avoid initiating or continuing consulting or counseling relationships if it is expected that the relationships can be of no benefit to clients, in which case rehabilitation counselors will suggest to clients appropriate alternatives.

R2.7 Rehabilitation counselors will recognize that families are usually an important factor in client's rehabilitation and will strive to enlist family understanding and involvement as a positive resource in promoting rehabilitation. The permission of clients will be secured prior to family involvement.

R2.8 Rehabilitation counselors and their clients will work jointly in devising an integrated, individualized rehabilitation plan which offers reasonable promise of success and is consistent with the abilities and circumstances of clients. Rehabilitation counselors will persistently monitor rehabilitation plans to ensure their continued viability and effectiveness, remembering that clients have the right to make choices.

R2.9 Rehabilitation counselors will work with their clients in considering employment for clients in only jobs and circumstances that are consistent with the clients' overall abilities, vocational limitations, physical restrictions, general temperament, interest and aptitude patterns, social skills, education, general qualifications and other relevant characteristics and needs. Rehabilitation counselors will neither place nor participate in placing clients in positions that will result in damaging the interest and welfare of either clients or employers.

Canon 3—Client Advocacy

Rehabilitation counselors shall serve as advocates for people with disabilities.

Rules of Professional Conduct

R3.1 Rehabilitation counselors will be obligated at all times to promote access for people with disabilities in programs, facilities, transportation, and communication, so that clients will not be excluded from opportunities to participate fully in rehabilitation, education, and society.

R3.2 Rehabilitation counselors will assure, prior to referring clients to programs, facilities, or employment settings, that they are appropriately accessible.

R3.3 Rehabilitation counselors will strive to understand accessibility problems of people with cognitive, hearing, mobility, visual and/or other disabilities and demonstrate such understanding in the practice of their profession.

R3.4 Rehabilitation counselors will strive to eliminate attitudinal barriers, including stereotyping and discrimination, toward people with disabilities and will enhance their own sensitivity and awareness toward people with disabilities.

R3.5 Rehabilitation counselors will remain aware of the actions taken by cooperating agencies on behalf of their clients and will act as advocates of clients to ensure effective service delivery.

Canon 4—Professional Relationships

Rehabilitation counselors shall act with integrity in their relationships with colleagues, other organizations, agencies, institutions, referral sources, and other professions so as to facilitate the contribution of all specialists toward achieving optimum benefit for clients.

Rules of Professional Conduct

R4.1 Rehabilitation counselors will ensure that there is fair mutual understanding of the rehabilitation plan by all agencies cooperating in the rehabilitation of clients and that any rehabilitation plan is developed with such mutual understanding.

R4.2 Rehabilitation counselors will abide by and help to implement "team" decisions in formulating rehabilitation plans and procedures, even when not personally agreeing with such decisions, unless these decisions breach the ethical Rules.

R4.3 Rehabilitation counselors will not commit receiving counselors to any prescribed courses of action in relation to clients, when transferring clients to other colleagues or agencies.

R4.4 Rehabilitation counselors, as referring counselors, will promptly supply all information necessary for a cooperating agency or counselor to begin serving clients.

R4.5 Rehabilitation counselors will not offer on-going professional counseling/case management services to clients receiving such services from other rehabilitation counselors without first notifying the other counselor. File review and second opinion services are not included in the concept of professional counseling/case management services.

R4.6 Rehabilitation counselors will secure from other specialists appropriate reports and evaluations, when such reports are essential for rehabilitation planning and/or service delivery.

R4.7 Rehabilitation counselors will not discuss in a disparaging way with clients the competency of other counselors or agencies, or the judgments made, the methods used, or the quality of rehabilitation plans.

R4.8 Rehabilitation counselors will not exploit their professional relationships with supervisors, colleagues, students, or employees, sexually or otherwise. Rehabilitation counselors will not condone or engage in sexual harassment, defined as deliberate or repeated comments, gestures, or physical contacts of a sexual nature unwanted by recipients.

R4.9   Rehabilitation counselors who know of an ethical violation by another rehabilitation counselor will informally attempt to resolve the issue with the counselor, when the misconduct is of a minor nature and/or appears to be due to lack of sensitivity, knowledge, or experience. If the violation does not seem amenable to an informal solution, or is of a more serious nature, rehabilitation counselors will bring it to the attention of the appropriate committee on professional ethics.

R4.10   Rehabilitation counselors possessing information concerning an alleged violation of this Code, will, upon request, reveal such information to the Commission on Rehabilitation Counselor Certification or other authority empowered to investigate or act upon the alleged violation, unless the information is protected by law.

R4.11   Rehabilitation counselors who employ or supervise other professionals or students will facilitate professional development of such individuals. They provide appropriate working conditions, timely evaluations, constructive consultation, and experience opportunities.

Canon 5—Public Statements/Fees

Rehabilitation counselors shall adhere to professional standards in establishing fees and promoting their services.

Rules of Professional Conduct

R5.1   Rehabilitation counselors will consider carefully the value of their services and the ability of clients to meet the financial burden in establishing reasonable fees for professional services.

R5.2   Rehabilitation counselors will not accept for professional work a fee or any other form of remuneration from clients who are entitled to their services through an institution or agency or other benefits structure, unless clients have been fully informed of the availability of services from other such sources.

R5.3   Rehabilitation counselors will neither give nor receive a commission or rebate or any other form of remuneration for referral of clients for professional services.

R5.4   Rehabilitation counselors who describe rehabilitation counseling or the services of rehabilitation counselors to the general public will fairly and accurately present the material, avoiding misrepresentation through sensationalism, exaggeration, or superficiality. Rehabilitation counselors are guided by the primary obligation to aid the public in developing informed judgments, opinions, and choices.

Canon 6—Confidentiality

Rehabilitation counselors shall respect the confidentiality of information obtained from clients in the course of their work.

Rules of Professional Conduct

R6.1   Rehabilitation counselors will inform clients at the onset of the counseling relationship of the limits of confidentiality.

R6.2   Rehabilitation counselors will take reasonable personal action, or inform responsible authorities, or inform those persons at risk, when the conditions or actions of clients indicate that there is clear and imminent danger to clients or others after advising clients that this must be done. Consultation with other professionals may be used where appropriate. The assumption of responsibility for clients must be taken only after careful deliberation and clients must be involved in the resumption of responsibility as quickly as possible.

R6.3   Rehabilitation counselors will not forward to another person, agency, or potential employer, any confidential information without the written permission of clients or their legal guardians.

R6.4   Rehabilitation counselors will ensure that there are defined policies and practices in other agencies cooperatively serving rehabilitation clients which effectively protect information confidentiality.

R6.5   Rehabilitation counselors will safeguard the maintenance, storage, and disposal of the records of clients so that unauthorized persons shall not have access to these records. All non-professional persons who must have access to these records will be thoroughly briefed concerning the confidential standards to be observed.

R6.6   Rehabilitation counselors, in the preparation of written and oral reports, will present only germane data and will make every effort to avoid undue invasion of privacy.

R6.7   Rehabilitation counselors will obtain written permission from clients or their legal guardians prior to taping or otherwise recording counseling sessions. Even with guardians' written consent, rehabilitation counselors will not record sessions against the expressed wishes of clients.

R6.8   Rehabilitation counselors will persist in claiming the privileged status of confidential information obtained from clients, where communications are privileged by statute for rehabilitation counselors.

R6.9   Rehabilitation counselors will provide prospective employers with only job relevant information about clients and will secure the permission of clients or their legal guardians for the release of any information which might be considered confidential.

Canon 7—Assessment

Rehabilitation counselors shall promote the welfare of clients in the selection, utilization, and interpretation of assessment measures.

Rules of Professional Conduct

R7.1   Rehabilitation counselors will recognize that different tests demand different levels of competence for administration, scoring, and interpretation, and will recognize the limits of their competence and perform only those functions for which they are trained.

R7.2   Rehabilitation counselors will consider carefully the specific validity, reliability, and appropriateness of tests, when selecting them for use in a given situation or with particular clients. Rehabilitation counselors will proceed with caution when attempting to evaluate and interpret the performance of people with disabilities, minority group members, or other persons who are not represented in the standardized norm groups. Rehabilitation counselors will recognize the effects of socioeconomic, ethnic, disability, and cultural factors on test scores.

R7.3   Rehabilitation counselors will administer tests under the same conditions that were established in their standardization. When tests are not administered under standard conditions, as may be necessary to accommodate modifications for clients with disabilities or when unusual behavior or irregularities occur during the testing session, those conditions will be noted and taken into account at the time of interpretation.

R7.4   Rehabilitation counselors will ensure that instrument limitations are not exceeded and that periodic reassessments are made to prevent stereotyping of clients.

R7.5   Rehabilitation counselors will make known the purpose of testing and the explicit use of the results to clients prior to administration. Recognizing the right of clients to have test results, rehabilitation counselors will give explanations of test results in language clients can understand.

R7.6   Rehabilitation counselors will ensure that specific interpretation accompanies any release of individual data. The welfare and explicit prior permission of clients will be the criteria for determining the recipients of the test results. The interpretation of assessment data will be related to the particular goals of evaluation.

R7.7   Rehabilitation counselors will attempt to ensure, when utilizing computerized assessment services, that such services are based on appropriate research to establish the validity of the computer programs and procedures used in arriving at interpretations. Public offering of an automated test interpretation service will be considered as a professional-to-professional consultation. In this instance, the formal responsibility of the consultant is to the consultee, but the ultimate and overriding responsibility is to clients.

R7.8   Rehabilitation counselors will recognize that assessment results may become obsolete. They make every effort to avoid and prevent the misuse of obsolete measures.

Canon 8—Research Activities

Rehabilitation counselors shall assist in efforts to expand the knowledge needed to more effectively serve people with disabilities.

Rules of Professional Conduct

R8.1   Rehabilitation counselors will ensure that data for research meet rigid standards of validity, honesty, and protection of confidentiality.

R8.2   Rehabilitation counselors will be aware of and responsive to all pertinent guidelines on research with human subjects. When planning any research activity dealing with human subjects, rehabilitation counselors will ensure that research problems, design, and execution are in full compliance with such guidelines.

R8.3   Rehabilitation counselors presenting case studies in classes, professional meetings, or publications will confine the content to that which can be disguised to ensure full protection of the identity of clients.

R8.4   Rehabilitation counselors will assign credit to those who have contributed to publications in proportion to their contribution.

R8.5   Rehabilitation counselors recognize that honesty and openness are essential characteristics of the relationship between rehabilitation counselors and research participants. When methodological requirements of a study necessitate concealment or deception, rehabilitation counselors will ensure that participants understand the reasons for this action.

Canon 9—Competence

Rehabilitation counselors shall establish and maintain their professional competencies at such a level that their clients receive the benefit of the highest quality of services the profession is capable of offering.

Rules of Professional Conduct

R9.1 Rehabilitation counselors will function within the limits of their defined role, training, and technical competency and will accept only those positions for which they are professionally qualified.

R9.2 Rehabilitation counselors will continuously strive through reading, attending professional meetings, and taking courses of instruction to keep abreast of new developments, concepts, and practices that are essential to providing the highest quality of services to their clients.

R9.3 Rehabilitation counselors, recognizing that personal problems and conflicts may interfere with their professional effectiveness, will refrain from undertaking any activity in which their personal problems are likely to lead to inadequate performance. If they are already engaged in such activity when they become aware of their personal problems, they will seek competent professional assistance to determine whether they should suspend, terminate or limit the scope of their professional activities.

R9.4 Rehabilitation counselors who are educators will perform their duties based on careful preparation so that their instruction is accurate, up-to-date and scholarly.

R9.5 Rehabilitation counselors who are educators will ensure that statements in catalogs and course outlines are accurate, particularly in terms of subject matter covered, bases for grading, and nature of classroom experiences.

R9.6 Rehabilitation counselors who are educators will maintain high standards of knowledge and skill by presenting rehabilitation counseling information fully and accurately, and by giving appropriate recognition to alternative viewpoints.

Canon 10—CRC Credential

Rehabilitation counselors holding the Certified Rehabilitation Counselor (CRC) designation shall honor the integrity and respect the limitations placed upon its use.

Rules of Professional Conduct

R10.1 Certified Rehabilitation Counselors will use the Certified Rehabilitation Counselor (CRC) designation only in accordance with the relevant *GUIDELINES* promulgated by the Commission on Rehabilitation Counselor Certification.

R10.2 Certified Rehabilitation Counselors will not attribute to the mere possession of the designation depth or scope of knowledge, skill, and professional capabilities greater than those demonstrated by achievement of the CRC designation.

R10.3   Certified Rehabilitation Counselors will not make unfair comparisons between a person who holds the Certified Rehabilitation Counselor (CRC) designation and one who does not.

R10.4   Certified Rehabilitation Counselors will not write, speak, nor act in ways that lead others to believe Certified Rehabilitation Counselors are officially representing the Commission on Rehabilitation Counselor Certification, unless such written permission has been granted by the said Commission.

R10.5   Certified Rehabilitation Counselors will make no claim to unique skills or devices not available to others in the profession unless the special efficacy of such unique skills or device has been demonstrated by scientifically accepted evidence.

R10.6   Certified Rehabilitation Counselors will not initiate or support the candidacy of an individual for certification by the Commission on Rehabilitation Counselor Certification if the individual is known to engage in professional practices which violate this Code.

ACKNOWLEDGEMENT

Referenced documents, statements, and sources for the development of this revised Code are as follows: National Rehabilitation Counseling Association Code of Ethics, National Academy of Certified Clinical Mental Health Counselors, and the Ethical Standards of the American Association for Counseling and Development. Portions of the Code are also derived from the American Psychological Association "Ethical Principles of Psychologists."

References

Adams, P., & Nelson, K. (1995). Introduction. In P. Adams & K. Nelson (Eds.), *Reinventing human services: Community and family centered practice* (pp. 1–14). New York: Aldine de Gruyter.

Adcock, R. L., & Lee, J. W. (1972). Principles of time management. In A. C. Beck & E. D. Hillmer (Eds.), *A practical approach to organization development through MBO* (pp. 282–285). Reading, MA: Addison-Wesley.

Allen, H., & Miller, D. (1988). Client death: A national survey of the experiences of certified rehabilitation counselors. *Rehabilitation Counseling Bulletin, 32,* 58–64.

Almagor, M. (1991). The relationship among fathers' physical disability, agreement regarding marital satisfaction, and perception of children's emotional state. *Rehabilitation Psychology, 36*(4), 241–254.

Alston, R., McCowan, C. J., & Turner, W. L. (1994). Family functioning as a correlate of disability adjustment for African Americans. *Rehabilitation Counseling Bulletin, 37,* 277–289.

Alston, R., & Turner, W. L. (1994). A family strengths model of adjustment to disability for African American clients. *Journal of Counseling & Development, 72,* 378–383.

Altarriba, J., & Santiago-Rivera, A. L. (1994). Current perspectives on using linguistic and cultural factors in counseling the Hispanic client. *Professional Psychology: Research and Practice, 25,* 388–397.

Althen, G. (1988). *American ways—A guide for foreigners in the United States.* Yarmouth, ME: Intercultural.

Amble, B., & Peterson, G. (1979). Rehabilitation counselors: The use of psychological reports. *Rehabilitation Counseling Bulletin, 23,* 127–130.

American Medical Association. (1989). *Encyclopedia of Medicine.* New York: Random House.

American Rehabilitation Counseling Association, Commission on Rehabilitation Counselor Certification, and National Rehabilitation Counseling Association. (1987). Code of professional ethics for rehabilitation counselors. *Journal of Applied Rehabilitation Counseling, 18*(4), 28–32.

Americans with Disabilities Act of 1990, 42 U.S.C. § 12101 *et seq.*

Amundson, N. (1989). A model for individual career counseling. *Journal of Employment Counseling, 26,* 132–138.

Anderson, D., & Berlant, J. (1995). Managed mental health and substance abuse services. In P. Kongstvedt (Ed.), *Essentials of managed health care.* Gaithersburg, MD: Aspen.

Andrew, J. (Ed.). (1994). *Disability handbook* (2nd ed.). Fayetteville: Department of Rehabilitation Education and Research, University of Arkansas.

Angell, D. L., De Sau, G. T., & Havrilla, A. A. (1969). Rehabilitation counselor versus coordinator: One of rehabilitation's great straw men. *NRCA Professional Bulletin, 9.*

Anthony, W. (1980). A rehabilitation model for rehabilitating the psychiatrically disabled. *Rehabilitation Counseling Bulletin, 24,* 6–21.

Anthony, W. (1993). Managed mental health care: Will it be rationed care or rational care? *Psychosocial Rehabilitation Journal, 16*(4), 120–123.

Argyle, M., & Dean, J. (1965). Eye contact, distance and affiliation. *Sociometry, 28,* 289–304.

Arnold, B., & Orozco, S. (1988). Physical disability, acculturation, and family interaction among Mexican Americans. *Journal of Applied Rehabilitation Counseling, 20*(2), 28–32.

Arnold, J., & Partridge, D. (1988). A note concerning psychological well-being and client experiences at an Employment Rehabilitation Centre. *Journal of Occupational Psychology, 61*, 341–346.

Arnold, M., & Case, T. (1993). Supporting providers of in-home care: The needs of families with relatives who are disabled. *Journal of Rehabilitation, 59*, 55–59.

Arvey, R., & Campion, J. (1982). The employment interview: A summary of recent research. *Personnel Psychology, 35*, 281–322.

Aston, S. J. (1984, December). *Prevalence of ocular anomalies in American Indians*. Paper presented at the annual meeting of the American Academy of Optometry, St. Louis, MO.

Atkins, B. J. (1988). An asset-oriented approach to cross-cultural issues: Blacks in rehabilitation. *Journal of Applied Rehabilitation Counseling, 19*, 45–49.

Atkinson, D. R., & Matsushita, Y. J. (1991). Japanese-American acculturation, counseling style, counselor ethnicity, and perceived counselor credibility. *Journal of Counseling Psychology, 38*, 473–478.

Baker, C. K., & Taylor, D. W. (1995). Assessment of African American clients: Opportunities for biased results. *Vocational Evaluation and Work Adjustment Bulletin, 29*, 46–51.

Barnow, B. (1996). Policies for people with disabilities in U.S. employment and training programs. In J. Mashaw, V. Reno, R. Burkhouser, & M. Berkowitz (Eds.), *Disability, work and cash benefits* (pp. 297–330). Kalamazoo, MI: W.E. Upjohn Institute for Employment Research.

Baruth, L. G., & Manning, M. L. (1992). Understanding and counseling Hispanic American children. *Elementary School Guidance and Counseling, 27*, 113–122.

Bayer, D. (1996). Interaction in families with young adults with a psychiatric diagnosis. *The American Journal of Family Therapy, 24*, 21–30.

Bayes, M. (1972). Behavioral cues of interpersonal warmth. *Journal of Counseling Psychology, 39*, 333–339.

Beardsley, M., & Rubin, S. (1988). Rehabilitation service providers: An investigation of generic job tasks and knowledge. *Rehabilitation Counseling Bulletin, 37*, 122–139.

Beauchamp, T. L., & Childress, J. F. (1983). *Principles of biomedical ethics* (2nd ed.). New York: Oxford University Press.

Becker, D., & Drake, R. (1994). Individual placement and support: A community mental health center approach to vocational rehabilitation. *Community Mental Health Journal, 30*, 193–206.

Benjamin, A. (1981). *The helping interview* (3rd ed.). Boston: Houghton Mifflin.

Bernstein, L., Bernstein, R., & Dana, R. (1974). *Interviewing: A guide for health professionals* (2nd ed.). New York: Appleton-Century-Crofts.

Berven, N. (1984). Assessment practices in rehabilitation counseling. *Journal of Applied Rehabilitation Counseling, 15*(3), 9–14.

Berven, N., & Driscoll, J. (1981). The effects of past psychiatric disability on employer evaluation of a job applicant. *Journal of Applied Rehabilitation Counseling, 12*, 50–54.

Biller, E., & White, W. (1989). Comparing special education and vocational rehabilitation in serving persons with specific learning disabilities. *Rehabilitation Counseling Bulletin, 33*(1), 4–17.

Billingsley, A. (1992). *Climbing Jacob's ladder*. New York: Simon & Schuster.

Billingsley, A., & Caldwell, C. H. (1991). The church, the family, and the school in the African American community. *Journal of Negro Education, 60*, 427–440.

Blackwell, T. L., Martin, W. E., & Scalia, V. A. (1994). *Ethics in rehabilitation: A guide for rehabilitation professionals*. Athens, GA: Elliott & Fitzpatrick.

Bloom, K., Buhrke, R., & Scott, T. (1988). Burnout and job expectations of state agency rehabilitation counselors in North Dakota. *Journal of Applied Rehabilitation Counseling, 19*, 32–36.

Blount, M., Thyer, B., & Frye, T. (1992). Social work practice with Native Americans. In D. Harrison, J. Wodarski, & B. Thyer (Eds.), *Cultural diversity and social work practices* (pp. 107–134). Springfield, IL: Charles C Thomas.

Bolton, B. (1981). Assessing employability of handicapped persons: The vocational rehabilitation perspective. *Journal of Applied Rehabilitation Counseling, 12,* 40–44.

Borgen, W., Amundson, N., & Biela, P. (1987). The experience of unemployment for persons who are physically disabled. *Journal of Applied Rehabilitation Counseling, 18,* 25–32.

Botterbusch, K. (1994). Summary of: Community support networks for persons with psychiatric disabilities. *Vocational Evaluation and Work Adjustment Bulletin, 27,* 57–61.

Bowe, F. (1987). *Out of the job market: A national crisis.* Washington, DC: President's Committee on Employment of People with Disabilities.

Bray, G. P. (1977). Reactive patterns in families of the severely disabled. *Rehabilitation Counseling Bulletin, 20,* 236–239.

Bray, G. (1980). Team strategies for family involvement in rehabilitation. *Journal of Rehabilitation, 46,* 20–23.

Brodwin, M. G., & Brodwin, S. K. (1993). Rehabilitation: A case study approach. In M. G. Brodwin, F. Tellez, & S. K. Brodwin (Eds.), *Medical, psychological and vocational aspects of disability* (pp. 1–19). Athens, GA: Elliot & Fitzpatrick.

Brodwin, M., Parker, R. M., & DeLaGarza, D. (1996). Disability and accommodation. In E. M. Szymanski & R. M. Parker (Eds.), *Work and disability* (pp. 165–207). Austin, TX: PRO-ED.

Burkhead, J. (1992). Computer applications in rehabilitation. In R. M. Parker & E. M. Szymanski (Eds.), *Rehabilitation counseling: Basics and beyond* (2nd ed., pp. 365–400). Austin, TX: PRO-ED.

Bush, D. W. (1992). Consulting psychologists in rehabilitation services. *Rehabilitation Education, 6,* 99–104.

Bushy, A. (Ed.). (1991). *Rural nursing, Volume 2.* Newbury Park, CA: Sage.

Calhoun, J., & Wilson, W. (1974). Behavior therapy and the minority client. *Behavior Therapy, 5,* 299–302.

Campbell, A. (1981). *The sense of well-being in America.* New York: McGraw-Hill.

Canelón, M. F. (1995). Job site analysis facilitates work reintegration. *American Journal of Occupational Therapy, 49,* 461–467.

Capuzzi, D., & Gross, D. R. (1995). *Counseling and psychotherapy: Theories and interventions.* Englewood Cliffs, NJ: Merrill.

Carkhuff, R. R., & Anthony, W. A. (1979). *The skills of helping.* Amherst, MA: Human Resource Development Press.

Casas, J. M., & Vasquez, M. J. (1989). Counseling the Hispanic client: A theoretical and applied perspective. In P. B. Pedersen, J. G. Draguns, W. J. Lonner, & J. E. Trimble (Eds.), *Counseling across cultures* (pp. 153–175). Honolulu: University of Hawaii.

Cassell, J. L., & Mulkey, S. W. (1985). *Rehabilitation caseload management: Concepts and practice.* Austin, TX: PRO-ED.

Chan, F., Berven, N. L., & Lam, C. S. (1990). Computer-based, case management simulations in the training of rehabilitation counselors. *Rehabilitation Counseling Bulletin, 33,* 212–228.

Chan, F., Hedl, J. J., Parker, H. J., Lam, C. S., Chan, T. N., & Yu, B. (1988). Differential attitudes of Chinese students toward people with disabilities: A cross-cultural perspective. *The International Journal of Social Psychiatry, 34,* 267–273.

Chan, F., Hua, M. S., Ju, J. J., & Lam, C. S. (1984). Factoral structure of the Chinese Scale of Attitudes Toward Disabled Persons: A cross cultural validation. *International Journal of Rehabilitation Research, 7,* 317–319.

Chan, F., Lam, C. S., Wong, D., Leung, P., & Fang, X. S. (1988). Counseling Chinese Americans with disabilities. *Journal of Applied Rehabilitation Counseling, 19*(4), 21–25.

Chan, F., McCollum, P. S., & Pool, D. A. (1985). Computer-assisted rehabilitation services: A preliminary draft of the Texas casework model. *Rehabilitation Counseling Bulletin, 28,* 219–232.

Chan, F., Rosen, A., Wong, D., & Kaplan, S. (1993). Evaluating rehabilitation counseling caseload management skills through computer simulations. *Journal of Counseling and Development, 71,* 493–498.

Chan, S. (1992). Families with Asian roots. In E. W. Lynch & M. J. Hanson (Eds.), *Developing cross-cultural competence: A guide for working with young children and their families* (pp. 181–257). Baltimore: Brookes.

Chartrand, J. (1991). The evolution of trait and factor career counseling. A person × environment fit approach. *Journal of Counseling and Development, 69,* 518–524.

Cheatham, H. E. (1990). Empowering Black families. In H. E. Cheatham & J. B. Tewart (Eds.), *Black families: Interdisciplinary perspectives* (pp. 373–393). New Brunswick, NJ: Transaction.

Cheung, F. K., & Snowden, L. R. (1990). Community mental health and ethnic minority populations. *Community Mental Health Journal, 26,* 277–291.

Cheung, P. (1995). Acculturization and psychiatric morbidity among Cambodian refugees in New Zealand. *International Journal of Social Psychiatry, 41,* 108–119.

Chubon, R. (1985). Quality of life measurement of persons with back problems: Some preliminary findings. *Journal of Applied Rehabilitation Counseling, 16,* 31–34.

Chubon, R. (1992). Defining rehabilitation from a systems perspective: Critical implications. *Journal of Applied Rehabilitation Counseling, 23*(1), 27–32.

Chung, D. K. (1992). Asian cultural commonalities: A comparison with mainstream American culture. In S. M. Furuto, R. Biswas, D. K. Chung, K. Murase, & F. Ross-Sheriff (Eds.), *Social work practice with Asian Americans* (pp. 27–44). Newbury Park: Sage.

Clark, S., & Kelley, S. D. (1992). Traditional Native American values: Conflict concordance in rehabilitation. *Journal of Rehabilitation, 58*(2), 23–28.

Code of professional ethics for rehabilitation counselors. (1988). *Rehabilitation Counseling, 31,* 255–268.

Cohen, R., & Lavach, C. (1995). Strengthening partnerships between families and service providers. In P. Adams & K. Nelson (Eds.), *Reinventing human services: Community and family centered practice* (pp. 261–277). New York: Aldine de Gruyter.

Connors, J. L., & Donnellan, A. M. (1993). Citizenship and culture: The role of disabled people in Navajo society. *Disability, Handicap and Society, 8,* 265–280.

Cook, D., & Ferritor, D. (1985). The family: A potential resource in the provision of rehabilitation services. *Journal of Applied Rehabilitation Counseling, 16*(2), 52–53.

Cooper, C., & Marshall, J. (1978). Sources of managerial and white collar stress. In C. Cooper & R. Payne (Eds.), *Stress at work.* New York: Wiley.

Corey, G., Corey, M. S., & Callahan, P. (1979). *Professional and ethical issues in counseling and psychotherapy.* Monterey, CA: Brooks/Cole.

Cormier, W. H., & Cormier, L. S. (1979). *Interviewing strategies for helpers: A guide to assessment, treatment, and evaluation.* Monterey, CA: Brooks/Cole.

Corrigan, P., & Kayton-Weinberg, D. (1993). Clinical care update: "Aggressive" and "problem-focused" models of case management for the severely mentally ill. *Community of Mental Health Journal, 29*(5), 449–458.

Cottone, R. R., Handelsman, M., & Walters, N. (1986). Understanding the influence of family systems on the rehabilitation process. *Journal of Applied Rehabilitation Counseling, 17,* 37–40.

Cottone, R. R., Simmons, B., & Wilfley, D. (1983). Ethical issues in vocational rehabilitation: A review of the literature from 1970 to 1981. *Journal of Rehabilitation, 49*, 19–24.

Crimando, W., & Riggar, T. (1996). *Utilizing community resources.* Delray Beach, FL: St. Lucie.

Crimando, W., & Sawyer, H. W. (1983). Microcomputers in private sector rehabilitation. *Rehabilitation Counseling Bulletin, 27*, 26–31.

Crisp, R. (1990). Return to work after spinal cord injury. *Journal of Rehabilitation, 56*, 28–35.

Cull, J., & Levinson, K. (1977). State rehabilitation administrators' views on psychological evaluation: A five year follow-up study. *Rehabilitation Literature, 38*, 203–204.

Cutler, F., & Ramm, A. (1992). Introduction to the basics of vocational evaluation. In J. Siefken (Ed.), *Vocational evaluation in the private sector* (pp. 31–66). Menomonie, WI: University of Wisconsin–Stout.

Dana, R. H. (1993). *Multicultural assessment perspectives for professional psychology.* Needham Heights, MA: Allyn & Bacon.

Danek, M., Conyers, L., Enright, M., Munson, M., Brodwin, M., Hanley-Maxwell, C., & Gugerty, J. (1996). Legislation concerning career counseling and job placement for people with disabilities. In E. M. Szymanski & R. M. Parker (Eds.), *Work and disability* (pp. 39–78). Austin, TX: PRO-ED.

Danek, M., Wright, G. N., Leahy, M. J., & Shapson, P. R. (1987). Introduction to rehabilitation competency studies. *Rehabilitation Counseling Bulletin, 31*, 84–93.

Dawis, R. (1976). The Minnesota Theory of Work Adjustment. In B. Bolton (Ed.), *Handbook of measurement and evaluation in rehabilitation.* Baltimore: University Park Press.

Dawis, R., & Lofquist, L. (1984). *A psychological theory of work adjustment.* Minneapolis: University of Minnesota Press.

DeLoach, C., & Greer, B. (1979). Client factors affecting the practice of rehabilitation counseling. *Journal of Applied Rehabilitation Counseling, 10*, 53–59.

Dew, D., Phillips, B., & Reiss, D. (1989). Assessment and early planning with the family in vocational rehabilitation. *Journal of Rehabilitation, 55*, 41–44.

Ditty, J., & Reynolds, K. (1980). Traditional vocational evaluation: Help or hindrance? *Journal of Rehabilitation, 46*, 22–25.

Dobren, A. (1994). An ecologically oriented conceptual model of vocational rehabilitation of people with acquired midcareer disabilities. *Rehabilitation Counseling Bulletin, 37*, 215–228.

Dolliver, R., & Nelson, R. (1975). Assumptions regarding vocational counseling. *Vocational Guide Quarterly, 24*, 12–19.

Douglas, R. (1994). The Americans with Disabilities Act after three years: Where are we? *Journal of Vocational Rehabilitation, 4*, 153–157.

Dozier, M., Lee, S., Kleir, S., Toprac, M., & Mason, M. (1993). A case management program in Texas revisited. *Psychosocial Rehabilitation Journal, 17*(2), 183–189.

Drotar, D., Crawford, P., & Bush, M. (1984). The family context of childhood chronic illness: Implications for psychosocial intervention. In M. Eisenberg, L. Sutkin, & M. Jansen (Eds.), *Chronic illness and disability through the life span: Effects on self and family* (pp. 103–129). New York: Springer.

Drucker, P. E. (1967). The effective decision. *Harvard Business Review, 45*(1), 92–98.

Dumas, A., & Sadowsky, D. (1984). A family training program for adventitiously blinded and low vision veterans. *Journal of Visual Impairment and Blindness, 78*, 473–478.

Dungee-Anderson, D., & Beckett, J. O. (1992). Alzheimer's disease in African American and White families: A clinical analysis. *Smith College Studies in Social Work, 62*, 155–168.

D'Zurilla, T. (1986). *Problem solving therapy.* New York: Springer.

Eastern Paralyzed Veterans Association. (1989). *Accessibility*. Jackson Heights, NY: Author.

Eigner, J., & Jackson, D. (1978). Effectiveness of a counseling intervention program for teaching career decision-making skills. *Journal of Counseling Psychology, 25*, 45–52.

Emener, W. (1979). Professional burnout: Rehabilitation's hidden handicap. *Journal of Rehabilitation, 45*, 55–58.

Emener, W., & McHargue, J. (1978). Employer attitudes toward the employment and placement of the handicapped. *Journal of Applied Rehabilitation Counseling, 9*, 120–125.

Emener, W., & Rubin, S. E. (1980). Rehabilitation counselor role and functions and sources of role strain. *Journal of Applied Rehabilitation Counseling, 11*, 57–59.

Engblom, E., Hamalainen, H., Ronnemaa, T., Vanttinen, E., Kallio, V., & Knuts, L. (1994). Cardiac rehabilitation and return to work after coronary artery bypass surgery. *Quality of Life Research, 3*, 207–213.

Equal Employment Opportunity Commission. (1995). *ADA enforcement guidance: Preemployment disability-related questions and medical examinations*. Washington, DC: Author.

Evans, D. R., Hearn, M. T., Uhlemann, M. R., & Ivey, A. E. (1989). *Essential interviewing: A programmed approach to effective communication* (3rd ed.). Pacific Grove, CA: Brooks/Cole.

Evans, L., Bishop, S., Matlock, L., Stranahan, S., Smith, G., & Halar, E. (1987). Family interaction and treatment adherence after stroke. *Archives of Physical Medical Rehabilitation, 68*, 513–517.

Faherty, B. (1990, July). Case management, the latest buzzword: What it is, and what it isn't. *Caring Magazine*, 20–22.

Falvo, D. R. (1991). *Medical and psychosocial aspects of chronic illness and disability*. Gaithersburg, MD: Aspen.

Feist-Price, S., & Ford-Harris, D. (1994). Rehabilitation counseling: Issues specific to providing services to African American clients. *Journal of Rehabilitation, 60*, 13–19.

Felton, J. S. (1993a). Medical terminology. In M. G. Brodwin, F. Tellez, & S. K. Brodwin (Eds.), *Medical, psychological and vocational aspects of disability* (pp. 21–34). Athens, GA: Elliot & Fitzpatrick.

Felton, J. S. (1993b). The physical examination. In M. G. Brodwin, F. Tellez, & S. K. Brodwin (Eds.), *Medical, psychological and vocational aspects of disability* (pp. 35–50). Athens, GA: Elliot & Fitzpatrick.

Felton, J., Perkins, D., & Lewin, M. (1969). *A survey of medicine and medical practice for the rehabilitation counselor*. Washington, DC: Rehabilitation Services Administration, Department of Health, Education and Welfare.

Flanagan, J. (1978). A research approach to improving our quality of life. *American Psychologist, 33*, 138–147.

Flannagan, T. W. (1977). Placement: Beyond the obvious. *Rehabilitation Counseling Bulletin, 21*, 116–120.

Flaskerund, J. H. (1986). The effects of culture-compatible intervention on the utilization of mental health services by minority clients. *Community Mental Health Journal, 22*, 127–141.

Fong, R. (1992). A history of Asian Americans. In S. M. Furuto, R. Biswas, D. K. Chung, K. Murase, & F. Ross-Sheriff (Eds.), *Social work practice with Asian Americans* (pp. 3–26). Newbury Park, CA: Sage.

Franz, J., & Crystal, R. (1985). A career development model for the juvenile diabetic: Implications for rehabilitation practice. *Journal of Applied Rehabilitation Counseling, 17*(1), 24–27.

Frazier, E. F. (1939). *The Negro family in the United States*. Chicago: University of Chicago Press.

Freeman, E. M. (1990). Theoretical perspectives for practice with Black families. In S. M. L. Logan, E. M. Freeman, & R. G. McRoy (Eds.), *Social work practice with Black families: A culturally specific perspective* (pp. 38–52). White Plains, NY: Longman.

Fugita, S., Ito, K. L., Abe, J., & Takeuchi, D. T. (1991). Japanese Americans. In N. Mokuau (Ed.), *Handbook of social services for Asian and Pacific Islanders* (pp. 61–77). Westport, CT: Greenwood Press.

Fuhriman, A., & Pappas, J. (1971). Behavioral intervention strategies for employment counseling. *Journal of Employment Counseling, 8,* 116–124.

Gade, E., & Toutges, G. (1983). Employers' attitudes toward hiring epileptics: Implications for job placement. *Rehabilitation Counseling Association, 26,* 353–356.

Galassi, J. P., & Galassi, M. D. (1978). Preparing individuals for job interviews: Suggestions from more than 60 years of research. *Personal Guidance Journal, 57,* 188–192.

Garber-Conrad, B. (1987). Rehabilitation in Canada's north. *Journal of Visual Impairment and Blindness, 81,* 164–165.

Gardner, J. (1991). Early referral and other factors affecting vocational rehabilitation outcomes for Workers' Compensation clients. *Rehabilitation Counseling Bulletin, 34,* 197–209.

Garrett, J. T., & Garrett, M. W. (1994). The pathway of good medicine: Understanding and counseling Native American Indians. *Journal of Multicultural Counseling and Development, 22,* 134–144.

Garza, R., & Gallegos, P. (1995). Environmental influences and personal choice: A humanistic perspective on acculturation. In A. M. Padilla (Ed.), *Hispanic psychology* (pp. 3–14). Thousand Oaks, CA: Sage.

Garzon, F., & Tan, S. Y. (1992). Counseling Hispanics: Cross-cultural and Christian perspectives. *Journal of Psychology and Christianity, 11,* 378–390.

Genther, R. W., & Moughan, J. (1977). Introverts' and extroverts' responses to non-verbal attending behaviors. *Journal of Counseling Psychology, 24,* 144–145.

Gerhardt, U. (1990). Patient careers in end-stage renal failure. *Social Science and Medicine, 30,* 1211–1224.

Gilbride, D., & Stensrud, R. (1992). Demand-side job development: A model for the 1990s. *Journal of Rehabilitation, 58,* 34–39.

Gill, W. S. (1972). The psychologist and rehabilitation. In J. G. Cull & R. E. Hardy (Eds.), *Vocational rehabilitation: Profession and process* (pp. 470–483). Springfield, IL.: Charles C Thomas.

Glasser, W. (1981). *Stations of the mind.* New York: Harper & Row.

Gleick, E. (1996, February 5). Rehab centers run dry. *Time Magazine, 147*(6), 44–45.

Goldberg, R. (1992). Toward a model of vocational development of people with disabilities. *Rehabilitation Counseling Bulletin, 35,* 161–173.

Goldberg, R., Bigwood, A., MacCarthy, S., Donaldson, W., & Conrad, S. (1972). Vocational profile of patients awaiting and following renal transplantation. *Archives of Physical Medicine and Rehabilitation, 53,* 28–33.

Goldberg, R., & Freed, M. (1973). Vocational adjustment, interest, work values, and career plans of persons with spinal cord injuries. *Scandinavian Journal of Rehabilitation Medicine, 5,* 3–11.

Goldman, L. (1971). *Using tests in counseling* (2nd ed.) New York: Appelton-Century-Crofts.

Goldstein, A. P. (1973). *Structured learning therapy.* New York: Academic Press.

Gomez, J., & Michaels, R. (1995). An assessment of burnout in human service providers. *Journal of Rehabilitation, 61*(1), 23–26.

Good Housekeeping. (1989). *The Good Housekeeping family health and medical guide.* New York: Hearst.

Goodwin, D. (1994). Nursing case management activities: How they differ between employment settings. *Journal of Nursing Administration, 24*(2), 29–34.

Goodwin, L. R., Jr. (1989). Private counseling: A primer. *Journal of Applied Rehabilitation Counseling, 20,* 41–46.

Goodyear, D. L., & Stude, E. W. (1975). Work performance: A comparison of severely disabled and nondisabled employees. *Journal of Applied Rehabilitation Counseling, 6,* 210–216.

Gottfredson, G., & Holland, J. (1996). *Dictionary of Holland Occupational Codes* (3rd ed.). Odessa, FL: Psychological Assessment Resources.

Grand, S. A., & Strohmer, D. C. (1983). Minority perceptions of the disabled. *Rehabilitation Counseling Bulletin, 27*, 117–119.

Granovetter, M. (1979). Placement as brokerage information problems in the labor market for rehabilitation workers. In D. Vandergoot & J. D. Worrall (Eds.), *Placement in rehabilitation* (pp. 83–101). Baltimore: University Park Press.

Green, J. W. (1995). *Cultural awareness in the human services: A multi-ethnic approach* (2nd ed.). Boston: Allyn & Bacon.

Greenwood, R., & Johnson, V. (1985). *Employer concerns*. Fayetteville: University of Arkansas, Arkansas Research and Training Center in Vocational Rehabilitation.

Greenwood, R., Johnson, V., & Schriner, K. (1988). Employer perspectives on employer-rehabilitation partnerships. *Journal of Applied Rehabilitation Counseling, 19*(1), 8–12.

Greenwood, R., Rubin, S., & Farley, R. (1980). *Systematic caseload management: Trainer's guide*. Fayetteville: University of Arkansas, Arkansas Research and Training Center in Vocational Rehabilitation.

Grossman, H. (1995). *Educating Hispanic students: Implications for instruction, classroom management, counseling and assessment* (2nd ed.). Springfield, IL: Charles C Thomas.

Groth-Marnat, G. (1984). *Handbook of psychological assessment*. New York: Van Nostrand Reinhold.

Haas, L., & Malouf, J. (1989). *Keeping up the good work: A practitioner's guide to mental health ethics*. Sarasota, FL: Professional Resource Exchange.

Hagner, D., Butterworth, J., & Keith, G. (1995). Strategies and barriers in facilitating natural supports for employment of adults with severe disabilities. *Journal of the Association of Persons with Severe Handicaps, 20*(2), 110–120.

Hagner, D., Fesko, S. L., Cadigan, M., Kiernan, W., & Butterworth, J. (1996). Securing employment: Job search and employer negotiation strategies in rehabilitation. In E. M. Szymanski & R. M. Parker (Eds.), *Work and disability* (pp. 309–340). Austin, TX: PRO-ED.

Hale, J., & Hunter, M. (1988). *From HMO movement to managed care industry: The future of HMOs in a volatile healthcare market*. Washington, DC: Monograph published by the InterStudy Center for Managed Care Research.

Hall, E. T. (1976a). *Beyond culture*. Garden City, NY: Anchor Press.

Hall, E. T. (1976b). How cultures collide. *Psychology Today, 10*, 66–74.

Hallover, D., Prosser, R., & Swift, K. (1989). Neuropsychological evaluation in the vocational rehabilitation of brain injured clients. *Journal of Applied Rehabilitation Counseling, 20*, 3–7.

Hampton, D. (1993). Implementing a managed care framework through care maps. *Journal of Nursing Administration, 23*(5), 21–27.

Hanley-Maxwell, C., Bordieri, J., & Merz, M. A. (1996). Supporting placement. In E. M. Szymanski & R. M. Parker (Eds.), *Work and disability* (pp. 341–364). Austin, TX: PRO-ED.

Hanna, W., & Rugovsky, E. (1992). On the situation of Afican-American women. *Journal of Applied Rehabilitation Counseling, 23*, 39–45.

Harrington, T., & O'Shea, A. (1984). *Guide for occupational exploration* (2nd ed.). Circle Pines, MN: American Guidance Service.

Hartigan, J., & Wigdor, A. (1989). *Fairness in employment testing: Validity generalizations, minority issues, and the GATB*. Washington, DC: National Academy Press.

Hathaway, S., & McKinley, C. (1970). *Minnesota Multiphasic Personality Inventory*. Minneapolis, MN: National Computer Systems.

Hays, P. (1996). Addressing the complexities of culture and gender in counseling. *Journal of Counseling and Development, 74*, 332–337.

Heinrich, R. K., Corbine, J. L., & Thomas, K. R. (1990). Counseling Native Americans. *Journal of Counseling and Development, 69*, 128–133.

Heinssen, R., Levendusky, P., & Hunter, R. (1995). Client as colleague: Therapeutic contracting with the seriously mentally ill. *American Psychologist, 50*(7), 522–531.

Henke, R. O., Connolly, S. G., & Cox, J. G. (1975). Caseload management: The key to effectiveness. *Journal of Applied Rehabilitation Counseling, 6*, 217–227.

Heppner, P., & Krauskopf, C. (1987). An information processing approach to personal problem solving. *The Counseling Psychologist, 15*, 371–447.

Herbert, J. T. (1989). Assessing the need for family therapy: A primer for rehabilitation counselors. *Journal of Rehabilitation, 55*(1), 45–51.

Herbert, J.T., & Wright, G. (1985). Attitudes of state vocational rehabilitation agencies toward counselor education. *Rehabilitation Counseling Bulletin, 28*(3), 155–160.

Herr, E. (1987). Education and preparation for work: Contributions of career education and vocational education. *Journal of Career Development, 13*, 16–30.

Herring, R. D. (1994). The clown or contrary figure as a counseling intervention strategy with Native American Indian clients. *Journal of Multicultural Counseling and Development, 22*, 153–164.

Hershenson, D. (1988). Along for the ride: The evaluation of rehabilitation counselor education. *Rehabilitation Counseling Bulletin, 31*, 204–217.

Hershenson, D. (1996). A systems reformulation of a developmental model of work adjustment. *Rehabilitation Counseling Bulletin, 40*, 2–9.

Herskovits, M. J. (1941). *The myth of the Negro past.* Boston: Beacon Press.

Hesketh, B., & Dawis, R. (1991). The Minnesota Theory of Work Adjustment: A conceptual framework. In B. Hesketh & A. Adams, *Psychological perspectives on occupational health and rehabilitation.* New York: Harcourt Brace Jovanovich.

Highlen, P. S., & Baccus, G. K. (1977). Effect of reflection of feeling and probe on client self-referenced affect. *Journal of Counseling Psychology, 24*, 440–443.

Hill, C. E., & Gormally, J. (1977). Effects of reflection, restatement, probe, and nonverbal behavior on client affect. *Journal of Counseling Psychology, 24*, 92–97.

Hill, R. B. (1971). *The strengths of Black families.* New York: Emerson Hall.

Hill, R. B. (1993). *Research on the African American family: A holistic perspective.* Westport, CT: Auburn House.

Hinkle, J. S. (1994). Practitioners and cross-cultural assessment: A practical guide to information and training. *Measurement and Evaluation in Counseling and Development, 27*, 103–115.

Hinman, S., Means, B., Parker, S., & Odendahl, B. (1988). *Job Seeking Skills Assessment.* Hot Springs, AR: Research and Training Center in Vocational Rehabilitation.

Hodges, M., & Knisley, M. (1995). Emerging questions for case management in behavioral health managed care systems. In L. Giesler (Ed.), *Case management for behavioral managed care* (pp. 74–93). Cincinnati, OH: National Association of Case Management.

Hoehn-Saric, R., Frank, J. D., Imber, S. D., Nash, E. H., Stone, A. R., & Battle, C. C. (1964). Systematic preparation of patients for psychotherapy: I. Effects on therapy behavior and outcome. *Journal of Psychological Research, 2*, 267–281.

Holland, J. (1994). *Self-Directed Search (Form R).* Odessa, FL: Psychological Assessment Resources.

Holmes, G., & Karst, R. (1989). Case record management: A professional skill. *Journal of Applied Rehabilitation Counseling, 20*(1), 36–40.

Hong, G. (1993). Contextual factors in psychotherapy with Asian Americans. In J. L. Chin, J. H. Liem, M. D. Ham, & G. Gong (Eds.), *Transference and empathy in Asian American psychotherapy: Cultural values and treatment needs* (pp. 3–14). Westport, CT: Greenwood.

Hornby, G., & Seligman, M. (1991). Disability and the family: Current status and future developments. *Counseling Psychology Quarterly, 4,* 267–271.

Huang, K. (1991). Chinese Americans. In N. Mokuau (Ed.), *Handbook of social services for Asian and Pacific Islanders* (pp. 79–96). Westport, CT: Greenwood Press.

Husby, R., Dahl, A., Dahl, C., Heiberg, A., Olafsen, O., & Weisaeth, L. (1985). Short-term dynamic psychotherapy: Prognostic value of characteristics of patients studied by a two year follow-up of 39 neurotic patients. *Psychotherapy & Psychosomatics, 43,* 8–16.

Hyde, A., & Goldman, C. (1993). Common family issues that interfere with the treatment and rehabilitation of people with schizophrenia. *Psychosocial Rehabilitation Journal, 16*(4), 63–74.

Hylbert, K., Sr., & Hylbert, K., Jr. (1979). *Medical information for human service workers* (2nd ed.). State College, PA: Counselor Education Press.

Isett, R., & Roszkowski, M. (1979). Consumer preferences for psychological report contents in a residential school and center for the mentally retarded. *Psychology in the Schools, 16,* 402–407.

Isom, R. (1995). *Case working: The integrated report writer and invoice maker.* Athens, CA: Elliott & Fitzpatrick.

Issacson, L., & Brown, D. (1977). *Career information, career counsleing, and career development.* Boston: Allyn & Bacon.

Ivey, A. (1988). *Intentional interviewing and counseling* (2nd ed.). Pacific Grove, CA: Brooks/Cole.

Jackson, G. G. (1991). The African genesis of the Black perspective in helping. In R. L. Jones (Ed.), *Black psychology* (2nd ed., pp. 533–558). Berkeley, CA: Cobb & Henry.

Jackson, T. (1991). *Guerrilla tactics in the new job market.* New York: Doubleday.

Jacobs, D., Charles, E., Jacobs, T., Weinstein, H., & Mann, D. (1972). Preparation for psychotherapy of the disadvantaged patient. *American Journal of Orthopsychiatry, 42,* 666–674.

Jacques, M. E., Burleigh, D. L., & Lee, G. (1973). Reactions to disabilities in China: A comparative, structural, and descriptive analysis. *Rehabilitation Counseling Bulletin, 16,* 206–217.

Jagger, L., Neukrug, E., & McAuliffe, G. (1992). Congruence between personality traits and chosen occupation as a predictor of job satisfaction for people with disabilities. *Rehabilitation Counseling Bulletin, 36,* 53–60.

James, W. H., & Hastings, J. F. (1993). Cross-cultural counseling: A systematic approach to understanding the issues. *International Journal for the Advancement of Counseling, 16,* 319–332.

Jamison, R., & Virts, R. (1989). The influence of family support on chronic pain. *Behavioral Research and Therapy, 28,* 283–287.

Janis, I., & Mann, L. (1977). *Decision-making.* New York: Free Press.

Joe, J. R., & Malach, R. S. (1992). Families with Native American roots. In E. W. Lynch & M. S. Hanson (Eds.), *Developing cross-cultural competence: A guide for working with young children and their families* (pp. 89–119). Baltimore: Brookes.

Johnson, M. (1993). *Moral imagination.* Chicago: The University of Chicago Press.

Johnson, S., & Atkins, B. (1987). Building bridges: Transition from school to work for youth who are disabled. *Journal of Applied Rehabilitation Counseling, 18,* 15–19.

Johnson, V., Greenwood, R., & Schriner, K. (1988). Work performance and work personality: Employers' concerns about workers with disabilities. *Rehabilitation Counseling Bulletin, 32*(1), 50–57.

Jongbloed, L. (1994). Adaptation to a stroke: The experience of one couple. *The American Journal of Occupational Therapy, 48,* 1006–1013.

Kadushin, A. (1972). *The social work interview.* New York: Columbia University Press.

Kelley, S., & Lambert, S. (1992). Family support in rehabilitation: A review of research, 1980–1990. *Rehabilitation Counseling Bulletin, 36,* 98–119.

Kim, H. C. (1994). *A legal history of Asian Americans, 1790–1990.* Westport, CT: Greenwood.

Kim, Y. O. (1995). Cultural pluralism and Asian Americans: Culturally sensitive social work practice. *International Social Work, 38*(1), 69–78.

Kirchman, M. (1986). Measuring the quality of life. *The Occupational Therapy Journal of Research, 6*(1), 21–31.

Kitano, H. H., & Daniels, R. (1995). *Asian Americans: Emerging minorities* (2nd ed.). New Jersey: Prentice-Hall.

Kitchener, K. S. (1984). Intuition, critical evaluation and ethical principles: The foundation for ethical decisions in counseling psychology. *The Counseling Psychologist, 12*(3), 43–55.

Kitchener, K. S. (1986). Teaching applied ethics in counselor education: An integration of psychological processes and philosophical analysis. *Journal of Counseling and Development, 64,* 306–310.

Kolata, G. (1993, January 4). A losing battle. *Chicago Tribune,* Tempo Section, pp. 1, 3.

Kosciulek, J. (1994). Relationship of family coping with head injury to family adaption. *Rehabilitation Psychology, 39*(4), 215–230.

Kosciulek, J. (1995). Impact of head injury on families: An introduction for family counselors. *The Family Journal in Counseling and Therapy for Couples and Families, 3,* 116–125.

Kosciulek, J., & Pichette, E. (1996). Adaptation concern of families of people with head injuries. *Journal of Applied Rehabilitation Counseling, 27,* 8–13.

Krause, J., & Crewe, N. (1987). Prediction of long-term survival of persons with spinal cord injury. *Rehabilitation Psychology, 32*(4), 205–714.

Kuhnert, K. (1989). The latent and manifest consequences of work. *The Journal of Psychology, 123*(5), 417–427.

Kulik, C., Oldham, G., & Hackman, J. R. (1987). Work design as an approach to person–environment fit. *Journal of Vocational Behaviors, 31,* 278–296.

Kunce, J. (1969). Vocational interest, disability, and rehabilitation. *Rehabilitation Counseling Bulletin, 12,* 204–210.

Kunce, J., & Angelone, E. (1990). Personality characteristics of counselors: Implications for rehabilitation counselor roles and functions. *Rehabilitation Counseling Bulletin, 34*(1), 4–15.

LaCrosse, M. B. (1975). Nonverbal behavior and perceived counselor attractiveness and persuasiveness. *Journal of Counseling Psychology, 22,* 536–566.

LaFromboise, T. D., Trimble, J. E., & Mohatt, G. V. (1990). Counseling intervention and American Indian tradition: An integrative approach. *The Counseling Psychologist, 18,* 628–654.

Landefeld, J. (1975). Speaking therapeutically. *Human Behavior, 9,* 56–59.

Landy, F. (1985). *Psychology of work behavior.* Homewood, IL: Dorsey.

Larsen, E. (1996, January 22). The soul of an HMO. *Time Magazine, 147*(4), 44–53.

Lassiter, S. M. (1995). *Multicultural clients: A professional handbook for health care providers and social workers.* Westport: Greenwood.

Leahy, M., Shapson, P., & Wright, G. (1987). Rehabilitation practitioner competencies by role and setting. *Rehabilitation Counseling Bulletin, 31*(2), 119–130.

Leahy, M., Szymanski, E., & Linkowski, D. (1993). Knowledge importance in rehabilitation counseling. *Rehabilitation Counseling Bulletin, 37*(2), 130–145.

Lehman, A. (1983). The well-being of chronic mental patients. *Archives of General Psychiatry, 40,* 369–373.

Lehman, A., Ward, N., & Linn, L. (1982). Chronic mental patients: The quality of life issue. *American Journal of Psychiatry, 139,* 1271–1276.

Leong, F. T. (1986). Counseling and psychotherapy with Asian Americans: Review of the literature. *Journal of Counseling Psychology, 33,* 196–206.

Leung, P., & Sakata, R. (1988). Asian Americans and rehabilitation: Some important variables. *Journal of Applied Rehabilitation Counseling, 19*(4), 16–20.

Li, D. J. (1965). *Ageless Chinese: A history.* New York: Charles Scribner's Sons.

Liem, J. H. (1993). Linking theory and practice. In J. L. Chin, J. H. Liem, M. D. Ham, & G. Hong (Eds.), *Transference and empathy in Asian American psychotherapy: Cultural values and treatment needs* (pp. 121–1137). Westport: Greenwood.

Lindenberg, R. (1980). Work with families in rehabilitation. In P. Power & A. Dell Orto (Eds.), *Role of the family in the rehabilitation of the physically disabled* (pp. 516–525). Austin, TX: PRO-ED.

Littlejohn-Blake, S. M., & Darling, C. A. (1993). Understanding the strengths of African American families. *Journal of Black Studies, 23,* 460–471.

Livneh, H. (1986). A unified approach to existing models of adaptation to disability: Part I—A model adaptation. *Journal of Applied Rehabilitation Counseling, 17*(1), 5–16.

Locke, D. C. (1992). *Increasing multicultural understanding: A comprehensive model.* Newbury Park, CA: Sage.

Locke, E., Saari, L., Shaw, K., & Latham, G. (1981). Goal setting and task performance: 1969–1980. *Psychological Bulletin, 90,* 125–152.

Loo, C., Tong, B., & True, R. (1989). A bitter bean: Mental health status and attitudes in Chinatown. *Journal of Community Psychology, 17,* 283–296.

Lopez, S. (1981). Mexican-American usage of mental health facilities: Underutilization considered. In A. Baron (Ed.), *Explorations in Chicano psychology* (pp. 139–164). New York: Praeger.

Louis Harris & Associates. (1986). *The ICD Survey of disabled Americans: Bringing disabled Americans into the mainstream.* New York: International Center for the Disabled.

Louis Harris & Associates. (1987). *The ICD Survey II: A nationwide survey of 920 employers.* New York: International Center for the Disabled.

Lowrey, L. (1987). Rehabilitation relevant to culture and disability. *Journal of Visual Impairment and Blindness, 81*(4), 162–164.

Lyles, M. R. (1992). Mental health perceptions of Black pastors: Implications for psychotherapy with Black patients. *Journal of Psychology and Christianity, 2,* 368–377.

Lynch, E. W. (1992). Developing cross cultural competence. In E. W. Lynch & M. J. Hanson (Eds.), *Developing cross cultural competence: A guide for working with young children and their families* (pp. 35–59). Baltimore: Brookes.

Lyon, J. (1993). Models of nursing care delivery and case management: Clarification of terms. *Nursing Economics, 11*(3), 163–169.

Mabe, A. R., & Rollin, S. A. (1986). The role of a code of ethical standards in counseling. *Journal of Counseling and Development, 54*(5), 294–297.

Mace, R. (1980). *Focus on research: Recreation for disabled individuals.* Washington, DC: George Washington University, Regional Rehabilitation Research Institute.

Mackenzie, A. (1990). *The time trap.* New York: American Management Association.

Mager, R. (1984). *Goal analysis* (2nd ed.). Belmont, CA: Fearon.

Maki, D., Pape, D., & Prout, H. (1979). Personality evaluation: A tool of the rehabilitation counselor. *Journal of Applied Rehabilitation Counseling, 10*, 119–123.

Malgady, R. G., & Rogler, L. H. (1987). Ethnocultural and linguistic bias in mental health evaluation of Hispanics. *American Psychologist, 42*, 228–234.

Manderscheid, R., & Henderson, M. (1995). Federal and state legislative and program directions for managed care: Implications for case management. In L. Giesler (Ed.), *Case management for behavioral managed care* (pp. 52–71). Cincinnati, OH: National Association of Case Management.

Marachnik, D. (1970). Assessing work potential of the handicapped in public schools. *Vocational Guide Quarterly, 18*, 225–229.

Marin, G. (1994). The experience of being a Hispanic in the United States. In W. Lonner & R. Malpass (Eds.), *Psychology and culture* (pp. 23–27). Boston: Allyn & Bacon.

Marsella, A. J. (1993). Vietnamese Americans. In N. Mokuau (Ed.), *Handbook of social services for Asian and Pacific Islanders* (pp. 117–130). Westport: Greenwood.

Marsh, D. (1992). *Families and mental illness: New directions in professional practice*. New York: Praeger.

Marshak, L., & Seligman, M. (1993). *Counseling persons with physical disabilities*. Austin, TX: PRO-ED.

Marshall, C. A., Martin, W. E., Thomason, T. C., & Johnson, M. J. (1991). Multiculturalism and rehabilitation counselor training: Recommendations for providing culturally appropriate counseling services to American Indians with disabilities. *Journal of Counseling and Development, 70*, 225–234.

Martin, W. (1991). Career development and American Indians living on reservations: Cross-cultural factors to consider. *The Career Development Quarterly, 39*, 273–283.

Martin, W. E., Frank, L. W., Minkler, S., & Johnson, M. (1988). A survey of vocational rehabilitation counselors who work with American Indians. *Journal of Applied Rehabilitation Counseling, 19*(4), 29–34.

Martin, W., & Swartz, J. (1996). Inclusion of cultural and contextual differentials in the rehabilitation assessment and placement process. *Journal of Job Placement, 2*(1), 23–27.

Mary, N. L. (1990). Reactions of Black, Hispanic, and White mothers to having a child with handicaps. *Mental Retardation, 28*, 1–5.

Maslach, C., & Florian, V. (1988). Burnout, job setting, and self-evaluation among rehabilitation counselors. *Rehabilitation Psychology, 33*(2), 85–93.

Mathews, S., & Fawcett, S. (1984). Building the capacities of job candidates through behavioral instruction. *Journal of Community Psychology, 12*, 123–129.

Matkin, R. E. (1980). Vocational rehabilitation during economic recession. *Journal of Applied Rehabilitation Counseling, 11*, 124–127.

Matkin, R. E. (1983). The roles and functions of rehabilitation specialists in the private sector. *Journal of Applied Rehabilitation Counseling, 14*, 14–27.

Matkin, R. E. (1995). Private sector rehabilitation. In S. Rubin & R. Roessler (Eds.), *Foundations of the vocational rehabilitation process* (4th ed.). Austin, TX: PRO-ED.

Matkin, R., Bauer, L., & Nickles, L. (1993). Personality characteristics of certified rehabilitation counselors in various work settings. *Journal of Applied Rehabilitation Counseling, 24*(3), 42–53.

May, P. (1982). Substance abuse and American Indians: Prevalence and susceptibility. *The International Journal of the Addictions, 17*(7), 1201.

Maze, M., & Mayall, D. (1991). *The enhanced guide for occupational exploration*. Indianapolis, IN: JIST Works.

McAdoo, H. P. (Ed.). (1981). *Black families*. Beverly Hills, CA: Sage.

McArthur, C. (1954). Analyzing the clinical process. *Journal of Counseling Psychology, 1*, 203–208.

McCarthy, H. (1986). Making it in able-bodied America: Career development in young adults with physical disabilities. *Journal of Applied Rehabilitation Counseling, 17,* 30–38.

McDavis, R. J., Parker, W. M., & Parker, W. J. (1995). Counseling African Americans. In N. Vacc, S. Devaney, & S. Wittner (Eds.), *Experiencing and counseling multicultural and diverse populations* (pp. 217–250). Bristol: Accelerated Development.

McDonald, R. (1989). The search for one-stop shopping. In L. Hubbard & P. McAnally (Eds.), *Case management: Historical, current, and future perspectives.* Cambridge, MA: Brookline.

McGinley, H., LeFevre, R., & McGinley, P. (1975). The influence of a communicator's body position on opinion change in others. *Journal of Personality and Social Psychology, 31,* 686–690.

McGowan, J. (1969). Referral, evaluation, and treatment. In D. Malikin & H. Rusalem (Eds.), *Vocational rehabilitation of the disabled: An overview* (pp. 111–128). Baltimore: University Park Press.

McGowan, J. F., & Porter, T. L. (1967). *An introduction to the vocational rehabilitation process.* Washington, DC: Department of Health, Education and Welfare, Vocational Rehabilitation Administration.

McIsaac, H., & Wilkinson, H. (1965). Clients talk about their caseworkers. *Public Welfare, 23,* 147–154.

McMahon, B. (1979). A model of vocational redevelopment for the mid-career physically disabled. *Rehabilitation Counseling Bulletin, 23,* 35–47.

McRoy, R. G. (1990). A historical overview of Black families. In S. M. L. Logan, E. M. Freeman, & R. G. McRoy (Eds.), *Social work practice with Black families: A culturally specific perspective* (pp. 3–17). White Plains, NY: Longman.

McWhirter, J. J., & Ryan, C. A. (1991). Counseling the Navajo: Cultural understanding. *Journal of Multicultural Counseling and Development, 19,* 75–82.

Merriam Webster's Ninth New Collegiate Dictionary. (1984). Springfield, MA: G&C Merriam Company.

Messer, S. B., & Winokur, M. (1980). Some limits to the integration of psychoanalytic and behavioral therapy. *American Psychologist, 35,* 818–827.

Millard, R. P. (1990). *The development and evaluation of an ethics in-service training program for rehabilitation practitioners.* Unpublished doctoral dissertation, Southern Illinois University, Carbondale.

Miller, D., & Starr, M. (1967). *The structure of human decisions.* Englewood Cliffs, NJ: Prentice-Hall.

Miller, L. (1972). Resource-centered counselor-client interaction in rehabilitation settings. In J. Bozarth (Ed.), *Models and functions of counseling for applied settings and rehabilitation workers.* Fayetteville: University of Arkansas, Arkansas Rehabilitation Research and Training Center in Vocational Rehabilitation.

Miller, L., & Roberts, R. (1979). Unmet counselor needs from ambiguity to the Zeigarnik effect. *Journal of Applied Rehabilitation Counseling, 10,* 60–65.

Miller, M. (1985). Counselor as hypothesis tester: Some implications of research. *Journal of Counseling and Development, 6,* 276–278.

Minton, E. (1977). Job placement: Strategies and techniques. *Rehabilitation Counseling Bulletin, 21,* 141–149.

Molinaro, D. (1977). A placement system develops and settles: The Michigan model. *Rehabilitation Counseling Bulletin, 21,* 121–129.

Moore, J. (1984). Impact of family attitudes toward blindness/visual impairment on the rehabilitation process. *Journal of Visual Impairment & Blindness, 78*(3), 100–105.

Morgan, C. A., & Bost, J. M. (1989). The secretary and the rehabilitation office. *Journal of Rehabilitation, 55,* 14–17.

Morrow, R. D. (1987). Cultural differences—Be aware! *Academic Therapy, 23*(2), 143–149.

Mowbray, C., Rusilowski-Clover, G., Arnold, J., Allen, C., Harris, S., McCrohan, N., & Greenfield, A. (1994). Project WINS: Integrating vocational services on mental health case management teams. *Community Mental Health Journal, 30*(4), 347–362.

Mueller, J. (1990). *The workplace workbook: An illustrated guide to job accommodation and assistive technology.* Washington, DC: Dole Foundation.

Mullins, J., Rumrill, P., & Roessler, R. (1995). The role of the rehabilitation placement professional in the ADA era. *Work: A Journal of Prevention, Assessment and Rehabilitation, 6, 3–10.*

Mund, S. (1981). Creativity and innovation in vocational rehabilitation counseling. *Journal of Applied Rehabilitation Counseling, 12, 32–35.*

Munro, J. D. (1985). Counseling severely dysfunctional families of mentally and physically disabled persons. *Clinical Social Work Journal,* pp. 18–31.

Murase, K. (1992). Models of service delivery in Asian American communities. In S. M. Furuto, R. Biswas, D. K. Chung, K. Murase, & F. Ross-Sheriff (Eds.), *Social work practice with Asian Americans* (pp. 101–120). Newbury Park, CA: Sage.

Murdick, N. L., Gartin, B. C., & Arnold, M. B. (1994). A method for the reduction of bias in educational assessment. *Journal of Instructional Psychology, 21*(1), 83–89.

Murphy, S. (1988). Counselor and client views of vocational rehabilitation success and failure: A qualitative study. *Rehabilitation Counseling Bulletin, 31*(3), 185–197.

Murray, H. (1943). *Thematic Apperception Test.* Cambridge, MA: Harvard University Press.

Muthard, J. E., & Salomone, P. R. (1969). The roles and functions of the rehabilitation counselor. *Rehabilitation Counseling Bulletin, 13* (Special Issue).

Nagi, S. (1969). *Disability and rehabilitation.* Columbus: Ohio University Press.

National Association of Rehabilitation Professionals in the Private Sector. (n.d.). *Standards and ethics.* Blue Jay: CA, Author.

National Association of State Directors of Development Disabilities Services. (1995). *Managed care and long-term supports for people with developmental disabilities.* Alexandria, VA: Author.

National Council on Disability. (1993). *ADA watch year one: A report to the President and the Congress on progress in implementing the Americans with Disabilities Act.* Washington, DC: Author.

National Rehabilitation Administrative Association. (1983). Code of ethics of the National Rehabilitation Administrative Association. *Administration and Supervision in Rehabilitation, 13*(1), 7.

National Rehabilitation Counseling Association, Ethics Sub-Committee. (1972). *Code of ethics for rehabilitation counselors.* Washington, DC: Author.

Neff, W. (1985). *Work and human behavior* (3rd ed.). New York: Aldine.

Nelson, S. H., McCoy, G. F., Stetter, M., & Vanderwagen, W. C. (1992). An overview of mental health services for American Indians and Alaskan Natives in the 1990s. *Hospital and Community Psychiatry, 43, 257–261.*

Nezu, A. (1987). A problem-solving formulation of depression: A literature review and proposal of a pluralistic model. *Clinical Psychology Review, 7, 121–144.*

Nickerson, K. J., Helms, J. E., & Terrell, F. (1994). Cultural mistrust, opinions about mental illness, and Black students' attitudes toward seeking psychological help from White counselors. *Journal of Counseling Psychology, 4*(1), 378–385.

Nishio, K., & Bilmes, M. (1987). Psychotherapy with southeast Asian American clients. *Professional Psychology: Research and Practice, 18*(4), 342–346.

Nochi, M. (1996). Family theories for rehabilitation practice: Their "figures" and "grounds." *Journal of Applied Rehabilitation Counseling, 27*(1), 27–32.

Novak-Amado, A., McAnally, L., & Hubbard-Linz, M. (1989). In M. Hubbard-Linz & P. McAnally (Eds.), *Case management: Historical, current, and future perspectives*. Cambridge, MA: Brookline.

Nugent, F. A. (1990). *An introduction to the profession of counseling*. Columbus, OH: Merrill.

Oka, T. (1994). Self-help groups in Japan: Trends and traditions. *Prevention in Human Services, 11*(1), 69–95.

O'Keeffe, J. (1994). Disability, discrimination, and the Americans with Disabilities Act. In S. Bruyere & J. O'Keeffe, *Implications of the Americans with Disabilities Act for psychology*. New York: Springer.

Okun, B. (1976). *Effective helping: Interviewing and counseling techniques*. North Scituate, MA: Duxbury Press.

Okun, B. (1987). *Effective helping interviewing and counseling techniques* (3rd ed.). Monterey, CA: Brooks/Cole.

Olsheski, J., & Growick, B. (1987). Factors related to the acceptance of rehabilitation services by injured workers. *Journal of Applied Rehabilitation Counseling, 18*, 16–19.

Orlansky, M. D., & Trap, J. J. (1987). Working with Native American persons: Issues in facilitating communication and providing culturally relevant services. *Journal of Visual Impairment and Blindness, 81*, 151, 153–155.

Orr, A. L. (1993). Training outreach workers to serve American Indian elders with visual impairment and diabetes. *Journal of Visual Impairment and Blindness, 87*(9), 336–340.

Osipow, S. (1987). Applying person-environment theory to vocational behavior. *Journal of Vocational Behavior, 31*, 333–336.

Osipow, S., & Fitzgerald, L. (1996). *Theories of career development* (4th ed.). Boston: Allyn & Bacon.

Pape, D. A., & Klein, M. A. (1986). Ethical issues in rehabilitation counseling: A survey of rehabilitation practitioners. *Journal of Applied Rehabilitation Counseling, 17*(4), 8–13.

Parent, W., & Everson, J. (1986). Competencies of disabled workers in industry: A review of business literature. *Journal of Rehabilitation, 52*, 16–23.

Parker, R., & Schaller, J. (1996). Issues in vocational assessment and disability. In E. M. Szymanski & R. M. Parker (Eds.), *Work and disability* (pp. 127–164). Austin, TX: PRO-ED.

Patterson, C. H. (1960). Psychological testing and the counseling process. In C. H. Patterson (Ed.), *Readings in rehabilitation counseling*. Champaign, IL: Stipes.

Patterson, C. H. (1970). Power, prestige and the rehabilitation counselor. *Rehabilitation Research and Practice Review, 1*, 1–7.

Payne, L. M. (1989). Preventing rehabilitation counselor burnout by balancing the caseload. *Journal of Rehabilitation, 55*, 20–24.

Pedersen, P. B. (1987). Ten frequent assumptions of cultural bias in counseling. *Journal of Multicultural Counseling and Development, 15*, 16–24.

Pernice, R., & Brook, J. (1994). Relationship of migrant status (refugee or immigrant) to mental health. *The International Journal of Social Psychiatry, 40*, 177–188.

Pickett, S. A., Vraniak, D. A., Cook, J. A., & Cohler, B. J. (1993). Strength in adversity: Blacks bear burden better than Whites. *Professional Psychology: Research and Practice, 24*, 460–467.

Pimentel, R. (1995). *The return to work process: A case management approach*. Chatsworth, CA: Milt Wright & Associates.

Plummer, F. M. (1976). Projective techniques. In B. Bolton (Ed.), *Handbook of measurement and evaluation in rehabilitation* (pp. 117–132). Baltimore: University Park Press.

Pollard, K. (1993). Faster growth, more diversity in U. S. Projections. *Population Today, 21*(2), 3, 10.

Ponchillia, S. V. (1993). The effect of cultural beliefs on the treatment of Native people with diabetes and visual impairment. *Journal of Visual Impairment and Blindness, 87*, 333–335.

Power, P. (1988). The family and the rehabilitation process: Counselor roles and functions. In S. Rubin & N. Rubin (Eds.), *Contemporary challenges to the rehabilitation counseling profession* (pp. 243–258). Baltimore: Brookes.

Power, P. (1991). *A guide to vocational assessment* (2nd ed.). Austin, TX: PRO-ED.

Power, P., & Dell Orto, A. (1980a). Particular disabilities and family influences. In P. Power & A. Dell Orto (Eds.), *Role of family in the rehabilitation of the physically disabled* (pp. 235–241). Baltimore: University Park Press.

Power, P., & Dell Orto, A. (1980b). General impact of child disability/illness on the family. In P. Power & A. Dell Orto (Eds.), *Role of the family in the rehabilitation of the physically disabled* (pp. 173–179). Baltimore: University Park Press.

Power, P., & Dell Orto, A. (1980c). Counselors' skills and roles with families experiencing varied disabilities or continued adjustment problems. In P. Power & A. Dell Orto (Eds.), *Role of the family in the rehabilitation of the physically disabled* (pp. 353–361). Baltimore: University Park Press.

Power, P., Hershenson, D., & Fabian, E. (1991). Meeting the documented needs of clients' families: An opportunity for rehabilitation counselors. *Journal of Rehabilitation, 57*, 11–16.

Prediger, D. J. (1993). *Multicultural assessment standards: A compilation for counselors*. Alexandria, VA: American Counseling Association.

Price, B. K., & McNeill, B. W. (1992). Cultural commitment and attitudes towards seeking counseling services in American Indian college students. *Professional Psychology: Research and Practice, 23*, 376–381.

PSI International. (n.d.). Quality-of-life research in rehabilitation. *Rehab Brief, 11*(1), 1–4.

Pumpian, I., Fisher, D., Certo, N., & Smalley, K. (1997). Changing jobs: An essential part of career development. *Mental Retardation, 35*(1), 39–48.

Pyke, J., & Atcheson, V. (1993). Social recreational services: Issues from a case management perspective. *Psychosocial Rehabilitation Journal, 17*(2), 121–130.

Ramund, B., & Stensman, R. (1988). Quality of life and evaluation of functions among people with severely impaired mobility and nondisabled controls. *Scandinavian Journal of Psychology, 29*, 137–144.

Rapp, C. (1995). The active ingredients of effective case management: A research synthesis. In L. Giesler (Ed.), Case management for behavioral managed care (pp. 5–46). Cincinnati, OH: NACM.

Rawls J., (1958). Justice as fairness. *The Philosophical Review, 67*, 164–194.

Rehabilitation Act Amendments of 1986, 29 U.S.C. § 701 *et seq.*

Rehabilitation Act of 1973, 29 U.S.C. § 701 *et seq.*

Remley, T. (1993). Rehabilitation counseling: A scholarly model for the generic profession of counseling. *Rehabilitation Counseling Bulletin, 37*(2), 182–186.

Rennick, P. (1975). Psychosocial evaluation of individuals with epilepsy. In G. Wright (Ed.), *Epilepsy rehabilitation* (pp. 81–103). Boston: Little, Brown.

Rhodes, E. R., Mason, R. D., Eddy, P., Smith, E. M., & Bums, T. R. (1988, November/Decenber). The Indian health service approach to alcoholism among American Indians and Alaskan Natives. *Public Health Reports, 103*, 621–627.

Richardson, T. Q., & Molinaro, K. (1996). White counselor self-awareness: A prerequisite for developing multicultural competence. *Journal of Counseling and Development, 74*, 238–242.

Riggar, T. F., & Patrick, D. (1984). Case management and administration, *Journal of Applied Rehabilitation Counseling, 15*, 29–33.

Roessler, R. (1987). Work, disability, and the future: Promoting employment for people with disabilities. *Journal of Counseling and Development, 66*(4), 188–190.

Roessler, R. (1980). Factors affecting client achievement of rehabilitation goals. *Journal of Applied Rehabilitation Counseling, 11,* 169–172.

Roessler, R. (1995). Quality of life: The ultimate outcome in rehabilitation. *Directions in Rehabilitation Counseling, 6*(3), 1–10.

Roessler, R., & Greenwood, R. (1987). Vocational evaluation. In B. Bolton (Ed.), *Handbook of measurement and evaluation in rehabilitation.* (pp. 151–168). Baltimore: Brookes.

Roessler, R., & Hiett, A. (1983). A comparison of job development strategies in rehabilitation. *Journal of Rehabilitation, 49*(1), 65–69.

Roessler, R., & Johnson, V. A. (1987). Developing job maintenance skills in learning disabled youth. *Journal of Learning Disabilities, 20*(7), 428–432.

Roessler, R., Mack, G., & Statler, J. (1975). *Experimental case management: A pilot manual for training case managers in services coordination projects.* Fayetteville: University of Arkansas, Arkansas Research and Training Center in Vocational Rehabilitation.

Roessler, R., & Rubin, S. (1992). *Case management and rehabilitation counseling.* Austin, TX: PRO-ED.

Roessler, R., & Rumrill, P. (1995). *Enhancing productivity on your job: The win-win approach to reasonable accommodations.* New York: National Multiple Sclerosis Society.

Rogers-Dulan, J., & Blacker, J. (1995). African American families, religion, and disability: A conceptual framework. *Mental Retardation, 33,* 226–238.

Rohe, D., & Athelstan, G. (1982). Vocational interests of persons with spinal cord injury. *Journal of Counseling Psychology, 29,* 283–291.

Rojewski, J. W. (1992). Key components of model transition services for students with learning disabilities. *Learning Disability Quarterly, 15,* 135–150.

Rosenberg, B. (1973). The work sample approach to vocational evaluation. In R. E. Hardy & J. G. Cull (Eds.), *Vocational evaluation for rehabilitation services.* Springfield, IL: Charles C Thomas.

Rounds, J., Dawis, R., & Lofquist, L. (1987). Measurement of person-environment fit and prediction of satisfaction in the theory of work adjustment. *Journal of Vocational Behavior, 31,* 297–318.

Rubenfeld, P. (1988). The rehabilitation counselor and the disabled client: Is a partnership of equals possible? In S. Rubin & N. Rubin (Eds.), *Contemporary challenges to the rehabilitation counseling profession* (pp. 31–44). Baltimore: Brookes.

Rubin, S. E., & Emener, W. G. (1979). Recent rehabilitation counselor role changes and role strain—A pilot investigation. *Journal of Applied Rehabilitation Counseling, 10,* 142–147.

Rubin, S. E., & Farley, R. C. (1980). *Intake interview skills for rehabilitation counselors.* Fayetteville: University of Arkansas, Arkansas Rehabilitation Research and Training Center.

Rubin, S. E., Matkin, R., Ashley, J., Beardsley, M., May, V. R., Onstott, K., & Puckett, F. (1984). Roles and functions of certified rehabilitation counselors. *Rehabilitation Counseling Bulletin, 27,* 199–224; 239–243.

Rubin, S. (1979, April). *Identification of essential diagnostic, counseling, and placement competencies: Implications for rehabilitation counselor education.* Paper presented at the American Personnel and Guidance Association Convention, Las Vegas, NV.

Rubin, S. E., Millard, R. P., & Wong, H. D. (1989). *Ethical case management practices.* Carbondale: Southern Illinois University, Rehabilitation Institute.

Rubin, S. E., Millard, R. P., Wong, H. D., & Wilson, C. A. (1990). *Ethical case management practices* (2nd ed.). Carbondale: Southern Illinois University, Rehabilitation Institute.

Rubin, S. E., Pusch, B. D., Fogarty, C., & McGinn, F. (1995). Enhancing the cultural sensitivity of rehabilitation counselors. *Rehabilitation Education, 9,* 253–264.

Rubin, S. E., & Roessler, R. (1992). *Case management and rehabilitation counseling* (2nd ed.). Austin, TX: PRO-ED.

Rubin, S. E., & Roessler, R. (1995). *Foundations of the vocational rehabilitation process* (4th ed.). Austin, TX: PRO-ED.

Ruiz, R., & Padilla, A. (1977). Counseling Latinos. *Personnel and Guidance Journal, 55,* 401–408.

Ryan, A. S., & Smith, M. J. (1989). Parental reactions to developmental disabilities in Chinese American families. *Child and Adolescent Social Work, 6,* 283–299.

Ryan, C., Sherman, P., & Judd, C. (1994). Accounting for case manager effects in the evaluation of mental health services. *Journal of Consulting and Clinical Psychology, 62*(5), 964–974.

Safilios-Rothschild, C. (1970). *The sociology and social psychology of disability and rehabilitation.* New York: Random House.

Salomone, P. (1996). Career counseling and job placement: Theory and practice. In E. M. Szymanski & R. M. Parker (Eds.), *Work and disability* (pp. 365–420). Austin, TX: PRO-ED.

Salomone, P., & Usdane, W. (1977). Client centered placement revisited: A dialogue. *Rehabilitation Counseling Bulletin, 21,* 85–91.

Salzman, M. (1995). Attributional discrepancies and bias in cross-cultural interactions. *Journal of Multicultural Counseling and Development, 23,* 181–193.

Santiago, J. (1992). The fate of mental health services in health care reform: II. realistic solutions. *Hospital and Community Psychiatry, 42,* 363–365.

Saravanabhavan, R. C., & Marshall, C. A. (1994). The older Native American Indian with disabilities: Implications for providers of health care and human services. *Journal of Multicultural Counseling and Development, 22,* 182–194.

Satcher, J. (1992). Responding to employer concerns about the ADA and job applicants with disabilities. *Journal of Applied Rehabilitation Counseling, 23,* 37–40.

Satcher, J., & Dooley-Dickey, K. (1992). *College students' guide to the Americans with Disabilities Act of 1990 (Title I).* Jackson: Mississippi State University, Career Development Project.

Saxe, L., & Goodman, L. (1988). *The effectiveness of outpatient vs. inpatient treatment: Updating the OTA report.* Hartford, CT: Prudential Insurance Co.

Scarnulis, E. (1989). Issues in case management for the 90s. In M. Hubbard-Linz & P. McAnally (Eds.), *Case management: Historical, current, and future perspectives.* Cambridge, MA: Brookline.

Schalock, R., Keith, K., Hoffman, K., & Karan, O. (1989). Quality of life: Its measurement and use. *Mental Retardation, 27*(1), 25–31.

Schene, A., & Gersens, V. (1986). Effectiveness and application of partial hospitalization. *Acta Psychiatrica Scandanavia, 74,* 335–340.

Schlenoff, D. (1974). Considerations in administering intelligence tests to the physically disabled. *Rehabilitation Literature, 35,* 362–363.

Schmidt, J. (1969). The use of purpose in casework practice. *Social Work, 14,* 77–84.

Schwawb, L. (1989). Strengths of families having a member with a disability. *Journal of the Multihandicapped Person, 2*(2), 105–117.

Sears, J. H. (1975). The able disabled. *Journal of Rehabilitation, 41,* 12–22.

Shank, M., & Turnbull, A. (1993). Cooperative family problem solving. In G. Singer & L. Powers (Eds.), *Families, disability, and empowerment* (pp. 231–254). Baltimore: Brookes.

Shapiro, J., & Wright, A. (1996, September 9). Can churches save America? *U.S. News & World Report*, pp. 46–53.

Shokoohi-Yekta, M., & Retish, P. M. (1991). Attitudes of Chinese and American male students towards mental illness. *The International Journal of Social Psychiatry, 37*, 192–200.

Siegel, H., Rapp, R., Lelliher, C., Fisher, J., Wagner, J., & Cole, P. (1995). The strengths perspective of case management: A promising inpatient substance abuse treatment enhancement. *Journal of Psychoactive Drugs, 27*(1), 67–72.

Simeonsson, R., & Bailey, D. (1986). Siblings of handicapped children. In J. Gallagher & P. Vietze (Eds.), *Families of handicapped persons* (pp. 67–77). Baltimore: Brookes.

Singer, G., Irvin, L., Irvine, B., Hawkins, N., Hegreness, J., & Jackson, R. (1993). Helping families adapt positively to disability. In G. Singer & L. Powers (Eds.), *Families, disability, and empowerment* (pp. 67–83). Baltimore: Brookes.

Singer, G., & Powers, L. (1993). Contributing to resilience in families. In G. Singer & L. Powers (Eds.), *Families, disability, and empowerment* (pp. 1–25). Baltimore: Brookes.

Sink, J. M., Porter, T. L., Rubin, S. E., & Painter, L. C. (1979). *Competencies related to the work of the rehabilitation counselor and vocational evaluator*. Athens: University of Georgia and the McGregor Company.

Sloane, R. B., Cristol, A. H., Pepernik, L., & Staples, R. F. (1970). Role preparation and expectation of improvement in psychotherapy. *Journal of Nervous and Mental Disease, 150*, 18–26.

Smart, J. F., & Smart, D. W. (1991). Acceptance of disability and the Mexican American culture. *Rehabilitation Counseling Bulletin, 34*, 357–367.

Smart, J. F., & Smart, D. W. (1993). Vocational evaluation of Hispanics with disabilities: Issues and implications. *Vocational Evaluation and Work Adjustment Bulletin, 26*(3), 111–122.

Smith, A., & Chemers, M. (1981). Perceptions of motivation of economically disadvantaged employees in a work setting. *Journal of Employment Counseling, 18*, 24–33.

Smith, E. (1977). Counseling Black individuals: Some stereotypes. *The Personnel and Guidance Journal, 55*, 390–396.

Smith, E. (1981). Cultural and historical perspectives in counseling Blacks. In D. Sue (Ed.), *Counseling the culturally different: Theory and practice* (pp. 141–185). New York: Wiley.

Smith, G., & Ashbaugh, J. (1995). *Managed care and people with developmental disabilities: A guidebook*. Alexandria, VA: National Association of State Directors of Developmental Disabilities Services.

Smith, L. M., & Godfrey, H. P. D. (1995). *Family support programs and rehabilitation: A cognitive-behavioral approach to traumatic brain injury*. New York: Plenum.

Smith, M. J., & Ryan, A. S. (1987). Chinese-American families of children with developmental disabilities: An exploratory study of reactions to service providers. *Mental Retardation, 25*(6), 345–350.

Smith, T. (1981). Employer concerns in hiring mentally retarded persons. *Rehabilitation Counseling Bulletin, 24*, 316–318.

Smits, S., & Ledbetter, J. (1979). The practice of rehabilitation counseling within the administrative structure of state-federal programs. *Journal of Applied Rehabilitation Counseling, 10*, 79–84.

Solly, D. (1987). A career counseling model for the mentally handicapped. *Techniques: A Journal for Remedial Education and Counseling, 3*, 294–300.

Starkey, P. D. (1969). Job placement: The rehabilitation counselor's dilemma. *Rehabilitation Counseling Bulletin, 12*, 211–213.

Stein, L., & Test, M. (1980). Alternative to hospital treatment: Conceptual model, treatment program, and clinical evaluation. *Archives of General Psychiatry, 37*, 393–397.

Steinhaur, P., Mushin, D., & Rae-Grant, Q. (1980). Psychological aspects of chronic illness. In P. W. Power & A. E. Dell Orto (Eds.), *Role of the family in the rehabilitation of the physically disabled* (pp. 128–144). Austin, TX: PRO-ED.

Stewart, C. J., & Cash, W. (1994). *Interviewing: Principles and practices.* Madison, WI: WCB Brown & Benchmark.

Stock, L. (1987). Native Americans: A brief profile. *Journal of Visual Impairment & Blindness, 81,* 152.

Stone, C. I., & Sawatzki, B. (1980). Hiring bias and the disabled interviewee: Effects of manipulating work history and disability information of the disabled job applicant. *Journal of Vocational Behavior, 16,* 96–104.

Stone, J., & Gregg, C. (1981). Juvenile diabetes and rehabilitation counseling. *Rehabilitation Counseling Bulletin, 24,* 283–291.

Strupp, H. H., & Bloxom, A. (1973). Preparation of lower class patients for group psychotherapy. *Journal of Consulting Clinical Psychology, 41,* 373–384.

Sudarkasa, N. (1980). African and Afro American-family structure: A comparison. *The Black Scholar, 2,* 37–60.

Sue, D. W. (1990). Culture-specific strategies in counseling: A conceptual framework. *Professional Psychology: Research and Practice, 21,* 424–433.

Sue, D., & Sue, S. (1987). Cultural factors in the clinical assessment of Asian Americans. *Journal of Consulting and Clinical Psychology, 55,* 479–487.

Sue, D. W., & Sue, D. (1990). *Counseling the culturally different: Theory and practice* (2nd ed.). New York: Wiley.

Sue, D., & Sue, D. M. (1995). Asian Americans. In N. A. Vacc, S. B. DeVaney, & J. Wittmer (Eds.), *Experiencing and counseling multicultural and diverse populations* (3rd ed., pp. 63–89). Bristol: Accelerated Development.

Sue, S., & McKinney, H. (1975). Asian Americans in the community mental health care system. *American Journal of Orthopsychiatry, 45,* 111–118.

Sue, S., & Zane, N. (1987). The role of culture and cultural techniques in psychotherapy: A critique and reformulation. *American Psychologist, 42,* 37–45.

Sullivan, W., Hartmann, D., & Wolk, J. (1995). Expanding horizons: Case management in employee assistance programs. *Alcoholism Treatment Quarterly, 12*(3), 43–54.

Sutton, J. (1985). The need for family involvement in client rehabilitation. *Journal of Applied Rehabilitation Counseling, 16,* 42–45.

Swisher, J., & Hylbert, K., Sr. (1973). The rehabilitation counselor and the physician. *Journal of Applied Rehabilitation Counseling, 4,* 68–75.

Szymanski, E. M., Linkowski, D., Leahy, M., Diamond, E., & Thoreson, R. (1993). Human resource development: An examination of perceived training needs of Certified Rehabilitation Counselors. *Rehabilitation Counseling Bulletin, 37*(2), 163–181.

Tache, J., & Selye, H. (1978). Our stress and coping mechanisms. In C. Spielberger & I. Sarason (Eds.), *Stress and anxiety* (Vol. 5). New York: Wiley.

Tanner, D. C., & Martin, W. E. (1986). Services and training needs in communicative problems and disorders for rehabilitation professionals serving Native Americans. *Journal of Rehabilitation Administration, 10,* 117–122.

Tate, D., Habeck, R., & Galvin, D. (1986). Disability management: Origins, concepts, and principles for practice. *Journal of Applied Rehabilitation Counseling, 17,* 5–11.

Tax Reduction and Simplification Act of 1977.

Tax Reform Act of 1976, 26 U.S.C. § 190 *et seq.*

Taylor, R., & Taylor, S. (1994). *The AUPHA manual of health services management.* Gaithersburg, MD: Aspen.

Taylor, S. J., & Bogdan, R. (1989). On accepting relationships between people with mental retardation and non-disabled people: Toward an understanding of acceptance. *Disabled Handicap & Society, 4,* 21–36.

Texas Rehabilitation Commission for the Blind. (1993). *Caseload management.* Austin, TX: Author.

Thomas, S. (1986). *Report writing in assessment and evaluation.* Menomonie, WI: Materials Development Center, University of Wisconsin–Stout.

Thomas, T. D., Thomas, G., & Joiner, J. G. (1993). Issues in the vocational rehabilitation of persons with serious and persistent mental illness: A national survey of counselor insights. *Psychosocial Rehabilitation Journal, 16*(4), 129–134.

Thomason, T. C. (1991). An introduction for non-Native American counselors. *Journal of Counseling and Development, 69,* 321–327.

Thurer, S. (1980). Vocational rehabilitation following coronary bypass surgery: The need for counseling the newly well. *Journal of Applied Rehabilitation Counseling, 1*(1), 94–98.

Todisco, M., & Salomone, P. R. (1991). Facilitating effective cross-cultural relationships: The White counselor and the Black client. *Journal of Multicultural Counseling and Development, 19,* 146–157.

Toupin, E. S. (1980). Counseling Asians in psychotherapy in the context of racism and Asian American history. *American Journal of Orthopsychiatry, 50*(1), 76–86.

Trimble, J. E., & Fleming, C. M. (1989). Proving counseling services for Native American Indians: Client, counselor, and community characteristics. In P. B. Pedersen, J. G. Draguns, W. J. Lonner, & J. E. Trimble (Eds.), *Counseling across cultures* (pp. 177–204). Honolulu: University of Hawaii Press.

Truax, C. B., & Wargo, D. G. (1969). Effects of vicarious therapy pretraining and alternate sessions on outcome in group psychotherapy with outpatients. *Journal of Consulting Clinical Psychology, 33,* 440–447.

Turnbull, A., Summers, J., & Brotherson, M. (1986). Family life cycle. In J. Gallagher & P. Vietze (Eds.), *Families of handicapped persons* (pp. 45–65). Baltimore: Brookes.

Turner, W. L., & Alston, R. J. (1994). The role of the family in psychosocial adaptation to physical disabilities for African Americans. *Journal of the National Medical Association, 86,* 915–921.

Tymchuk, A. J. (1981). Ethical decision making and psychological treatment. *Journal of Psychiatric Treatment and Evaluation, 3,* 507–513.

Tymchuk, A. J. (1982). Strategies for resolving value dilemmas. *American Behavioral Scientist, 26*(2), 159–175.

Tymchuk, A. J., Drapkin, R., Major-Kingsley, S., Ackerman, A. B., Coffman, E. W., & Baum, M. S. (1982). Ethical decision making and psychologists' attitudes toward training in ethics. *Professional Psychology, 13*(3), 412–421.

Uba, L. (1992). Cultural barriers to health care for Southeast Asian refugees. *Public Health Reports, 107,* 544–548.

Uba, L. (1994). *Asian Americans.* New York: Guilford.

Uba, L., & Sue, S. (1991). Nature and scope of services for Asian and Pacific Islander Americans. In N. Mokuau (Ed.), *Handbook of social services for Asian and Pacific Islanders* (pp. 3–19). Westport, CT: Greenwood Press.

U.S. Bureau of the Census. (1988). *1980 Census of Population: Asian and Pacific Islander Population in the United States.* Washington, DC: U.S. Government Printing Office.

U.S. Bureau of the Census. (1993). *1990 Census of Population: Asian and Pacific Islanders in the United States.* Washington, DC: U.S. Government Printing Office.

U.S. Chamber of Commerce. (1981). *Analysis of workers' compensation laws*. Washington, DC: Government Printing Office.

U.S. Department of Commerce. (1994). *1990 Census of Population: Characteristics of American Indians by Tribe and Language*. Washington, DC: U.S. Government Printing Office.

U.S. Department of Justice. (1996). *A Guide to Disability Rights Laws*. Washington, DC: U.S. Government Printing Office.

U.S. Department of Labor. (1979). *General Aptitude Test Battery*. Washington, DC: U.S. Government Printing Office.

U.S. Department of Labor. (1991). *Dictionary of Occupational Titles* (4th ed.). Washington, DC: U.S. Government Printing Office.

U.S. Department of Labor. (Annual). *Occupational Outlook Handbook*. Washington, DC: U.S. Government Printing Office.

Urban Institute. (1975, June 10). *Executive Summary of the Comprehensive Needs Study of Individuals with the Most Severe Handicaps*. Washington, DC: Author.

Usdane, W. M. (1976). The placement process in the rehabilitation of the severely handicapped. *Rehabilitation Literature, 37*, 162–167.

Vander Kolk, C. (1995). Future methods and practice in vocational assessment. *Journal of Applied Rehabilitation Counseling, 26*(2), 45–50.

Vandergoot, D., & Engelkes, J. (1980). The relationship of selected rehabilitation counseling variables with job-seeking behaviors. *Rehabilitation Counseling Bulletin, 24*, 173–177.

Vandergoot, D., & Swirsky, J. (1980). Applying a systems view to placement and career services in rehabilitation: A survey. *Journal of Applied Rehabilitation Counseling, 11*, 149–155.

Vargo, F. (1983). Adaptation to disability by the wives of spinal cord males: A phenomenological approach. *Journal of Applied Rehabilitation Education, 15*(1), 28–32.

Vash, C. (1984). Evaluation from the client's point of view. In A. Halpern & J. Fuhrer (Eds.), *Functional assessment in rehabilitation* (pp. 253–267). Baltimore: Brookes.

Velton, E., & Bondi, J. (1973). Effect of stomach surgery on work ability. *Journal of Applied Rehabilitation Counseling, 4*, 3–7.

Vocational Evaluation and Work Adjustment Association Code of Ethics. (1980, Spring). *Vocational Evaluation and Work Adjustment Bulletin, 13*(1), 8.

Vogel, V. J. (1987). The blackout of Native American cultural achievements. *American Indian Quarterly, 11*(1), 11–35.

Wadas, T. (1993). Case management and caring behavior. *Nursing Management, 24*(9), 40–45.

Walls, R., & Dowler, D. (1987). Client decision making: Three rehabilitation decisions. *Rehabilitation Counseling Bulletin, 30*(3), 136–147.

Walters, J., & Neugeboren, B. (1995). Collaboration between mental health organizations and religious institutions. *Psychiatric Rehabilitation Journal, 19*, 51–57.

Warren, N. C., & Rice, L. N. (1972). Structuring and stabilizing psychotherapy for low-prognosis clients. *Journal of Consulting and Clinical Psychology, 39*, 173–181.

Wechsler, D. (1974). *The Wechsler Intelligence Scale for Children–Revised*. San Antonio: Psychological Corp.

Wechsler, D. (1997). *Wechsler Adult Intelligence Test* (3rd ed.). San Antonio: Psychological Corp.

Weisenstein, G. R. (1979). Barriers to employability of the handicapped: Some educational implications. *Journal of Research Development Education, 12*, 57–70.

Weldon, K., & McDaniel, R. (1982). The effectiveness of the Testing Orientation Procedure on achievement scores of disadvantaged youths. *Vocational Evaluation Work Adjustment Bulletin, 15*, 94–97.

Welfel, E. R. (1987). A new code of ethics for rehabilitation counselors: An achievement or a constraint? *Journal of Applied Rehabilitation Counseling, 18*(4), 9–11.

Welfel, E. R., & Lipsitz, N. E. (1984). The ethical behavior of professional psychologists: A critical analysis of the research. *The Counseling Psychologist, 12*(3), 31–42.

Westin, M., & Reiss, D. (1979). The family's role in rehabilitation: "Early Warning System." *Journal of Rehabilitation, 45*, 26–29.

Wheaton, J., & Berven, N. (1994). Education, experience, and caseload management practices of counselors in a state vocational rehabilitation agency. *Rehabilitation Counseling Bulletin, 38*(1), 44–58.

White, A. (1953). The patient sits down. *Psychosomatic Medicine, 15*, 256–257.

White, J. L. (1984). *The psychology of Blacks: An Afro-American perspective*. Englewood Cliffs, NJ: Prentice-Hall.

Whitehouse, F. A. (1975). Rehabilitation clinician. *Journal of Rehabilitation, 41*, 24–26.

Whittington, H. (1992). Managed mental health: Clinical myths and imperatives. In S. Feldman (Ed.), *Managed mental health services*. Springfield, IL: Charles C Thomas.

Widgery, R., & Stackpole, C. (1972). Desk position, interviewee anxiety, and interviewer credibility. *Journal of Counseling Psychology, 19*, 173–177.

Willey, D. A. (1979). Caseload management for the vocational rehabilitation counselor in a state agency. *Journal of Applied Rehabilitation Counseling, 9*, 152–158.

Willis, W. (1992). Families with African American roots. In E. W. Lynch & M. J. Hanson (Eds.), *Developing cross-cultural acceptance: A guide for working with young children and their families* (pp. 121–150). Baltimore: Brookes.

Wilson, L. L., & Stith, S. M. (1991). Culturally sensitive therapy with Black clients. *Journal of Multicultural Counseling and Development, 19*, 32–43.

Wise, R., Charner, I., & Randour, M. (1976). A conceptual framework for career awareness in career decision-making. *Counseling Psychology, 6*, 47–52.

Wittman, J., Strohmer, D., & Prout, H. (1989). Problems presented by persons of mentally retarded and borderline intellectual functioning in counseling: An exploratory investigation. *Journal of Applied Rehabilitation Counseling, 20*(2), 8–13.

Wodarski, J. (1992a). Social work practice with Hispanic Americans. In D. F. Harrison, J. Wodarski, & B. Thyer (Eds.), *Cultural diversity and social work practice* (pp. 71–105). Springfield, IL: Charles C Thomas.

Wodarski, J. (1992b). Social work with Asian-Americans. In D. Harrison, J. Wodarski, & B. Thyer (Eds.), *Cultural diversity and social work practice* (pp. 45–69). Springfield, IL: Charles C Thomas.

Wong, D., & Chan, C. (1994). Advocacy on self-help for patients with chronic illness: The Hong Kong experience. *Prevention in Human Services, 11*(1), 117–139.

Wong, H. D. (1990). *Ethical dilemmas encountered by rehabilitation counselors and independent living service providers*. Unpublished doctoral dissertation, Southern Illinois University, Carbondale.

Wright, B. (1960). *Physical disability—A psychological approach*. New York: Harper & Brothers.

Wright, B. (1968). The question stands, should a person be realistic? *Rehabilitation Counseling Bulletin, 11*, 291–296.

Wright, B. (1980). Developing constructive views of life with a disability. *Rehabilitation Literature, 41*, 274–279.

Wright, G. (1980). *Total rehabilitation*. Boston: Little, Brown & Company.

Wright, G. N., Leahy, M. J., & Shapson, P. R. (1987). Rehabilitation Skills Inventory: Importance of counselor competencies. *Rehabilitation Counseling Bulletin, 31*(2), 107–118.

Wright, T. J. (1988). Enhancing the professional preparation of rehabilitation counselors for improved services to ethnic minorities with disabilities. *Journal of Applied Rehabilitation Counseling, 19*, 4–10.

Young, T. K. (1994). *The health of Native Americans: Toward a bicultural epidemiology*. New York: Oxford University Press.

Zadny, J. (1980). Employer reactions to job development. *Rehabilitation Counseling Bulletin, 24*, 161–169.

Zadny, J., & James, L. (1976). Another view on placement: State of the art 1976. *Portland State University Studies on Placement and Job Development for the Handicapped* (Studies in Placement Monograph No. 1., March). Portland, OR: Portland State University Regional Rehabilitation Research Institute.

Zadny, J., & James, L. (1977). Time spent on placement. *Rehabilitation Counseling Bulletin, 21*, 31–35.

Zuniga, M. E. (1992). Families with Latin roots. In E. W. Lynch & M. Hanson (Eds.), *Developing cross cultural competence: A guide for working with young children and their families* (pp. 151–179). Baltimore: Brookes.

Author Index

Subject Index